THE ADHD BOOK OF LISTS

A Practical Guide for Helping Children and Teens with Attention Deficit Disorders

Sandra F. Rief

Illustrated by Ariel Rief

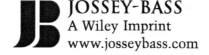

JOSSEY-BASS
A Wiley Imprint
www.josseybass.com

Published by Jossey-Bass
A Wiley Imprint
989 Market Street, San Francisco, CA 94103-1741   www.josseybass.com

Jossey-Bass books and products are available through most bookstores. To contact Jossey-Bass directly, call our Customer Care Department within the U.S. at 800-956-7739, outside the U.S. at (317) 572-3993 or fax (317) 572-4002.

Jossey-Bass also publishes its books in a variety of electronic formats. Some content that appears in print may not be available in electronic books.

The author has provided the websites and phone numbers for teacher use only. The publisher cannot guarantee the accuracy or completeness of the information found in these sites and is not responsible for errors or omissions or results obtained from use of the information.

Permission granted by the National Initiative for Children's Healthcare Quality to publish the information in List 6-5 and Appendix items A-8, A-9, A-10, A-25, and A-26.

Art in Appendix items A-11 and A-12 is taken from Microsoft® clip art.

Library of Congress Cataloging-in-Publication Data
Rief, Sandra F.
   The ADHD book of lists : a practical guide for helping children and
teens with attention deficit disorders / Sandra F. Rief ; illustrated by
Ariel Rief.—1st ed.
      p. cm.
Includes bibliographical references.
   ISBN 978-0-7879-6591-4 (pbk.)
   1. Attention-deficit-disordered children—Education—United
States—Handbooks, manuals, etc. 2. Hyperactive
children—Education—United States—Handbooks, manuals, etc.   I. Title:
Attention deficit hyperactivity disorder book of lists.   II. Title.
   LC4713.4.R57 2003
   371.93—dc21   2003004061

FIRST EDITION
PB Printing 13 12

DEDICATION

In memory of my beloved son, Benjamin—with the hope and prayer that all of our children will have a healthy, bright, and happy future.

ACKNOWLEDGMENTS

My deepest thanks and appreciation to:

- My precious, loving family members, who not only provide me with constant support and joy, but also were very instrumental in writing this book:
  - Gil, my oldest son and outstanding copy editor
  - Ariel, my youngest son and talented illustrator
  - Itzik, my wonderful husband and chart designer
  - Jackie, my lovely daughter and new teacher in the family—for her fresh ideas and enthusiasm
  - Sharon, Jason, Mom, and Ben for their great feedback, help, and encouragement
- All of the wonderful, dedicated educators I have had the great fortune to work with and meet over the years. Thank you for sharing with me your creative strategies, ideas, and insights.
- The extraordinary parents (especially the wonderful volunteers in CHADD and other organizations worldwide) whose tireless efforts have raised awareness of ADHD, and as a result, improved the care and education of our children.
- All of the children who have touched my heart and inspired me throughout the years. It is because of you that I love what I do.
- All of the researchers and practitioners in the different fields dedicated to helping children with ADHD and their families.
- Bernice Golden (editor) for her guidance and help and Diane Turso (development editor) for all her hard work on several of my books.
- Lesley Iura and Carolyn Uno, my wonderful editors at Jossey-Bass, for making it such a pleasure to write this book.

ABOUT THE AUTHOR

Sandra F. Rief (B.A., M.A., University of Illinois) is an award-winning educator with over 20 years of experience teaching in public schools. She is a nationally and internationally recognized speaker, consultant, and teacher-trainer specializing in instructional and behavioral strategies for meeting the needs of children with learning, attention, and behavioral challenges. Sandra resides with her family in San Diego, California. Currently she is working as a consultant with the New York City schools and is on the faculty of the ADHD project of the National Initiative for Children's Healthcare Quality (NICHQ). She is a former member of CHADD's National Professional Advisory Board.

Sandra is the author of several books, including: *How to Reach and Teach ADD/ADHD Children* (The Center for Applied Research in Education, 1993); *How to Reach and Teach All Students in the Inclusive Classroom*, co-authored with Julie Heimburge (The Center for Applied Research in Education, 1996); *The ADD/ADHD Checklist—An Easy Reference for Parents and Teachers* (Prentice Hall, 1998); *Alphabet Learning Center Activities Kit*, co-authored with Nancy Fetzer (The Center for Applied Research in Education, 2000); and *Ready . . . Start . . . School—Nurturing and Guiding Your Child Through Preschool and Kindergarten* (Prentice Hall Press, 2001).

She has also developed and presented a number of educational videos, including: *ADHD: Inclusive Instruction and Collaborative Practices*; *How to Help Your Child Succeed in School—Strategies and Guidance for Parents of Children with ADHD and/or Learning Disabilities*; *Successful Classrooms: Effective Teaching Strategies for Raising Achievement in Reading and Writing* (with Linda Fisher and Nancy Fetzer); and *Successful Schools: How to Raise Achievement and Support At-Risk Students* (with Linda Fisher and Nancy Fetzer).

For information about Sandra's resources, speaking/consulting, and online course "Reaching and Teaching Students with ADHD," visit her website http://www.sandra rief.com or call 800-682-3528.

ABOUT THIS BOOK

Awareness of ADHD has skyrocketed since I first wrote *How to Reach and Teach ADD/ADHD Children* back in 1993; however, there is still a tremendous amount of misinformation, myths, and controversy surrounding this disorder. Fortunately, much scientific progress has been accomplished through more than 6,000 worldwide studies on children with ADHD. Recent advances in brain research and genetics particularly have shed new light on the subject. In the first part of this book, I will share the research-validated information that is most widely accepted at this time by medical and mental health professionals with expertise in the field.

Why has there been such an interest in this population of children, warranting so much research? According to Dr. Harlan Gephart, current Chairperson of the American Board of Pediatrics and clinical professor of pediatrics at the University of Washington Medical School in Seattle, "ADHD is the most common neurobehavioral disorder of childhood and accounts for more referrals to mental health counselors and pediatric services than any other childhood disorder."

Because ADHD is considered a chronic health-care condition (similar to children with asthma) requiring ongoing management, ADHD is currently the focus of the NICHQ (National Initiative for Children's Healthcare Quality). The goal of this initiative is to maximize the quality of care, as well as improve collaborative efforts (home/school/clinical) and outcomes for children with this disorder. It is very gratifying to see the efforts that are being taken to ensure that primary health-care providers conduct a quality diagnosis according to the American Academy of Pediatrics (AAP) guidelines, and work closely with both the parents and the school to care and manage their ADHD patients.

My perspective is always that of an educator. Over the past decade, I have had the privilege of participating in numerous conferences on ADHD (including international conferences in Brazil, Canada, Costa Rica, Israel, Colombia, and South Africa). It is clear that ADHD is not just a concern or "an issue" in the United States. Teachers and parents in other countries face the same kinds of challenges and frustrations; they, too, are desperately seeking ways to best help their children with ADHD to achieve success.

What is important to understand about ADHD is the fact that it is a *real* disorder, one that often presents serious challenges to a child's life (and that of his or her family). ADHD can significantly impair successful functioning in school, home, and other settings, and is associated with a variety of negative outcomes when it goes unrecognized and untreated. Consequently, we mustn't trivialize ADHD, but, rather, do our best to understand it. We need to learn the most effective treatments, strategies, and supports to help manage the disorder, intervene early, and optimize the child's current and future success.

There is much that can be done to help those with ADHD. Most of this book focuses on specific strategies, supports, and interventions that have been found to be effective in minimizing the typical problems associated with ADHD and helping these children achieve success. I'm very fortunate to have spent most of my career teaching at a school that was a model in "inclusive education." Our staff was firmly committed to reaching and teaching *all* students; and we were very successful in doing so. A number of strategies or recommendations in this book come from what I have learned from my many students with ADHD and their families.

In addition, I have had the privilege these past few years of observing hundreds of classrooms and working with scores of educators across the country. I am grateful for the openness of these wonderful teachers (and parents) whom I have met, who so willingly share their ideas, strategies, struggles, and successes. Their stories and insights have inspired and taught me so much.

In essence, the content in much of this book comes from a lot of hands-on experience teaching students who have ADHD, and from many experts and practitioners I have learned from, particularly in the fields of education, psychology, and medicine. Much of what is shared is simply "good teaching" or positive "parenting" practices that would be useful for *all* children. However, the strategies and suggestions are of *particular benefit* to children and teens with ADHD (and those with other learning, attention, or behavioral challenges).

It is my hope that readers will find this book to be a useful resource in teaching, parenting, or treating children or teens with ADHD.

Sandra F. Rief

A NOTE FROM THE AUTHOR

The official term for the disorder at this time is Attention-Deficit/Hyperactivity Disorder (AD/HD). You may see it in print with or without the slash. In the past, the term ADD was commonly used. Some people still prefer to use ADD if the individual does not have the hyperactive characteristics. However, **ADHD** is the most current term or abbreviation, and it is inclusive of *all types* of the disorder:

- the predominantly inattentive type (those without hyperactivity)
- the predominantly hyperactive/impulsive type
- the combined type

So, please be aware that all references to ADHD include those individuals who may be predominantly inattentive and do not have the hyperactive behaviors.

Cross References: For your convenience, I have provided numerous cross references to related lists throughout the book. These are indicated by the list numbers in parentheses following individual items. Additional cross references are provided as separate bulleted items and at the end of many sections under "Related Lists." You will find that these cross references are an invaluable tool for finding related topics in *The ADHD Book of Lists*.

SOURCES AND RESOURCES

Gephart, Harlan R. "AD/HD: Diagnosis, Treatment, and Advocacy." A Supplement to *Drug Benefit Trends*, vol. 13, supplement C. December 2001.

CONTENTS

SECTION 1:
UNDERSTANDING, DIAGNOSING, AND TREATING ADHD

Section 2:
Preventing and Managing Behavior Problems: Strategies, Supports, and Psycho-Social Interventions

SECTION 3:
INSTRUCTIONAL STRATEGIES, ACCOMMODATIONS, AND SUPPORTS

SECTION 4:
STUDY SKILLS/LEARNING STRATEGIES, ORGANIZATION, AND HOMEWORK TIPS

SECTION 5:
ACADEMIC DIFFICULTIES IN READING, WRITING, AND MATH

SECTION 6:
COLLABORATIVE CARE AND PRACTICES TO SUPPORT STUDENTS WITH ADHD

SECTION 7:
SPECIAL EDUCATION, RELATED SERVICES, OR OTHER SCHOOL SUPPORTS AND ACCOMMODATIONS FOR STUDENTS WITH ADHD

SECTION 8:
UNDERSTANDING, SUPPORTING, AND IMPROVING OUTCOMES FOR INDIVIDUALS WITH ADHD

APPENDIX:
CHARTS, FORMS, AND VISUAL PROMPTS

UNDERSTANDING, DIAGNOSING, AND TREATING ADHD

1-1
DEFINITIONS AND DESCRIPTIONS OF ADHD

The following are descriptions of ADHD as defined by some of the leading researchers and authorities on attention deficit disorders. As ADHD continues to be studied intensively, with more and more information learned each year, these descriptions perhaps may be refined in the future. At this time, the majority of the scientific community believes the following.

- ADHD is a neuro-biological behavioral disorder characterized by chronic and developmentally inappropriate degrees of inattention, impulsivity, and, in some cases, hyperactivity.

- ADHD is a chronic disorder that interferes with a person's capacity to regulate activity level (hyperactivity), inhibit behavior (impulsivity), and attend to tasks (inattention) in developmentally appropriate ways.

- ADHD is a neurological inefficiency in the area of the brain that controls impulses, and is the center of "executive functions." (1-2)

- ADHD is a performance disorder, a problem of being able to produce or act upon what one knows.

- ADHD is a physiological disorder causing difficulty with self-regulation and goal-directed behavior.

- ADHD is a developmental delay or lag in inhibition, self-control, and self-management.

- ADHD is a brain-based disorder that arises out of differences in the central nervous system (CNS)—both in structural and neurochemical areas.

- ADHD is a pattern or constellation of behaviors that are so pervasive and persistent that they interfere with daily life.

- ADHD is a dimensional disorder of human behaviors that all people exhibit at times to certain degrees. Those with ADHD display the symptoms to a significant degree that is maladaptive, and developmentally inappropriate compared to others that age.

- ADHD is the most common neurobehavioral disorder of childhood and among the most prevalent chronic health conditions affecting school-aged children, with core symptoms including inattention, hyperactivity, and impulsivity.

- ADHD is a developmental disorder of self-control. It consists of problems with attention span, impulse control, and activity level.

- ADHD represents a condition that leads individuals to fall to the bottom of a normal distribution in their capacity to demonstrate and develop self-regulatory and self-control skills.

1-1 (*continued*)

- ADHD is a medical condition caused predominantly by genetic factors that result in certain neurological differences. It comes in various forms.
- ADHD is a disability of inhibition (being able to wait, stop responding, and not responding to an event). Inhibition involves motor inhibition, delaying gratification, turning off or resisting distractions in the environment while engaged in thinking.
- ADHD is a neuro-biological behavioral disorder causing a high degree of variability and inconsistency in performance, output, and production.

SOURCES AND RESOURCES

American Academy of Pediatrics. "Clinical Practice Guideline: Diagnosis and Evaluation of the Child With AD/HD," *Pediatrics*, vol. 105, no. 5, May 2000.

Barkley, Russell A. *ADHD and the Nature of Self-Control*. New York: The Guilford Press, 1997.

Barkley, Russell A. *Attention Deficit Hyperactivity Disorder: A Handbook for Diagnosis and Treatment*, 2nd ed. New York: The Guilford Press, 1996.

Barkley, Russell A. *Taking Charge of ADHD*. New York: The Guilford Press, 2000.

Castellanos, F. Xavier. "Approaching a Scientific Understanding of What Happens in the Brain in AD/HD," CHADD: *Attention*, vol. 4, no. 1, Summer 1997, 30–35.

CHADD. "Fact Sheet #1—The Disorder Named AD/HD." Landover, MD: CHADD.

Gephart, Harlan R. "AD/HD: Diagnosis, Treatment, and Advocacy." A Supplement to *Drug Benefit Trends*, vol. 13, supplement C. December 2001.

Goldstein, Sam. "The Facts About ADHD: An Overview of ADHD." (http://www.samgoldstein.com/articles/9907.html)

Goldstein, Sam. "Categorical or Dimensional Models: Which Is Best for ADHD?" (http://www.samgoldstein.com/articles/0011.html)

National Institute of Mental Health. "Attention Deficit Hyperactivity Disorder." (http://www.nimh.nih.gov/publicat/adhd.cfm)

1-2
ADHD AND THE "EXECUTIVE FUNCTIONS"

When discussing difficulties associated with ADHD, many of them center on the ability to employ the "executive functions" (EF) of the brain. The following are definitions and descriptions of what is referred to as "executive functioning."

Executive functions are:

- The management functions of the brain.
- The covert, self-directed actions individuals use to help maintain control of themselves and accomplish goal-directed behavior.
- The variety of functions within the brain that activate, organize, integrate, and manage other functions.
- Brain functions that have to do with self-regulation.
- The "overseers" of the brain.
- The higher-order cognitive processes involved in the regulation of behavior, inhibition of impulses, sequential thinking, planning, and organizing.

According to Russell Barkley (2000b), the deficit in inhibition (the core of ADHD) impairs the development of these executive functions. Apparently, in children with ADHD, the executive functions (at least some of them) are developmentally delayed compared with other children of the same age.

EXECUTIVE FUNCTION COMPONENTS

It has not as yet been determined exactly what constitutes the executive functions of the brain. However, they are believed by many to involve:

- Working memory (holding information in your head long enough to act upon it)
- Organization of thoughts, time, and space
- Planning
- Arousal
- Activation
- Sustaining alertness and effort
- Self-regulation
- Emotional self-control
- Internalizing speech/language (using your inner speech to guide your behavior)
- Prioritizing

1-2 (*continued*)

- Inhibiting verbal and nonverbal responding
- Cognitive flexibility
- Quickly retrieving and analyzing information
- Sequential thinking
- Developing and following through on a plan of action
- Strategy monitoring and revising, which involves making decisions based upon task analyses, planning, and reflection
- Complex, goal-directed problem-solving

When executive functions are immature and not working well, a number of challenges can result, particularly with regard to schoolwork. Weaknesses in executive functioning may cause difficulties to varying degrees with:

- Planning how to tackle assignments
- Problem-solving strategies
- Goal-directed behavior
- Sense/awareness of time
- Organization skills
- Time management
- Handling negative emotions (for example, frustration, anger)
- Motor control (for example, handwriting/fine motor)
- Persevering on tasks
- Delaying immediate gratification for long-term gain
- Study skills
- Using learning strategies
- Interpreting social cues
- Attentiveness
- Staying focused and blocking out distractions
- Making decisions based on thoughtful weighing of consequences and sound judgment
- Completing long-term projects
- Planning for the future
- Recalling information and memory
- Memorization skills:
  - Academic and learning tasks
  - Processing speed
  - Verbal fluency
  - Motivation

It is important to realize that executive function weaknesses cause academic challenges (mild to severe) for most students with ADHD, irrespective of how intelligent, gifted, and capable they may be. Consequently, most children and teens with attention deficit disorders will need some supportive strategies and/or accommodations to compensate for their deficit in executive functioning (whether these are part of a written plan or not).

SOURCES AND RESOURCES

Barkley, Russell A. *Taking Charge of ADHD—Revised.* New York: The Guilford Press, 2000a.

Barkley, Russell A. Presentation at Schwab Foundation for Learning, May 2000b. (http://www.schwablearning.org/pdfs/2200_7-barktran.pdf)

Brown, Thomas. *Attention Deficit Disorders and Co-morbidities in Children, Adolescents, and Adults.* Washington, DC: American Psychiatric Press, 2000.

Dendy, Chris A. Ziegler. *Teaching Teens with ADD and ADHD.* Bethesda, MD: Woodbine House, 2000.

Dendy, Chris A. Ziegler. "5 Components of Executive Function," CHADD: *Attention,* February 2002. (attention@chadd.org)

Fowler, Mary. *Maybe You Know My Teen.* New York: Broadway Books, 2001.

Parker, Harvey. *Put Yourself in Their Shoes.* Plantation, FL: Specialty Press, Inc., 1999.

1-3
THE OFFICIAL DIAGNOSTIC CRITERIA
FOR ADHD (DSM-IV)

The official criteria for a diagnosis of ADHD is found in the *Diagnostic and Statistical Manual*, 4th edition (DSM-IV), published by the American Psychiatric Association in 1994. The DSM-IV criteria:

- Guides the current diagnosis for attention deficit disorders.
- Lists nine symptoms under the category of *inattention*.
- Lists nine symptoms under *hyperactivity and impulsivity*.

The criteria states that the individual must exhibit six or more (out of the nine) symptoms in the inattention category, and/or six (out of the nine) symptoms of hyperactivity and impulsivity.

The following are the symptoms listed in DSM-IV:

Inattention

1. Often fails to give close attention to details or makes careless mistakes in schoolwork, work, or other activities.

2. Often has difficulty sustaining attention in tasks or play activities.

3. Often does not appear to listen when spoken to directly.

4. Often does not follow through on instructions and fails to finish schoolwork, chores, or duties in the workplace (not due to oppositional behavior or failure to understand instructions).

5. Often has difficulty organizing tasks and activities.

6. Often avoids, dislikes, or is reluctant to engage in tasks requiring sustained mental effort (such as schoolwork or homework).

7. Often loses things necessary for tasks or activities (for example, toys, school assignments, pencils, books, or tools).

8. Is often easily distracted by extraneous stimuli.

9. Often forgetful in daily activities.

Hyperactivity/Impulsivity

1. Often fidgets with hands or feet or squirms in seat.

2. Often leaves seat in classroom or in other situations in which remaining seated is expected.

3. Often runs about or climbs excessively in situations in which it is inappropriate (in adolescents or adults, may be limited to subjective feelings of restlessness).

4. Often has difficulty playing or engaging in leisure activities quietly.

5. Is often "on the go" or often acts as if "driven by a motor."

6. Often talks excessively.

7. Often blurts out answers before questions have been completed.

8. Often has difficulty awaiting turn.

9. Often interrupts or intrudes on others (for example, butts into conversations or games).

Additional Criteria

- Some hyperactive-impulsive or inattentive symptoms that cause impairment must have been present before age 7 (showing an early onset).

- The behaviors/symptoms have been evident for at least the past six months.

- Symptoms cause some impairment in two or more settings (for example, at school and at home).

- There must be clear evidence of clinically significant impairment in social, academic, or occupational functioning.

- Symptoms must be maladaptive and inconsistent with the individual's developmental level.

- Symptoms are not better accounted for by another mental disorder.

The diagnosis of ADHD differentiates between three different types of the disorder:

- AD/HD—*predominantly hyperactive/impulsive type* (without the inattention symptoms being significant)

- AD/HD—*predominantly inattentive type* (without the hyperactive/impulsive symptoms being significant)

- AD/HD—*combined type* (the most common type of AD/HD, defined by the individual meeting both the criteria of inattention and hyperactivity/impulsivity)

RELATED LISTS

- See Lists 1-14, 1-15, 1-18, and 1-19 for more information regarding the diagnosis of ADHD.

- See Lists 1-2, 1-5, 4-3, 5-1, 5-6, and 5-13 for more about core and secondary symptoms that are common difficulties and impairments in individuals with ADHD.

Note: DSM-IV criteria for ADHD was field tested on school-aged children, mostly boys. It is possible that when future editions of the DSM are published (DSM-V), there may be different or more specific diagnostic criteria for targeted populations (for example, children under 6, adults, girls).

1-3 (continued)

SOURCES AND RESOURCES

American Psychiatric Association. *Diagnostic and Statistical Manual of Mental Disorders* (4th edition). Washington, DC, 1994: 83–84.

CHADD. "Fact Sheet #1—The Disorder Named AD/HD." Landover, MD: CHADD.

1-4

WHAT IS CURRENTLY KNOWN AND UNKNOWN ABOUT ADHD

WE KNOW . . .

- ADHD has been the focus of a tremendous amount of research. There are literally thousands of studies and scientific articles published (nationally and internationally) on ADHD.

- ADHD has been recognized as a very real, valid, and significant disorder by the U.S. Surgeon General, the National Institutes of Health, the U.S. Department of Education, the Centers for Disease Control and Prevention, and the major medical and mental health associations (for example, the American Medical Association, the American Psychiatric Association, the American Academy of Child and Adolescent Psychiatry, the American Psychological Association, and the American Academy of Pediatrics).

- The evidence from an overwhelming amount of worldwide research indicates that ADHD is a neuro-biological disorder. (1-7)

- Recent estimates of the prevalence of ADHD in school-aged children range from 3–12%. Most agree that probably somewhere between 4–7% of children are affected.

- Degrees of ADHD range from mild to severe.

- There are different types of ADHD with a variety of characteristics. No one has all of the symptoms or displays the disorder in the exact same way. (1-3, 1-5)

- Symptoms vary in every child, and even within each child with ADHD the symptoms may look different from day to day.

- Approximately two-thirds of individuals (children/teens) with ADHD have an additional coexisting disorder. (1-11)

- Many children/teens with ADHD "slip through the cracks" without being identified or receiving the intervention and treatment they need. This is particularly true of ethnic minorities and girls.

- ADHD is diagnosed at least three times more frequently in boys than girls. It is believed (and research is showing) that *many* more girls actually have ADHD and are not being diagnosed. (1-13)

- The challenging behaviors exhibited by children with ADHD stem from their physiological, neuro-biological disorder. Rarely are these behaviors willful or deliberate. Children with ADHD are generally not even aware of their behaviors and how they affect others.

1-4 (continued)

- Children with ADHD are more likely than their peers to be suspended or expelled from school; retained a grade or drop out of school; have trouble socially and emotionally; and experience rejection, ridicule, and punishment.

- ADHD is a lifelong disorder. Most children with ADHD (about 80%) continue to have substantial symptoms into adolescence, and as many as 67% continue to exhibit symptoms into adulthood. (1-12, 8-7, 8-8)

- The prognosis for ADHD is alarming *if not treated*. Without interventions, children with this disorder are at risk for serious social, emotional, behavioral, and academic problems.

- The prognosis for ADHD *when treated* is positive and hopeful. With intervention, most children who are diagnosed and provided with the help they need will be able to successfully manage the disorder.

- There are countless successful individuals with ADHD in every profession and "walk of life."

- ADHD isn't new. It has been around, recognized by clinical science, and documented in the literature since 1902 (having been renamed several times). Some of the previous names for the disorder were: Minimal Brain Damage, Minimal Brain Dysfunction, Hyperactive Child Syndrome, and ADD with or without Hyperactivity.

- Children and teens with ADHD do much better when they are provided with activities that are interesting, novel, and motivating.

- Children with ADHD can usually be taught effectively in general education classrooms with proper management, supports, and assistive strategies.

- Children and teens with ADHD perform much better when they are able to receive stronger and more immediate rewards/reinforcers. Their impairment in inhibition and the nature of impulsivity make it much more difficult for them to persist and maintain motivation while working for long-term goals and rewards.

- ADHD is *not* a myth. It is *not* a result of poor parenting or lack of caring, effort, and discipline.

- ADHD is *not* laziness, willful behavior, or a character flaw.

- There is no "quick-fix" or "cure" for ADHD.

- A number of other problems or disorders (for example, learning, medical/health, social, emotional) may cause symptoms that *look like* ADHD, but are not ADHD. (1-10)

- A number of factors can intensify the problems of someone with ADHD or lead to significant improvement (such as the structure in the environment, support systems available, level of stress).

- Stimulant medications that affect the neurotransmitters in the central nervous system (CNS) are known to reduce the symptoms and impairment of ADHD. (1-23, 1-24)

- ADHD exists across all populations, regardless of gender, race, or ethnicity.

- There are racial and ethnic disparities in access to health-care services. As such, ethnic minorities with ADHD are often underserved and not receiving adequate help and treatment.

WE ALSO KNOW . . .

- Behavior-management techniques and strategies that are effective in the home and school for children with ADHD (2-1 through 2-16)
- Classroom interventions, accommodations, and teaching strategies that are most helpful for students with ADHD (3-1 through 5-14)
- Specific "parenting strategies" that are most effective with children who have ADHD (2-12, 2-13, 2-14, 2-15, 4-5, 4-7, 4-9, 8-2)
- The treatments that have been proven effective in reducing the symptoms and improving functioning of children/teens with ADHD (1-22, 1-23, 1-24, 2-16)
- Many additional strategies that are helpful for individuals with ADHD, such as organization and time management and stress reduction/relaxation (4-4 through 4-7, 8-9)

Points to Keep in Mind

- ADHD can be managed best by a multimodal treatment and a team approach. (1-22, 1-24, 1-25, 6-1, 6-2, 6-3, 6-4, 6-5)
- It takes a team effort of parents, school personnel, and health/mental health-care professionals to be most effective in helping children with ADHD.
- No single intervention will be effective for treating/managing ADHD. It takes vigilance, ongoing treatment/intervention plans, as well as revision of plans and going "back to the drawing board" frequently.
- The teaching techniques and strategies that are necessary for the success of children with ADHD are good teaching practices and helpful to *all* students in the class.
- A lot of help and resources are available for children, teens, and adults with ADHD, as well as those living with and working with individuals with ADHD. (1-22, 2-17, 6-3, 6-4, 8-5, 8-10)
- We are learning more and more each day due to the efforts of the many researchers, practitioners (educators, mental health professionals, physicians) committed to improving the lives of individuals with ADHD.

WHAT IS UNKNOWN ABOUT ADHD

There is still a great deal we do not yet know about ADHD, including:

- The causes (although there are more accepted theories supported by a growing body of scientific evidence). (1-8)
- How to prevent ADHD.

1-4 (*continued*)

- An easy, conclusive diagnosis for ADHD and coexisting conditions.

- What may prove to be the best, most effective treatments and strategies for helping individuals with ADHD.

- Just in the past few years there has been interest regarding ADHD in adulthood. This has generated a lot of research and more information and treatment approaches for this population.

- ADHD in the early childhood years (younger than age 6) is an area in need of more research.

- Gender issues and differences in ADHD (diagnosis and treatment of girls) has gained recognition; so have cultural variables with regard to ADHD. Hopefully, with all of the research and study taking place about attention deficit disorders, we can look forward to learning more in the near future.

1-5
BEHAVIORAL CHARACTERISTICS OF ADHD

In addition to the diagnostic criteria listed in the 4th edition of the *Diagnostic and Statistical Manual* (DSM-IV) (see List 1-3), a more detailed list of symptoms and characteristics associated with ADHD is provided here.

THE PREDOMINANTLY INATTENTIVE TYPE OF ADHD

- This type of ADHD was called "ADD without hyperactivity" or "undifferentiated ADD" in the past. Many people prefer to still use the term ADD rather than ADHD when referring to those who do not have the classic hyperactive symptoms, but display the predominantly inattentive symptoms of the disorder.

- These are the children and teens who often "slip through the cracks" and are not so easily identified or understood. Since they do not exhibit the disruptive hyperactive/impulsive behaviors that get our attention, it is easy to overlook these students and misinterpret their behaviors and symptoms as "not trying" or "being lazy."

- It is common to display any of the following behaviors at times, in different situations, to a certain degree. Those who truly have an attention deficit disorder have a history of showing many of these characteristics—far above the "normal" range developmentally—resulting in significant difficulty in performance. The nature of these inattentive symptoms tends to impact heavily upon academic performance and achievement.

Characteristics and Symptoms of Inattention

- Easily distracted by extraneous stimuli (for example, sights, sounds, movement in the environment)
- Does not seem to listen when spoken to
- Difficulty following directions
- Significant difficulty sustaining attention and level of alertness (especially on work requiring mental effort or tasks that are tedious, perceived as boring, or not of one's choosing)
- Difficulty concentrating and attending to task (often needs direct assistance with refocusing and redirection)
- Often loses his or her place when reading
- Can't stay focused on what he or she is reading (especially if text is difficult, lengthy, boring, not choice reading material)
- Forgets what he or she is reading and needs to reread frequently
- Tunes out—may appear "spacey"

1-5 (*continued*)

- Daydreams (thoughts are elsewhere)
- Often confused
- Often feels overwhelmed
- Great difficulty initiating or getting started on tasks
- Fails to finish work—many incomplete assignments
- Difficulty working independently—needs high degree of focusing attention to task
- Gets bored easily
- Often sluggish or lethargic (may fall asleep easily in class)
- Does not pay attention to details and makes many careless errors (for example, with math computation, spelling, written mechanics—capitalization and punctuation)
- Poor study skills
- Inconsistent performance—one day is able to perform a task, the next day cannot
- Disorganized—loses/can't find belongings (papers, pencils, books); desks, backpacks, lockers, and rooms may be total disaster areas
- Difficulty organizing (for example, planning, scheduling, preparing for activities/tasks, time management)
- Little or no awareness of time—often underestimates length of time a task will require to complete (4-3)
- Procrastinates
- Forgetful; difficulty remembering
- Slow and minimal written output and production
- Displays weak "executive functions" (1-2)
- May have many reading, math, or written language difficulties (5-1, 5-6, 5-13)

PREDOMINANTLY HYPERACTIVE/IMPULSIVE TYPE OF ADHD

Those individuals with this type of ADHD have a significant number of hyperactive and impulsive symptoms. They may have some, but not a significant number of inattentive symptoms.

Children and teens with ADHD have limited ability to inhibit their responses and control behavior. They will exhibit many of the following characteristics and symptoms (but not all of them). Even though each behavior is normal in children at different ages to a certain degree, in those with ADHD, the behaviors *far exceed* that which is normal developmentally (in frequency, level, and intensity).

Characteristics and Symptoms of Hyperactivity

- In constant motion—running and climbing excessively in situations where it is inappropriate
- Always "on the go" and highly energetic

- Can't sit still (jumping up and out of chair, falling out of chair, sitting on knees, standing up out of seat)
- A high degree of unnecessary movement (pacing, tapping feet, drumming fingers)
- Restlessness
- Always seems to need something in hands; finds/reaches for nearby objects to play with and/or put in mouth
- Fidgets with hands or feet
- Squirms in seat
- Makes inappropriate/odd noises
- Roams around the classroom—isn't where he or she is supposed to be
- Has difficulty playing quietly
- Has a hard time staying within own boundaries and intrudes in other people's space
- Excessively talkative
- Has difficulty "settling down" or calming self

Characteristics and Symptoms of Impulsivity

- Blurts out verbally—often inappropriately
- Has great difficulty with raising hand and waiting to be called on
- Often interrupts or intrudes on others
- Can't wait for his or her turn in games and activities
- Can't keep hands/feet to self
- Can't wait or delay gratification—wants things *now*
- Knows the rules and consequences, but repeatedly makes the same errors/infractions of rules
- Gets in trouble because he or she can't "stop and think" before acting (responds first, thinks later)
- Has trouble standing in lines
- Doesn't think or worry about consequences, so tends to be fearless or gravitate to "high risk" behavior (for example, jumping from heights, riding bike into street without looking); hence, a high frequency of injuries
- Accident prone—breaks things
- Has difficulty inhibiting what he or she says, making tactless comments; says whatever pops into head and talks back to authority figures
- Begins tasks without waiting for directions (before listening to the full direction or taking the time to read written directions)
- Hurries through tasks (particularly boring ones) to get finished and makes numerous careless errors

1-5 (*continued*)

- Gets easily bored and impatient
- Does not take time to correct/edit work
- Often disrupts and bothers others
- Constantly drawn to something more interesting or stimulating in the environment
- May hit when upset or grab things from others (not inhibiting responses or thinking of consequences)

High Degree of Emotionality

- Easily angered—has a "short fuse"
- Temper outbursts
- Moody
- Easily frustrated
- Gets upset and annoyed quickly
- Irritable
- Loses control easily
- Overly reactive

Other Common Characteristics

- Has difficulty relating to others—gets along better with younger children
- Has difficulty with transitions and changes in routine/activity
- Becomes easily overstimulated
- Displays aggressive behavior
- Immature social skills
- Difficult to discipline
- Can't work for long-term goals or payoffs
- Low self-esteem
- Poor handwriting, fine-motor skills, written expression, and output
- Often overly sensitive to sounds, textures, or touch (may be tactile defensive)
- Has difficulty with motivation
- Receives a lot of negative attention/interaction from peers and adults
- Has difficulties with learning and school performance—not achieving or performing to level that is expected (given child's/teen's apparent ability)
- Language and communication problems (for example, not sticking to topic, not fluent verbally)
- Memory problems
- Has difficulty with complex motor sequences

Points to Keep in Mind

■ A child/teen may receive the diagnosis of the predominantly inattentive type of ADHD and still have *some* of the hyperactive/impulsive symptoms; or be diagnosed as having the predominantly hyperactive/impulsive type of ADHD, yet still have *some* of the inattentive characteristics.

■ Many specialists and researchers now believe that the *key problem* associated with ADHD is centered in the ability to inhibit responses, to curb immediate reactions, to "stop . . . think . . . and plan" before acting. The individual with ADHD, therefore, does not fully utilize his or her "executive functions" for self-management. See List 1-2 on executive functions.

■ Many girls go undiagnosed, often perceived as just "spacey," when they actually have the predominantly inattentive type of ADHD. (1-13)

■ There is a high frequency of coexisting learning disabilities with ADHD. The multidisciplinary school team should evaluate students when there are signs of any learning problems. (1-18, 6-2, 7-1, 7-2, 7-4)

1-6
ADHD STATISTICS AND RISK FACTORS

ADHD is associated with a number of risk factors. The fact that having ADHD places one at risk for developing academic, behavioral, and social difficulties becomes apparent when viewing the research and statistics, which are indeed alarming. Compared with their peers of the same age, youth with ADHD experience:

- More serious accidents
- More school failure and dropout
- More delinquency and altercations with the law
- Higher teen pregnancy (starting earlier and using less contraception)
- Earlier experimentation and use of alcohol and tobacco

Having ADHD increases the risk for other psychiatric disorders as well. Approximately 70% of children/teens with ADHD have (or will develop) at least one other major disorder causing impairment. (1-11)

The following statistics apply to individuals with ADHD:

- Until recently, most of the literature estimated that approximately 3–7% of school-age children have ADHD. Current estimates indicate that as many as 4–12% of all school-aged children may be affected, according to the American Academy of Pediatrics.
- Nearly 7% of elementary-age children in the United States have been diagnosed with ADHD, according to the first nationwide survey conducted by the Centers for Disease Control and Prevention, which was reported in May 2002.
- ADHD affects approximately 5% of the adult population (Murphy and Barkley, 1996).
- 3.5 million children meet the criteria for ADHD, yet only 50% of these children are diagnosed and treated.
- Up to 50% of ADHD adolescents may have either oppositional disorder or conduct disorder.
- The number of boys diagnosed with ADHD outnumbers girls between 3 and 4 to 1.
- As many as 30–50% may be retained in a grade at least once.
- Almost 35% of children with ADHD quit school before completion.
- For half of ADHD children, social relationships are seriously impaired.
- At least 25–35% of ADHD teens display antisocial behavior or conduct disorder. Consequently, a far greater percentage of ADHD youth end up in the juvenile court system than the general population.

- Within their first two years of independent driving, adolescents with a diagnosis of ADHD have nearly four times as many auto accidents and three times as many citations for speeding as young drivers without ADHD.

- At least three times as many teens with ADHD have failed a grade, been suspended, or expelled from school.

- If one twin has symptoms of ADHD, the risk that the other will have the disorder is between 55–92%, with as high as 92% odds for identical twins.

- There is a 45–50% chance that if a child has ADHD, one of the biological parents has ADHD as well.

- Approximately 50–65% of children with ADHD continue to have symptoms as they reach adulthood. The vast majority (even though they do not meet all the criteria for the full diagnosis) continue to have impairment.

SOURCES AND RESOURCES

American Academy of Pediatrics. *Understanding ADHD* and the *ADHD Toolkit*. Chicago: American Academy of Pediatrics. (www.aap.org)

Barkley, Russell A. *Taking Charge of ADHD—Revised.* New York: The Guilford Press, 2000a.

Barkley, Russell A. Presentation at Schwab Foundation for Learning, June 2000b. (http://www.schwablearning.org/pdfs/2200_7-barktran.pdf)

Biederman, J., et al. *American Journal of Psychiatry*, 1991.

Burland, J. *Parents and Teachers as Allies: Recognizing Early-Onset Mental Illness in Children and Adolescents.* Arlington, VA: National Alliance for the Mentally Ill, 2001.

Centers for Disease Control and Prevention. "Prevalence of Attention Deficit Disorder and Learning Disability." National Center for Health Statistics. May 21, 2002. (http://www.cdc.gov/nchs/releases/02news/attendefic.htm)

Consortium of international scientists: International Consensus Statement on ADHD, January 2002. (http://www.chadd.org)

Gephart, Harlan. "Self-Management Concepts Applied to ADHD in Children." *Northwest Bulletin: Family & Child Health*, vol. 16, no. 2, Spring 2002.

Murphy, K., and R. Barkley. *Comprehensive Psychiatry*, 37, 393–401; 1996.

Safer et al. *Pediatrics*, 98, 1084–1088; 1996.

1-7
WHAT THE RESEARCH IS REVEALING ABOUT ADHD

Teams of researchers around the world are involved in searching for answers about ADHD. The following is a summary of the current evidence about ADHD, based upon the research from metabolic, brain-imaging, and molecular genetic studies.

There is an overwhelming amount of evidence that ADHD is neuro-biological in nature. There are brain differences in those with ADHD, both in structural and neuro-chemical areas. Though much has been learned about this disorder over the past decade, there is still much to learn. In the years to come, the scientific community may perhaps solve the puzzle of ADHD.

Differences in the Brain

- Numerous studies measuring electrical activity, blood flow, and brain activity have found differences between those with ADHD and control groups (those without ADHD), including:
  - Decreased activity level and lower metabolism levels in certain regions of the brain (mainly the frontal region and the basal ganglia).
  - Lower metabolism of glucose (the brain's energy source) in the frontal region.
  - Decreased blood flow to certain brain regions.

- These differences have been identified using brain activity and imaging tests/scans (MRIs, SPECT, EEG, BEAMS, PET, Functional MRIs). *Note:* Imaging and other brain tests are *not* used in the diagnosis of ADHD. To date, a comprehensive history of the problem remains the best way to identify the disorder.

- There is very strong scientific evidence that ADHD may be due to imbalances (lower levels) in dopamine, one of the neurotransmitters or brain chemicals, and/or reduced metabolic rates in certain regions of the brain. Dopamine is believed to function as a brain messenger that travels across the synapses of the brain, affecting the braking mechanism or inhibitory circuits in the brain. Dopamine pathways in the brain, which link the basal ganglia and frontal cortex, appear to play a major role in ADHD.

- Children with ADHD may have disturbances in their dopamine signaling systems.

- Brain-imaging studies indicate that children with ADHD have specific brain structures that are about 5–10% smaller than those unaffected by ADHD.

Genetic Research

- Much of the recent research involves molecular genetic studies. One type is "whole-genome scanning" studies that genotype DNA in entire families to look for patterns and differences.

- Other genetic research involves "candidate-gene" studies that seek specific forms of genes, which show up more often in children with ADHD compared with those unaffected by ADHD.

- Researchers have found at least two candidate genes associated with ADHD. One of those genes, the dopamine transporter gene (DAT1), is involved in regulating the amount of dopamine available in the brain.

  - Researchers have found differences between the structure of the DAT1 gene in families with ADHD and "normal" control families.

  - There is belief that the DAT1 gene in some individuals with ADHD may be causing an "overactive dopamine pump," sucking up dopamine too fast and not leaving it in the synapse long enough.

- A second recently found gene that may be involved with ADHD apparently makes specific nerve cells less sensitive to dopamine. It is suspected that because ADHD is a complex disorder with multiple traits, multiple genes are involved and will be discovered in the future.

Landmark MTA Study

- There has been significant research with regard to treatments for ADHD and their relative effectiveness. The longest and most thorough study of the effects of ADHD interventions was the 1999 Multimodal Treatment Study of Children with ADHD (MTA) by the National Institute of Mental Health (NIMH). (1-23)

- Researchers found that medication treatment alone and medication combined with behavior treatment worked significantly better (than just behavior alone or community care alone) at reducing the symptoms of ADHD. There was overwhelming evidence as to the effectiveness of well-managed use of stimulant medication in the treatment of ADHD.

- Stimulant medications have been proven to be very effective as treatment in improving the core symptoms of at least 70–80% of children and adults with ADHD. (More recent estimates are higher—up to 90%.)

ADHD in Certain Populations

- In very recent years there have been several research studies addressing ADHD in early childhood, in adulthood, and gender differences (ADHD in girls and women). Far more studies are needed in these areas. The coming years should shed more light about ADHD in these populations, so that the disorder will be better diagnosed, understood, and treated.

- Recent research has found that ADHD symptoms can reliably be diagnosed in children 4–6 years old.

- Recent studies of adults have found nearly equal numbers of males and females with ADHD. *Note:* ADHD is identified at least three times more frequently in boys than girls.

1-7 (*continued*)

■ There is growing evidence that symptoms of ADHD in girls, particularly girls with the predominantly inattentive type, are not always evident until puberty. *Note:* This has important implications in the DSM diagnostic criteria currently being used for ADHD.

SOURCES AND RESOURCES

Barkley, Russell A. "Attention-Deficit Hyperactivity Disorder," *Scientific American.* (http://www.sciam.com/1998/0998issue/0998barkley.html)

Castellanos, F. Xavier. "Approaching a Scientific Understanding of What Happens in the Brain in AD/HD," CHADD: *Attention*, vol. 4, no. 1, Summer 1997, 30–35. (attention@chadd.org)

Ellison, Anne Teeter. "Research Update: Recent Scientific Findings," CHADD: *Attention*, vol. 8, no. 4, February 2002, 15. (attention@chadd.org)

Fine, Lisa. "Research: Paying Attention," *Education Week*, May 2001. (http://www. edweek.org/ew/ewstory)

Goldstein, Sam. "The Facts about ADHD: An Overview of Attention-Deficit Hyperactivity Disorder." (http://www.samgoldstein.com/articles/9907.html)

Harman, Patricia. "One-on-One with Russell Barkley," CHADD: *Attention*, vol. 6, no. 4, March/April 2000, 12–14. (attention@chadd.org)

Jensen, Peter S. "AD/HD: What's Up, What's Next?" CHADD: *Attention*, vol. 8, no. 6, June 2001, 24–27. (attention@chadd.org)

Lombroso, Paul, Larry Scahill, and Matthew State. "The Genetics of Attention Deficit Hyperactivity Disorder," CHADD: *Attention*, vol. 5, no. 1, Spring 1998, 25–30. (attention@chadd.org)

MTA Cooperative Group. "A 14-month Randomized Clinical Trial of Treatment Strategies for AD/HD," *Archives of General Psychiatry*, 56:1073–1086; 1999.

Nadeau, Kathleen and Patricia Quinn. "Future Directions in Understanding Girls and Women with AD/HD," *ADDvance*, vol. 5, no. 3, February/March 2002.

National Institute of Mental Health ADHD reprint (http://www.nimh.nih.gov/publicat/ adhd.ctm)

Ringeisen, Heather. "AD/HD and the National Institute of Mental Health: Where Are We Now and Where Are We Going?" CHADD: *Attention*, vol. 7, no. 3, November/December 2000, 10–13. (attention@chadd.org)

1-8
PROBABLE CAUSES OF ADHD

ADHD has been researched extensively in the United States and a number of other countries. There have been literally thousands of well-designed and controlled scientific studies trying to determine the causes and most effective treatments for children, teens, and, more recently, adults. To date, the causes of ADHD are not fully known or understood. However, based on the enormous amount of research, there is a lot of consensus in the scientific community about most *probable causes*, which include the following.

HEREDITY

This is the most common cause based on the evidence.

- Heredity accounts for about 80% of children with ADHD.
- ADHD is known to run in families. (Research studied identical and fraternal twins, adopted children, and families.)
- It is believed that a genetic predisposition to the disorder is inherited. The child likely inherits a biochemical condition in the brain, which influences the expression of ADHD symptoms.
- Children with ADHD will frequently have a parent, sibling, grandparent, or other close relative with ADHD, or whose history indicates he or she had similar problems and symptoms during childhood.
- See List 1-6, ADHD Statistics and Risk Factors, regarding the prevalence of ADHD in parents and siblings.

PRENATAL, DURING BIRTH, OR POSTNATAL TRAUMA/INJURY

Trauma to the developing fetus during pregnancy or birth, which may cause brain injury or abnormal brain development, can cause ADHD. Trauma might include:

- Fetal exposure to alcohol, cigarettes/nicotine, and other toxic elements
- Exposure to high levels of lead
- Multiple pregnancy complications, such as toxemia and premature birth
- Brain injury from disease or trauma

Current research (as reported by NIMH) suggests that drugs like crack and cocaine may affect the normal development of brain receptors and that drug abuse may harm the receptors.

1-8 (*continued*)

ILLNESSES AND BRAIN INJURY

■ Researchers say that no more than 5% of those with ADHD are believed to acquire the disorder through illness or postnatal brain damage. However, ADHD may be caused by:

  ▪ Trauma or head injury to the frontal part of the brain

  ▪ Certain medical conditions such as thyroid disorder and illnesses that affect the brain (such as encephalitis)

DIMINISHED ACTIVITY AND LOWER METABOLISM IN CERTAIN BRAIN REGIONS

■ There is less brain activity taking place in the frontal regions of the ADHD brain (the areas known to be responsible for controlling activity level, impulsivity, attention) compared with the non-ADHD population. Studies revealed this brain region to have less:

  ▪ Blood flow

  ▪ Metabolism of glucose

  ▪ Electrical activity

■ These studies are based upon:

  ▪ PET scans

  ▪ EEGs

  ▪ Neuro-imaging and magnetic resonance imaging

CHEMICAL IMBALANCE OR DEFICIENCY IN NEUROTRANSMITTERS

■ A significant amount of research indicates that those with ADHD may have a deficiency or inefficiency in brain chemicals (called neurotransmitters) in the part of the brain (frontal lobe) that is responsible for attention, inhibiting impulses and behavior, and motor control.

■ It is believed stimulant medications work well to reduce ADHD symptoms (as they are suspected to stimulate the production of neurotransmitters to better normalize the brain chemistry).

SLIGHT STRUCTURAL BRAIN DIFFERENCES

■ There is evidence of some possible structural differences in certain brain regions believed responsible for ADHD.

- Scientists have found through neuro-imaging studies that the frontal lobe and basal ganglia are about 10% reduced in size and activity in individuals studied with ADHD.

OTHER POSSIBLE CAUSES

- It is generally believed that factors in the environment (for example, the amount of structure versus chaos; the effective management techniques being used; the types of supports in place) affect the severity of the symptoms and behaviors displayed, and the risk for developing more significant problems. However, these environmental factors are *not* found to be the *cause* of ADHD.

- Research has not supported many of the other suggested causes that are popular in the media (such as diet, food additives, sugar). (1-26)

- For more related information about possible causes, see List 1-7.

SOURCES AND RESOURCES

Barkley, Russell A. "Attention-Deficit Hyperactivity Disorder," *Scientific American*. (http://www.sciam.com/1998/0998issue/0998barkley.html)

Castellanos, F. Xavier. "Approaching a Scientific Understanding of What Happens in the Brain in AD/HD," CHADD: *Attention*, vol. 4, no. 1, Summer 1997, 30–35.

CHADD. "Fact Sheet—The Disorder Named AD/HD." Landover, MD: CHADD. (http://www.chadd.org/fs/fs1.htm)

Goldman, L. S., M. Genel, R. Bezman et al. "Diagnosis and Treatment of Attention-Deficit/Hyperactivity Disorder in Children and Adolescents," *Journal of the American Medical Association*, vol. 279, no. 14, April 8, 1998.

Goldstein, Sam. "The Facts about ADHD: An Overview of Attention-Deficit Hyperactivity Disorder." (http://www.samgoldstein.com/articles/9907.html)

NIMH ADHD reprint (http://www.nimh.nih.gov/publicat/adhd.ctm)

"Understanding and Identifying Children with ADHD: First Steps to Effective Intervention" (http://www.ldonline.org/ld-indepth/add_adhd/ael_firsteps.html)

1-9
POSITIVE TRAITS AND CHARACTERISTICS IN MANY PEOPLE WITH ADHD

- Highly energetic
- Verbal
- Spontaneous
- Creative and inventive
- Artistic
- Persistent and tenacious
- Innovative
- Imaginative
- Warmhearted
- Compassionate and caring
- Accepting and forgiving
- Inquisitive
- Resilient
- Make and create fun
- Know how to enjoy the present
- Empathetic
- Sensitive to needs of others
- Resourceful
- Gregarious
- Not boring

- Enthusiastic
- Intelligent and bright
- Humorous
- Outgoing
- Ready for action
- Willing to take a risk and try new things
- Good at improvising
- Enterprising
- Sees different aspects of a situation—has an interesting perspective
- Able to find novel solutions
- Charismatic
- Observant
- Negotiator
- Full of ideas and spunk
- Can think on their feet
- Intuitive
- Good in crisis situations
- Passionate

1-10
ADHD "LOOK ALIKES"

Not everyone who displays symptoms of ADHD has an attention deficit disorder. There are a number of other conditions and factors (medical, psychological, learning, psychiatric, emotional, social, environmental) that can cause inattentive, hyperactive, and impulsive behaviors. These other possible causes that produce symptoms, which may "mimic" or be confused with ADHD, need to be considered and ruled out.

Points to Keep in Mind

- It is very possible that ADHD is only *part* of the diagnostic picture, and that *in addition* to ADHD there are other coexisting conditions or disorders.

- There is a high rate of "comorbidity" with ADHD, which means there are at least two co-occurring disorders. Studies show that as high as two-thirds of children with ADHD may have an additional coexisting disorder. (1-11) This, of course, makes treatment, intervention, and management more complicated.

- Making an accurate and complete diagnosis requires a skilled, knowledgeable professional who is aware of conditions that produce similar symptoms as ADHD, and can identify and address other conditions or disorders that may coexist.

The following can cause some of the symptoms that may look like ADHD:

- Learning Disabilities (LD)
- Sensory impairments (hearing, vision, motor problems)
- Mood disorders (Depression, Dysthymia)
- Substance use and abuse (of alcohol and drugs)
- Oppositional Defiant Disorder (ODD)
- Conduct Disorder (CD)
- Allergies
- Post-Traumatic Stress
- Anxiety disorder
- Obsessive–Compulsive disorder
- Sleep disorders
- Bipolar disorder (Manic–Depressive)
- Thyroid problems
- Rare genetic disorders (such as Fragile X Syndrome)
- Seizure disorders
- Lead poisoning
- Hypoglycemia
- Anemia
- Fetal Alcohol Syndrome (FAS)/Fetal Alcohol Effects
- Chronic illness
- Language disorders
- Tourette syndrome (Tourette's disorder)
- Pervasive developmental disorder
- Autism
- Asperger's syndrome
- Developmental delays
- Sensory integration dysfunction

1-10 (*continued*)

- Low intellectual ability
- Very high intellectual ability
- Severe emotional disturbance

- Side effects of medications being taken (such as antiseizure medication, asthma medication)

The following factors can also cause a child/teen to be distracted, unable to concentrate, and have acting-out behaviors:

- If the child/teen is living in high-stress situations such as:
  - Physical/sexual abuse
  - Divorce and custody battles
  - Victim of bullying/peer pressure and other peer/social issues
  - Home life is chaotic, unpredictable, unstable, and/or neglectful with inappropriate expectations placed on the child
- If the child/teen is in a highly unpleasant school environment, which may include:
  - Pervasive negative climate
  - Low expectations for academic achievement
  - Poor instructional strategies
  - Nonstimulating and unmotivating curriculum
  - Ineffective classroom management

1-11
ADHD AND COEXISTING (OR ASSOCIATED) DISORDERS

As pointed out in other lists (1-4, 1-7, 1-10), ADHD is often accompanied by one or more other psychiatric, psychological, developmental, and/or medical disorders or conditions.

COMORBIDITY

- The word "comorbidity" is the technical or medical term for having coexisting disorders.

- Estimates vary as to the rate of comorbidity with ADHD. Most sources cite that between one-half to two-thirds of children/teens diagnosed with ADHD have at least one other major disorder.

- In the landmark Multimodal Treatment Study of Children with ADHD (1999), researchers found that two-thirds of children with ADHD also met criteria for at least one other psychiatric disorder, and those other disorders caused significant impairment above and beyond the impairment caused by ADHD.

- The most common coexisting disorders with ADHD are: Oppositional Defiant Disorder, Conduct Disorder, Anxiety Disorder, Depression, and Learning Disabilities.

- See List 1-10, ADHD "Look Alikes," for other possible conditions to be aware of that may resemble or coexist with ADHD.

- Because of the high degree of coexisting conditions with ADHD, the American Academy of Pediatrics recommends in its Guidelines that primary-care practitioners screen for the presence of other diagnoses, as part of the diagnostic process for ADHD.

- In order to effectively treat the child, a differential diagnosis needs to be made by skilled professionals to tease out what may be ADHD and any other accompanying condition or disorder the child may have.

The prevalence reported of individuals with ADHD who have additional coexisting disorders varies among sources. The following statistics are provided by leading experts and other sources (including the CHADD Fact Sheet on "AD/HD and Co-Existing Disorders").

COEXISTING DISORDERS IN THOSE DIAGNOSED WITH ADHD

- Oppositional Defiant Disorder (ODD)—ranging from 40–65%
- Anxiety Disorder—ranging from 25–40% of children/adolescents and 25–40% of adults

1-11 (continued)

- Conduct Disorder (CD)—ranging from 10–25% of children, 25–50% of adolescents, and 20–25% of adults

- Bipolar (manic/depressive illness)—ranging from 1–20%

- Depression—ranging from 10–30% in children and 10–47% in adolescents and adults

- Tics/Tourette's Syndrome—about 7% of those with ADHD have Tics or Tourette's Syndrome, but 60% of Tourette's Syndrome patients also have ADHD

- Learning Disabilities (LD)—ranging from 20–60%, with most estimating between one-third and one-half of children with ADHD having a coexisting learning disability (The Centers for Disease Control and Prevention [CDC] reported in May 2002 that about one-half of the school-aged children diagnosed with ADHD have been identified with an accompanying learning disability.)

- Sleep Problems—more than 50% of ADHD children need more time to fall asleep; nearly 40% may have problems with frequent night wakings; and more than half have trouble waking in the morning

- Secondary Behavioral Complications—up to 65% of children with ADHD may display secondary behavioral complications such as noncompliance, argumentativeness, temper outbursts, lying, blaming others, and being easily angered

Points to Keep in Mind

- Most all children with ADHD have some kind of school-related problems (achievement, performance, social).

- It is believed that having ADHD predisposes that person to the above-mentioned disorders. Therefore, the diagnostic process should include screening for possible comorbidities (for example, through interview, questionnaires, and rating scales that may indicate or alert the diagnostician to symptoms of other coexisting disorders).

- ADHD falls under the category of Disruptive Behavior Disorder in the *Diagnostic and Statistical Manual of Mental Disorders*, 4th Edition (DSM-IV). Also in this category are the commonly co-occurring disorders of Oppositional Defiant Disorder (ODD) and Conduct Disorder (CD).

The criteria for receiving the diagnosis of Oppositional Defiant Disorder (ODD) requires a pattern of negative, hostile, and defiant behavior that has been evident for a while (at least 6 months); occurs more frequently than is typical in individuals of comparable age and developmental level; and causes significant impairment in social, academic, or occupational functions.

Like the DSM criteria for being diagnosed with ADHD, there is a list of symptoms, and the child/teen must display a significant number of them, such as:

- Often loses temper
- Often argues with adults

- Often actively defies or refuses adult requests or rules
- Often deliberately annoys people
- Often blames others for his or her own mistakes or misbehavior
- Often touchy or easily annoyed by others
- Often angry and resentful
- Often spiteful or vindictive

Conduct Disorder is the most serious form of Disruptive Behavior Disorders in children and teens, and involves a pattern of delinquent behavior. Some of the characteristics include:

- Aggression to people and animals (often bullies, threatens, or intimidates others; often initiates physical fights; has used a weapon that can cause serious physical harm to others; has been physically cruel to people or animals; has stolen while confronting a victim; has forced someone into sexual activity)
- Destruction of property (has deliberately engaged in fire-setting with the intention of causing serious damage; has deliberately destroyed others' property)
- Deceitfulness or theft
- Serious violations of rules
- Conduct Disorder can have an early onset of antisocial behavior (before age 10) or a later onset. These children have delinquent behaviors and—coupled with ADHD—are difficult to treat. It is critical to intervene as early as possible, as without the proper medical, psychosocial, and other support/intervention, their prognosis is poor.

Note: Children with ADHD are at a much higher risk than the average child of developing a more serious disruptive behavior disorder. It is important that we recognize the risk and implement early interventions. Parents, educators, and medical/mental health-care providers should be alert to signs of other disorders and issues that may exist or emerge (often in the adolescent years), especially when current strategies and treatments being used with the ADHD child/teen are no longer working effectively. This warrants further diagnostic assessment.

SOURCES AND RESOURCES

American Academy of Pediatrics Clinical Practice Guideline. "Diagnosis and Evaluation of the Child with Attention-Deficit/Hyperactivity Disorder," *Pediatrics*, 2000; 105:1158–1170.

Anastopoulos, Arthur, E. Paige Temple, and Ericka Klinge. "The Key Components of a Comprehensive Assessment of Attention-Deficit/Hyperactivity Disorder." (http://www.ldonline.org/ld-indepthadd_adhd/adhd_assess.html)

1-11 (*continued*)

Baren, Martin. "The Assessment of ADHD in School-Aged Children," *CME/CE Supplement to: Drug Benefit Trends*, vol. 13, December 2001.

Barkley, Russell A. *Taking Charge of ADHD—Revised*. New York: The Guilford Press, 2000.

CHADD. "Fact Sheet 5: AD/HD and Co-Existing Disorders," *Attention*, vol. 7, no. 1, July/August 2000, 31–37.

Diagnostic and Statistical Manual of Mental Disorders, 4th edition. Washington, DC: American Psychiatric Association, 1994.

Green, M., M. Wong, D. Atkins et al. *Diagnosis of Attention Deficit/Hyperactivity Disorder. Technical Review 3*. AHCPR publication 99-0050. Rockville, MD: US Dept of Health and Human Services, Agency for Health Care Policy and Research, 1999. AHCPR publication 99-0050

Multimodal Treatment Study of Children with ADHD. *Archives of General Psychiatry*, 56:1088–1096; 1999.

National Center for Health Statistics 2002 News Release. "New CDC Report Looks at Attention-Deficit/Hyperactivity Disorder," May 2002. (http://www.cdc.gov/nchs/releases/02news/attendefic.htm)

National Institute of Mental Health. Attention Deficit Hyperactivity Disorder. (http://www.nimh.nih.gov/publica/adhd.ctm)

Parker, Harvey. *Put Yourself in Their Shoes—Understanding Teenagers with Attention Deficit Hyperactivity Disorder*. Plantation, FL: Specialty Press, Inc., 1999.

Pelham, William E. *Attention Deficit Hyperactivity Disorder: Diagnosis, Nature, Etiology, and Treatment*. Buffalo, NY: University of Buffalo Center for Children and Families, 2002.

Pliszka, S. R., C. L. Carlson, and J. M. Swanson. *ADHD with Comorbid Disorders: Clinical Assessment and Management*. New York: The Guilford Press, 1999.

"Summary of the Practice Parameters for the Assessment and Treatment of Children and Adolescents with Conduct Disorders," *American Academy of Child and Adolescent Psychiatry*. (http://aacap.org/clinical/Condct%7E1.htm)

Wilens, Timothy E. *Straight Talk About Psychiatric Medications for Kids*. New York: The Guilford Press, 1999.

1-12
DEVELOPMENTAL COURSE OF ADHD ACROSS THE LIFESPAN

It is now known that ADHD is not just a childhood disorder. In most cases, a child with ADHD will continue to have symptoms as a teenager. In fact, the majority of children with ADHD will have the disorder as an adult as well. (1-6, 8-8)

One notable finding reported by a leading researcher and authority on ADHD, Russell Barkley, Ph.D., of the University of Massachusetts Medical Center, is that ADHD causes a "developmental lag" of approximately 30% in the area of self-control and inhibition. This means that a 10-year-old child with ADHD is functioning more like a 7-year-old in his or her emotional control, ability to inhibit impulses, and self-regulate. Though children with ADHD develop in these areas, they lag behind their peers.

This developmental lag is important to realize about children and teens with ADHD. As parents and teachers lament that 15-year-old John needs to "act his age," remember that if John has ADHD, his ability to self-manage and demonstrate "responsible behavior" most likely is that of an 11-year-old (30% younger).

SYMPTOMS ACROSS THE AGE LEVELS

Infancy and Toddler Stages

- ADHD is typically diagnosed in school-aged children. However, there is evidence that even in infancy, toddler, and early childhood years, there are indicators that a child may be "at-risk" for eventually being diagnosed with ADHD (or another developmental disorder).

- "Difficult temperaments" characterize many infants and toddlers who may be children with ADHD. According to Goldstein (2000), studies indicate approximately 5–10% of all infants exhibit difficult temperament; and as high as 70% of "temperamentally difficult" infants experience later childhood problems of learning, behavior, and socialization.

The following are signs to watch for in infancy that may be symptomatic of future difficulties:

- Irritability
- Shrill, frequent crying
- Overactive and restless
- Sleep problems

- Fussy eater
- Difficulty adapting well to changes in the environment
- Difficulty nursing and feeding

1-12 (*continued*)

- Colicky
- Hard to please
- Hard to establish and maintain on a schedule

In the toddler years, early indicators may include:

- Excessively active
- Picky eater
- Sleep problems
- Fussiness and irritability
- Higher degree of crying
- Temper tantrums
- Noncompliance
- Poorly adapting to changes
- Clumsiness/being accident prone
- Speech and language problems

Preschool and Kindergarten Years

See List 8-6 for information and strategies specific to children of preschool and kindergarten age range.

In these early years when the child is now in social and educational environments with other children for half-day or full-day programs, more signs and symptoms of possible ADHD, learning disabilities, or other developmental disorders may become evident. Parents, teachers, pediatricians, and day-care providers should be alert to children in this age group who exhibit a number of the following difficulties compared with other children that age.

Symptoms and indicators in preschool and kindergarten include:

- Very short attention span (much more apparent than in the average child that age)
- Trouble sitting/staying with the group (such as circle time with class on the rug)
- Can't listen long to stories
- Moodiness
- Speech and language difficulties (understanding or expressing self in language)
- Motor-skill problems
- Overly reactive (cries easily, temper tantrums)
- Poor self-control when frustrated or angry
- Highly impulsive
- Excessively active
- Not interested in playing with other children or has great difficulty doing so
- Difficulty holding and using a crayon, pencil, or scissors
- Avoids writing or any fine-motor task
- Argumentative and uncooperative

- Has trouble following one- or two-step directions
- Excessively timid and avoids interaction with others
- Seems overly sensitive to noise or touch
- Seems to get easily overstimulated and has trouble calming
- Aggressiveness
- Clumsiness/accident prone
- Fearless behavior
- Trouble adapting to changes of routine or new environments
- Difficulty following class rules and teacher directions

It is recommended that when children in these early years show signs of a difficult temperament and possible developmental disorders, early intervention should be initiated in order to reduce the risk of many future problems developing. This would involve:

- Providing information and guidance to parents on positive strategies and supports to implement in the home (for example, behavioral, learning, language, motor, environmental).
- Referring the child for evaluation, if indicated.
- Obtaining any needed services (such as speech and language therapy or occupational therapy).

Elementary School Years

- ADHD is typically diagnosed in the elementary school years when the expectations for academic and behavioral/social performance (following rules, sitting quietly, paying attention, working cooperatively and productively, and so on) become problematic.
- Elementary school children with ADHD have been the subject of a great deal of research. All of the lists in this book are relevant to children of this age range.

Middle School Years

For many youngsters, these are very difficult and painful years. It is a period of time when:

- There is rapid growth and development, causing many to feel awkward and unattractive in their changing bodies.
- The overriding concern is to "fit in" with peers and be accepted.
- Children are trying to gain more independence, so they challenge their parents' authority.
- They must also cope with the expectations of multiple teachers and harder academic and self-management demands (being an independent learner, more organized and responsible, and having mastered their "basic skills").

1-12 (*continued*)

In addition, middle schoolers with ADHD:

■ Have all the normal struggles as their peers, but theirs is often a much greater challenge because of their ADHD symptoms and behaviors, affecting their social and school success.

■ Have all of the same behaviors that can be found in the elementary school child with ADHD.

■ May have some of the behaviors and issues described below as seen in older teens.

See List 8-7 for more information and strategies to help this age group of children/young teens with ADHD.

High School/Teen Years

During this period, teens with ADHD generally have a change in their symptoms. For example, the overt hyperactivity is usually seen now manifested as restlessness or fidgetiness. Other problems and coexisting conditions/disorders (such as signs of depression) may emerge.

The following are commonly seen in teens with ADHD:

■ Time-awareness/time-management issues (lateness, procrastination)

■ Forgetfulness

■ Disorganization

■ Difficulty waking up and falling asleep

■ Easily bored (and falls asleep in class)

■ Impulsive

■ Difficulty paying attention

■ Immaturity

■ Poor planning and goal-directed behavior

■ Irritability

■ Gravitates to "high-risk behaviors" and associates with peers with similar problems and behaviors

■ Argumentative, talks back to authority figures

■ Emotionally reactive

■ Social/behavioral problems

■ Doesn't take responsibility for actions

■ Higher-than-average amount of speeding tickets, traffic violations, and accidents

■ Academic difficulties

- Significant problems in school keeping up with projects and managing the "work load"
- Problems in the workplace or out-of-school functions/activities

Note: Studies show that by adolescence, the child may have a history of failure in academic performance (about 58%) and marked difficulties in social relationships. An estimated 35% of teens with ADHD quit school. (1-6)

According to Flick (2000), the typical adolescent is faced with five basic developmental demands:

1. Achieving independence
2. Establishing an identity
3. Developing close interpersonal ties
4. Coping with his or her sexuality
5. Completing his or her education/training to decide on a vocation/occupation

Many teens with ADHD may actually be deficient or delayed in meeting some of these five basic developmental demands.

See List 8-7 for more information and strategies specific to adolescents with ADHD.

Adults

It has only been in recent years that ADHD in adulthood has been studied, and that attention has been focused on the diagnosis and treatment of the disorder in this population. It used to be the belief that ADHD was a childhood disorder that was outgrown. Of course, we now know that to be untrue. In fact:

- Approximately 60–70% of children diagnosed with ADHD continue to have ADHD as adults.
- ADHD is a disorder that persists across the lifespan.

Note: So many adults who struggled (academically, socially, emotionally, and behaviorally) as a result of their disorder spent their lives mislabeled and misunderstood. Fortunately, we are learning more about ADHD and how it impacts across the lifespan. Adults with ADHD benefit from diagnosis and treatment, just as children do. Many parents realize that they themselves have the disorder when their child is struggling and evaluated for ADHD.

In addition to the symptoms of childhood (1-2, 1-3, 1-5), adults with ADHD often exhibit some of the following difficulties:

- Antisocial behavior
- Educational underattainment
- Vocational underattainment
- Depression

1-12 (*continued*)

- Anxiety
- Substance abuse
- Low frustration tolerance
- High levels of stress
- Long-term relationship problems
- Mood disorders
- Employment difficulties
- Chronic time-management difficulties (procrastination, lateness)
- Pattern of short-lived interests
- Frequent moves and/or job changes
- Sleep-arousal problems
- Money-management problems (such as impulsive purchases, poor budgeting)
- Poor memory/forgetfulness
- Emotional volatility
- Excessively impatient
- Undertake many projects simultaneously
- Difficulty staying focused in conversations
- Drawn to situations of high intensity

See List 8-8 for more information and strategies for the adult population.

Points to Keep in Mind

- Even though ADHD generally persists from childhood throughout adulthood, it does not limit one's future. The above-mentioned list gives "risk factors" and simply means that children with ADHD are more predisposed to these traits than the rest of the population. As such, it is important not to be overwhelmed with concern.

- There are countless adults with ADHD who are highly successful in every profession and "walk of life." Having ADHD does not mean one can't live a normal, happy life; graduate from high school, college, or vocational school (or even medical school or law school); raise a family; and have a career of choice.

- With diagnosis and intervention, ADHD can be managed properly, significantly minimizing the risk factors. This is a time of good fortune for those with ADHD. We understand so much more than in the past about how to help—the strategies, supports, and treatments that enable those with ADHD (children, teens, and adults) to be successful.

- Adults have far more options than children since they can create or find an environment that is ADHD-friendly. Those who seize the opportunity are able to utilize their strengths, talents, and passion to excel in their chosen career and hobbies.

■ The types of supports, treatments, and therapies that are needed by many individuals with ADHD vary at different times and stages of life. (1-22)

SOURCES AND RESOURCES

Anderson, Sheila. "ADHD and the Role of Parents," *Drug Benefit Trends*, vol. 13, Sup. C, December 2001.

CHADD. "Fact Sheet: AD/HD in Adults." (http://www.chadd.org/facts/add_facts07.htm)

Dendy, Chris Zeigler. *Teenagers with ADD*. Bethesda, MD: Woodbine House, 1995.

Flick, Grad L. *How to Reach & Teach Teenagers with ADHD*. Paramus, NJ: The Center for Applied Research in Education, 2000.

Fowler, Mary. *Maybe You Know My Teen*. New York: Broadway Books, 2001.

Goldstein, Sam. "Young Children at Risk: The Early Signs of AD/HD," February 2000. (www.samgoldstein.com)

Goldstein, Sam. "The Facts About ADHD: An Overview of Attention-Deficit Hyperactivity Disorder," July 1999. (http://www.samgoldstein.com/articles)

Goldstein, Sam. "Update on Adult ADHD." February 2001. (www.samgoldstein.com)

Hallowell, Edward, and John Ratey. *Driven to Distraction*. New York: Pantheon Books, 1994.

Jones, Clare. *Sourcebook for Children with Attention Deficit Disorder—A Management Guide for Early Childhood Professionals and Parents*. Tucson, AZ: Communication Skill Builders, 1991.

Nadeau, Kathleen. *Adventures in Fast Forward*. New York: Brunner/Mazel Publishers, 1996.

National Institute of Mental Health ADHD reprint (http://www.nimh.nihgov/publicat/adhd.ctm)

Reimers, Cathy, and Bruce Brunger. *ADHD in the Young Child—Driven to Redirection*. Plantation, FL: Specialty Press, Inc., 1999.

Rief, Sandra. *Ready . . . Start . . . School—Nurturing and Guiding Your Child Through Preschool and Kindergarten*. Paramus, NJ: Prentice Hall Press, 2001.

1-13
GIRLS WITH ATTENTION DEFICIT DISORDERS

Point to Keep in Mind

- Many girls with ADHD have gone undiagnosed (or misdiagnosed) for years because they frequently do not have the typical hyperactive symptoms seen in boys that signal a problem and get attention. In the past few years, much more attention has been given to girls with the disorder.

- Girls who do have the combined symptoms of ADHD are very recognizable because their behavior is so significantly out of norm for other girls. But, on the whole, most girls have the predominantly inattentive type of the disorder.

- The following are typical characteristics of girls with ADHD:
  - Tend to be compliant in school and do not exhibit many of the disruptive behaviors more common in boys.
  - Are often very good at trying to make themselves invisible to cover up their difficulties.
  - Are often overlooked or labeled/written off as being "space cadets," "ditzy," or "scattered."
  - Have a real and serious problem (affecting them academically, socially, and emotionally) that is often unrecognized.

Much of what we are now aware of and beginning to understand about females with ADHD comes from the work of Nadeau, Quinn, Littman, Solden, and others who have strongly advocated on the behalf of this population. Because of their leadership, the scientific community is now looking at gender issues in ADHD. These studies have recently begun to reveal the significance of gender differences and issues, and will undoubtedly result in changes and improvements in the diagnosis and treatment for girls with this disorder.

As Nadeau, Quinn, and Littman (1999) explain, girls:

- Have more internal and often less external (observable) symptoms.
- Have greater likelihood of anxiety and depression.
- Experience a lot of academic difficulties, peer rejection, and self-esteem issues.
- Are more likely to be hyperverbal than hyperactive.

There are special issues that need to be explored in more depth regarding girls with ADHD:

- There is less likelihood of symptoms showing up before age 7.

- Symptoms tend to increase rather than decrease at puberty.

- Girls are likely underdiagnosed because the current diagnostic criteria requires evidence of symptom onset before 7 years of age.

- Hormones from puberty onward have a great influence on girls with ADHD.

- Premenstrual syndrome (PMS) presents additional problems, worsening ADHD symptoms by adding to disorganization and emotionality.

Be aware that:

- Girls who may have done well academically in elementary school often have trouble achieving academically once they enter the middle school years.

- The demands of "executive functioning" in these higher grades create a lot of stress. (1-2)

- Girls tend to try very hard to please teachers and parents. They often work exceptionally hard (compulsively so) to achieve academic success.

- Impulsivity in girls can lead to binge eating and engaging in high-risk/high-stimulation activities (such as smoking, drinking, drugs, sexual promiscuity, unprotected sex).

Rather than (or in addition to) the classic symptoms boys display (hyperactivity, impulsivity, inattention, and executive functions), girls with ADHD are often characterized by the following:

- Hypersocial behavior
- Hyperverbal behavior (cannot stop talking, chatting, and commenting on everything)
- Much giggling and "silly" behavior
- Irritability and dysphoric tendencies
- Mood swings
- Temper tantrums
- Feeling shy, timid, and withdrawn
- Becoming easily overwhelmed
- Being self-critical
- Being anxious
- Hair-twirling, nail-biting, picking at cuticles
- Depression
- Low self-esteem
- Tendency to unleash frustrations at home that were kept hidden at school

1-13 (continued)

- Academic passivity—giving up easily
- Introversion

Just a few years ago the first big study of ADHD in girls was published (Biederman et al., 1999). The study indicates that girls, like their male peers, also have social problems. They tend to have poor family relationships, greater addiction to substances than their male counterparts, and significant learning problems. Fifty percent of the girls studied had significant secondary co-occurring conditions.

Female social rules place a greater value on cooperating, listening, care-taking, and maintaining relationships. According to Giler (2001), ADHD females appear to have specific problems in five areas that may cause them to struggle socially:

1. Appearing uninterested because of poor listening skills.
2. Displaying poor management or expression of anger or moods.
3. Bragging or being outspoken and appearing self-involved.
4. Forgetting appointments or being late.
5. Failing to show interest by not remembering or checking with their friends about their feelings, relationships, or reactions to events that have occurred in their friends' lives.

Verbal expression and processing problems common in many children with ADHD may have a negative impact on girls with this disorder, as so many of girls' interactions heavily involve verbal demands.

Note: For more in-depth information about the issues and treatment of girls of all ages and women with ADHD, see the excellent books and other publications by Nadeau, Littman, Quinn, Solden, and others; as well as *ADDvance: A Magazine for Women with ADD* (edited by Nadeau and Quinn). View their website at http://www.ADDvance.com.

SOURCES AND RESOURCES

Biederman, J., S. Faraone, E. Mick et al. "Clinical Correlates of ADHD in Females: Findings from a Large Group of Girls Ascertained from Pediatric and Psychiatric Referral Services," *Journal of the American Academy of Child and Adolescent Psychiatry*, 38 (8), 966–975; 1999.

Giler, Janet Z. "Are Girls with AD/HD Socially Adept?" CHADD: *Attention*, vol. 7, no. 4, February 2001, 28–31.

Littman, Ellen. "We Understand Far Too Little About Girls with ADHD," *ADDvance*, vol. 3, no. 6, July/August 2000, 17–21.

Nadeau, Kathleen. "Elementary School Girls with AD/HD," CHADD: *Attention*, vol. 7, no. 1, July/August 2000, 44–49.

Nadeau, Kathleen. "Middle School Girls with AD/HD," CHADD: *Attention*, vol. 7, no. 2, September/October 2000, 61–71.

Nadeau, Kathleen, Ellen Littman, and Patricia Quinn. *Understanding Girls with AD/HD.* Silver Spring, MD: Advantage Books, 1999.

Nadeau, Kathleen, and Patricia Quinn. "Gender Differences in the Diagnosis of AD/HD," *ADDvance*, vol. 5, no. 2, November/December 2001, 17–22.

Quinn, Patricia, and Kathleen Nadeau. "Understanding Preschool Girls with AD/HD," CHADD: *Attention*, vol. 6, no. 5, May/June 2000, 42–45.

Solden, Sari. *Women with Attention Deficit Disorder.* Grass Valley, CA: Underwood Books, 1995.

1-14
MAKING THE DIAGNOSIS: A COMPREHENSIVE EVALUATION FOR ADHD

The diagnosis of ADHD is not a simple process. There isn't yet any laboratory test (such as blood) or single measure to determine if a person has ADHD; nor can any particular piece of information alone confirm or deny the existence of ADHD. Though in future years there may well be the use of genetic testing, brain imaging, and/or other more conclusive tools and methods used for diagnostic purposes, currently this is not the case.

THE DIAGNOSIS

- The cornerstone of an ADHD diagnosis is meeting the criteria for Attention Deficit/Hyperactivity Disorder as described in DSM-IV. (1-3)
- The diagnosis is made by gathering and synthesizing information obtained from a variety of sources in order to determine if there is enough evidence to conclude that the child meets *all* of the criteria for having ADHD (as defined in the DSM-IV).
- According to the criteria in DSM-IV, the child must:
  - Exhibit at least six of the nine characteristics of *inattention*, or at least six of the nine characteristics of *hyperactivity/impulsivity*.
  - Show evidence of symptoms *before age 7*, which have lasted *longer than six months*.
  - The symptoms must be to a degree that is "maladaptive and inconsistent with the child's developmental level," and serious enough to be affecting the successful functioning of the child in at least two settings (for example, home and school).
- The evaluator must collect and interpret data from multiple sources, settings, and methods. The diagnostician must use his or her clinical judgment to determine:
  - There are a sufficient number of ADHD symptoms present.
  - These symptoms are presently causing impairment in the child's life and affecting the child's successful functioning in more than one setting (at home, school, social situations in other environments).
  - These symptoms have existed a significant amount of time (at least some since early childhood), and other factors, disorders, or conditions do not better account for these symptoms.
- It is *not sufficient* for a child to be seen by a community physician who has only seen the child for a brief office visit and has not gathered and analyzed the necessary diagnostic data from the parents, school, and other sources. An appropriate evaluation for

ADHD takes time. In a clinical setting the diagnostic process will likely require a *minimum* of two visits.

- Until recently, it would have been advised that a child only be evaluated by a specialist, a professional with much expertise in attention deficit disorders. This is still recommended with more complex cases (such as probable comorbidity or coexisting conditions).

- However, since May 2000, when the American Academy of Pediatrics (AAP) published guidelines for the diagnosis of ADHD, far more pediatricians and primary-care practitioners are familiar with and capable of conducting the comprehensive evaluation required to diagnose and treat attention deficit disorders.

- As pediatricians and primary-care doctors continue to receive more training in implementing these guidelines, there should be far more consistency in effective diagnostic practices for ADHD. Hopefully, children will benefit by receiving more appropriate evaluations, and consequently, effective treatment and management.

- The ADHD National Initiative for Child Healthcare Quality (NICHQ), described in List 6-5, shows much promise in demonstrating that such care can be provided with excellent results.

The AAP Guideline Recommendations, which are intended to provide a framework for diagnostic decision-making, include the following:

1. If a child 6 to 12 years of age exhibits inattention, hyperactivity, impulsivity, academic underachievement, or behavior problems, primary-care clinicians should initiate an evaluation for ADHD.

2. The diagnosis of ADHD requires that a child meet the criteria for ADHD in the *Diagnostic and Statistical Manual of Mental Disorders*, 4th edition.

3. The assessment of ADHD requires evidence directly obtained from parents or caregivers regarding the core symptoms of ADHD in various settings, the age of onset, duration of symptoms, and degree of functional impairment.

4. The assessment of ADHD also requires evidence directly obtained from the classroom teacher (or other school professional) regarding the core symptoms of ADHD, duration of symptoms, degree of functional impairment, and coexisting conditions. A physician should review any reports from a school-based multidisciplinary evaluation where they exist, which will include assessments from the teacher or other school-based professionals.

5. Evaluation of the child with ADHD should include assessment for coexisting conditions.

6. Other diagnostic tests are not routinely indicated to establish the diagnosis of ADHD but may be used for the assessment of coexisting conditions.

1-14 (_continued_)

WHAT ARE THE COMPONENTS OF A COMPREHENSIVE EVALUATION FOR ADHD?

Here are the main components in the diagnostic process.

History

An evaluation for ADHD will require taking a thorough history. The history is obtained through:

- Interviewing the parents/guardians and child (This is a key component.)
- Using questionnaires (generally filled out by parents prior to office visits)
- Reviewing previous medical and school records

By using these techniques and instruments, the evaluator obtains important data regarding:

- The child's medical history (prenatal, birth, illnesses, injuries)
- The child's developmental and school history
- Family medical and social history
- Any significant family circumstances

Other Information

This is gathered through _interview_ and _questionnaires_ with parents (and the child, as age appropriate). (1-19)

Behavior Rating Scales

These are useful in determining the degree to which various ADHD-related behaviors/symptoms are observed in different key environments (such as home and school). In addition to teachers and parents, rating scales may be filled out by others (e.g., school counselor, special education teacher, child-care provider, other relative) who spend time with the child. (1-19)

Gathering Current School Information

A critical part of the diagnostic process is reviewing information supplied by the school. Teachers may be asked to report their observations about the child through rating scales, questionnaires, narrative statements, phone interviews, or other measures.

No one is in a better position than the teacher to report on the child's school performance, functioning, and behaviors compared to other children of that age and grade. The teacher's observations and perceptions regarding the child's ability to exhibit self-control, follow rules and directions, stay focused and on-task, initiate and follow-through on assignments, and so on, is critical information. (1-14, 1-15)

Review of School Records

School history of behaviors indicating ADHD, as well as history of academic achievement and performance, may be obtained through:

- Past report cards
- Bus and office referrals
- Standardized achievement tests
- Work samples (particularly writing samples)
- Past Student Support Team (SST) referrals and action plans
- Any psycho-educational assessments or individualized testing

Observations

Directly observing the child's functioning in a variety of settings can provide helpful diagnostic information. Most useful are observations in natural settings where the child spends much of his or her time (such as school). How a child behaves and performs in an office visit is often not indicative of how that same child performs and behaves in a classroom, playground, cafeteria, or other natural setting.

As clinicians do not have the time to make visits to observe the child in the school setting, school personnel can make some observations and provide those observational reports to the evaluating doctor. (1-15, 1-17, 1-18)

Physical Exam

A clinical evaluation for ADHD generally includes a routine pediatric examination to rule out other medical conditions that could produce ADHD symptoms. Based on the child's physical exam, as well as medical history (through interview and questionnaire), a physician may look for evidence of other possible causes for the symptoms or additional issues that may need to be addressed (such as sleep disturbances, bedwetting, anxiety, depression).

Most other medical tests (blood work, EEG, CT scans) are not done in an evaluation for ADHD. It is the physician's responsibility to determine the need for additional medical testing and/or referral to other specialists if indicated.

1-14 (continued)

Performance Tests

Different tests are sometimes used in a comprehensive evaluation to try obtaining more information about how a child functions on various performance measures. Some clinicians use:

■ Computerized tests that measure the child's ability to inhibit making impulsive responses and to sustain attention and focus on tasks

■ Other measures of performance (for example, evaluating ability to organize and pay attention to visual stimuli on paper–pencil tasks)

Note: These kinds of performance tests are not standard practice or routinely done in most ADHD assessments. They are not necessary for making the diagnosis.

Academic and Intelligence Testing

If there is indication of possible learning disabilities, a request for a psycho-educational evaluation is appropriate and recommended. (7-1, 7-2, 7-14) An evaluator should have at least a general indication of a child's academic achievement levels and academic performance. This can partly be determined through:

■ A review of the student's report cards

■ Standardized test scores

■ Classroom work samples

■ Informal screening measures

■ Teacher/parent/student report

If a child does struggle academically, this should alert the evaluator to the possibility of coexisting learning disabilities. In order to determine if the child has learning disabilities, a psycho-educational assessment would need to be administered. This typically involves:

■ Assessment of cognitive abilities

■ A battery of individualized achievement tests to determine academic strengths and weaknesses

■ Various processing tests (such as measuring memory and sequencing skills, visual-motor integration)

WHO IS QUALIFIED TO EVALUATE A CHILD FOR ADHD?

A number of professionals have the qualifications to assess for attention deficit disorders:

■ Psychiatrists

- Clinical psychologists
- Clinical social workers
- Pediatricians
- Family practitioners
- Neurologists
- Other qualified medical and mental health professionals

In addition to clinical evaluations for ADHD, many schools/school districts are qualified to conduct school-based assessments. (1-18) School psychologists are the key diagnosticians in the school-based assessment, along with other school personnel on the multidisciplinary team involved in the assessment and gathering of information.

ADVICE TO PARENTS

In selecting a professional to evaluate your child, be sure to investigate, be proactive, and question that individual about the methods he or she will be using in the diagnostic process. This professional must:

- Adhere to recommended diagnostic guidelines for ADHD by the American Academy of Pediatrics and DSM-IV diagnostic criteria.
- Conduct an evaluation that is comprehensive and multidimensional.
- Be knowledgeable about ADHD and coexisting conditions.
- Take adequate time to comfortably answer questions about assessment, treatment, and management to the parents' satisfaction.

RELATED LISTS

- See Lists 1-16, 6-4, 6-5, 8-5, and 8-10 for additional information and guidance for parents.

SOURCES AND RESOURCES

"American Academy of Pediatrics Clinical Practice Guideline: Diagnosis and Evaluation of the Child with Attention-Deficit/Hyperactivity Disorder," *Pediatrics* 105:1158–1170; 2000. (www.aap.org/policy/ac002.html)

Anastopoulos, Arthur, E. Paige Temple, and Ericka Klinge. "The Key Components of a Comprehensive Assessment of Attention-Deficit/Hyperactivity Disorder." (http://www.ldonline.org/ld-indepthadd_adhd/adhd_assess.html)

Baren, Martin. "The Assessment of ADHD in School-Aged Children," *CME/CE Supplement to: Drug Benefit Trends*, vol. 13; December 2001.

1-14 (*continued*)

"Diagnosis and Treatment of Attention Deficit Hyperactivity Disorder," National Institutes of Health Consensus Development Statement. (http://odp.od.nih.gov/consensus/cons/110/110_statement.htm)

Gephart, Harlan. "Attention-Deficit/Hyperactivity Disorder: Diagnosis, Treatment, and Advocacy," *CME/CE Supplement to: Drug Benefit Trends*, vol. 13; December 2001.

Herrerias, C., J. Perrin, and M. Stein. "The Child with ADHD: Using the AAP Clinical Practice Guideline," *American Family Physician*, vol. 63, no. 9; May 1, 2001.

National Institute of Mental Health ADHD reprint (http://www.nimh.nih.gov/publica/adhd.ctm)

1-15
THE SCHOOL'S ROLE AND RESPONSIBILITIES IN THE DIAGNOSIS OF ADHD

As described in List 1-14, the diagnosis of ADHD is dependent upon gathering sufficient information to get a clear picture of how ADHD symptoms observed (currently and in previous years) affect the child in key environments. Obviously the school—where the child spends much of his or her life—is a key environment.

Points to Keep in Mind

■ Besides the presence of symptoms, the evaluator must obtain sufficient information in order to determine the degree of impairment the symptoms are causing (for example, academic functioning and productivity, behavioral problems, ability to make and keep friends, social/emotional functioning, and so forth). Teachers and other school personnel who interact and observe the child on a daily basis are in the best position to provide this information.

■ Parents have a right to expect the school to be supportive and responsive in the diagnostic process. Schools need to provide information requested by the child's physician or mental health professional conducting a clinical evaluation for ADHD. It will be necessary for parents to sign a release-of-information form before school personnel can communicate with other professionals outside of school, or provide documentation and data regarding the child.

■ School personnel should be prompt and thorough in providing any information requested for an evaluation (such as behavioral rating scales). (1-15, 1-19)

■ It is also helpful (and may be requested) for the teacher to write a paragraph or two indicating how he or she views the child in relation to other students in the classroom (regarding behavior, social skills, work production/output, and so on).

■ School personnel can provide insight and helpful data to the evaluator regarding the child's functioning by making observations in the classroom and other school settings (such as the playground and lunchroom).

■ Information indicating the existence of symptoms in previous school years (and age of onset of symptoms) is gathered in the history and review of school records. A great deal of useful data is located in the student's school records/cumulative file, including:

  ▪ Past report cards

  ▪ District/state achievement testing

  ▪ Any other school evaluations (such as psycho-educational, speech/language)

  ▪ Past and current Individual Education Plans (IEPs)

1-15 (*continued*)

- In addition, disciplinary referrals (which may be among the records of guidance counselors and/or administrators) may provide information about the student's behavioral problems in school.

- Copies of work samples, particularly written samples and curriculum-based assessment, are also good indicators of a child's levels of performance and production. When providing work samples, particularly of writing, it is helpful to also include a scoring guide (rubric) for that product so evaluator knows how that piece of work compares to grade-level expectations.

- It is highly recommended that schools provide information to the physician in a manner that takes into account the physician's limited time. A one- or- two-page summary of the child's school history and current performance is helpful.

- Teachers should be willing to speak and confer with whomever is conducting the evaluation. It is very beneficial for the physician (or other evaluator) and teacher to speak directly with each other (either face-to-face or by phone). *Note:* If a child is receiving an outside evaluation for ADHD and the school is *not* requested to send information, and no attempt is made to communicate with or obtain input from the school, it is an *inappropriate evaluation* for ADHD. The evaluator is *not* following recommended diagnostic guidelines by the American Academy of Pediatrics, or acquiring sufficient evidence to meet ADHD diagnostic criteria as determined by the American Psychiatric Association.

- See List 1-18 for information regarding a school-based evaluation.

- School personnel need to be alert and aware of the high rate of coexisting conditions and disorders with ADHD. (1-11) Often those students who exhibit very significant behavioral challenges have ADHD and another coexisting mental health disorder needing treatment. It is important for the school to facilitate referrals to appropriate community agencies and medical/mental health-care professionals, when indicated.

- The child/teen should be evaluated by the school's multidisciplinary team if the student is known to have ADHD that is impairing educational performance (this includes behavioral, not just academic performance). (7-1 through 7-4)

- The school is responsible for determining educational impairment.

- The school has the responsibility of initiating and following through with a comprehensive evaluation if the child is suspected of having ADHD or any other disability impairing educational performance. (This includes behavioral, not just academic performance.) If the child is eligible, the school is then responsible for providing supports and services under either of the two federal laws: IDEA or Section 504 of the Rehabilitation Act of 1973. (7-1 through 7-4)

- Remember that approximately 50% of children with ADHD also have coexisting learning disabilities. If a student with ADHD is struggling academically, the school should consider the probability of learning disabilities and provide a more comprehensive psycho-educational evaluation. (7-2, 7-4)

1-16
PURSUING AN EVALUATION FOR ADHD: RECOMMENDATIONS FOR PARENTS

There is no need to seek an evaluation for possible ADHD if the child's symptoms or behaviors are not causing a problem in functioning. Just because a child displays some of the characteristics of ADHD does not give reason to pursue an evaluation unless those symptoms are affecting how well the child is performing academically, socially, or behaviorally in daily life.

Points to Keep in Mind

■ Remember that the symptoms of ADHD are all normal in and of themselves. It is when symptoms displayed by a child are more extreme and causing problems for the child (at school, home, other settings) that the parent has cause for concern. The behaviors associated with ADHD should be problematic (causing some degree of impairment) to go through the evaluation process.

■ It is very common for parents to become aware and concerned about their child's "problematic behaviors" when the child starts school and faces the demands of an academic environment.

■ For many children it is not until third or fourth grade that they start to really struggle in school. This is when the academic work and expectations for independent learning, on-task behavior, and self-control intensify.

■ Sometimes the student manages to function adequately in an elementary school setting, but falls apart at the middle school level or even higher. When looking at the student's elementary school history, the behaviors/symptoms were evident but under control. Now, clearly something needs to be done to help the child.

■ At whatever stage, when parents are concerned about symptoms that are affecting the child's functioning and suspect that it may be the result of ADHD or another disorder or disability, parents should pursue an evaluation. At any point, parents should communicate their concerns with their child's primary-care physician and teachers.

■ Parents should make an appointment to meet with the classroom teacher(s), asking for their input and observations regarding the child's academic achievement, performance or production, and behavior. Parents may ask the teacher(s) to implement a few reasonable interventions to help with any of the above concerns, and find out how they can assist and support at home.

■ As ADHD is both a medical and behavioral disorder, parents may decide to have their child evaluated for ADHD by a physician or mental health professional outside of school (a clinical evaluation).

1-16 (*continued*)

- There are a number of community professionals who have the skills and qualifications to evaluate a child for ADHD. Some professionals (child psychiatrists, child neurologists, developmental/behavioral pediatricians) have a great deal of expertise in ADHD. It is recommended that children with more complex issues (likelihood of co-occurring conditions) should be evaluated by a specialist.

Primary-care physicians will be involved in the clinical evaluations of most average, uncomplicated cases of ADHD:

- The American Academy of Pediatrics (AAP) published guidelines regarding the evaluation and treatment of children with ADHD. (1-14) These guidelines are what primary-care physicians use in the diagnosis of ADHD, based upon the DSM-IV criteria. (1-3)

- The AAP recommends that primary-care doctors initiate an evaluation for ADHD when patients 6–12 years of age exhibit inattention, hyperactivity, impulsivity, academic underachievement, and/or behavioral problems.

- Primary-care doctors are to use DSM-IV criteria, requiring the evaluator to establish the existence of core symptoms in various settings; age of onset and duration of symptoms; and degree of functional impairment at home and school.

- Pediatricians and general practitioners should no longer be diagnosing ADHD after a simple office visit; and they should never be diagnosing ADHD without gathering data and communicating with the school.

Note: Even though the AAP guidelines have been available since May 2000, not all primary-care physicians are following them in their diagnostic process. If parents have their child evaluated for ADHD by their primary-care doctor, it is strongly recommended that they question their doctor about whether or not he or she follows the AAP guidelines for diagnosing and treating ADHD.

Points to Keep in Mind

- For any appropriate clinical evaluation of ADHD, the school will be called upon to supply the necessary data (such as records, reports, observation forms, rating scales, work samples) to the doctor, psychiatrist, social worker, psychologist, or whichever medical or mental health professionals are conducting the evaluation. (1-15)

- It is highly recommended that parents initiate the IEP process and request an evaluation from the school if their child is experiencing learning problems or appears to be underachieving. (7-4) Remember, approximately 50% of children with ADHD also have a coexisting learning disability.

- A school-based assessment can be done concurrent with, before, or after the doctor's evaluation for ADHD. It is often best to coordinate efforts.

- In pursuing a school evaluation, parents should let the teacher know why they want their child evaluated. Parents should speak with the school psychologist, school nurse, principal, special education teacher, or school counselor regarding this request for testing.

- It is likely that the parent will be asked to first meet with the school's Student Support Team (SST). (6-2) This is appropriate as long as the meeting is scheduled in a timely manner, and parents agree to first meet with the school team. During the SST meeting, information and concerns are reviewed by the classroom teacher, support staff, administrator, and parents.

- The SST meeting is recommended protocol, particularly if the child has never before been referred for a special education evaluation, and there has not yet been an intervention plan developed to address the student's difficulties in the classroom.

- It is especially helpful to first have an SST meeting when considering an evaluation for ADHD for the following reasons:

  - The options of a clinical evaluation and/or school-based screening or assessment can be discussed.

  - The school can share with parents its role in the assessment of ADHD, and obtain parental permission (in writing) to begin gathering data (child's school history and current functioning) and so forth.

  - It is likely to ensure better coordination and communication if parents and school staff meet first prior to initiating the diagnostic process.

- A school-based screening or evaluation may be initiated at the time of the SST meeting if review of information indicated it is appropriate. (1-18)

- When parents submit to the school a request for evaluation, which is their right under federal law (7-1, 7-2, 7-4), it formally opens an IEP timeline to begin the assessment and special education process.

- Parents may also request a Section 504 evaluation. (7-1, 7-3)

- As long as the school arranges to meet with the parents in a reasonable time frame, it is often best if parents channel their concerns and request for testing through the SST (if one exists at the school). However, parents may choose not to go through this process and request school testing at any time. It is recommended to make this request in writing.

- The school evaluation team has the responsibility of determining if a child has a disability under federal law, and whether or not a child meets eligibility criteria, which will entitle the student to special education or related services under IDEA or Section 504. (7-1, 7-2, 7-3, 7-4)

- Parents seeking professionals to evaluate (and treat) their child may wish to do their homework first by contacting and speaking with other parents of children/teens who have ADHD (such as through the local chapter of CHADD).

- School nurses and school psychologists are also excellent resources and very knowledgeable in most cases about health-care providers in the community who have expertise in ADHD.

1-17
IF YOU SUSPECT A STUDENT HAS ADHD: RECOMMENDATIONS AND INFORMATION FOR TEACHERS AND OTHER SCHOOL PERSONNEL

When you observe a student displaying inattentive, hyperactive, and impulsive behavior in the classroom, you should automatically attempt to deal with those behaviors by using strategies proven to be effective. These strategies include, for example, environmental structuring, cueing and prompting, study skills assistance, and behavior-modification techniques.

Obviously, this is simply good teaching practice, as all students who display the need should be provided behavioral/academic help and support. School professionals should consider the following when they wish to initiate an evaluation for students suspected of having ADHD:

- Keep records of interventions you are attempting, anecdotal records regarding the student's behaviors and classroom performance, work samples, as well as any phone contacts and conferences with parents.

- Communicate with the previous year's teacher(s) to see if your areas of concern were also of issue the prior year; and if so, find out what strategies and interventions were used successfully or unsuccessfully by that teacher.

- Consult informally with appropriate support staff (such as school counselor, school nurse, psychologist, or special education teacher). Always share your concerns and ask for advice and assistance as needed.

Many schools use a Student Support Team (SST) process as protocol for the next step (6-2), which basically consists of the following:

1. Generally, the teacher submits a meeting request form/referral to the SST chair.

2. The SST meeting is then scheduled to discuss the child, share information and strategies, and develop a plan of action to support the student.

3. In many districts, the SST process requires that the teacher first document interventions already implemented, and communicate/share concerns with the parents prior to bringing up the child for discussion at an SST meeting.

4. Parents are typically invited to the SST meeting as part of the team.

5. Teachers and other team members will be asked to bring to the meeting any documentation or data collected on the student that may be helpful in sharing how the child is functioning academically, behaviorally, socially, and emotionally.

At the SST meeting, support staff, the classroom teacher(s), parents, and an administrator generally:

1. Review the student's school history and other relevant information.

2. Share about the child's strengths, interests, and areas of difficulty.

3. Discuss interventions implemented both in the past and currently.

4. Strategize next-step interventions and develop a plan of action, which may include implementing some more interventions in school (for example, counseling, social skills group, non-special education academic supports, behavioral contracts/plans, and so forth).

5. This is often the time (while discussing the child's behaviors and areas of difficulty at school and home) when if the school suspects ADHD, an evaluation is recommended to parents.

6. At this time, parents are generally informed about the diagnostic process and given the options—if they are interested—on how to proceed with a clinically based or school-based screening or assessment. (1-14, 1-15, 1-16, 1-18)

Note: It is vital that teachers be cautious in the way in which they express to parents their concern that a child might have ADHD, as there are liabilities that may be incurred if it is not done properly. In fact, some states and school districts restrict what school personnel are permitted to discuss with parents. It is suggested that teachers check the protocol at their school. A team is the best forum for discussing whether the child's behaviors are indicative of what may possibly be ADHD and recommending an evaluation to parents. At minimum, one other school professional (for example, a school nurse, counselor, or psychologist) should join the teacher.

Following are some possible statements to use in communicating with parents:

■ "These are the behaviors we have been observing that have been causing your child difficulty at school and affecting his/her learning (or school performance)." *Note:* Ask parents whether they have observed these kinds of behaviors at home and whether they have similar concerns.

■ "Sometimes there are physiological causes for these kinds of difficulties (with paying attention, self-control, impulsive behavior, being highly active and restless). Of course, the only way to know that is through an evaluation."

■ "You may want to consider sharing these concerns with your child's doctor (or having your child evaluated)."

When meeting with parents prior to the child being diagnosed with a disorder, teachers should:

■ Avoid language that appears to diagnose or label the child as having ADHD.

■ Share objective information and descriptions of the child's behavior and performance.

■ Communicate their concern and caring for the child.

1-17 (*continued*)

- Emphasize the difficulties the *student* is having, not the problems the child is causing the *teacher*.

- Be sensitive to differences in cultural values and norms when speaking with parents of a different race, ethnicity, or cultural background.

Points to Keep in Mind

- Parents must understand that diagnosing ADHD is not simple. It requires the collection of significant data that must be interpreted to determine if the child meets the diagnostic criteria for ADHD.

- A school-based evaluation for ADHD can be conducted for *educational purposes*. (1-18)

- For a medical/clinical diagnosis of ADHD to be made, the parents will need to have the school supply data to the physician/mental health professional conducting the assessment. Of course, any possible medical conditions that may cause symptoms of ADHD or "look-like" ADHD would have to be determined or ruled out by a medical professional, not school professionals. (1-10)

- If parents wish to pursue any evaluation (school-based or clinically-based), they will be asked to sign permission forms to enable the school to start gathering appropriate information (such as teacher rating scales, questionnaires, observation forms, screening devices, informal/formal diagnostic testing). (1-15, 1-19)

- If the team decides to pursue a special education evaluation, the procedures and paperwork for an IEP will be initiated. (7-1, 7-2, 7-4)

Caution to Teachers

- Do not tell parents that you think their child has ADHD and should, therefore, be seen by their doctor.

- Do not attempt to diagnose ADHD.

- Do not recommend that the child be placed on medication or discuss medication with parents. If parents bring up the topic and ask you questions, suggest they share such questions with medical professionals.

- Do not share with parents your personal beliefs or biases about ADHD treatment approaches.

- Learn as much as you can about ADHD. Utilize a team approach and make any referrals or suggestions that the child possibly has ADHD through the team.

- Be prepared to let parents know how *you* will implement strategies and supports to help their child (regardless of any outside treatments the parents may pursue).

- Teachers need to *objectively describe* what they see regarding the child's behavior and performance in the classroom.

1-18
SCHOOL-BASED ASSESSMENT FOR ADHD

Some school districts are very proactive and involved in helping to identify, diagnose, and provide effective interventions for students with ADHD. These school districts generally have specified procedures and a process for school-based screening or evaluation of students for ADHD. The following steps (or variations) are typical in such school-based ADHD screening or assessment:

■ Most school-based screening or evaluation for ADHD begins with the Student Support Team (SST) process, with parents as members of the team. See List 6-2 for more about SST meetings, including the steps generally required of teachers prior to scheduling an SST meeting for a student.

■ In the case of a child suspected of having ADHD, teachers may be advised to carefully observe the student in comparison to other children in the classroom (degree of off-task behavior, out-of-seat behavior, completion of assignments) and start documenting or collecting evidence of difficulties in school performance (work samples, anecdotal records of behavioral incidents).

■ Teachers and parents will be asked to discuss their concerns and observations about the child's behavior, academic performance, social–emotional adjustment and coping skills, organization and study habits, and so forth.

■ During this meeting, the SST determines whether core symptoms (inattention, impulsivity, hyperactivity) are a concern in the school setting, as well as at home. If so, an initial screening for ADHD is recommended. Parents are provided information about steps the school can take in the diagnostic process for possible ADHD.

■ At the SST meeting, a plan of action is developed that includes some specific strategies or interventions the teacher agrees to try for a period of time (usually three to six weeks). The action plan may also involve other school supports. Parents are asked to sign a release-of-information form and give written permission to the school if they wish to proceed. This begins a period of initial screening for ADHD, which may involve:

  ▪ Review of cumulative school records (including report card grades and teacher comments, absences, standardized assessment, curriculum-based assessment, work samples).

  ▪ Classroom observation by at least one other person other than the classroom teacher.

  ▪ Observation, when possible, of the child in other school settings (cafeteria, P.E., playground).

  ▪ Vision and hearing screening.

  ▪ Screening scales or rating scales for teachers and parents to fill out, indicating the existence and degree of symptoms and impairment at home and at school.

  ▪ Questionnaires or a structured parent interview (to gather developmental, health, family, and school history).

1-18 (*continued*)

- Generally it is the school psychologist who has the primary responsibility for gathering the data and interpreting the information.

- Some districts designate a time frame (such as six to eight weeks or eight to ten weeks) to complete the following: gather all of the above information (and perhaps additional testing such as aptitude and/or achievement); review the data; implement and determine the effectiveness of strategies/interventions tried; and reconvene the SST to decide appropriate next steps.

- These next steps might include:

  - Continuing strategies and interventions proving to be effective.

  - Choosing a new or revised set of strategies/interventions to implement.

  - Initiating a medical referral (and sending a summary of the two preceding items to the child's physician, with written parental consent).

  - Initiating a referral for special education.

  - Providing supports, information, training, and referrals for parents.

- If screening instruments indicate possible ADHD and classroom interventions are not successful in resolving the student's difficulties, the school will generally recommend a medical and/or special education referral.

- In some school districts, if the child appears to have ADHD after careful review of the information gathered from screening and data review, their protocol is as follows:

  - Make a medical referral.

  - Send the completed packet of information and brief summary page to the physician (with parental permission).

  - Obtain a physician's statement in writing that the child has ADHD in order to be considered eligible for special education under "other health impaired" criteria (OHI).

  - Request the physician to describe how the symptoms, which led to the diagnosis, might adversely affect the student's educational performance.

- If the school team (which includes parents as members of the team) is able to determine that the ADHD symptoms are having an adverse impact on the student's educational performance, the child is entitled under law to reasonable school accommodations and special education or related services, if needed.

- Because ADHD is on the list of "other health impairments" under special education law (IDEA), a student whose ADHD symptoms are causing significant educational impairment would meet the eligibility criteria under OHI and would be entitled to special education and related services. (7-1, 7-2)

- Most districts require a medical diagnosis of ADHD to qualify a student for special education under the category of "other health impaired." However, this is a gray area under IDEA law and varies from state to state, district to district, depending on how OHI eligibility is interpreted.

- Because of these variations, a school-based assessment (without a physician statement or medical diagnosis) may or may not be sufficient for qualifying a student under OHI (for educational purposes only).

- To determine eligibility for accommodations under Section 504 of the Rehabilitation Act of 1973, the school team is also responsible for a 504 assessment. (7-1, 7-3)

- The SST also serves as the 504 team in most schools. The ADHD screening/assessment procedures described above are sufficient for determining if a child has "a physical or mental condition that significantly limits a major life activity (learning)."

- If a child meets that criteria under Section 504, then the SST/504 team can write a 504 Accommodation Plan for the student, which contains reasonable accommodations and supports that will be implemented to help the student. (7-3)

- During the school-based screening or evaluation for ADHD, it often becomes apparent that the child is also experiencing problems with learning, speech and language, motor skills, or other areas. Remember, there are a number of common coexisting conditions and disorders with ADHD. When this is the case, a referral for special education and assessment of all areas of concern should take place under IDEA (the IEP process). (7-2, 7-4)

- Teacher information that is valuable in an ADHD diagnosis (clinical or school-based) includes such insights and observations regarding:
  - The child's rate of progress, general school performance, and adjustment
  - Current problems seen in the classroom or other school settings
  - Environmental, instructional, and behavioral strategies/interventions that seem to be most effective
  - How well the student interacts with others
  - The child's strengths, interests, and motivators
  - Work performance, production, and output
  - Organizational skills and time management
  - On-task behavior
  - Ability to inhibit behavior and exhibit self-control
  - The child's apparent learning styles

- Parent information that is valuable in an ADHD diagnosis (clinical or school-based) includes insights and observations regarding:
  - The child's difficulties in learning, behavior, health, and social interactions
  - The child's strengths, interests, and motivators
  - Responses to discipline and discipline techniques used in the home

1-18 (*continued*)

- How the child responds when upset, angry, or frustrated
- How the child gets along with others (siblings, neighborhood children)
- The child's feelings (worries, fears)
- In addition, parents' input is needed regarding:
  - The concerns of others who spend much time with their child (baby-sitters, child-care providers, other relatives, friends, teachers)
  - Medical history
  - Early developmental history
  - Family history
  - School history
  - Behavioral history
  - Recent stress events (serious illness in family, death, divorce, family moved, and so on)

RELATED LISTS

- See Lists 1-14 and 1-19 for more information on this topic.

1-19
PARENT AND TEACHER RATING SCALES, QUESTIONNAIRES, AND INTERVIEW QUESTIONS

There are a variety of different questionnaires and rating scales that are published and available for use by evaluators in obtaining information from parents and teachers.

Some of these scales and questionnaires include:

- NICHQ Vanderbilt Assessment Scale—Parent and Teacher Informant scales
  Note: The Vanderbilt Teacher scale can be found in the Appendix. All of the Vanderbilt scales (parent, teacher, and follow-up) can be downloaded from the website of the National Initiative for Children's Healthcare Quality (AAP ADHD Toolkit) at www.nichq.org.
- Conners' Teacher Rating Scale and Conners' Parent Rating Scale—Revised
- ACTeRs (ADD-H Comprehensive Teacher's Rating Scale)
- Behavior Assessment System for Children—Teacher Rating Scales (BASC-TRS)
- Comprehensive Behavior Rating Scale for Children
- Child Behavior Checklist—Teacher's Report Form (Achenbach)
- Devereux Behavior Rating Scale
- Child Attention Profile
- The SNAP Teacher and Parent Rating Scale
- Pittsburgh Modified Conners Teacher Rating Scale
- Parent/Teacher Disruptive Behavior Disorder (DBD) Rating Scale
- Attention Deficit Disorders Evaluation Scale (ADDES)
- School Situations Questionnaire
- Home/School Situations Questionnaire

Rating scales list a number of items that teachers or parents rate according to the frequency they observe the child exhibiting those specific behaviors or problems. Sometimes the ratings range from "never" to "almost always," or from "not at all" to "very much." Some rating scales are numerical (ranging from 1–5 or 0–4). The scales are standardized and enable the evaluator to compare a child's behavioral symptoms with those of other children of that age/developmental level.

Points to Keep in Mind

- In some of the instruments used, various situations in the home or school are described, and the parents/teachers rate if they see the child presenting difficulty in any of those situations and to what degree (mild to severe).

1-19 (*continued*)

- The types of behaviors that teachers are asked to rate the child/teen in comparison with other students in the class focus on the existence or degree of:
  - Disruptive behavior
  - Demanding behavior
  - Excitability
  - Moodiness
  - Compliant, cooperative behavior
  - Oppositional behavior
  - Organization skills
  - Distractibility
  - Forgetfulness
  - Independent work habits
  - On-task behavior
  - Talkativeness
  - Activity level
  - Fidgetiness
  - Aggressiveness
  - Ability to interact and get along with other children, adults, and authority figures
  - Ability to change activities and handle transitions/changes in routine
  - Ability to get started on tasks
  - Ability to pay attention to details
  - Ability to complete work
  - Ability to follow directions and class rules
  - Ability to wait his or her turn
  - Ability to sustain attention to tasks requiring mental effort
  - Ability to control emotions
  - Ability to display self-control and inhibit behavior/impulses
  - Ability to concentrate and pay attention
  - Ability to play quietly
- Teachers should be prepared to share with the evaluator information to questions they may be asked, such as the following:
  - Describe the child's strengths and interests.
  - Describe the child's difficulties.
  - Describe the current educational functioning levels and performance.

- Has the child had any testing or school assessments?
- Does the child receive any special education services?
- What services are available at the school?
- Has the child ever repeated a grade?

■ Parents will be asked similar questions related to their observations in the home or other settings.

■ Questionnaires and interviews with parents (and often the child) may elicit information regarding:

- Other diagnoses or problems the child has had, as well as treatments
- Family information and history of medical, psychiatric, psychological problems and diagnoses of parents and other family members
- School information and history (for example, presenting problems, concerns, academic performance, any testing, support services or interventions)
- The parents' child-management/discipline style
- The child's interactions with family members, friends, and others
- Other family stressors
- Medical history (prenatal, illnesses, allergies, hospitalizations, medications, surgeries, and injuries)
- Developmental history (approximate dates of milestones reached in various language, motor, self-help, adaptive, and learning skills)
- Other problems the child is experiencing or problems in the past that may be relevant
- Child/teen's strengths/interests
- Parents' observations of how well the child can modulate his or her behavior (for example, sit still during meal time; play games with siblings; handle frustrations; refrain from interrupting; how well the child can organize, pay attention, and persist through tasks such as homework or chores)

1-20
ADHD AND ITS EFFECT ON THE FAMILY

It is important to be aware of the challenges that exist in the home when one or more children (or parent) have ADHD, as this disorder significantly affects the entire family. Unfortunately, teachers are generally unaware or underestimate the struggles these families face—typically, a much higher degree of stress than the average family, along with depression or other pathology in one or more family members.

Note: Remember, it is likely that more than one family member has this disorder (and coexisting conditions). See List 1-6.

The following are reasons why ADHD causes so much stress in families:

■ There are generally major issues surrounding the battle with homework as well as morning and evening routines (getting ready for school, bedtime).

■ Living with a child who has ADHD often takes a heavy toll on marriages:

  ▪ Parents are generally in different stages of a "grieving process" about having a child who does not fit the norm and has a disability.

  ▪ It is common for parents to disagree about treatment, discipline, management, structure, and so forth.

  ▪ Parents are known to blame one another for the child's problems or to be highly critical of one another in their parenting or spousal role. This causes a great deal of marital stress and a higher rate of divorce.

  ▪ Often it is the mother who must cope with the brunt of the issues throughout the day, which is physically and emotionally exhausting.

  ▪ The situation is even more challenging in single-parent homes.

■ As any parent of a toddler knows, when the child needs constant supervision and monitoring, it is very time-consuming and interferes with one's ability to get things done as planned (housework, chores, and so on).

■ Parents of children who have ADHD are constantly faced with needing to defend their parenting choices as well as their child. They must listen to "negative press" about this disorder and reject popular opinion in order to provide their child with necessary interventions and treatment.

■ Parents must deal with criticism and "well-meaning advice" from grandparents, other relatives, friends, and acquaintances regarding how they should be disciplining and parenting their child. This causes a lot of parental self-doubt and adds to the stress they are already living with day in and day out.

- Frequently, the family must deal with social issues, such as the exclusion of the child from out-of-school activities. It is painful when the child is not invited to birthday parties, or has difficulty finding someone to play with and keeping friends.

- Siblings are often resentful or jealous of the central role their ADHD sibling plays in the family's schedule, routines, and activities, as well as the extra time and special treatment the child receives. In addition, siblings are acutely aware and feel hurt and embarrassed when their brother or sister has acquired a negative reputation in the neighborhood and school.

- Parents have a much higher degree of responsibility in working with the school and being proactive in the management of their child. Further, it is crucial that they fully educate themselves about ADHD in order to successfully advocate their child's needs. (8-5, 8-10)

Points to Keep in Mind

- In many cases, other family members who have ADHD were never diagnosed and have been struggling to cope with their own difficulties without proper treatment and support. That is why the clinicians who specialize in treating children with ADHD say it is so important to view treatment in the context of the family. Learning about the family (communication, disciplinary practices, and so on) helps in designing a treatment plan that is most effective for the child.

- It is very common that parents will recognize for the first time what they have been suffering with over the years (undiagnosed ADHD) when their son or daughter is diagnosed with the disorder. This can be most helpful and result in a positive change in the family dynamics. (8-8)

- Without question, families of children with ADHD need support and understanding. Fortunately, there are far more supports available now than a decade ago. See Lists 6-4 and 8-10 on supports that parents need.

SOURCES AND RESOURCES

http://www.chadd.org

http://www.addhelpline.org

http://www.adhd.com

http://www.add.org

http://www.oneaddplace.com

http://www.schwablearning.org

See List 8-10 for more websites.

1-21
THE IMPACT OF ADHD ON SCHOOL PERFORMANCE AND SUCCESS

ADHD generally causes the most difficulty and impairment in school performance. This disorder can significantly affect children and teens in various aspects of school functioning (academic, behavioral, and social).

Please note that every student has different educational needs. Their ADHD symptoms may or may not affect them in the following areas, and, if so, to varying degrees. Much of the content in this book addresses specific strategies, techniques, and supports in the following areas, which are problematic for many students with ADHD:

- Organization and study skills
- Planning for short-term assignments
- Planning for long-term projects and assignments
- Various disruptive, aggressive, and/or annoying behaviors, resulting in a much higher degree of negative attention and interaction from classmates, teachers, and other school personnel
- Social skills and peer relationships (ability to work well in cooperative learning groups and get along with peers in work or play activities)
- Classwork completion to acceptable grade-level standards
- Homework completion (turned in on time and to acceptable grade-level standards)
- Listening and following directions
- Following class and school rules
- Participating and engaging in classroom instruction/activities
- Working independently (seat work)
- Being prepared with materials for class and homework
- Ability to cope with daily frustrations
- Time awareness and time-management skills
- Issues with low self-esteem
- Building and maintaining friendships
- Written expression/output
- Handwriting and fine-motor skills
- Spelling
- Proofing and editing written work

- Note-taking
- Test-taking
- Reading comprehension
- Reading fluency (generally when there is a coexisting learning disability)
- Math computation
- Listening comprehension
- Short-term memory
- Anger management
- Problem solving and conflict resolution

Fortunately, there are numerous strategies that can be employed by teachers (and parents) to help children build these skills and enhance their school performance. See lists throughout this book.

1-22
A COMPREHENSIVE TREATMENT PROGRAM FOR ADHD

Once a child is identified and diagnosed with ADHD, there are many ways to help the child and the family. The most effective approach is a multifaceted treatment that might involve the following types of interventions:

- Medical
- Psychological (behavioral)
- Educational

Note: There are only two treatments that are scientifically proven to be effective in the management of ADHD: (1) stimulant medication and (2) parent training/behavioral therapy.

Points to Keep in Mind

- Parents are the child's primary case managers. They need to find appropriate professionals and build a team to help with the care and management of their ADHD child.
- Most positive outcomes are achieved when collaboration occurs between:
  - Parents
  - School personnel
  - Physician
  - Mental health professionals
  - The child
- Since ADHD often lasts throughout one's lifetime, a person may need some of the supports and interventions at different times in his or her life (assistance from educators, mental health professionals, physicians, tutors, coaches).

Key Components of the Multimodal Treatment Program

- *Medical/pharmacological intervention*—Pharmacological treatment involves the use of medication to manage ADHD symptoms. (1-23, 1-24, 1-25)
- *Behavior modification and specific behavior management strategies* implemented at home and school. A number of these techniques and strategies are addressed in Section 2. (2-1 through 2-17)
- Educational supports and accommodation.

Counseling of Various Kinds

- *Parent counseling/training*—This is a crucial part of any treatment plan, as parents must learn and be provided with:

- Accurate and reliable information about ADHD in order to understand the impact and developmental course of the disorder, the treatment options, and available resources to help manage ADHD.

- A new set of skills for managing their child's challenging behaviors.

- Training in effective behavioral techniques and how to structure the home environment (and other aspects of their child's life).

■ *Family counseling*—The whole family is often affected in the homes of children with ADHD. (1-20) Family therapy can address issues that affect other family members (parents and siblings) and improve family relationships.

■ *Individual counseling*—The child may benefit from learning coping techniques, self-monitoring/self-regulation strategies, problem-solving strategies, and how to deal with stress and anger.

■ *Psychotherapy (for adults)*—This may help the adult with a history of school, work, personal, and relationship problems talk about his or her feelings and deal with self-defeating patterns of behavior.

■ *Vocational counseling*—This is often an important intervention for teens and adults.

■ *Social skills training*—This training is usually provided in small groups with curriculum addressing specific skills that children with ADHD tend to have difficulties with. Skills include such behaviors as:

- Waiting for a turn

- Listening and responding

- Understanding body language and vocal tones

- Ignoring teasing

- Sharing and cooperating

Note: Social-skills training programs teach specific skills through discussion and role-playing, then provide the opportunity for the child to practice the skills repeatedly in the natural setting where the skill is required (what is referred to as the "point of performance"). (2-16)

■ *Numerous school interventions* (environmental, academic, instructional, behavioral) to accommodate the child's needs. See lists throughout this book addressing these topics.

■ *Special education or related services*, if needed. (7-1 through 7-4)

■ *Special school services and accommodations*—Various interventions and "safety nets" that may be available at the school such as homework assistance, mentoring, academic tutorials, computer lab, and so on.

■ *Teacher/school staff awareness training about ADHD.* (6-3)

■ *Physical outlet* (swimming, martial arts, gymnastics, track and field, dance, hiking, sports).

- *Note:* Team sports such as soccer or basketball may be better than other team sports (such as baseball) that require a lot of waiting for a chance to move and participate.

1-22 (*continued*)

- Children with ADHD are often more successful in individual sports rather than team sports. Activities such as martial arts (such as aikido) are often recommended because they increase the child's ability to focus and concentrate.

- *Recreation and enhancement of areas of strength*—Involve the child/teen in activities that build upon his or her strengths and interests (arts/crafts, sports, scouts, dance, music, acting/performing arts).

- *Organizational/time-management coaching*—This is becoming a popular intervention for adolescents and adults with ADHD. It basically involves acquiring the support of a coach who helps organize the ADHD individual with:
  - Scheduling
  - Breaking down work tasks into reasonable and manageable short-term goals
  - Checking in regularly and keeping the ADHD client on target with his or her individual short- and long-term goals
  - See Lists 4-4 through 4-9 and 8-8.

- *Support groups*—It is often helpful for parents to interact with other parents who have children with ADHD:
  - Parent support groups are excellent sources of information, assistance, and networking.
  - CHADD maintains support groups/local chapters throughout the United States.
  - Parents can also find information and connections with other parents on the Internet (websites and chat rooms related to ADHD).
  - See Lists 6-4, 8-5, and 8-10.

Note: Children/teens with ADHD may also benefit from meeting and speaking with peers who also have the same disorder and challenges.

Points to Keep in Mind

- When pursuing any treatment, seek out doctors and therapists who are knowledgeable and experienced specifically with treating individuals with ADHD. (1-16, 8-5)

- Ongoing teamwork and communication between parents, school personnel, physicians, and therapists is critical in any treatment plan. See the ADHD Management Plan form (by NICHQ) in the Appendix that illustrates collaborative partnership in establishing goals, plans to reach the goals, and multimodal treatment.

- If ADHD-like symptoms are causing the child difficulty, school interventions should be implemented at once (regardless of whether or not the child has been diagnosed with ADHD). Parents should be encouraged to pursue an evaluation. A proper diagnosis is most helpful in understanding the child and, thus, better meeting that child's needs.

- All professionals working with the child/family need to have a knowledge base about ADHD and focus on the issues from a positive approach. Interventions should be designed to help the child recognize and draw upon his or her strengths, and build within the child a sense of control over his or her own behaviors.

■ Parents should stay clear of professionals who tend to cast blame upon anyone (child, parents, school) or view ADHD from a negative perspective. Goldstein (2000) makes a very powerful point when he advises:

> "Treatment planning must not only include identifying strategies to manage problematic symptoms and behaviors, but also finding strategies to build on what's right, to facilitate self-esteem, self-confidence, resilience, and a sense of self-efficacy. The discussion of treatment planning must equally focus on what is *right* with the child as upon what is wrong."

■ Parents need to be educated about ADHD and treatments and their legal rights in the educational system so they can effectively advocate for their child—both in the educational and health-care systems. (7-1 through 7-5, 8-5, 8-10)

■ Children, especially teens, should be included as active partners in the entire treatment program. They need to understand the reason for various interventions and how those treatments are intended to positively affect their daily lives. The child/teen must be respectfully included in this process and understand so that they will be motivated to cooperate and participate in (not sabotage) the treatment.

SOURCES AND RESOURCES

Gephart, Harlan. "AD/HD: Diagnosis, Treatment, and Advocacy," *Drug Benefits Trends*, vol. 13, Supplement C; December 2001.

Goldstein, Sam. "ADHD as a Disorder of Self Regulation," Special CHADD Handout, October 7–9, 1999. (http://www.samgoldstein.com/articles/9910.html)

Goldstein, Sam. "From Assessment to Treatment: Developing a Comprehensive Plan to Help Your Child with ADHD," September 2000. (http://www.samgoldstein.com/articles/0009.html)

Hinshaw, S. P., R. G. Klein, and H. Abikoff. Childhood Attention Deficit Hyperactivity Disorder: Nonpharmacologic and Combination Approaches. In P. E. Nathan and J. M. Gorman (eds.), *A Guide to Treatments that Work*. New York: Oxford University Press, 1998.

Hinshaw, Stephen. "Psychosocial Intervention for AD/HD: How Well Does it Work?" CHADD: *Attention*, vol. 6, no. 4; March/April 2000, 30–34.

Leslie, Laurel. "Treatments for ADHD" (http://sandiegoadhd.org/clinicians/treatment/treatment_index.htm)

Pelham, W. E., and G. Fabiano. "Behavior Modification," *Child and Adolescent Psychiatric Clinics of North America*, vol. 2, 671–688, 2000.

1-22 (*continued*)

Pelham, William E., Jr. *ADHD: Diagnosis, Nature, Etiology, and Treatment.* Buffalo, NY: University of Buffalo, Center for Children and Families, 2002.

"Study Explores Treatment Options for AD/HD," CHADD: *Attention*, vol. 6, no. 4, March/April 2000, 37–39.

"Understanding and Identifying Children with ADHD: First Steps to Effective Intervention" (http://www.ldonline.org/ld_indepth/add_adhd/ael_firsteps.html)

1-23
RESEARCH-VALIDATED TREATMENTS
FOR ADHD

There are no quick fixes or "cures" for ADHD. There are, however, treatment approaches known to be effective. A multimodal approach, with a combination of interventions (medical, psycho-social, and educational) has the greatest long-term effectiveness in the treatment and management of ADHD.

Because ADHD is for most individuals a chronic and lifelong disorder, there are various treatments that may be needed at different stages or times in a person's life. List 1-22 addresses components of a comprehensive, multimodal treatment plan for ADHD.

Points to Keep in Mind

- Some treatment approaches are known to be more effective than others, based upon extensive research and empirical studies. Research data gathered over thirty years has proven that the use of stimulant medications in the treatment of ADHD accounts by far for the greatest amount of behavioral improvement in children with ADHD. Based on the evidence, the benefits of medication greatly outweigh the risks of treatment.

- The research also demonstrates that behavioral treatments are highly beneficial (but to a lesser degree than medication in improvement of symptoms).

- Psycho-stimulant medications (also called simply "stimulants") are the most widely used class of medication for the management of symptoms related to ADHD. (1-24) Stimulant treatment significantly improves in the short-term many of the core symptoms and related behaviors of ADHD, including:
  - Decreased activity levels and impulsivity
  - Increased attention to task and concentration
  - Increased amount and accuracy of school work produced
  - Decreased negative behavior in social interactions
  - Decreased verbal/physical hostility

A RESEARCH-VALIDATED STUDY

The National Institute of Mental Health (NIMH) supported the largest ADHD study that had ever been conducted, called the Multimodal Treatment Study of Children with Attention-Deficit Hyperactivity Disorder (MTA, 1999). This landmark government-sponsored research study:

1-23 *(continued)*

- Was the longest and most thorough study of the effects of medication and behavioral treatments for children diagnosed with ADHD

- Involved nearly 600 elementary school children with ADHD between the ages of 7 and 9, from a range of socioeconomic backgrounds

- Took place at six different university medical centers around the United States and Canada

- Randomly assigned children to four different treatment programs:

    1. Used medication management alone

    2. Used behavioral treatment alone

    3. Used a combination of both medication and behavioral treatment

    4. Received routine community care from physicians not involved with the study

Results of this important study showed that:

- The group of children who received carefully managed medical treatment (monthly office visits, close communication with parents and teachers in determining effectiveness of prescription, adjustment based upon that feedback) had the greatest improvements in ADHD symptoms.

- Improvements were greater than those children who received only the behavioral treatments; and the behavioral interventions were very intensive, involving:

    - A combination of parent training sessions in behavioral management

    - Teacher consultations

    - A summer treatment program

    - A paraprofessional aide placed in the child's class for a few months

- Although children in the "behavioral treatment only" group also improved in ADHD-related behaviors, the carefully managed and supervised medication-only group made much greater improvements with their treatment in comparison.

- The group of children who received a combination of well-managed medication treatment and behavioral treatment also had very significant improvements.

- Children treated by a physician who was carefully managing and supervising the medication treatment (alone) or in combination with behavioral treatments showed fewer ADHD symptoms than those who received only behavioral treatments or regular medical treatment in the community.

- Careful monitoring of medication (involving communication with parents and school personnel along with monthly follow-up) was shown to make a significant difference in the effectiveness of treatment.

- The community treatment physician generally saw children in office visits one or two times a year and there was little if any interaction with teachers in the management of the medication.

■ The combination program of medicine and behavioral treatments was most effective in improving areas such as:

- Academic performance

- Patient anxiety

- Child–parent interaction

- Oppositional behavior

- Enabling improvement of symptoms with generally lower doses of medication required

■ The American Academy of Pediatrics Guidelines on ADHD recommend stimulant medication and/or behavior management or behaviorial treatments as appropriate.

■ Well-managed drug therapy with stimulant medications is highly effective. The most effective treatment (in and of itself) in improving the symptoms of ADHD is during the period of time the medication is within the child's body. Once the medication wears off, the symptom-relief also wears off.

■ There is disagreement among the experts and other professionals as to whether or not stimulant medication should be the first-line treatment for all children who have ADHD as a primary diagnosis. Certainly in school settings, the following should be implemented without delay when a child exhibits ADHD-like behaviors and difficulties:

- Environmental engineering/accommodations

- Behavioral interventions and supports

- Other key instructional and academic strategies and accommodations

WHAT DOES THE RESEARCH SHOW ABOUT PSYCHO-SOCIAL TREATMENTS FOR ADHD?

The following information is summarized from Hinshaw (2000), one of the key MTA researchers.

Of the various psycho-social therapies (play, psychotherapy), research has proven only one type of therapy effective in treating ADHD—behavioral therapy/behavior modification. Lists in Section 2 will address the various strategies and techniques recommended in behavior therapy. Among the behavior therapies found to be effective for children with ADHD are:

■ *Direct Contingency Management*

- Positive and negative contingencies are applied directly to the child in carefully structured and engineered environments (residential settings, special education classes, summer treatment programs).

- Children consistently earn rewards when demonstrating appropriate target behaviors and prudent consequences (such as response cost or timeout) for misbehaviors.

1-23 (continued)

- The therapy is provided directly by teachers, counselors, or others working with the child in that setting.

- *Clinical Behavior Therapy*—This is the most common form of behavioral therapy, involving a therapist training parents and teachers in behavior-modification and management techniques. The research validates the importance of training parents of ADHD children to implement parenting practices with appropriate behavior-management techniques. There are better outcomes for the child when parents and teachers focus on:

  - Prompting and positively attending to appropriate behavior

  - Applying consistent corrective consequences to inappropriate behaviors

  - Coordinating programs between home and school (Daily Report Cards)

  - In order for clinical behavior therapy to be an effective treatment for children with ADHD, the adults (parents/teachers) must be committed, active participants in the recommended treatment.

- *Social Skills Training*—Research has shown benefits for children with ADHD when they are directly taught specific social skills, have numerous and repeated opportunities to rehearse or practice those skills (especially at the point of performance or real-life settings), and are rewarded for the use of those skills. (2-16)

Although medication is known to have the greatest effect in ADHD symptom improvement, it is not the treatment of choice for everyone, nor does it teach a child necessary skills (coping, behavioral, social–emotional, academic). There are some children for whom medication does not work, and there are a number of families who do not wish to use medication as part of the treatment plan. Psycho-social and educational interventions are needed for most children with ADHD and may be the only available treatment options for many.

SOURCES AND RESOURCES

American Psychiatric Association. *ADHD Fact Sheet*, March 2001.

Gephart, Harlan. "AD/HD: Diagnosis, Treatment, and Advocacy." *Drug Benefits Trends*, vol. 13, Sup. C, December 2001.

Hinshaw, S. P., R. G. Klein, and H. Abikoff. Childhood Attention Deficit Hyperactivity Disorder: Nonpharmacologic and Combination Approaches. In P. E. Nathan and J. M. Gorman (eds.), *A Guide to Treatments that Work*. New York: Oxford University Press, 1998.

Hinshaw, Stephen. "Psychosocial Intervention for AD/HD: How Well Does it Work?" CHADD: *Attention*, vol. 6, no. 4, March/April 2000.

MTA Cooperative Group. "Fourteen-month Randomized Clinical Trial of Treatment Strategies for Attention-Deficit Hyperactivity Disorder," *Archives of General Psychiatry*, 56, 1073–1086; 1999.

MTA Cooperative Group. "Effects of Comorbid Anxiety, Poverty, Session Attendance, and Community Medication Treatment Outcome in Children with AD/HD," *Archives of General Psychiatry*, 56, 1088–1096; 1999.

MTA study (http://www.nimh.nih.gov/events/mtaqu.ctm)

Pelham, W. E., T. Wheeler, and A. Chronis. "Empirically Supported Psychosocial Treatments for Attention-Deficit Hyperactivity Disorder," *Journal of Clinical Child Psychology*, 27, 190–205; 1998.

Ringeisen, Heather. "AD/HD and the National Institute of Mental Health: Where Are We Now and Where Are We Going?" CHADD: *Attention*, vol. 7, no. 3, November/ December 2000, 10–13.

"Study Explores Treatment Options for AD/HD," CHADD: *Attention*, vol. 6, no. 4, March/April 2000, 37–39.

Swanson, J. M., K. McBurnett et al. "Effect of Stimulant Medication on Children with Attention Deficit Disorder: A Review of Reviews," *Exceptional Children*, 60, 154– 162; 1993.

1-24
MEDICATION TREATMENT AND MANAGEMENT

Medications have been used for decades to treat symptoms of ADHD. Though none of them cure the disorder, they do temporarily control the symptoms. Most effective in both children and adults are the stimulants (also called psychostimulants).

PSYCHOSTIMULANT (STIMULANT) MEDICATIONS

- These are the most commonly prescribed medications for ADHD and should be the first choice of medications used in treating children with ADHD. Stimulant medications have been used for children and studied for about fifty years.

- It is suspected that these stimulant medications increase the production of neurotransmitters in the brain to a more normalized level, enabling the child to better focus attention and regulate his or her activity level and impulsive behaviors. See Lists 1-7 and 1-8, which explain how researchers believe these medications work within the brain to reduce symptoms and improve functioning.

- There are various kinds of stimulant medications:
  - *Methylphenidate* (Ritalin®, Metadate®, Methylin®, Focalin®, Concerta™)
  - *Dextroamphetamine* (Dexedrine®, Dexedrine Spansule®, Dextrostat®)
  - *Mixed amphetamine salts* (Adderall®)

- Methylphenidates are among the most carefully studied drugs on the market. Hundreds of research studies and thousands of children have been involved in evaluating the use of these drugs in the treatment of ADHD. They are known to be highly effective and considered safe. Methylphenidate has been used successfully since 1955.

- Methylphenidates come in long-acting (up to 12 hours), intermediate-acting (up to 6 hours), and short-acting (up to 4 hours) forms.

- Stimulant (psychostimulant) medications have proven to be beneficial in the treatment of ADHD. In approximately 80–90% of children treated with stimulant medication, symptoms and impairment improve to various degrees. Each stimulant has a high response rate. A child who does not respond well (with symptom improvement) with one stimulant medication will often respond well to another.

- Choice of initial stimulant medication (to be tried) is a matter of physician and parent preference.

- The various types of stimulants have different onsets of action and drop-off slopes, duration of effects, and release systems into the body.

- Ritalin®, Dexedrine®, and generic methylphenidate come in short- and intermediate-acting forms.

- The short-acting form of the medication:
  - Starts to work about 20–30 minutes from the time it is taken.
  - Metabolizes quickly and is effective for approximately 3–4 hours.
  - Generally requires an additional dosage to be administered at school.
  - Often requires a third dose to enable the child to function more successfully in the late afternoon/evening hours.
- The long-acting form of the medication:
  - Provides a smoother sustained level of the drug throughout the day.
  - Minimizes fluctuations in blood levels.
  - May be beneficial for those children (particularly adolescents) who are embarrassed about or forgetful in going to the school nurse/office for a midday dose.
- *Benefits of stimulant medications:* In many cases, the improvement seen in school is dramatic when a child with ADHD receives a therapeutic dosage of a stimulant medication. The positive effects are often seen in improved ability to:
  - Control impulses and emotions
  - Inhibit behaviors and regulate activity level
  - Initiate and complete tasks
  - Sustain mental effort and increase work production
  - Pay attention and stay focused
  - Organize oneself
  - Interact with others
  - Tolerate frustrations
  - Other positive effects (such as improved handwriting and academic accuracy)
- *Adverse side effects from stimulant medications:* There are some possible side effects that may occur with stimulant medications, including:
  - Stomach aches
  - Headaches
  - Irritability
  - Loss of appetite
  - Difficulty falling asleep
  - Rebound effect may occur (see below)
  - A small number of children develop or unmask latent tics (involuntary muscle movements) in the form of facial grimaces, sniffing, coughing, snorting, or other vocal sounds. *Note:* These are rare and in most cases tics do not continue if the medication is stopped.
- There may also be an initial slight effect on height and weight gain. According to Wilens (1999), the vast majority of children ultimately achieve normal height and

1-24 (*continued*)

weight as young adults. By nature of their ADHD, these children tend to mature and grow at a later stage of their life (usually later adolescence).

- *Rebound phenomenon:* This is a worsening of ADHD symptoms (moodiness, irritability, less compliance, more activity) as the medication wears off. It usually lasts for about 15–45 minutes and can generally be altered by the physician adjusting the dosage or the times when medication is given, or prescribing a different medication.

- It is noted that typically the time when the stimulant is wearing off and rebound is observed takes place when the child goes through a significant transition time of the day (with change of expectations and structure).

- Often the child is on the bus ride home from school, in an after-school child-care environment, or at home expected to do homework or other activities when ADHD symptoms take a turn for the worse. So, it is not known if the worsening of ADHD symptoms observed is entirely due to the drug wear-off or other factors.

- *Titration phase:* When a child begins medication treatment, it requires what is known as a titration phase. This involves:

  - Close monitoring of symptoms and behavioral changes (at home and school) while progressively changing the doses and the timing of medication administered.

  - The attempt to achieve optimal effects from the medication with a minimum of side effects.

  - Starting typically with a low dose and raising it every few days until an optimal response is seen (improvement in symptoms and impairment at school and at home).

  - Time until the physician is able to determine the appropriate therapeutic prescription.

  - The titration process beginning again whenever a different choice of stimulant medication is tried.

  - Communication and feedback from teachers and parents to the physician. (1-25, 6-1)

TRICYCLIC ANTIDEPRESSANTS

- This is another group of medications that is also believed to work by acting on neurotransmitters in the brain. These, too, are used in the treatment of children with ADHD as a second-line choice of medication. This class of medications is often prescribed for a child who cannot tolerate or is not responding to a stimulant medication, or to a child with signs of depression, anxiety, or tics, as well as ADHD. This category includes the medications:

  - Imipramine (Tofranil®)

  - Desiprimine (Norpramine®)

  - Amytriptyline (Elavil®)

  - Nortriptyline (Pamelor®)

■ The tricyclic antidepressants take some time to build up in the bloodstream and reach a therapeutic level.

■ *Benefits:* These medications also reduce the symptoms of hyperactivity and impulsivity. They help with:

- Mood swings

- Emotionality

- Anxiety

- Depression

- Sleep disturbances

- Tics

■ *Possible side effects are:*

- Dry mouth

- Constipation

- Dizziness

- Confusion

- Increase in blood pressure

- Rapid or irregular heart rate

- Fatigue

■ There are less commonly used medications for treating ADHD. These include among others:

- Clonidine (Catapres®)

- Buproprion (Wellbutrin®)

■ Sometimes the child is best treated with a combination of medications. This is common practice for children with comorbid (coexisting) conditions. (1-11) Medication management can be quite complex for these children.

■ Whenever a child is being treated with medication, there are important things that teachers and parents need to be aware of, observing for, and reporting to the physician. (1-25)

Note: Parents should consult with the physician/medical professionals about any medication issues or concerns. This list is meant as a general reference only.

SOURCES AND RESOURCES

Adesman, Andrew. "Does My Child Need Ritalin?" CHADD: *Attention,* vol. 7, no. 5, April 2001, 37–38.

Greenhill, Laurence L. "ADHD and Medication Management," *Drug Benefit Trends,* vol. 13, Supplement C; December 2001.

1-24 (*continued*)

Jensen, Peter S. "Medication Strategies for ADHD," Presentation to NICHQ (National Initiative for Children's Healthcare Quality), September 12–13, 2001.

"Medication Management of Children and Adults with AD/HD," *The CHADD Information and Resource Guide to AD/HD*. Landover, MD: CHADD, 2001.

Swanson, J. M., K. McBurnett et al. "Effect of Stimulant Medication on Children with Attention Deficit Disorder: A Review of Reviews," *Exceptional Children*, 60, 154–162; 1993.

"Treatment for ADHD," Child and Adolescent Services Research Center & Developmental Services Division of Children's Hospital and Health Center, San Diego, 2001. (http://sandiegoadhd.org/clinicians/treatment/treatment_index.htm)

Wender, Esther. "Managing Stimulant Medication for AD/HD," *Pediatrics in Review*, vol. 22, no. 6; June 2001.

Wilens, Timothy E. *Straight Talk about Psychiatric Medications for Kids*. New York: The Guilford Press, 1999.

1-25
IF A CHILD/TEEN IS TAKING MEDICATION: ADVICE FOR SCHOOL STAFF AND PARENTS

WHAT TEACHERS NEED TO KNOW

Parents do not easily make the decision to try their child on medication. Typically, parents agonize over the decision and frequently avoid the medical route for years. No parent wants to have a child take a "drug." Parents often are fearful and feel guilty.

The school's role is to support any child receiving medication treatment. School personnel need to be aware of and sensitive to the issues involved with medicating children and fully cooperate as appropriate. Teachers in particular need to be involved with:

■ Close observation of the child

■ Communication with parents, doctors, and the school nurse

■ Making sure the child is receiving the medication as prescribed on time

Generally it is the school nurse who acts as the liaison between the parent and teacher in helping to manage the medication at school. Coordination and communication between all parties involved is essential for optimal results.

The teacher is an integral part of the therapeutic team because of his or her unique ability to observe the child's performance and functioning (academically, socially, and behaviorally) on medication during most of the day. Teachers will need to monitor and observe students on medication carefully and report changes in:

■ Academic performance

■ Work production

■ Ability to stay on-task

■ Behavior

■ Relationships

■ Any possible side effects the child may be experiencing

These observations and feedback are necessary in helping the physician to regulate the dosage and/or determine if the medication has the desired positive effects. Teachers should feel free to contact the parent, physician, and school nurse with input, observations, and any concerns they might have.

Physicians (or their office personnel) should be initiating contact with the teacher in managing the medication and asking for feedback through:

1-25 (*continued*)

■ Phone calls, e-mail

■ Completion of a teacher assessment follow-up behavior rating scale or medication monitoring form

■ Other information (such as work samples)

It is also important for teachers to understand that:

■ Medication(s), dosages, and times to be administered are often changed or adjusted until the right "recipe" or combination is found for the child.

■ Children metabolize medication at different rates.

■ Children may experience some side effects.

■ Teachers will need to observe and communicate if the child is having recurring academic, social, or behavioral problems at certain times of the day.

Points to Keep in Mind

■ If a student is prescribed a short-acting stimulant medication requiring a dosage to be taken during school hours, it is important that medication be given on time (which is generally administered during the lunch period or right after lunch). With Ritalin®, for example, the peak action is approximately two hours after the child has received it; the effects dissipate in about four hours.

■ Be aware that some children experience a "rebound effect" when the medication wears off. (1-24) When the next prescribed dose is not given on time, these children are found crying, fighting, or otherwise "in trouble" on the playground or cafeteria, and disruptive upon returning to the classroom. It takes approximately thirty minutes for the next school dose of medication to take effect. Careful timing to avoid this rebound effect will help considerably.

■ Many children/teens have a hard time remembering to go to the office at the designated time for medication because of the very nature of ADHD. It becomes the responsibility of the teacher, school nurse, counselor, and/or office staff to help with the administration of medication. Ways to remind the student (or alert the teacher that the student needs to take a midday dose) may include:

  ▪ A beeper watch or watch alarm for the student (or the teacher).

  ▪ "Coded" verbal reminders over the intercom.

  ▪ Private signals from the teacher to the student.

  ▪ Scheduling a natural transition of activities at that time and setting a clock, radio, or other signal to indicate that time of day.

  ▪ A sticker chart kept where the medication is dispensed, rewarding the child for remembering.

- Color-coded cards given to the child by the teacher or attached to his or her desk.
- "Sticky" notes placed near the teacher's schedule or in a plan book reminding the teacher to quietly direct the student to leave the room for medication.

■ It is very important to provide these reminders to students discreetly, without breaking confidentiality or discussing medication in front of other students. Pairing the medication time with a daily activity (for example, on the way to the cafeteria) is also a common and effective technique because it helps establish a consistent schedule.

■ In the nurse's absence, the office staff should be provided with a list of children who take medication, sending for the child if he or she does not come in to receive it.

■ Long-acting forms of medication eliminate the need for a midday dose at school. Parents/physicians should be notified if the child is having difficulty receiving the dose at school on time (due to resistance or forgetfulness). A long-acting prescription may be a better choice of medication for this child.

■ Medication therapy is most effective when combined with:
- Educational strategies and interventions
- Behavior-modification techniques and supports
- Parental awareness and training
- Counseling
- Management of the child's environment

WHAT PARENTS NEED TO KNOW

■ If a child is on medication, it is important that parents take responsibility for making sure he or she receives it as prescribed in the morning—on time and consistently.

■ Parents need to supervise that the child take the medication and not leave it as the son's or daughter's responsibility to remember to do so.

■ Close monitoring and management of the medication is crucial. If it is administered haphazardly and inconsistently, the child is better off without it.

■ Be aware of the possible side effects. Realize that appetite is one of those side effects, so make sure to discuss with the doctor and plan the child's meal times (such as breakfast) accordingly.

■ Be responsive to calls from the school regarding medication. Be sure the school has the permission forms and filled prescriptions they need on hand.

■ Communicate with the school nurse and teacher(s). Obviously, the purpose for treating the child with medication is optimal school performance and functioning. This requires teamwork and close communication between the home, school, and physician.

1-25 (*continued*)

- Be sure to take the child for all of the follow-up visits that are scheduled with his or her doctor. These are necessary for monitoring the medication's effectiveness.

- Parents must educate themselves about the medication treatment/intervention. They should talk to their physician and ask all the questions they need. There are excellent books and other resources available on medication treatments for ADHD. Check the local bookstore or library for books on ADHD. See Sources and Resources in List 1-24 and throughout this book.

- When a child is started on medication therapy, there is always a trial period when the physician is trying to determine the appropriate medication and dosage (titration). (1-24) Some are fortunate to find immediate and dramatic improvement. Others will take longer, and some will not benefit from or be able to tolerate the medication. However, in approximately 80–90% of children with ADHD, medication is found to be effective.

- See Lists 1-4, 1-7, and 1-23 for research evidence regarding the effectiveness of medication therapy in the treatment of ADHD, and about how medications are believed to work within the brain to relieve symptoms and improve functioning.

- Most schools have specific policies and procedures for administering medication:

  - A signed consent form on file

  - Medication in the original, labeled prescription bottle/container

  - Medication stored in a locked place

  - Maintaining careful records of the dosage, time of dispensing, and person administering the medication

- Also, the time of administration is often restricted (may vary only by thirty minutes before or after the prescribed time on the doctor's written order).

- Because the commonly prescribed stimulants are classified by the Drug Enforcement Administration as "Schedule II" medications, there are strict laws regarding how they are prescribed and dispensed. The Federal Drug Administration has restrictions that pharmacists must follow. This makes it more difficult for refilling prescriptions. For example:

  - The medication cannot be "called in."

  - Doctors can only write a prescription for one month at a time.

- It is important that parents pay close attention and communicate with the school nurse to make sure the school has the medication needed. It helps if parents are reminded well before the school's supply of medication runs out, so they have plenty of time to renew the prescription and deliver it to school.

- *Note:* Long-acting forms of the medication have the advantage of eliminating the need to keep a prescription at school, as well as the benefit of continuing to have a positive effect on symptoms during after-school activities.

- Children taking medications should be aware that the *medication* is not in control of their behavior—*they* are. The medication helps them put on the brakes and allows them to make better choices.

- For parents who are concerned about stimulant medications leading to increased rates of drug use in adolescence or adulthood, the research shows the opposite to be true. Studies indicate that children who have never been treated for ADHD have higher rates of drug use in later years, and children who are treated with medication therapy for ADHD show lower rates of drug use and alcohol abuse than non-medicated ADHD children.

1-26
ALTERNATIVE AND UNPROVEN TREATMENTS FOR ADHD

There are many alternative treatments parents may hear about that supposedly cure or improve the symptoms of ADHD. It can be quite enticing to parents of ADHD children who hear that a certain non-medical product or treatment can improve their child's behaviors and symptoms. However, the only proven treatments to date are medication and behavior therapy. (1-7, 1-23)

Many parents are reluctant or opposed to treating their child with medication. The many advertisements (magazines, TV, radio, Internet) making claims about various products/treatments that cure ADHD symptoms can sound very convincing and believable. Parents may be drawn to these other treatments that they feel are safer than medication or a better option in helping their child.

- Parents need to be cautious and informed consumers when considering alternative treatments. Be aware that:
  - Most make their claims based upon a small sample of people "studied."
  - Most tend to use testimonials in their advertisement of the product or treatment effectiveness.
  - Various products that are "natural" may be harmful (not having been through the scientific process to test for safety).
  - Those treatments that are advertised as miraculous or groundbreaking are generally bogus.
- Some of these treatments warrant further study, but for now remain unproven because they have not met scientific standards for evaluating the effectiveness of the treatment. This involves:
  - Controlled research studies
  - Measurement techniques enabling the scientific community to evaluate the findings
  - Peer reviews by other professionals prior to publication of results in scientific journals
  - Replicated studies by other teams of researchers to see if they achieve similar results
- Some of the various alternative treatments include:
  - Special diets (restricted sugar, additives)
  - Supplements of megavitamins, antioxidants, and minerals
  - Chiropractic skull manipulation and bone realignment
  - Treatment for *Candida* yeast infection

- Biofeedback
- Sensory integration training
- Herbal remedies
- Hypnosis
- Vestibular stimulation
- Anti-motion sickness medicine
- Optometric vision training
- Auditory training

■ Among the unproven treatments, a few (such as biofeedback) may have some benefit for ADHD children. However, though it has been used for a number of years, biofeedback is limited in its scientific support. Biofeedback is intended to train the child with ADHD to increase and decrease various types of brainwave activity associated with ADHD (such as sustained attention). It generally involves about 40 to 80 sessions and is an intensive, expensive treatment.

■ The popular belief that ADHD is due to too much sugar and can be managed by elimination diets has been studied, with the following results:

- There is no evidence from these studies that diets restricting sugar improve ADHD symptoms in most children.
- The National Institute of Health (NIH) concluded after review of the research and data available that restricted diet only seemed to help about 5% of children with ADHD—mostly either young children or children with food allergies.
- For the most part, dietary interventions have been disproven as effective in treating ADHD.

■ Parents are advised to consult with physicians and other resources before embarking on alternative treatments that may be expensive, time-consuming, and lack evidence of safety or effectiveness.

SOURCES AND RESOURCES

CASRC (Child and Adolescent Services Research Center) & Developmental Services Division of Children's Hospital and Health Center, San Diego, 2001 (http://sandiegoadhd.org/clinicians/treatment/treatment_index.htm)

CHADD "Fact Sheet 6: Assessing Complementary and/or Controversial Interventions," (http://www.chadd.org/fs/fs6.htm)

Ingersoll, Barbara, and Sam Goldstein. *Attention Deficit Disorder and Learning Disabilities: Realities, Myths and Controversial Treatments.* New York: Doubleday, 1993.

Preventing and Managing Behavior Problems: Strategies, Supports, and Psycho-Social Interventions

2-1
TARGET BEHAVIORS FOR STUDENTS WITH ADHD

Students with ADHD need positive behavioral supports and visual prompts to cue and remind them of expected behaviors. The following target behaviors may be used in conjunction with any of the behavioral forms in the Appendix and in Lists 2-7 and 2-9. Teachers should select and tailor target behaviors as appropriate.

Some target behaviors are also specific to the home for parents to include on a behavioral plan, earning the student tokens, points, or money based upon the success of his or her performance.

Note: In the Appendix are a number of illustrations that are representative of behavioral expectations. Enlarge or shrink to size and use the illustrations together with the target behaviors. They are appropriate for customizing behavioral charts/monitoring forms and for use as visual cues/prompts (desk copy, chart size).

The following are lists of variations of possible target behaviors/goals appropriate for use with positive behavioral support plans, daily report cards, and various monitoring forms. Teachers may wish to select from the optional wording of target behaviors. Notice that they are all stated in positive terms—what you want the student *to be doing*, instead of what you want the child *to stop doing*.

SCHOOL TARGET BEHAVIORS

On-Task Behavior and Showing Effort

- Completes work
- Turns in homework
- Turns in at least 80% of homework on time
- Turns in completed assignments
- On-task/working (no more than two reminders)
- Remains on-task until work is completed (no more than one prompt/reminder)
- Shows good effort on tasks
- Uses time allotted for assignments
- Completes or almost completes assignment(s) by the end of the work period
- Completes 80% of assignments on time

2-1 (continued)

- Completes assignment(s) with 80% accuracy
- Works quietly (no more than two reminders or prompts)
- Completes all steps in morning routine with no more than one reminder
- Starts seat work right away (no more than one prompt/reminder)
- Gets started on assignments right away (within two minutes)
- Appears attentive and listening (eyes on speaker, not talking/making noises)
- Participates in group activities
- Participates in lessons/activities
- Participates in activities without complaining
- Participates in class discussions (stays on topic, no interrupting, disagrees politely)
- Participates when called upon
- Stays on-task when other students are being disruptive, provocative, and/or disciplined

Cooperation and Appropriate Interactions with Others

- Waits patiently without interruptions or disruptions to classroom routines
- Uses appropriate language (no foul, rude, or sexual language)
- Talks in a normal volume (no more than one reminder)
- Accepts directions from staff without argument
- Refrains from arguing about behavior points
- Refrains from language that is threatening or insulting
- Refrains from fighting or using provocative gestures
- Engages in appropriate social interactions that treat self and others with respect
- Gets along with peers (no fighting, teasing, or put-downs)
- Respects adults (polite, no arguing or talking back)
- Appropriate interaction with adults (words/manners)
- Uses appropriate language in class (no cursing, put-downs, or teasing)
- Keeps hands, feet, and objects to self (no more than one reminder)
- Solves problems peacefully
- Works cooperatively
- Plays cooperatively
- Gets along with peers (no complaints of teasing/name calling, threatening, touching others' belongings without permission)
- Asks for help appropriately
- Shows effort to solve problems before seeking teacher help

- Asks permission before handling other people's property
- No referrals from lunch, recess, or the bus
- Shares with classmates (no more than one prompt/reminder)
- Allows classmates to do their work without bothering (no more than one complaint or reminder)
- Refrains from taking or destroying objects in school or other people's belongings

Following Directions

- Follows instructions
- Follows directions given by a staff member
- Listens to teacher directions
- Obeys class rules (with no more than two violations)
- Follows teacher directions (with two or fewer reminders)
- Listens and pays attention when teacher is talking (eyes on teacher, able to respond to the question "What did I say?")
- Follows cafeteria rules (no more than one rule infraction or reminder)
- Follows playground rules
- Follows bus rules
- Follows rules in hallways
- Follows rules in bathroom
- Follows rules in _____ (music class, P.E.)
- Follows rules of game(s)
- Follows rules in line (with no more than one reminder)
- Responds to adult requests/directions with no more than two prompts or reminders
- Receives a positive report from visiting teachers and specialists

Showing Preparedness, Readiness to Work, and Time-Management and Organization Skills

- On-time and ready
- Ready to work (has all needed materials, books)
- Prepared with all needed materials
- Assignments recorded in planner/assignment sheet
- Brings all needed materials
- Maintains personal belongings in a responsible manner
- Arrives on time
- Organizes materials according to checklist

2-1 (*continued*)

Being in the Proper Location

- Stays in seat
- Sits appropriately in assigned area (no more than one reminder/prompt)
- Stays with group
- Stays in class (does not leave without permission)
- Enters room quietly and goes to right place (no more than one reminder)
- Participates and stays with group
- Remains in assigned desk or classroom location during any instructional activity
- Remains in assigned areas of the building and grounds during the day
- If with an escort, remains with a staff member or within the requested distance at all times

Following Rules and Demonstrating Self-Control Behaviors

- Makes transitions within time given
- Gets teacher's attention appropriately
- Waits turn without interrupting
- Remains in seat during work period
- Refrains from blurting (no more than one calling out/blurting response per period)
- Raises hand and asks permission to speak
- Listens quietly

Visual Prompts

See the illustrations in the Appendix to use in conjunction with these behavioral expectations for school.

- Eyes (on teacher, work, speaker)
- Work quietly
- Quiet mouths
- Lips quiet (zipped)
- In seat
- On-task
- Pay attention
- Raise hand to speak
- Listen to teacher
- Follow directions
- Materials ready

- Cooperate
- Friendly words
- Get along with classmates
- Sit appropriately (facing forward, bottom in chair, feet on floor, chair legs on floor—no tipping)
- Sit appropriately on rug (head up, facing forward, hands in lap, legs crossed)
- Ears ready to listen
- Hands and feet to self
- Do your work
- Finish your work
- Turn in work

HOME TARGET BEHAVIORS

- Completes morning routine of checklist by 7:45 A.M.
- Completes bedtime routine of checklist by 9:30 P.M.
- Follows directions right away (with no more than two reminders)
- Follows directions within x minutes
- Brings home all needed books, materials, and assignment calendar
- Has assignment calendar/planner filled out accurately and completely
- Brings home daily report card from school
- Waits without interrupting while parent is on the phone (no more than one reminder)
- Gets along with siblings (no more than x reminders/redirections)
- Gets along with siblings (x or fewer fights or arguments)
- Solves problems peacefully without fighting
- Begins homework according to schedule with no more than two reminders
- Begins homework according to schedule without arguing
- Shows effort on homework
- Completes homework (or works on homework until parent determines he or she has spent sufficient amount of time and effort)

SOURCES AND RESOURCES

Pelham, William E. *ADHD: Diagnosis, Assessment, Nature, Etiology, and Treatment.* Buffalo, NY: Center for Children and Families, University at Buffalo, 2002. (http://wings.buffalo.edu/adhd)

2-2
REWARDS AND POSITIVE REINFORCERS FOR SCHOOL

The following are possible rewards that may be used with classroom (group) and individual behavior-management/modification programs. (2-1, 2-7, 2-9, Appendix)

For any social, activity, or material reward to be effective in motivating a child, it must have meaning and value to that student. Teachers have to discover (for example, through observation, inventory, or questioning) what the child likes. Particularly for students with ADHD, rewards must be changed frequently (or the child provided a menu of different reinforcers from which to choose) in order to maintain interest.

Social Reinforcers

■ Positive teacher attention and verbal praise

■ Praise given in writing (notes written on student's papers or sticky notes placed on student's desk; notes mailed to student)

■ Positive phone calls directly to student

■ Positive notes and calls to parents

■ Teacher smiles; a gentle pat on the back; thumbs up; high five; shaking the child's hand

■ Class applause or cheering of student, high fives, and compliments/praise

■ Class privilege of social status (such as team captain, class messenger)

■ Recognition at awards assemblies

■ Name being called on the school intercom recognizing something positive the student accomplished

■ Choice of seating for the period, day, or week (near friends)

■ Being awarded "Star of the Day" or "Student of the Week"

Activity Reinforcers/Privileges

■ Tutoring a younger child

■ Playing a game with friend(s)

■ First in line for dismissal (lunch, recess, and so on)

■ Early dismissal of one to two minutes for lunch/recess/passing to next class

■ Special activity (field trip, party, assembly, movie, school performance)

■ Lunchtime activities or privileges (choice of seating/eating in special location, games)

■ Earning time in class to catch up on work with teacher or peer assistance, if needed

- Listening to student's choice of music
- Extended lunchtime
- Extra P.E., music, art, or computer time
- A special game of choice (in class or recess/P.E. time)
- Breakfast or lunch with teacher, vice principal, principal, or other staff member
- Ice cream, popcorn, or pizza party for the class or group of students achieving a certain goal
- Privileges or responsibilities that are desirable (office assistant, taking care of class pet, taking attendance, ball monitor, passing out papers, sharpening pencils, operating AV equipment, and so on)
- Getting awarded a "no homework pass" for the evening, "good for removing 3 items from assignment" coupon, or "one late assignment accepted as on-time" coupon. (See the example in the Appendix.)
- Extra time/access to go to gym (to shoot baskets) or library/computer lab
- Opportunity to take a break and run a few laps, dance to a song, use playground equipment, and so on
- Free/earned time (individual or class) for activities of choice, such as games, listening to music, drawing, working on special project, accessing learning/interest centers
- Playing with clay or other craft materials
- Working at an art center with various supplies
- Taking off one bad grade from daily assignments that are recorded
- Taking one problem off a test
- Extra-credit opportunities to raise grades
- Studying with a friend
- Decorating a bulletin board or corner of the room
- Leading a game
- A chance to tell appropriate jokes in class
- Listening-post access to hear a story or book on tape
- Drawing cartoons
- Free reading (including books of choice, magazines, comic books)
- Computer/Internet access
- Center activity of choice
- Work on school projects (painting school mural, gardening)

Material Reinforcers

- School supplies (special pencils, pens, erasers, folders)
- Stickers, stars, badges, certificates

2-2 (*continued*)

- Food treats—preferably healthy snacks (pretzels, popcorn, crackers, frozen ice sticks, trail mix, juice, fruit)
- Treasure-chest items (small toys, trinkets, and so on)
- Magazines/books
- Class money, tickets, or points redeemable at auctions/lotteries or class stores
- Free tickets awarded to school dances, concerts, plays, and sporting events
- Coupons from businesses in the community for discounts toward purchases or free items

2-3
CLASSROOM-MANAGEMENT TIPS

The best management involves anticipating potential problems and avoiding them through careful planning. The following are the key components and strategies for effective classroom management necessary for creating a positive, productive learning environment.

Note: In the Appendix are a number of illustrations that are representative of behavioral expectations. Enlarge or shrink to size and use the illustrations together with the target behaviors. They are appropriate for customizing behavioral charts/monitoring forms and for use as visual cues/prompts (desk copy, chart size).

Establish a classroom environment that:

■ Is structured and well organized (clear schedule, routines, rules, careful planning of seating and physical space)

■ Is calm and predictable

■ Has clear rules/behavioral guidelines

■ Has clearly defined, taught, and practiced procedures that become automatic routines of classroom operation

■ Focuses on the use of positive reinforcement for appropriate behavior

■ Backs up behavioral limits/boundaries with fair corrective consequences that are enforced predictably and consistently

■ Is respectful and mutually supportive

■ Is warm, welcoming, and inclusive

■ Is flexible enough to accommodate individual needs of students

■ Has high academic and behavioral expectations

■ Builds upon students' skills of self-management (while supporting those who struggle in this area)

■ Is emotionally as well as physically safe. Students are not fearful of making a mistake or looking/sounding foolish and, consequently, are willing to risk participation.

■ See List 2-4, Environmental Accommodations and Supports in the Classroom.

Rules and Behavioral Expectations

■ Limit to a few (four or five) rules/behavioral standards.

■ State them positively (rather than saying "Don't . . .").

2-3 (*continued*)

- Make sure they are observable behaviors. ("Keep hands, feet, and objects to yourself"; "Be on time and prepared for class")
- Clearly state the behavior you want.
- Define concretely what the behaviors should "look like" and "sound like."
- Discuss, model, and practice those expectations.
- Role-play the desired behaviors.
- Post them in words/pictures and refer to them frequently. (See visual prompts in the Appendix.)
- Remind students of rules/expectations before start of activity.
- Ask individual students to repeat the rules/expectations.
- Clearly communicate your rules and expectations in writing to parents as well as students.
- Reward students for rule-following behavior.
- Remind students of your expectations with established visual/auditory prompts and signals.

Smooth classroom management is dependent upon the teaching of very specific and consistent procedures and routines.

Teach Procedures

- Decide upon your specific classroom procedures and write those down. Use the form in the Appendix entitled "Classroom Procedures: What Do You Expect Students to Do When . . .?"
- Teach your procedures until they become so well established and automatic that they become routine. Plan procedures for the start of the school day/class period (from entering class and morning routine) all the way through dismissal at the end of class/day. See example of the morning routine in visual format in the Appendix.
- Model, role-play, and practice all procedures at the beginning of the school year until they become automatic.
- Monitor, review, and reteach as needed throughout the year.

Teacher Proximity and Movement

- Circulate and move around the room frequently.
- Use your physical proximity and positioning for managing disruptive students; seat them closer to you for easy eye contact within close cueing/prompting distance (to place a hand on a shoulder, to point to a visual reminder on desk). Walk or stand near student(s) prone to misbehave.

- Use your movement as an effective management strategy. Create a floor plan of furniture and desk arrangement that enables easy access for all students and paths for walking among students frequently.

Use Signals

- Establish visual and auditory signals for getting students to stop what they are doing and give you their attention; transitioning from one activity to the next; and so on. Flash the lights; use a clapping pattern; play a bar of music; call out a signal word; hold up your hand; or other similar signals are examples.
- Provide students with some form of nonverbal signal to cue "I need help!" when they are working independently.

Visually Prompt

- Always maintain a visual schedule of the day/week and activities or routine, and refer to it frequently.
- See the Appendix for samples of visual prompts for routines and behavioral expectations.
- Post all student weekly/monthly jobs and responsibilities.

Monitor Student Behavior

- Scan the room frequently and stay alert as to what students are engaged in at all times. Provide positive feedback ("I like the way . . .").
- Develop the skill of "having eyes in the back of your head." Monitor and be aware of what students are doing in all parts of the room.
- Positively reinforce students engaged appropriately ("I see Karen and Alicia busy on their assignment. Well done.").
- Address inappropriate behavior when scanning (gentle reminder, eye contact and "the teacher look").
- Redirect students by mentioning their name, getting eye contact, and using a calm but firm voice.

Provide Positive Attention and Reward Appropriate Behavior

- Attend to students far more frequently when they are doing what they are supposed to be doing rather than when caught in a rule violation.
- Be sure to give at least three times more positive attention and comments to students than negative/corrective feedback. Strive for a 9:1 ratio of positive to negative!
- Use a high degree of positive verbal reinforcement of appropriate behaviors and sincere praise that is specific about the behavior exhibited ("Great job cooperating with your group and finishing the assignment on time").

2-3 (*continued*)

- Be generous with sincere praise.

- Frequently acknowledge and recognize good work, behavior, and social performance.

- Give positive, specific, and descriptive feedback to students. For example: "I see that Marcus is in his chair facing forward with his book open to the right page. Good job, Marcus." Or "I like the way Michael is standing in line quietly with his hands and feet to himself. Thank you, Michael."

- Remind yourself frequently to "catch them being good!"

- Many older students would be humiliated if teachers praised them openly in front of peers; however, they still need and appreciate the positive feedback. Provide positive attention and recognition through notes and quiet statements before/after class. Try using a sticky pad to jot down comments to students and place them on their desk.

- Establish positive reinforcement systems for classroom management. (2-7)

- Provide students with rewards for good behavior. The most common and effective, in most cases, is the use of activity reinforcers: "When you finish ____, you'll get to do ____."

- See List 2-2 for possible reinforcers/rewards for the classroom.

Negative Consequences

- Provide fair and reasonable consequences for misbehavior.

- Enforce with predictability in a calm, non-emotional manner.

- Try to handle inappropriate behavior as simply and promptly as possible.

- Use a hierarchy of negative consequences or mild punishments. Address only the child's behavior, not the child himself or herself.

- Deliver consequences using as few words as possible. Act without lecturing. Discussions about behavior can occur later.

- See List 2-8, Disciplining Students: Addressing Misbehavior.

Plan for Individual Student Support

- Carefully assign peer partners.

- Be willing to implement individual behavioral plans and supports for students in need. (2-1, 2-9)

- Enlist the help of support staff for more behaviorally challenging students. (6-1, 6-2, 6-3)

Ignore Some Behaviors

- Choose to ignore minor inappropriate behavior that is not intentional. Not every behavior warrants teacher intervention.

■ Teachers will have to be tolerant and flexible with ADHD students, allowing extra movement, fiddling with objects, and behaviors of which these students have significant physiological difficulty controlling.

Positive Teaching Behaviors

■ Model respectful language, tone of voice, and body language.

■ Position yourself at the door and greet students as they enter the room.

■ As students enter the room, immediately direct them to routine warm-up activities (journal entries, interpreting brief quotation on board, writing sentences using vocabulary words, two to three math problems) to avoid students having to wait undirected for instruction to begin.

■ Provide effective and respectful requests, redirection, and corrective feedback.

■ Use humor to de-escalate potential problems.

■ Avoid lecturing, nagging, criticism, and sarcasm.

■ Do not take a child's inappropriate behavior personally.

■ Be well planned and organized.

■ Share control. Do not be a "controlling teacher."

■ Discuss inappropriate behavior with students in private, when possible.

Transitions

■ Prepare for and provide structure and supervision during transitions, changes of routine, and unstructured situations. (2-5)

■ Teach and practice the procedures involved in a transition requiring movement of materials, furniture, and/or student.

Involve Parents

■ Communicate frequently with parents, keeping them well informed as to all aspects of what is being studied in school, work requirements, and their child's performance.

■ Forge a partnership with parents. (4-8, 6-1, 8-1, 8-4)

■ See the home/school communication forms in the Appendix.

Points to Keep in Mind

■ Effective classroom management goes hand in hand with good teaching/instruction. Students will generally demonstrate appropriate behavior when there is:
  ▪ Engaging, meaningful learning activities/instruction
  ▪ Pacing to avoid frustration and boredom
  ▪ Little lag time when students are waiting to find out what they are doing next

■ See Lists 3-2, 3-3, 3-4, and 3-7.

2-3 (continued)

- Assign to students any classroom-management jobs and responsibilities that they are capable of doing themselves (cleaning up, passing out and collecting papers, gathering materials, taking attendance and lunch count).

- The key to effective classroom management is building positive relationships with students. Most children typically work hard to please teachers whom they like, trust, and respect. It is important for teachers to make the time and effort to know their individual students and build a relationship, demonstrating that they truly care about their lives and success.

- Good classroom management requires all the steps needed to address individual student needs. See List 2-9 for individualized behavioral supports and interventions.

- Employ techniques suggested in List 2-10 to aid calming and avoid escalation of problems.

- See List 2-6 for giving directions and increasing student compliance.

- See List 2-11 for dealing with "challenging" or "difficult" behaviors.

2-4
ENVIRONMENTAL ACCOMMODATIONS AND SUPPORTS IN THE CLASSROOM

The following strategies are essential to effective classroom management and preventing behavioral problems. They also address the needs of diverse learners and accommodating individual learning styles. See Lists 2-3, 2-5, 3-4, and 3-9 for additional information and strategies related to this topic.

■ Physically arrange the classroom with options for seating; for example, single-desk options as opposed to two-person desks/tables for those students who need more buffer space. Typically, for students with ADHD, table formations where desks are clustered with four to six students per group and facing each other is not recommended. More optimal desk formations are:

  ■ U-shaped/horseshoes

  ■ E-shaped

  ■ Straight rows

  ■ Staggered rows (groups of four students per row in the center with slanted groups of two students per row on the peripheries)

■ The key to furniture arrangement is the ability of the teacher to easily access (with as few steps as possible) each student without obstruction. The best classroom-management strategy is teacher proximity—moving among the students, monitoring, cueing, and giving feedback.

■ Students with ADHD should be seated in the following ways:

  ■ Close to the center of instruction

  ■ Surrounded by and facing positive role models and well-focused students

  ■ Within teacher cueing and prompting distance

  ■ Away from high-traffic areas and distracters (noisy heaters/air conditioners, doors, windows, pencil sharpeners)

■ For children who have discomfort and trouble sitting in their seats, try seat cushions. Two recommended cushions are *Movin' Sit Jr.* and *Disc O'Sit Jr.* Both are inflatable "dynamic" seat cushions that accommodate a child's need for squirming and wiggling in the chair (see the resources).

■ There are a number of other options to sitting in one's seat to work. For example, allowing a child to sit on a beanbag chair with paper attached to a clipboard may increase productivity and motivation.

■ Avoid "open classrooms" or loft-type situations.

■ Have informal areas of the classroom (carpet area, soft cushions, beanbag chairs).

2-4 (*continued*)

- Use carpet squares for seating away from desks (on the floor near the teacher) if the room is not carpeted.
- If the room is not carpeted, insert old tennis balls on the tips of each chair leg to reduce the noise level.
- Establish rules and procedures for movement within the classroom (when it is okay to get up, get a drink, sharpen pencils, and so on).
- Define areas of the room concretely.
- Designate physical boundaries with colored masking tape on the carpet, floor, or tables.
- Make use of storage bins for "center" activities and materials.
- Store materials in clearly labeled bins, shelves, tubs, trays, and/or folders. (3-6)
- Provide easy access to materials and independent learning activities.
- Post all schedules, calendars, and assignments.
- Have pictures and/or a list of rules and daily routine. See the Appendix for a pictorial example of a morning routine.
- Use furniture, shelves, and partitions to divide space.
- Remove any unnecessary furniture from the classroom, creating additional free space.
- Have comfortable lighting and room temperature.
- Keep a portion of the room free from distracters. Provide desk organizers to help children easily locate materials.
- Provide a lot of visual prompts, models, and displays for student reference (including visual depictions of procedures, routines, and rules). See the Appendix.
- Use tools such as timers (various kinds), bells, and so on, for signaling changes of activity. See the visual CD *Time Timer* available at www.timetimer.com.
- Use a minute timer to designate how much time is allotted for transitions. Meeting the expectation can result in class or table privileges; failure to meet expectation may result in time owed.
- Allow ADHD students an alternative desk or chair in the room (two-seat method).
- Reduce visual distractions such as unnecessary writing on the board.
- Reduce or minimize auditory distractions whenever possible.
- Use a listening post for books on tape, stories, and music as appropriate.
- Be sure desks and tables are positioned so that all students can see the board and overhead screen, or at least are able to move their chairs easily to do so.
- Permit the student(s) who cannot sit for very long to stand near the desk while working at certain times (if productive).
- Build in stretch breaks or exercise breaks after sitting any length of time.

- Experiment with background music at different times of the day and for various activities and purposes (to calm and relax, motivate, and stimulate thinking). Try a variety of instrumental cassettes/CDs, including environmental sounds (such as rain forest), Baroque music, classical, jazz, show tunes, etc. (3-9)

- Permit students to use earphones to block out noise during seatwork, test-taking, or other times of the day. Some teachers purchase sets of earphones to be used for this purpose, or allow a child to bring to school his or her own earphones. It is encouraged that *all* students experiment with and be allowed to use these tools (not just students with special needs). (3-9)

- Have designated quiet times of the day.

- The room environment should be well organized, visually appealing, arranged for maximum use of space, and show student work/ownership.

- Be aware of glare in the classroom and its effects on visibility.

- Be sure desks are adjusted (raised or lowered) so that each student can sit at a desk and chair of the appropriate height. Make sure furniture is stable, not wobbly.

- Reduce the clutter and unnecessary visual overload in the classroom.

- Provide "office areas" or "study carrels" for seating options during certain times of the day as needed. These should be encouraged and experimented with by *all* students in the class so seating in these areas is never viewed as punitive or for students with special needs only.

- Purchase or construct privacy boards to place on tables while taking tests, or other times of the day to block visual distractions and limit the visual field.

- Provide some students extra workspace and/or storage space.

- Turn off the lights at various times of the day for calming (particularly after P.E. and recess). (2-10)

- Kidney-shaped tables are ideal for small-group instruction.

- Certain aromas are sometimes used that have various effects. For example, peppermint, spearmint, and lemon are three scents that are supposed to increase one's alertness.

- Allow students to move to a quiet corner or designated area of the room if needed.

- Create an environment of safety, inclusiveness, success, emotional well-being, acceptance, tolerance, calmness, high interest, fun, and humor.

- Be open, flexible, and willing to make changes in seating when needed.

- Be sensitive to the physical needs of students (need for a drink of water, snacks, use of restroom, movement/stretching) that may interfere with learning.

SOURCES AND RESOURCES

Karges-Bone, Linda. *Beyond Hands-On*. Carthage, IL: Teaching & Learning Co., 1996.

2-4 (continued)

Movin' Sit Jr. and *Disc O' Sit Jr.* are available through several companies such as Therapro, 800-257-5376. (www.theraproducts.com)

Rief, Sandra. *The ADD/ADHD Checklist: An Easy Reference for Parents and Teachers.* Paramus, NJ: Prentice Hall, 1998.

The Brain Store, 800-325-4769 (www.thebrainstore.com), catalog has a wide variety of resources, including the following musical selections: *Accelerating Learning: Soundwave 200*™ (Steve Halpern); *Music for the Classroom* (Gary Lamb); *The Sound Health Series: Music for Learning and Thinking* (Richard Lawrence and Joshua Leeds); and *Baroque Music to Empower Learning & Relaxation* (Optimal Learning®).

2-5
PREVENTING BEHAVIOR PROBLEMS DURING TRANSITIONS AND "CHALLENGING TIMES" OF THE SCHOOL DAY

- Students with ADHD typically have the greatest behavioral difficulties during transitional times of the day in the classroom, as well as the school settings outside of the classroom that are less structured and supervised (playground, cafeteria, hallways, bathrooms).

- Prepare for changes in routine (assemblies, substitute teachers, field trips) through discussion and modeling expectations. Avoid catching students off-guard.

- Maintain a visual schedule that is reviewed and referred to frequently. When changes are to occur in the schedule, point them out in advance.

Classroom Transitions

- Communicate clearly when activities will begin and when they will end.

- Give specific instructions about how students are to switch to the next activity.

- Be sure to clearly teach, model, and have students practice and rehearse all procedures that will occur in changes of activities. This includes such things as the students' quick and quiet movement from their desks to the carpet area, putting away/taking out materials, and so forth.

- Use **signals** for transitions (playing a bar of music on a keyboard, flashing lights, ringing a bell, beginning a clapping pattern, saying prompts such as "1,2,3 . . . eyes on me"). A signal indicates that an activity is coming to an end and children need to finish whatever they are doing. Some teachers signal and tell students they will have a brief amount of time (three to five minutes) to finish what they are working on before the next activity or to clean up. They then set a timer for that amount of time. Primary-grade teachers typically use songs or chants for transitions (for cleaning up, moving to the rug).

- Provide direct teacher guidance and prompting to those students who need it during transitions.

- Reward smooth transitions. Many teachers use individual points or table points to reward students or rows/table clusters of students who are ready for the next activity. The reward is typically something simple like being the first row or table to line up for recess.

- Be organized in advance with prepared materials for the next activity.

2-5 (continued)

Transitioning from Out-of-Classroom Activities Back to the Classroom

■ Meet the students after lunch, P.E., recess, and other activities outside of the classroom and walk them quietly into the classroom.

■ Set a goal for the class (everyone enters class after lunch/recess and is quiet and ready to work by a certain time). On successful days of meeting that goal, the class is rewarded by a move on a behavior chart. See the Connect-the-Dots Chart in the Appendix.

■ Use relaxation and imagery activities or exercises for calming after recess, lunch, and P.E. Playing music, singing, and/or reading to students at these times is also often effective. (8-9)

Out-of-Classroom School Settings

■ Teach, model, and practice appropriate behaviors and expectations for out-of-class activities (in the cafeteria, passing in hallways, during assemblies).

■ Assign a buddy or peer helper to assist during these transitional periods and out-of-classroom times.

■ It is important to have schoolwide rules/behavioral expectations so that all staff members calmly and consistently enforce through positive and negative consequences. (2-16)

■ Schoolwide incentives and positive reinforcers ("caught being good" tickets redeemable for school prizes) are helpful in teaching and motivating appropriate behaviors outside of the classroom.

■ For students who have behavioral difficulty on the bus, an individual contract or including the bus behavior on a daily report card should be arranged (with the cooperative efforts of the school, bus driver, and parent).

■ Special contracts or some type of individualized behavior plan with incentives for appropriate behavior may need to be arranged for the playground, cafeteria, or other such times of the day. See List 2-9 and the Appendix for examples of various contracts.

■ If using a daily report card or monitoring form of some type (see the Appendix), days on which there are no reports of behavioral referrals in out-of-classroom settings can result in bonus points on the report card.

■ Increase supervision outside of the classroom, and provide more choices of activities that children can engage in (hula hoops, jump rope, board games, library/computer, supervised games).

■ It is important that all staff members are aware of the struggles children with ADHD have in nonstructured environments. Awareness training of ADHD should be provided for personnel involved with supervision outside of the classroom.

■ Staff members should identify and positively target those students in need of extra support, assistance, and careful monitoring outside of the classroom.

- Increase supervision during passing periods, lunch, recess, and school arrival/dismissal.

- It is helpful to have organized clubs and choices for students before and after school, and during the break before and after lunch.

- One of the biggest transitions students face is the move from one grade level to the next, particularly the change from elementary to middle school, and middle school to high school. Prepare students (especially those with ADHD) by visiting the new school, meeting with counselors and/or teachers, practicing the locker combination, receiving the schedule of classes in advance, and practicing the walk from class to class.

2-6
TIPS FOR GIVING DIRECTIONS AND INCREASING STUDENT COMPLIANCE

- Wait until it is quiet and you have students' attention before giving instructions. Do not talk over students' voices.

- Walk over to touch or physically cue certain students for their focus prior to giving directions. (3-2, 3-4)

- Face students when you talk.

- Use a signal in class that indicates students are to stop what they are doing and pay attention to you prior to your giving instructions.

- Give concise, clear verbal directions (to the point). Speak in simple, short sentences, avoiding a lot of unnecessary talk.

- Provide multisensory instructions, such as visual cues and graphics along with simple verbal explanations. Write on the board a few key words, picture cues, phrases, and page numbers.

- Use a buddy system for clarification and assistance with directions, as needed.

- Avoid multiple-step instruction. Provide, whenever possible, one instruction at a time.

- If multi-step directions are used, always clearly delineate the steps and sequence (1, 2, 3 . . .) of the directions in writing.

- Write assignments and directions needed on the board in a consistent spot, and leave them there for reference.

- Always check for understanding of directions by having individual students volunteer to repeat or rephrase your directions to the whole class.

- Use student partners for clarification of directions: "Tell your partner what we are going to be doing on page 247."

- Provide for a discreet means of clarifying directions without calling attention to and embarrassing individual students who need extra help. For example, use private signals.

- Model what to do, showing the entire class. Leave visual models in the classroom as reference.

- Read written directions to the class and have students color highlight or circle or underline key words in the directions.

- Give frequent praise and positive feedback when students are following directions and/or making a good attempt to do so.

- Provide follow-up after you give directions (check student's work, praise a job well done).

- Break down tasks into smaller steps, simplifying directions for each phase of the task/assignment.
- Keep in mind that you may often need to provide more assistance and structure to enable students with ADHD to follow directions. Remember, it is characteristic of children and teens with ADHD to have difficulty:
  - Disengaging from activities (particularly fun ones) that they have not completed
  - Responding and following through without prompting and cueing
  - Utilizing recall and memory
- Make sure to give complete directions, including what you expect students to do if they have any questions and when they are finished with the task/assignment.
- For students who have difficulty following directions, obtain eye contact and give directions from a closer proximity.
- Focus on what behavior you want *started*, rather than *stopped*. Before issuing commands or directives to a child, think in terms of what you want to see the child doing instead of what he or she is currently doing.
- Use what is referred to as "alpha commands," which are clear and well stated; avoid "beta commands," which are unclear and poorly stated.
- Remember that what may be misinterpreted in children as noncompliant behavior (deliberately disobeying an adult) is often due to the adult's poorly issued directions or commands. With poorly stated directions, noncompliance may actually be due to the child's lack of understanding, forgetting, misinterpreting the direction, or not processing all that was said.

The following are some *do's and don'ts* when giving directions/commands to students. See the sources and resources for more information on this topic.

Do not:

- Give a string or chain of multiple directions/commands.
- Keep repeating the direction.
- Use vague language that is open to interpretation and lacks enough precise information ("Behave appropriately." "Clean up." "Get ready." "Be respectful.").
- Continue to talk and elaborate after giving a direction/command.
- State in the form of a question ("Would you open your books to page . . .?" "Isn't it time to get busy?" "Why don't you go back to your seat now?").

Do:

- Get the child's direct attention (get close, say child's name, obtain eye contact).
- State directions/commands in the form of what students are to do ("Look at the chart." "Pick up your pencils." "Turn to your assignment calendar.").
- Be specific in what you expect to see ("Eyes looking at me." "Bottoms in your chair." "Book open to page 21." "Desks cleared except for pencil.").

2-6 (*continued*)

- Use a firm, matter-of-fact, and neutral tone of voice.
- Give one direction/command at a time.
- Wait a minimum of five seconds to allow time to comply, without additional verbalizing, restating, or adding a new direction.
- Praise and positively reinforce immediately after child follows the direction.
- Repeat the direction after the appropriate amount of "wait time" using the words: "You need to . . ."
- Praise/positively reinforce if the child follows the direction.
- Provide a mild negative consequence if the child still does not comply.

SOURCES AND RESOURCES

Forehand, R., and R. McMahon. *Helping the Noncompliant Child.* New York: The Guilford Press, 1981.

Goldstein, Sam. "The Importance of Positive Directions for Children with ADHD" (http://www.samgoldstein.com/articles/0201.html)

Walker, Hill M., and Janet Eaton Walker. *Coping with Noncompliance in the Classroom.* Austin, TX: Pro-Ed Publishers, 1991.

2-7
CLASS (GROUP)
BEHAVIOR-MANAGEMENT SYSTEMS

Effective behavior management requires a focus on positive incentives and reinforcement opportunities in the classroom. As described in List 2-8, teachers *do* need to implement mild corrective consequences for addressing student misbehavior and enforcing their behavioral expectations. However, skilled and experienced teachers know that positive-based classroom systems for motivating and rewarding cooperative, rule-following behavior are essential.

Points to Keep in Mind

- Most teachers use what is referred to as "contingencies" in managing and motivating students. This basically involves such statements as:
  - "When you finish ____, you may then ____."
  - "First ____ needs to be done, and then you may ____."
  - "You may ____ as long as you ____."
  - "When the class has ____, we will get to ____."
  - "If we ____, we'll be able to then ____."

- In essence, students must do the less desirable task or activity first in order to get, do, or participate in something they want.

- Teachers also reward appropriate behavior through the use of social reinforcers (recognition and praise). Most effective is having positive attention and recognition given by peers (as well as the teacher):
  - "Nice job, Johnny! Let's give him a round of applause."
  - "Way to go, Nicole! Stand up and take a bow."
  - High fives from classmates

- There are several varieties of class (group) reinforcement systems teachers may choose to use that may best fit their style of teaching, comfort level, and the interest of their students. (These are described later in this list.)

- It is recommended that schools provide the time and opportunity for teachers to share with colleagues the various class behavior-management and incentive systems they are using.

- The best incentives in a classroom are those involving activity reinforcers. Students are motivated throughout the day to earn time to participate in rewarding activities of choice (games, high-interest learning centers, time to work on special projects):

2-7 (*continued*)

- "Choice time" for fun, preferred activities can be awarded as frequently as needed by the developmental age of the group (twice a day, daily, weekly—"Freaky Fun Friday").

- Students with ADHD need the opportunity to earn the reward of participation more frequently than most classmates. They often are penalized for their difficulties with work production, having to miss rewarding activities in order to complete unfinished assignments.

- When this is the case, more support and accommodations may be needed to help ADHD students get caught up with their work.

GROUP POSITIVE-REINFORCEMENT SYSTEMS

Table/Team Points

- Points are given for specific behaviors being demonstrated.

- Any tables/teams earning a target number (*x* amount) of points earns the reward or privilege.

- This is not table/team competition. Each table/team can earn the reward or privilege if meeting the goal.

Table/Team Competition

- Points are given to any table/team demonstrating the target behaviors.

- At the end of the day/week, the table or team with the most points earns the reward or privilege.

Marbles in a Jar

- Teacher catches students engaged in appropriate behaviors and reinforces by putting a marble (or something similar) in a jar.

- When the jar is filled, the class earns a reward.

- This is a particularly effective technique for rewarding quick and smooth transitions.

Chart Moves

- A chart is created for the class or group. See the Connect-the-Dots Chart in the Appendix.

- The class is reinforced for meeting a set goal by moving a place on the chart. (2-1)

- When the chart is filled, the group earns the reward.

Token Economy System

- Students have the chance to earn tokens, points, tickets, or class money. These are later redeemable at a class store, auction, or raffle.

- A menu of rewards is developed with corresponding price values attached. (2-2)

- Rewards may include: small school supplies, other items students at that grade level like, "free homework assignment" coupons, and various privileges. See the Appendix for sample homework coupons.

- Students can spend their earned tokens, points, or money at designated times during class auctions or shopping at the class store.

- Token economy systems allow a teacher to fine or charge students ($10 class currency for forgetting book at home and needing to borrow another; $10 late to class).

- *Note:* Teachers must award generously and frequently for positive behaviors to students with ADHD, so that the students are not overly fined for rule infractions or forgetfulness. This would result in frustration, losing motivation, and the program not being effective.

- If using a monetary system, the teacher must give students the opportunity to earn class money for basic expectations throughout the day (coming to school—$10; bringing homework—$10 for each subject; doing nightly reading, indicated by parent signature in student planner—$10; on-task for class work—$10 each subject; plus bonuses at teacher's discretion).

- At the end of the week, fines are subtracted from the earned money. Students spend their money on purchases in the class store, perhaps every other week.

Probability Reinforcers

- Teachers who give raffle tickets for demonstrating target behaviors or meeting certain goals have students write their names on the tickets and place them in a container.

- Drawings are held daily or weekly.

- Names drawn receive prizes or privileges.

- Students know that the more tickets they have, the greater the chance of winning a reward.

Group Response Cost

- A target behavior that the whole class is working to improve is selected (for example, in seat/in place unless having permission to be elsewhere; appropriate language—no cursing/swearing). See List 2-1 for other possible target behaviors.

- A certain number of points or tokens are automatically given at the beginning of each day/class period or once a week (on Mondays).

- A goal is set that would represent an improvement in the target behavior. A point/token is removed every time the inappropriate behavior occurs.

- Successfully meeting the goal is determined by how many points/tokens the class needs to have remaining at the end of the time frame chosen.

- If they meet the goal, the class earns the selected reward.

2-7 (*continued*)

- The success level is gradually raised (at least five remaining points, then ten) until the behavior has significantly improved. Then a different behavior can be selected.

- See the Appendix for an example of a response cost chart. There are many variations of response cost systems. The key is that students are working to keep what they have been given up front. For example, at the beginning of the day, the teacher may automatically give 15 minutes of free time to the class to be used at the end of the day. Specific misbehaviors that occur during the day will result in one-minute loss of time from the free minutes given. The net positive balance will be awarded at the end of the day.

- Of course, the teacher has the discretion to add bonus minutes during the day for exceptionally good behavior to increase the motivation.

Level Systems

- Some classrooms (usually special education classes) find a level system effective.

- Each child in the class earns points for specified behaviors throughout the day; for example, in proper location, on-task, respect for property, appropriate language/verbal interactions, and appropriate physical interactions.

- Depending upon the number of points earned, the child has access to different levels of rewards at the end of the day (or at the end of the week).

- For example, earning 85% or higher of the possible points would enable that student access to the highest level of choices. During activity time, these students would have the choice of most desirable activities, materials, places to sit/play, and other privileges.

- Students earning lower percentages of possible points also have reinforcing activity time, but their choices are more limited.

RELATED LISTS

- See List 2-18 for many excellent tools and strategies on this topic.

- See Lists 2-3, 2-4, 2-5, and 2-11 for more strategies in classroom management, preventing behavioral problems, and tips for dealing with "challenging" students.

2-8
DISCIPLINING STUDENTS: ADDRESSING MISBEHAVIOR

What Is Punishment?

- An aversive experience following misbehavior in an effort to reduce the behavior (in frequency, intensity, or duration).
- A reactive strategy—after the fact.
- A response to misbehavior, but one that does not teach replacement behaviors.

That is why the focus of positive classroom discipline is on proactive efforts to:

- Establish the structure and climate for success.
- Effectively teach appropriate behavioral expectations.
- Motivate students to cooperate through the abundance of positive reinforcements available in the classroom.
- See Lists 2-3, 2-4, 2-5, 2-7, 2-16, and 8-1.

However, in addition to positive consequences, negative or corrective consequences are also necessary components of effective behavior management. In fact, with ADHD students, research shows that reward-only programs are not effective in changing or modifying behavior.

Note: Response-cost techniques are found to be highly effective in behavior modification with students who have ADHD. (2-7, 2-9)

Proactive teachers do the following:

- Carefully plan a hierarchy of consequences for addressing misbehavior.
- Inform students, parents, and administrators of the classroom behavioral plan.
- Make sure students know in advance what kinds of consequences they can expect from misbehavior.

Students need to know that a teacher will enforce behavioral expectations with speed, predictability, and consistency. Corrective consequences in a classroom should begin with mild and quiet interventions such as:

- Positioning yourself near the student (proximity).
- A gentle touch on the shoulder.
- Whispering a reminder or directive to the student.
- Private, pre-arranged signals.

2-8 (*continued*)

- Nonverbal cues (making eye contact; giving the "teacher look" to convey disapproval of inappropriate behavior; pointing to or tapping on visual prompts). See the Appendix for sample visual prompts.
- Gentle, verbal reminders and warnings such as:
  - "Steve, remember to raise your hand, please."
  - "Anna, the rule is ____. That's a warning."
  - "Vincent, where are you supposed to be right now?"
  - "Jared, next time ask permission before you ____."
- Issuing a direct command:
  - "Susan, get busy doing problems 1 to 10 now."
  - "Brianna, I need you in your seat and facing forward."

After clear warnings, infractions of the rules need to result in a minor penalty of some type such as:

- Losing time from a preferred activity.
- Losing access to a preferred object for a period of time (can't use certain equipment or materials).
- Brief delay (a minute or two of having to wait before participating in a desired activity).
- Positive practice/do-overs, such as:
  - If caught running from the classroom into the hallway, sending them back to the class door and having them walk appropriately.
  - If speaking rudely, saying, "Try that again, please—politely and respectfully this time."
- Fining, loss of points, demerits, and response costs.
- Owing time (a few minutes of recess, from preferred activity, or after school/class), and during such time the student is to pay back any time owed in a certain manner (sitting at seat quietly with desk cleared and nothing to do but wait).
- Various forms of brief timeout or time-away from class participation, or from the chance to earn positive reinforcement, such as:
  - Head down at desk (could involve counting to a certain number)
  - Being moved a few feet away from the group temporarily (to sit in chair rather than on the rug but still within view of group)
  - Timeout location in classroom (away from view of group and without the opportunity for positive reinforcement)
  - Timeout/time-away location in a neighboring buddy class that has been arranged to exchange students for this purpose
  - Timeout in other school location that has supervision and is designed to be nonreinforcing for this purpose

- *Note:* Timeout/time-away should usually start with no more than a few minutes, with additional time added or a longer timeout period assigned for continued behavioral infractions.

■ Have the student record behavioral infractions in a log or notebook.

■ Have the student fill out a form of some type describing the behavior, requiring that he or she reflect on the behavioral choices made, and what he or she needs to do differently next time.

■ At a time when you can sit with the student, debrief the behavior (go through the behavioral form the student was asked to complete). Set up short-term goals to work on. See the example in the Appendix.

■ Restitution or fixing the problem:

  - If student makes a mess, he or she has the responsibility of cleaning it up.

  - If student hurts someone's feelings or was disrespectful, he or she must apologize verbally or in writing.

■ Teacher/student conference

■ Parental contact:

  - Phone call from the teacher

  - Phone call during the day to the parent with the student needing to discuss the inappropriate behavior with his or her parent in teacher's presence

  - Note home

  - Communication via daily report card

  - Parent conference with teacher

  - Parent conference with teacher and administrator

■ In-school suspension

■ Out-of-school suspension

The following is a sample of a fourth-grade classroom hierarchy of corrective consequences that follows the schoolwide discipline plan/policy:

■ *First infraction*—Warning

■ *Second infraction*—Warning (student also receives a fine in the class token economy system). (2-7)

■ *Third infraction*—5 minutes of timeout in the classroom. At timeout (a desk in the back of the room), the student fills out a form describing what behavior resulted in his or her timeout and how the student plans to change or correct his or her behavior upon returning to the group.

■ *Fourth infraction*—Teacher fills out a referral form describing the student's behavior. The student is sent with the referral to a buddy class for 15 minutes of timeout in that classroom.

2-8 (*continued*)

■ *Fifth infraction*—The student is sent to the administrator and receives an In-School Suspension (ISS). This typically involves being placed in another classroom for the rest of the day with work to do.

Points to Keep in Mind

■ Always handle mild misbehaviors in the classroom. More serious infractions would, of course, require the involvement of the administrator.

■ Be aware of students with disabilities who receive more significant disciplinary action (such as those involving suspensions of more than ten days in a school year). (7-5)

■ Key to positive discipline is finding time to teach and practice problem solving, conflict resolution, and pro-social skills. (2-11, 2-16)

■ Utilize classroom (group) behavior systems and supports. (2-7)

■ Many students with ADHD need some kind of individual plan to monitor and reinforce target behaviors. See Lists 2-1 and 2-9 and the samples in the Appendix.

2-9
INDIVIDUALIZED BEHAVIOR MANAGEMENT, INTERVENTIONS, AND SUPPORTS

Children and teens with ADHD typically need far closer monitoring, a higher rate and frequency of feedback, and more powerful incentives to modify their behavior than the average child.

In addition to classroom (group) behavior-management systems (see 2-7), students with ADHD benefit from individual daily and/or weekly monitoring and reinforcement plans. There are several samples in the Appendix, which will be described in this list.

When designing an individual plan as an intervention for a student, it must be:

- Tailored to address the specific behavior and work performance weaknesses of the child/teen.

- Tied to a motivating choice of rewards (specific objects, privileges, activities) the child/teen really wants and will work hard to attain.

- Reviewed frequently and revised when it begins to lose its effectiveness.

- Implemented consistently.

Points to Keep in Mind

Note: The information and recommended strategies/interventions in this list are very useful for implementing in conjunction with IEPs, Behavior Intervention Plans, and 504 or SST action plans. (6-2, 7-4, 7-5)

- There are numerous behaviors that may be selected or targeted for intervention. (2-1)

- Goals can be set based upon any of the key behaviors the child/teen needs to improve in order to function with greater success at school and meet classroom expectations of work and behavioral performance.

- When choosing possible reinforcements (rewards or incentives), see the suggestions in Lists 2-2 and 2-14.

- Students with ADHD need to be in classrooms that provide structure and support for success. They also need teachers who skillfully employ group behavior-management strategies, including both positive reinforcement for expected behaviors, and reasonable, predictable consequences for misbehavior. (2-3, 2-4, 2-8, 8-1)

- Children and teens with ADHD need teacher awareness of how to prevent problems and intervene when behavior is inappropriate in a manner that helps a student regain self-control and does not trigger an escalation of problem behavior. (2-6, 2-10, 2-11)

2-9 (*continued*)

■ Such teacher strategies and interpersonal skills are particularly necessary when a student is emotionally fragile, overreactive, and/or has a tendency to be oppositional and confrontational.

■ The illustrations in the Appendix may be used for tailoring any monitoring form or daily/weekly report card for a student. Pictures may be shrunk to icon size or enlarged for poster size. They serve as visual prompts or reminders of specific target behaviors that are the student's goals for improvement.

INDIVIDUALIZED INTERVENTIONS

The following are individualized interventions beneficial for students with ADHD. Refer to the forms found in the Appendix for samples of all of the following.

Goal Sheets

■ See Student Goal Sheet in the Appendix. For example:

   ▪ "I would like to improve ____."

   ▪ "This is my plan for reaching my goal of ____."

■ The child/teen identifies one goal to work on for the day or week (such as "organize my desk or locker"; "no fights"; "get caught up with my incomplete math assignments"). The student also plans the specific steps he or she will take to reach the goal. Sometimes the teacher or counselor meets briefly in the morning with the student to discuss the goal and offer encouragement. At the end of the day, they meet again and reward success.

Daily Report Cards

■ Daily report cards (DRCs) have been research validated as a very effective intervention for students with ADHD. They are highly recommended because they provide:

   ▪ Close monitoring of targeted behaviors.

   ▪ The frequency and intensity of positive reinforcement children/teens with ADHD need.

   ▪ A means of measuring and determining improvement in functioning (for example, IEP goals).

   ▪ Increased communication with parents.

   ▪ A means of reporting student performance throughout the day to parents and physicians, which is a useful tool in determining the effectiveness of medication on a child's functioning.

   ▪ See the DRC pages from NICHQ in the Appendix (A-8 through A-10). These were adapted from the Center for Children and Families, University of Buffalo, and are part of a 10-page packet developed by William E. Pelham, Jr., Ph.D., a researcher and leader in the field of behavioral interventions for children with ADHD.

■ To download the full packet on daily report cards, go to Dr. Pelham's website at the Center for Children and Families, University of Buffalo, State University of New York:

http://wings.buffalo.edu/psychology/adhd/. It is also available at www.nichq.org, under "ADHD Toolkit."

Options for Rewarding Successful Performance on Daily Report Cards

■ There are different options for rewarding students with a daily/weekly report card. Many DRCs use a leveled system of rewards as described in "How to Establish a Home–School Daily Report Card" in the Appendix. The greater the percentage of points earned, the higher the level of privileges or number of rewards that can be selected from the menu.

■ As shown on the reward form sample in the Appendix, receiving 75–89% of possible "plus" marks (or yes marks) earns the child the privilege of choosing two things from the reward menu. Higher percentages earn more; lower percentages earn fewer.

■ Another option for rewarding based upon performance on the daily report card is having the reward contingent upon the student successfully achieving a goal for the day or week (a target percentage of possible points).

■ When starting the program, it is important to make sure the child has immediate success. As such, the target goal should be very much within the child's reach (depending on the baseline of frequency of behaviors). For example, 70% of possible points may be the goal; if the child reaches the goal for the day, the predetermined reward is delivered.

■ First determine approximately how frequently the behavior you wish to improve is occurring. Count or measure the behavior over a period of a few days or a week to get an average.

■ As explained in the Appendix, parents provide the rewards; however, a teacher may need to provide the rewards at school as well.

■ It is important that reinforcement is provided consistently and as promised. A coordinated system between home and school is the most effective.

Varieties of DRC and Monitoring Forms

Refer to the following forms in the Appendix, which are described here for clarification:

■ The *Classroom Behavioral Chart* is an example of a daily report card (DRC) form.
  ▪ Behaviors are selected for monitoring and marked by the teacher at the end of the various time intervals designated on the chart.
  ▪ After subtracting the number of minuses from the number of pluses, the student's total net points for the day are determined.
  ▪ The child is rewarded based upon his or her performance.

■ The *Student Weekly Progress Report* is an example of a DRC that includes each day of the week on one form.
  ▪ Conduct and classwork are monitored throughout the week and one to four points are awarded based upon specific criteria of performance.
  ▪ The student is rewarded when achieving the daily or weekly goal.

2-9 (*continued*)

- The leveled reward can also be used instead of a target percentage goal.
- The *Student Daily Behavioral Report* is an example of a DRC formatted in a circle rather than a matrix to add novelty.
- The *Behavior Rating Sheet* is an example of a behavior monitoring form.
  - The teacher selects one or more behaviors to monitor during a time frame of school (one class period, mornings only, afternoons only, full day).
  - The student is rated on a 1–5 scale, and for overall behavior and performance for the day.
- The *Daily Performance Record* is a monitoring form per subject with teacher rating.
  - Behavior (good, average, poor)
  - Turned in homework? (yes/no)
  - Prepared for class? (yes/no)
  - Used class time effectively? (yes, somewhat, no)
- The *Weekly Behavior Report* is a simplified format of two behaviors ("I followed rules; I did my work") monitored three times a day (before recess, after recess, after lunch). The goal is set for a certain number of points or smiley faces that must be received in order to earn a predetermined reward.
- The *Student-Generated Progress Report* is a self-monitoring form. The student evaluates himself or herself and then the teacher initials if in agreement. The student and teacher monitor and evaluate behavior in class, homework completion, classwork quality/production, and notebook organization.
- The *Connect-the-Dots Chart* is an example of a "chart moves" strategy that involves:
  - Selecting a goal (target behavior).
  - When the goal is met, the child advances on his or her chart, in this case by connecting to the next dot.
  - When the chart is filled (all dots connected), the reward is earned.
  - The form in the Appendix shows how this can be a class chart (group goal) or an individualized chart (for a single student).

Student Contracts

These involve a written agreement among the student, teacher, and parent (or other parties). Included are:

- The criteria for successful performance of the agreed-upon behavior(s).
- What the reward will be if the student fulfills his or her agreement successfully.
- When the contract will be reviewed.
- In some cases, contracts include a penalty clause that indicates not only the reward but what the consequences will be for failing to perform the identified behavior(s).

See the two contract examples in the Appendix.

Token Economy System

■ This system includes any of the plans and techniques that involve awarding something immediately (points, plastic chips, stickers) for demonstrating a positive targeted behavior that is later redeemed (cashed in) for a privilege or reward.

■ Token economy systems often include "response cost" as well. This means also losing or deducting points/tokens for targeted misbehaviors.

■ Although emotionally fragile students may get upset with fines and deductions, it is a technique known to be effective with ADHD children/teens.

■ It is very important that when using response costs there are far more points/tokens being earned than taken away, or the incentive to meet the behavioral goal will disappear and the child will give up.

Response Costs

See the Response Cost Chart in the Appendix. The technique is described on the chart and is also explained here:

1. Select a problematic behavior to monitor (such as blurting/calling out, getting into arguments or fights, teasing, or being out of seat without permission) during a specific time frame (such as math class or mornings).

2. Record the frequency of the behavior during a few days to a week in order to get a baseline average of how often it typically occurs.

3. Use the chart, starting with whichever of the three point columns (50, 25, or 10) is most appropriate, based on the average baseline of occurrences.

4. Use the point column that most closely fits your need, and adjust from there. For example, if the baseline is 20, then use the 25 point column but start at the 20 box and deduct points from there.

5. Cross out one point each time the inappropriate target behavior occurs.

6. Start with a goal that is easy to achieve. For example, if starting at 20, mark the goal as 4, meaning that 16 points (but not more) can be deducted for misbehavior and the student will still earn a reward. This indicates a 20% improvement in the baseline performance.

7. Using the technique on this form, raise the goal for success *gradually* until the behavior has improved to a manageable level.

Note: Rather than using points, a response cost strategy can involve (a) giving the child a certain number of plastic chips or tokens during a period of time; (b) identifying which behavior will result in loss of a token (talking back, being out of seat, hitting); (c) removing a chip or token for each incident of inappropriate behavior; (d) giving the child a reward if he or she has any chips left at end of the time period.

RELATED LIST

■ See List 2-18 for more information about these individualized interventions and many other useful strategies on behavioral management.

2-10
STRATEGIES TO AID CALMING AND AVOID ESCALATION OF PROBLEMS

Always watch for warning signs of students becoming frustrated, agitated, or overly stimulated. Be aware of triggers to misbehavior and make adjustments with regard to task demand, environmental conditions, and so forth, as described in Lists 2-3 and 2-4.

When a student is showing signs that he or she is beginning to lose control, intervene at once.

- Provide a cue or prompt (stand near student and place a gentle hand on shoulder).
- Use a prearranged private signal (such as a nonverbal cue) as a reminder to settle down.
- Divert the child's attention, if possible.
- Redirect to a different location, situation, or activity (run an errand/message to the office; bring a note to a neighboring class; ask to help pass out materials; sharpen a can of spare pencils).
- Cue the student to use relaxation techniques (visualization, deep breathing, counting slowly, progressive muscle relaxation) as described in List 8-9.
- Prompt the student to use self-talk that is first taught as a self-regulation strategy ("I am calm and in control." "I need to chill out." "I can handle this. Just relax and stay calm.").
- Remind the student about rewards and consequences.
- Provide the student time and a means to regroup, regain control, and avoid the escalation of behaviors.

Points to Keep in Mind

- Provide an area that a student can access briefly as a preventive (not punitive) measure before behaviors escalate to a higher level.
- Consider creating a calming area equipped with such items as a fish tank or lava lamp, stuffed animal, soothing music (on a tape recorder with headset), stress ball, pillows, or perhaps a rocking chair.
- Such an area is designed as a "take-a-break" or "cool down" spot. Some teachers give these room locations names such as "Hawaii" (or some other name that the class agrees is a pleasant, relaxing reference).
- Students are directed to or asked if they need to visit the cool-down area for a short amount of time when feeling agitated or angry ("Would you like to go to Hawaii for a few minutes?"). *Note:* This is *not* a "timeout," which is a negative, corrective consequence that must be time away from anything rewarding.

- To relieve stress and aid in calming, it often helps to do physical activities (brisk walking, jogging, swinging, pushing/pulling activities, pounding/manipulating clay, and so on).
- One strategy for calming described by Harmin (2-18) is teaching students to regain self-control by using the "clock watch," which requires the following steps:
  - Stand near their desk.
  - Take a deep breath.
  - Face the wall clock and watch it go around one or two minutes.
  - Then sit down and get back to work.
- To aid calming:
  - Speak softly and slowly.
  - Watch your body language (relaxed).
  - Offer choices.
  - Try to defuse a potential situation and provide support.

RELATED LIST

- See List 2-11 for related strategies.

2-11
TIPS FOR DEALING WITH "CHALLENGING" OR "DIFFICULT" BEHAVIORS

Note: The following tips and strategies are appropriate for both the home and the school.

- Watch for and prevent triggers of misbehavior (time of day, the activity/expectations) and begin a plan of early intervention. (2-17)

- Increase the immediacy and frequency of positive feedback and reinforcement.

- Make a conscious effort to provide at least three times more positive than negative feedback.

- Plan a response and avoid "reacting" to challenging behavior (especially when you are in an emotional state).

- Do not feel compelled to give an immediate response in dealing with situations until you are in a calm, thinking state. Feel free to quietly and privately say to the child/teen, "We will deal with this after class." Or "I'm upset right now. I need time to think about this before we discuss the consequence of your behavior. I'll get back to you."

- Praise, encourage, and reward increments of improvement in behavior and work performance.

- Realize that you cannot control anyone else's behavior.

- Change what you *can* control . . . yourself (your attitude, body language, voice, strategies, expectations, and the nature of the interaction).

- Be firm, fair, and consistent.

- Physically relax your body before dealing with situations. Take a few deep breaths. Unfold your arms and relax your jaw. Cue yourself to be calm.

- Disengage from power struggles. Remember that you cannot be forced into an argument or power struggle. You only enter into one if you choose to do so (it takes two). Say, for example, "I am not willing to argue about this now. I will be free to discuss it later if you wish after class."

- Affirm and acknowledge a student's feelings ("I see you're upset." "I understand that you are angry now." "I can see why you would be frustrated.").

- Express your confidence in students' ability to make good choices.

- Avoid "why" questions ("Why did you do that?").

- Use "what" questions ("What are you supposed to be doing right now?" "What do you want?" "What is your plan to solve the problem?" "What can I do to help you?" "What would you like to see happen?").

- Remember that children/teens with ADHD are typically not deliberately trying to aggravate you.

- Do not take their behavior personally.

- Remind yourself that behaviors are stemming from their neuro-biological disorder.

- Be consistent in providing corrective consequences. (2-8)

- Deal with behavior as discretely as possible.

- Remain calm (relax body, uncross arms, lower voice), communicating your hope that they will choose to cooperate.

- Remind students of the rules.

- Try to maintain your sense of humor.

- Send "I messages." ("I feel ____ when you ____ because ____." "I want/need you to ____.")

- Speak privately, away from an audience.

- Avoid nagging, scolding, and lecturing.

- Do not take the bait.

- Use the "broken record" technique. Respond by repeating your directions with the same words and in a calm, neutral voice. Use the words "however" and "nevertheless." For example: "I understand you are feeling ____. However . . ." or "That may be____. Nevertheless . . ."

- Do not demand or threaten.

- Avoid being judgmental in your interactions.

- Do all you can to build the relationship.

- Take time to actively listen to the child. Be attentive. Listen without interjecting your opinions. Ask a lot of open and clarifying questions. Rephrase and restate what was said.

- Take an interest in the child/teen's life.

- Show caring and empathy.

- Try to determine if there is another underlying problem (poor reading skills; conflict with someone that needs to be resolved; and so on).

- Work together on establishing goals and identifying positive reinforcers that will be meaningful and motivating to the child/teen. (2-2, 2-9, 2-14)

- Forge a strong home–school alliance with a positive behavioral plan in place.

- Use individualized behavior-modification plans. (See List 2-9 and samples in the Appendix.)

- Provide choices ("I can't make you ____. But your choices are either ____ or ____.").

- It is okay to call for a break. For example, parents may go to a different room, take an exercise break, or do something else away from each other.

2-11 (*continued*)

- Discuss, problem-solve, and negotiate solutions when both parties have had time to cool down and are in a calm, thinking mode.

- Teach problem-solving strategies (identifying the problem, brainstorming possible solutions, evaluating pros and cons, choosing one and trying it, reviewing effectiveness, trying another if it wasn't working).

- If the child/teen appears on the verge of a "meltdown," try prompting the child to use self-calming, self-regulation techniques. See List 2-10 for strategies to aid calming and avoid escalation of problems.

- If student is motivated by power and status, seek opportunities for him or her to assume a leadership role in the classroom or school.

- Seek opportunities for the student to feel more connected to the school as a positive contributor. For example, train and assign him or her as:
  - Peer tutor to a younger student
  - Teacher-assistant in a lower-grade classroom
  - Peer mediator on the kindergarten playground
  - Assistant in the computer lab

2-12
PROACTIVE PARENTING: POSITIVE DISCIPLINE AND BEHAVIOR-MANAGEMENT STRATEGIES

Discipline means "teaching" responsible behavior. Children must learn appropriate, prosocial behavior in order to live and interact successfully with others. Of course, this is a key responsibility of parenting.

BASIC GUIDELINES

The following are basic guidelines for positive discipline and effective behavior management for the home:

- Provide structure, routine, and predictability.

- Set limits and let your child know you mean business.

- Establish a few specific, important rules/expectations that are clearly understood by all members of the household.

- Your responses to your child's behaviors and misbehaviors should be predictable, not random.

- Establish clear-cut consequences in advance with your child that are logical, reasonable, and fair. Enforce them with consistency.

- Use contingencies in establishing boundaries. This basically involves the age-old "Grandma's rule"—"First you eat your vegetables, then you get dessert." Examples:

  - "As soon as you _____, you may _____."

  - "Once you have _____, you will then be able to _____."

  - "You have done your homework. Now you get to go play."

- Children with ADHD receive far more than average negative attention from parents and teachers because misbehavior captures our attention. Notice and pay attention to your child when he or she is behaving appropriately.

- Make it a goal to catch your child "being good" at least three times more frequently than when you need to respond to misbehavior.

- Be specific in acknowledging and praising:

  - "I really appreciate how you cleaned up without being reminded."

  - "I noticed how well you were sharing and taking turns when you played with Bobby."

- Always reward or give positive attention to the behaviors you want to increase or continue to occur.

2-12 (*continued*)

- Immediately reinforce desired behavior with a positive consequence. That means something your child likes (praise, smiles, hugs, privileges, points/tokens earned toward a reward) would follow the behavior.

- Establish rewards and punishments that are easy to do and as simple as possible.

- Children with ADHD require more external motivation than other children, as their internal controls are less mature. Therefore, they will need more frequent, immediate, and potent rewards for their effort.

- Realize that children with ADHD have trouble delaying gratification and cannot wait very long for reinforcers. Working toward a long-range goal or "pay-off" is not going to be effective. It is better to use more frequent, smaller rewards, but ones that are still motivating.

- Token economy systems are effective for children with ADHD. It is worth the effort to learn how to implement such a system at home. It involves the following:
  - Rewarding the child with tokens of some kind (poker chips or points) for performing a number of behaviors.
  - These behaviors would include things they would normally be expected to do, such as being ready for the school bus on time; clearing the table after dinner; feeding the dog or other chores; remembering to bring home all books and the assignment calendar for homework.

- A menu of reinforcers is created with the child, which includes material things (certain toy, book, CD, special dessert) and privileges (inviting a friend to sleep over) the child values. (2-14) A point value is assigned for each item on the list. The child can "purchase" the reward from the tokens earned.

- Rewards will have to be changed frequently as well. Children with ADHD will not stay interested in the same rewards or incentives; they respond best to novelty. Therefore, a menu with a choice of privileges and small-ticket items that are meaningful to the child should be available.

- With a token economy system, the child can also be fined (lose tokens) for targeted behaviors (each incident of fighting with sibling; talking back). It is crucial in such a system to ensure that the child is earning far more tokens/points than he or she is losing, or it simply will not work.

- Daily report cards, contracts, or behavior-monitoring forms of some kind between home and school are necessary for many children/teens with ADHD. See the Appendix for several examples, and List 2-9.

- Negative consequences or punishments are also effective in changing behavior; however, use far more positives than negatives.

- When punishments are required, they should not be harsh. The purpose is to *teach* your child through its use and enforcement.

■ Consequences should be enforced as soon as possible following the infraction of rules—usually one warning, not several.

■ The best consequences are those that are logically related to the offense and natural results of the child's actions.

■ Some effective punishments include:

- Ignoring (particularly attention-getting behaviors)

- Verbal reprimands (not yelling and screaming)

- Removal of privileges (for example, TV time)

- Response costs (receiving a "fine" or penalty such as removal of some points or tokens earned, in a token economy system)

- Timeout (isolation for a brief amount of time)

■ When delivering consequences, do so in a calm but firm voice. State the consequence without lecturing. Be direct and to the point.

■ If using a timeout, choose a location that is boring for your child, as well as safe but away from the reinforcement of other people and activities. It should be clear to your child what behaviors will result in timeout. Typically, a reasonable amount of time is one minute per year of age. Set a timer.

■ Punishments must have a clear beginning and ending that you are able to control.

■ When punishing, be careful to focus on the *behavior* that is inappropriate. Do not attack the child as "being bad" or criticize his or her character.

■ Anticipate and plan in advance (with your spouse) how to handle challenging behaviors. Avoid responding and punishing when you are very angry. You do not want to dole out a punishment you will regret later because it is too harsh, inappropriate, or impossible to enforce.

■ Avoid getting pulled into a power struggle or a shouting match with your child. Disengage. Do not be afraid to say, "I'm too angry to talk about this right now. We will discuss this later." Take time to step back, calm down, and think before you act.

■ When calm, discuss the situation.

PREVENTIVE STRATEGIES

■ Remind through gentle warnings:

- "The rule is ____."

- "Next time ____."

- "Remember to ____."

■ Use "do statements" rather than "don't statements." (Say "Walk in the house" rather than "Don't run in the house.")

2-12 (*continued*)

- Learn to communicate more effectively. (2-13)

- Talk about, acknowledge, and label feelings—your child's and your own.

- Organize and arrange the home environment in a way that will optimize the chances for success and avoid conflict. (4-5, 4-7, 8-4)

- Set up routines (morning routines [getting ready for school], mealtime routines, homework routines, and bedtime routines) and adhere to them as closely as possible.

- Remove items or objects you do not want your impulsive/hyperactive child to touch or play with. "Child-proof" the house.

- Avoid fatigue—your child's and your own.

- Try to give your ADHD child as much of his or her own space as possible. Be observant. Notice when your child is becoming agitated, overly stimulated, or angry, and intervene. Try redirecting your child's attention and focus on something else.

- Only give your child chores and responsibilities that he or she is developmentally able to handle—what he or she is capable of, *not* what other kids of his or her age or other siblings can do.

- Provide the supports to enable your child to follow-through with chores and responsibilities. Remember that forgetfulness, procrastination, and disorganization are part of the ADHD picture. Your child will need reminders, help getting started, and so forth.

- Provide physical outlets. Your child needs to release energy and participate in physical activities (running, swimming, gymnastics, dancing, bike riding, playing ball).

- Maintain flexibility and a sense of humor!

- Monitor and supervise.

- Prepare your child for changes in the home, such as redecorating, visitors/house guests, and changes in parent work schedules. Talk about the change and avoid surprises.

- Purchase toys, books, games, and so on that are developmentally appropriate for your child and not too frustrating.

- Avoid competitive activities and/or prepare for games and activities that involve competition. Walk your child through the strategies of what to do if he or she loses a game. Reinforce good sportsmanship, explaining that one cannot always win. When playing games, praise and reward behavior that required your child to display self-control.

- Provide your child with training in social skills. (2-16)

- Provide a limited number of choices. Do not allow your child to dump out all of his or her toys; choose from all the music/video tapes; or examine all the books before choosing one for you to read with him or her. Allow your child to choose from only a few at one time.

- Be aware of siblings who are teasing and provoking your ADHD child, and intervene.

- See List 2-15, Preventing Behavior Problems Outside of the Home.

Points to Keep in Mind

- Try to keep calm and avoid discipline that is reactive (not thought out in advance).

- Prioritize and focus on what is important. You cannot make an issue out of everything.

- No matter how exhausted or frustrated you are, maintain your authority as a parent and follow through on what you need to do.

- Avoid sarcasm, ridicule, criticism, nagging, screaming, or physical punishment.

- Plan ahead which behaviors you will work toward increasing and how you will reward (positively reinforce those behaviors).

- It is far more difficult to manage the behaviors of children with ADHD than most other children. Be willing to seek professional help to find more effective strategies and guidance. Get referrals from other parents of children with similar needs. Find a mental health professional who is familiar with ADHD and experienced in dealing with hyperactive and impulsive behaviors.

- Parents of children with ADHD must become far more skilled in specialized behavior-management principles and techniques than other parents in order to know how to cope with and handle the daily challenges and behavioral difficulties resulting from their child's disorder.

- There are numerous resources available that address this topic of effective discipline and behavior-management strategies. (2-18)

- See List 2-11, Tips for Dealing with "Challenging" or "Difficult" Behaviors.

2-13
FOLLOWING DIRECTIONS: TIPS FOR PARENTS TO IMPROVE CHILDREN'S LISTENING AND COMPLIANCE

- Get your child's attention directly before giving directions. This means face-to-face and direct eye contact (not just calling out what you expect your child to do).

- You may need to walk over to touch or physically cue your child prior to giving directions.

- Do not attempt to give directions or instructions if you are competing with the distraction of TV, music, and video games. First turn those off to gain the child's attention and focus.

- Show your child what you want him or her to do. Model and walk through the steps. Check that your child understands.

- Depending on the developmental level of your child, one direction at a time is often all your son or daughter is capable of remembering and following-through on. Do not give a series of directions.

- Provide multisensory instructions by using a visual chart of tasks or chores your child is expected to do.

- A helpful technique for young children is to draw pictures on a chart hanging in the room that shows the sequence of morning or evening activities. For example: (1) clothing (to get dressed); (2) cereal bowl (to show eating breakfast); (3) hairbrush and toothbrush. As your child completes the task, he or she moves a clothespin down the chart next to that corresponding picture.

- Always check for understanding of directions. Have your child repeat or rephrase what you asked him or her to do.

- Use color to get your child's attention with anything you put in writing (key words, pictures, and so on).

- Write down the task you want done (words or pictures) and give that written direction or task card to your child for easy reference.

- Keep directions clear, brief, and to the point. Reduce unnecessary talking and elaboration.

- Be sure to give frequent *praise* and *positive feedback* when your child follows directions and/or is making a good attempt to do so.

- Provide follow-up when you give directions (inspect, check your child's work, and praise a job well done).

- Reward your child for following directions, as appropriate. For example: "You did a great job straightening up your room. You get to . . . (choose a game, have a snack)."
- Try not to lose your temper when your child fails to follow directions. Remember that it is characteristic of children with ADHD to have difficulty:
  - Disengaging from activities (especially fun ones) that they are in the middle of and have not completed
  - Responding and following-through without structuring, adult prompting, and cueing
  - Utilizing recall/memory
- Examine what you asked your son or daughter to do and see if you provided enough structure and assistance to enable him or her to follow-through with the directions given.
- It is easy to forget that even though they are at an age when they *should* remember and be able to do a task independently, children/teens developmentally may not be able to do so, and thus need some of the supports that a younger child would normally require.
- Provide support by working alongside your child on a task together.
- Try turning unpleasant chores and tasks into more pleasant or motivating experiences by making a game of it whenever possible. For example, try "Beat the Clock" challenges, such as "Let's see if you can finish putting all of your toys away while the commercials are still on (or before the alarm goes off, the song ends)."
- Break down tasks into smaller steps that you want to get done. Give one step at a time.
- Focus on the behavior you want *started*, rather than *stopped*. Before issuing a directive or command to your son or daughter, think in terms of what you want to see your child doing instead of what he or she is currently doing.
- Use what is referred to as "alpha" commands, which are clear and well stated. Avoid "beta commands," which are unclear and poorly stated. What you may interpret as your child's noncompliance may actually be the result of you not effectively communicating your directions.

Do's and Don'ts

The following are some do's and don'ts when giving directions/commands to children. See the sources and resources for more information on this topic.

- **Do not** give a direction or command until you know you have your child's attention.
- **Do** get your child's direct attention by getting close and obtaining eye contact (even if it means gently turning his or her face to look at you).
- **Do not** assume your child heard you.
- **Do** ask your child to repeat the direction back to you.
- **Do not** give a string or chain of multiple directions/commands.
- **Do** give one direction at a time.

2-13 (*continued*)

- **Do not** use vague language that is open to interpretation and lacks enough precise information ("Clean your room." "Get ready." "Be nice to your brother.").

- **Do** be precise in what you mean. For example, "Clean your room" means:
    1. Clothes hung in closet or folded/placed in drawers
    2. Bed made
    3. Toys in storage bins

- **Do not** continue to talk, explain, and elaborate after giving a direction or command.

- **Do** state what you want and then stop talking and give your child the chance to comply without interruption.

- **Do not** state your direction/command in the form of a question, such as:
    - "Would you get in your pajamas, please?"
    - "Isn't it time to get busy on your homework?"
    - "Why don't you leave your brother alone?"
    - "Are you ready to turn off the lights?"

- **Do** give your direction/command as a direct statement and be specific. For example:
    - "Get in your pajamas now."
    - "Lights off in 15 minutes."
    - "Sit with your bottom in the chair."
    - "Hang up the wet towel, please."

- **Do not** bark orders or use either an intimidating, wimpy, or emotional tone of voice.

- **Do** use a firm, matter-of-fact, and neutral tone of voice.

- **Do not** repeat, continue to verbalize, add new directions, or intervene in any manner without waiting a minimum of 5 seconds after issuing a directive/command. If your child does not comply with the direction the first time given, it is recommended (after the minimum of 5 seconds) to state the direction/command again. This time use the words: "You need to . . ." Praise/positively reinforce if your child follows the direction this time, and provide a mild negative consequence (loss of privilege—e.g., TV time) if your child still does not comply.

- **Do** wait a reasonable amount of time (depending on the situation) to enable your child to comply and follow your direction.

- **Do not** let it go unnoticed or unappreciated when your child follows directions appropriately.

- **Do** be sure to praise and positively reinforce immediately after your child follows the direction.

Points to Keep in Mind

- Avoid threats, ultimatums, criticism of your child's character/personality, sarcasm, and belittling.

- Do not respond or give consequences when your emotions are in high gear. It is better to tell your child that you are angry/upset now and need to cool down first before addressing the situation.

- Use questioning techniques that communicate your empathy and your desire to better understand your child ("This is a hard time for you, isn't it?" "Help me understand why . . ." "I'm guessing that ____. Is this correct?").

- Use "what" questions such as "What should you be doing now?" "What are your choices?" "What do you (or we) need to do to solve the problem?" "What do you need from me in order to help you?"

RELATED LISTS

- See Lists 2-11, 2-12, 2-18, and 3-4 for more related strategies.

SOURCES AND RESOURCES

Barkley, Russell A. *Your Defiant Child.* New York: The Guilford Press, 1998.

Barkley, Russell A. *Taking Charge of ADHD.* New York: The Guilford Press, 2000.

Forehand, R., and R. McMahon. *Helping the Noncompliant Child.* New York: The Guilford Press, 1981.

Goldstein, Sam. "The Importance of Positive Directions for Children with ADHD" (http://www.samgoldstein.com/articles/0201.html)

Regan, Claire. "Get Your Kids to Listen Up," *McCall's*, April 1998.

Robinson, Kristin. "Compliance—It's No Mystery," CHADD: *Attention*, July/August, 2000.

Taylor, John F. *From Defiance to Cooperation.* Roseville, CA: Prima Publishing, 2001.

Walker, Hill M., and Janet Eaton Walker. *Coping with Noncompliance in the Classroom.* Austin, TX: Pro-Ed Publishers, 1991.

2-14
REWARDS AND POSITIVE REINFORCERS
FOR HOME

Here are possible rewards to use with a behavioral-modification/management plan. See Lists 2-1 and 2-9, and the Appendix for examples of such plans, programs, and techniques that motivate and reinforce cooperative, responsible behavior.

Points to Keep in Mind

■ Any social, activity, or material reward will only work to motivate your child if it has meaning, value, and appeal to your son or daughter. Take time to find out from your child what he or she would like on a "menu" of reinforcers. Change that menu as often as necessary to maintain interest.

■ It is important to catch your child being good (demonstrating appropriate behavior). Acknowledge positive behavior and interact with your child at those times. Be generous with social reinforcers. (2-11, 2-12)

SOCIAL REINFORCERS

■ Positive attention from parents (acknowledgment, relaxed time together, talking)

■ Physical signs of affection from parents (hugs, kisses, cuddling)

■ Smiles

■ Thumbs-up sign/high fives

■ Piggyback rides

■ Cheering

■ Specific praise such as:

  ▪ "I like it when you . . ."

  ▪ "That sure was grown up of you when . . ."

  ▪ "That was great the way you . . ."

  ▪ "It makes me so happy when you . . ."

  ▪ "I'm so proud of how you . . ."

  ▪ "Thank you for . . ."

  ▪ "I can really tell you worked hard on . . ."

  ▪ "Let's show Mom . . ."

  ▪ "Let's make a copy of this for Grandma . . ."

  ▪ "Let's hang this up somewhere special . . ."

- "Great job on how you . . ."
- "I can't wait to tell Dad how you . . ."
- "I knew you could do it!"

ACTIVITY REINFORCERS AND PRIVILEGES

Note: Some of these activities are also social reinforcers.

- Playing a special game (indoor, outdoor)
- An outing (park, restaurant, ice cream shop, beach, zoo)
- Extended bedtime
- Time earned for watching TV, phone privilege, computer/Internet access, playing
- Special time alone with parent (out for breakfast, shopping, ice cream, ball game, building something)
- Freedom from chores
- Crafts (building models, making jewelry, and so on)
- Drawing or painting
- Selecting a meal for dinner
- Baking cupcakes, cookies, and so on
- Riding a bike
- Extra story/reading time with parent
- Going to a movie
- Going to a sporting event
- Extended curfew
- Participating in a school activity that costs money, such as a ski trip
- Participating in any sports activity of choice (swimming, skating, golfing, tennis, and so on)
- Going shopping
- Going to an arcade
- Listening to music
- Talking on the phone
- Driving privileges (parent driving to a place of child's choice or keys to the car for teens with drivers' licenses)
- Playing musical instruments
- Gymnastics, dance
- Club participation
- Renting a movie or video game

2-14 (*continued*)

- Camping
- Playing computer games
- Spending time with a special person (grandparent, favorite aunt/uncle)
- Staying overnight at a friend's or relative's house
- Inviting a friend (to visit/play, for lunch/dinner, to sleep over)

MATERIAL REINFORCERS

- Toys
- Art supplies
- Collectibles (baseball cards)
- Snacks/dessert
- Jewelry
- Books/magazines
- Games
- CDs or tapes
- DVDs or videos

- Clothing or accessories
- Puzzles
- Pets
- Sports equipment
- Wanted items for the child's room
- Money
- Any purchase of choice (within price range)

Note: Some reinforcers are recommended for daily rewards (for example, watching TV); some for weekly rewards (for example, video rental); and others for longer-range incentives the older child is working and saving up to earn.

2-15
PREVENTING BEHAVIOR PROBLEMS OUTSIDE OF THE HOME

Many parents of children with ADHD dread having to take their children shopping with them, or to other places outside of the home where behavior issues often emerge. The behavioral controls expected in some of these environments can be more than children with ADHD are able to handle.

The following recommendations help prevent—or at least reduce—potential behavior problems that can occur outside of the home:

- Teach, model, and practice appropriate behaviors and manners that you expect your child to display outside of the home (follow directions; clean up after self; walk/don't run inside the building; say "please" and "thank you").

- Anticipate and prepare for potential problems.

- Remember how any change of routine can be stressful and unnerving, which is why children with ADHD need preparation:

  - Give advance notice; avoid catching them off guard.

  - Talk about what to expect.

  - Provide your child enough time to get ready.

- Before going into public places (stores, doctor's offices, restaurants, church or temple, movie theaters) or visiting other people's homes:

  - Talk to your child about behavioral expectations.

  - State the rules simply.

  - Have your child repeat the rules back to you.

  - Give written directions if appropriate.

- Establish reward(s) that your child will be able to receive if he or she behaves appropriately and follows the rules. Remind your child of the contingency: "If you ____, you will be able to earn ____."

- Try not to put your child in situations that are too taxing on his or her self-control and attention span. Avoid places that you know will be too stimulating or difficult to supervise and manage the behavior.

- If your child is on medication, consider scheduling activities to coincide with the optimal effects of the medication.

- Avoid taking out your child when he or she is tired and needs a nap.

- Let your child know the negative consequences if he or she behaves inappropriately. Be prepared to enforce. Mean what you say!

2-15 (continued)

- When entering a public place (such as a department store) with your child, scout around for an isolated location that can be used for a timeout, if necessary.
- Remove your child from the situation when he or she is behaving inappropriately or showing signs of losing control.
- Supervise. Supervise. Supervise.
- Be prepared with a "bag of tricks." Knowing the nature of ADHD—how children bore easily and need to be kept busy—do not leave the house without toys, books, audiotapes, and games that can occupy your child and keep him or her entertained. Keep the "bag of tricks" replenished to maintain novelty and interest.
- Give your child feedback when you are with him or her outside of the home: "I'm proud of how well you are ____. It looks like you'll probably earn the ____ we talked about."
- If he or she is beginning to lose control, prompt your child to use previously taught self-regulation techniques ("Let's calm down. Take three deep breaths. Now count to ten slowly.").
- Prompt your child to use "self-talk" or other self-regulation strategies if showing signs of losing control in public places (take a few deep breaths; push an imaginary stop button; repeat to himself or herself, "I need to calm down. . . . Put on the brakes").
- Avoid shopping without building in the opportunity for your child to get something small.
- Talk with your child about the natural consequences of inappropriate behavior (friends or their parents won't want to invite him or her to their house again; other children will get angry and not want to play).
- Provide your child with social skills training to learn and practice skills for positively interacting with others. (2-16)

RELATED LIST

- See List 2-11, Tips for Dealing with "Challenging" or "Difficult" Behavior.

2-16

SOCIAL SKILLS INTERVENTIONS AND TEACHING PROSOCIAL BEHAVIOR

Children and teens with ADHD frequently have difficulty with interpersonal relationships, which can be a source of great pain and low self-esteem for the child and family. Although children and teens with ADHD are usually aware of the social skills they should exhibit, they often struggle *applying* them. This list addresses social skills issues along with strategies/interventions known to be effective.

Some common weaknesses in children/teens with ADHD that negatively affect their interactions and social acceptance are:

- Poor self-control and problem-solving skills. They are easily provoked to fighting, arguing, name calling, and inappropriate means of resolving conflicts.
- Poor self-awareness. They are often unaware of their own behaviors that others find annoying or intrusive.
- Difficulty controlling the noise level.
- Emotions interfere with activities.
- Poor communication skills (such as listening to others).

INTERVENTIONS FOR SOCIAL SKILLS PROBLEMS

Research indicates that the most effective interventions for addressing interpersonal/social skills difficulties in children/teens with ADHD are multimodal. These involve a combination of:

- School interventions
- Child interventions
- Parent interventions and training
- Medication intervention (if indicated)

School Interventions

- Within the classroom there is no better place and structure for teaching and practicing appropriate social skills than in the context of cooperative learning groups, as research has proven them effective not only in increasing student learning, but also:
  - Positive/supportive relationships
  - Student acceptance
  - Ability to see other points of view

2-16 (*continued*)

■ Some elementary schools provide social skills training through various lessons and units taught by the classroom teacher to the whole class, or in sessions facilitated and presented by the counselor (either in the classroom or small-group sessions outside of the classroom). There are some excellent programs and social skills curriculum on the market from which to choose, such as those listed in Sources and Resources.

■ Many schools are implementing character education programs focusing on teaching and positively reinforcing prosocial values and behaviors to create a positive schoolwide climate. These include such character traits as:

Trustworthiness	Fairness
Respect	Caring
Responsibility	Citizenship
Leadership	Courtesy
Honesty	Sharing
Dependability	Friendship
Moral courage	Sportsmanship
Empathy	Persistence
Integrity	Initiative

■ There are numerous ways of teaching and positively reinforcing targeted prosocial traits/behaviors throughout the school. Besides classroom lessons and activities, there can be schoolwide assemblies, messages over the intercom, and schoolwide/community campaigns. There are also schoolwide activities such as the following:

  ▪ All teachers spend time at the beginning of the week or month discussing a particular value or social skill (such as courtesy) with their students.

  ▪ All adults on campus wear a badge that has the social skill topic/word of the month printed it.

  ▪ Staff members are given a certain amount of "I Got Caught" tickets that they are to distribute to any student they happen to observe on campus exhibiting the targeted social skill behavior of the week or month (being respectful, courteous, fair, and so on).

  ▪ Students who receive tickets write their names on them and place the ticket inside the school box designated for that purpose. Once a day or week there is a raffle with prizes going to students whose names are drawn.

■ Some middle schools are teaching social skills in their P.E. programs through various formats:

  ▪ The specific social skill (encouragement, giving/accepting compliments, sportsmanship) is taught in 3- or 4-week units.

  ▪ Skills are discussed in terms of what it looks and sounds like when you display those skills, as well as the rationale for using them. For example, the following can represent what *encouragement* looks like: thumbs up, pat on back, smile, high five. The following can represent what *encouragement* sounds like: "Nice try." "You can do it." "Way to go."

- The skills are then practiced and reinforced through a number of entertaining and motivating cooperative games and activities.

- Students receive positive reinforcement in a variety of ways for exhibiting those skills.

- Students are responsible for processing and evaluating how well they and their group performed regarding the use of the specific social skill.

■ Increase student awareness of appropriate skills by modeling, giving positive attention, and reinforcing student displays of prosocial behavior both in and out of the classroom setting.

■ Provide corrective feedback in a manner that is neither judgmental nor embarrassing, but rather focuses on teaching positive social skills.

■ Help children weak in social skills by carefully pairing them with positive role models and assigning them to groups that will be more supportive. Sometimes teachers will need to try facilitating friendships for certain students who tend to be socially isolated.

■ In any context or format that social skills are being taught, do the following:

- Explain the need for learning the skill. This can be done through discussion and reinforced by visual displays (posters, photos).

- Demonstrate appropriate and inappropriate skills through positive and negative examples.

- Have students role-play and rehearse the appropriate skill.

- Ask students to look for and observe the skill being displayed in different settings.

- Provide many opportunities to *practice* the skill being taught in authentic, real-world activities.

■ In the context of these settings (or in debriefing afterward), provide coaching, positive reinforcement for appropriate use, and corrective feedback/consequences for inappropriate behavior.

■ There are various systems for positively reinforcing the use of prosocial skills in school settings: daily report card, individual contract, and school rewards (social, activity, material, privileges) contingent upon the display of targeted social skills. (2-1, 2-2, 2-7, 2-9, 2-14, Appendix)

■ Take photos of groups or individuals engaged in cooperative behavior and display them in a prominent place as a visual cue.

■ Some specific social skills that may be targeted for explicitly teaching, monitoring, coaching, and positively reinforcing include:

- How to listen to others without interrupting

- How to disagree

2-16 (*continued*)

- How to give and receive praise/compliments
- How to participate in a conversation without dominating it
- How to enter into a conversation or activity with others
- How to share and take turns
- How to ask for help
- How to play a game and accept losing appropriately
- How to apologize
- How to use an appropriate tone of voice and volume for a particular setting or situation
- General manners—using respectful, polite verbal and body language
- It is important for schools to establish and maintain a positive climate and culture with a belief in inclusive education—that all children belong and are part of the community.
- Many schoolwide interventions (conflict resolution, peer mediation, character education programs, cooperative learning) can be employed to increase the social functioning and interpersonal relationships of students.

Child Interventions

- Often children with ADHD are not so socially accepted because they have poor skills in playing various games/sports. It helps to involve them in as many opportunities as possible to build their skills and competencies so that peers will want to include them in their play and sport activities.
- Children/teens with social skills difficulties need direct intervention in building their social competence, particularly in peer relationships. Social skills training programs are an excellent means of doing so.
- Social skills programs commonly address some of the following:
  - Greeting others
  - Listening and responding
  - Showing interest by smiling and asking questions
  - Working and playing cooperatively
  - Learning to join an ongoing activity (a game in progress)
  - Ignoring teasing
  - Managing anger/using effective coping strategies
  - Following instructions and rules
  - Being aware of feelings (self and others)
  - Giving and accepting positive feedback

- Giving and accepting negative feedback
- Solving problems peacefully/nonaggressively

- Social skills programs are designed to teach specific skills within a small group (children and teens generally of same age range). The trainer uses a social skills training curriculum (see below). Most effective programs have sessions involving:
    - A *brief* introduction to the skill, including examples/non-examples, role-play, and rehearsal.
    - The bulk of the session involves actually playing an indoor or outdoor game/activity.
    - Children are prompted and coached on the use of the skill.
    - There is a short debriefing with feedback and reinforcement demonstrating the use of the targeted skill.

- Use of the skill with feedback and contingent reinforcement applied in authentic situations (playing a game) is a critical component of effective social skills programs.

- Any social skill taught should be one that can be generalized across settings. This requires that they be practiced and reinforced at school, home, and so forth.

- Training programs can be implemented in a variety of settings (after-school programs, summer treatment programs, clinical settings, learning centers/recreation centers).

- Children who have a deficit in specific social skills need direct, explicit teaching, and frequent opportunities to practice those appropriate skills.

- Those children/teens who know the appropriate skills but do not perform them due to inhibition problems, need a lot of external reinforcement (behavioral modification techniques) to help them exhibit better self-control in order to *use* the skills.

- Another component of child interventions is teaching the child/teen some cognitive approaches and other methods to help improve interpersonal relationships/social skills, and self-regulation of behavior. This includes training in:
    - Problem-solving techniques
    - Conflict resolution
    - Anger management
    - Relaxation strategies (8-9)

Parent Interventions

- Because interpersonal relationships are heavily affected at home as well as among peers, parents of children/teens with ADHD need to be part of the intervention plan, which includes training and skill building in:
    - Behavior-management techniques and positive discipline (2-12)
    - Dealing with challenging behaviors effectively (2-11)
    - Communicating with effective messages, directions, and commands (2-13)
    - Avoiding escalation of problems (2-10)

2-16 (*continued*)

- Parents must be provided with information about ADHD, as well as resources and supports in their community.

- Parents can help their children by:

  - Seeking a well-designed social skills training program for their child.

  - Orchestrating, when necessary, opportunities for their child to socialize and play with other children.

  - Reinforcing the prosocial skills being taught at school and any other social skills training in which the child may be participating.

- Parents may try bringing to their child's attention the inappropriateness of some of their social behaviors, and the effect they have on maintaining friendships. However, it is recommended to have such conversations at a time when it is calm at home (a more "teachable moment"), not when emotions are running high.

- In some communities there are centers or clinics specializing in multimodal treatment approaches for children/teens with ADHD. They may offer a variety of services and supports for both children and their parents. For example, children may be participating in a social skills training group in one room, while parents are in a different room in a parent-training session with a facilitator and group of other parents.

Medication Intervention

- Medication is found to be helpful for many children/teens with ADHD by enabling them to better benefit from psycho-social interventions (behavior modification, ability to apply problem-solving/conflict-resolution strategies, managing anger/emotions, and so on).

SOURCES AND RESOURCES

Bos, Candace S., and Sharon Vaughn. *Strategies for Teaching Students with Learning and Behavior Problems.* Needham Heights, MA: Allyn & Bacon, 1994.

Cohen, Cathi. *Raise Your Child's Social IQ.* Silver Spring, MD: Advantage Books, 2000.

Cunningham, Charles E., R. Bremner, and M. Secord-Gilbert. "The Community Parent Education Program (COPE Program): A School-Based Family Systems Oriented Course for Parents of Children with Disruptive Behavior Disorders." Hamilton, Ontario: McMaster University and Chedoke-McMaster Hospitals. Available through Center for Children and Families, University of Buffalo. (http://wings.buffalo.edu/psychology/adhd)

Fisher, Linda, Nancy Fetzer, and Sandra Rief. *Successful School: How to Raise Achievement and Support At-Risk Students.* (video) San Diego, CA: Educational Resource Specialists. (www.sandrarief.com)

Flick, Grad L. *ADD/ADHD Behavior-Change Resource Kit.* Paramus, NJ: The Center for Applied Research in Education, 1998.

Giler, Janet Z. *Socially ADDept™—A Manual for Parents of Children with ADHD and/or Learning Disabilities.* Santa Barbara, CA: CES Publications, 2000.

Goldstein, Arnold, Robert P. Sprafkin, N. Jane Gershaw, and Paul Klein. *Skillstreaming the Adolescent—A Structured Learning Approach to Teaching Prosocial Skills.* Champaign, IL: Research Press, 1980.

Jackson, J., D. Jackson, and C. Monroe. *Getting Along with Others.* Champaign, IL: Research Press, 1983.

Koplewicz, Harold S. "Managing Social Skills All Day, Every Day," CHADD: *Attention*, April 2002.

McGinnis, Ellen, and Arnold Goldstein. *Skillstreaming the Elementary School Child.* Champaign, IL: Research Press, 1984.

McGinnis, E., and Arnold Goldstein. *Skillstreaming in Early Childhood—Teaching Prosocial Skills to the Preschool and Kindergarten Child.* Champaign, IL: Research Press, 1990.

Novotni, Michele, with Randy Petersen. *What Does Everybody Know That I Don't? Social Skills Help for Adults with Attention Deficit/Hyperactivity Disorder (AD/HD).* Plantation, FL: Specialty Press, 1999.

PeaceBuilders Program®. Tucson, AZ: Heartsprings, Inc., 1992.

Pelham, William E. *ADHD: Diagnosis, Nature, Etiology, and Treatment.* Buffalo, NY: Center for Children and Families, 2002. (http://wings.buffalo.edu/psychology/adhd)

Sheridan, Susan B. *The Tough Kid Social Skills Book.* Longmont, CO: Sopris West, 1995.

Shure, Myrna B. *I Can Problem Solve—An Interpersonal Cognitive Problem-Solving Program.* Champaign, IL: Research Press, 1992.

Teeter, Phyllis Anne. "Building Social Skills in Children with ADD: A Multimodal Approach," CHADD: *Attention*, Summer 1997.

Walker, H. M., S. McConnell, D. Holmes, B. Todis, J. Walker, and N. Golden. *The Walker Social Skills Curriculum: The ACCEPTS Program.* Austin, TX: Pro-Ed, 1983.

Note: There are highly effective summer treatment programs for children with ADHD that utilize a strong behavioral and social skills component, along with parent training and other aspects of a multimodal approach. For information about such programs in the United States and Canada, check out this website: http://summertreatmentprogram.com.

2-17
COMMON TRIGGERS OR ANTECEDENTS TO MISBEHAVIOR

Students may misbehave for any number of reasons. When conducting a Functional Behavioral Assessment as described in List 7-5, try to determine what factors may be triggering the behaviors of concern. By determining the conditions or events that preceded the student's misbehaviors, you can more effectively intervene and support the student.

Many behavioral problems can be prevented or significantly reduced by anticipating the triggers and adjusting the antecedents. These include various conditions or triggers such as the following.

Environmentally Based

- Uncomfortable conditions (too noisy, crowded, hot, or cold)
- When there is a lack of:
  - Structure
  - Organization
  - Predictability
  - Interesting materials
  - Clear schedule
  - Visual supports

Physically Based

- When the child is not feeling well (ill, overly tired, hungry/thirsty)
- Medication related:
  - When wearing off
  - Change of prescription/dosage

Related to a Specific Activity or Event

- Losing a game
- Music class
- Change of routine without warning
- Cooperative learning groups and sharing of materials
- Tasks that student perceives as boring, lengthy, frustrating, repetitive

Related to a Performance/Skill Demand

- To remain seated
- To read independently
- To write a paragraph
- Having to wait patiently for a turn
- To hurry and complete a task
- Any behavioral/performance expectation that is a struggle for that individual student

Related to a Specific Time

- First period
- Before or after lunch
- Transition times of day
- Later afternoon

Other

- When given no choices/options
- When embarrassed in front of peers
- When having difficulty communicating
- When given no assistance or access to help on difficult tasks
- When recently teased by classmate(s)

2-18

SOURCES AND RESOURCES FOR BEHAVIORAL MANAGEMENT

There are many excellent resources available that address classroom management, positive discipline, behavioral interventions and supports, and related topics. In addition to the following, there are recommended resources in List 2-16, Social Skills Interventions and Teaching Prosocial Behavior.

SOURCES AND RESOURCES

Barkley, Russell A. *Taking Charge of ADHD—Revised.* New York: The Guilford Press, 2000.

Barkley, Russell A., and Christine M. Benton. *Your Defiant Child.* New York: The Guilford Press, 1998.

Belvel, Patricia, and Maya Jordan. *Rethinking Classroom Management: Strategies for Prevention, Intervention, and Problem Solving.* Thousand Oaks, CA: Corwin Press, 2003.

Bender, William N., Gregory Clinton, and Renet L. Bender. *Violence Prevention & Reduction in Schools.* Austin, TX: Pro-Ed, 1999.

Bluestein, Jane. *21st Century Discipline—Teaching Students Responsibility and Self-Management.* Torrance, CA: Fearon Teacher Aids, 1998.

Brooks, Robert, and Sam Goldstein. *Raising Resilient Children.* Lincolnwood, IL: Contemporary Books, 2001.

Canter, Lee, and Marlene Canter. *Succeeding with Difficult Students.* Santa Monica, CA: Lee Canter & Associates, 1993.

Chernow, Fred B., and Carol Chernow. *Classroom Discipline and Control.* Englewood Cliffs, NJ: Prentice Hall, 1981.

Crawford, D., and F. Schrumpf. *Creating the Peaceable School: A Comprehensive Program for Teaching Conflict Resolution.* Champaign, IL: Research Press, 1994.

Cruz, Lisa, and Douglas Cullinan. "Awarding Points, Using Levels to Help Children Improve Behavior," *Teaching Exceptional Children,* vol. 33, no. 3, Jan./Feb. 2001.

DeBruyn, Robert, and Jack Larson. *You Can Handle Them All: A Discipline Model for Handling Over 100 Different Misbehaviors at School and at Home.* Manhattan, KS: The Master Teacher, 1984.

DeRoche, Edward, and Mary M. Williams. *Educating Hearts & Minds: A Comprehensive Character Education Framework.* Thousand Oaks, CA: Corwin Press, 2001.

Elias, M. J., E. E. Tobias, and B. S. Friedlander. *Emotionally Intelligent Parenting: How to Raise a Self-Disciplined, Responsible, Socially Skilled Child.* New York: Harmony/Random House, 1999.

Elias, Maurice, Joseph E. Zins et al. *Promoting Social and Emotional Learning.* Alexandria, VA: Association for Supervision and Curriculum Development, 1997.

Fay, Jim, and Foster W. Cline. *Discipline with Love and Logic Resource Guide.* Golden, CO: The Love & Logic Press, Inc., 1997.

Fay, Jim, and David Funk. *Teaching with Love and Logic: Taking Control of the Classroom.* Golden, CO: The Love & Logic Press, 1995.

Flick, Grad L. *ADD/ADHD Behavior-Change Resource Kit.* Paramus, NJ: The Center for Applied Research in Education, 1998.

Fouse, Beth, and Maria Wheeler. *A Treasure Chest of Behavioral Strategies for Individuals with Autism.* Arlington, TX: Future Horizons, 1997.

Garber, Stephen, Marianne Garber, and Robyn Spizman. *Good Behavior—Over 1,200 Sensible Solutions to Your Child's Problems from Birth to Age 12.* New York: St. Martin's Paperbacks, 1987.

Geddes, Betsy. *Handling Misbehavior in Your Classroom.* Portland, OR: Geddes Consulting, 1995.

Glasser, Howard, and Jennifer Easley. *Transforming the Difficult Child: The Nurtured Heart Approach.* Tucson, AZ: Center for the Difficult Child Publications, 1998.

Goldstein, Sam. *Understanding and Managing Children's Classroom Behavior.* New York: John Wiley & Sons, 1995.

Goldstein, Sam, and Michael Goldstein. *Managing Attention Deficit Disorder in Children.* New York: John Wiley & Sons, 1998.

Goleman, Daniel. *Emotional Intelligence.* New York: Bantam, 1995.

Gootman, Marilyn E. *The Caring Teacher's Guide to Discipline: Helping Young Students Learn Self-Control, Responsibility, and Respect.* Thousand Oaks, CA: Corwin Press, 2001.

Gray, Carol et al. *The Original Social Story Book.* Jenison (MI) Public Schools. Arlington, TX: Future Horizons, Inc., 1993.

Greene, Ross W. *The Explosive Child.* New York: Quill-Harper Brothers Publishers, 2001.

Harmin, Merrill. *Strategies to Inspire Active Learning.* White Plains, NY: Inspiring Strategies Institute, 1998.

2-18 (*continued*)

Heininer, Janet E., and Sharon K. Weiss. *From Chaos to Calm: Effective Parenting of Challenging Children with ADHD and Other Behavioral Problems.* New York: Perigee Books, a division of Penguin Putnam, 2001.

Hodgdon, Linda. *Solving Behavior Problems in Autism—Improving Communication with Visual Strategies.* Troy, MI: Quirk Roberts, 1999.

Hutchinson, Sharon W., Jane Y. Murdock, Ramona D. Williamson, and Mary E. Cronin. "Self-Recording Plus Encouragement Equals Improved Behavior," *Teaching Exceptional Children*, vol. 32, May/June 2000.

Illes, Terry. *Positive Parenting Practices for Attention Deficit Disorder.* Jordan School District, Utah, 2002.

Jenson, William R., Ginger Rhode, and H. Kenton Reavis. *The Tough Kid Book (Practical Classroom Management Strategies).* Longmont, CO: Sopris West, 1995.

Jenson, William R., Ginger Rhode, and H. Kenton Reavis. *The Tough Kid Tool Box.* Longmont, CO: Sopris West, 1995. (This book of forms, charts, etc., accompanies *The Tough Kid Book.*)

Johnson, D., and R. Johnson. *Teaching Students to Be Peacemakers.* Edina, MN: Interaction Book Co., 1991.

Johnson, Lewis R., and Christine E. Johnson. "Teaching Students to Regulate Their Own Behavior," *Teaching Exceptional Children*, vol. 31, no. 4, March/April 1999, 6–10.

Jones, Fred. *Tools for Teaching.* Santa Cruz, CA: Fredric H. Jones & Associates, Inc., 2000.

Kamps, D., and M. Tankersley. "Prevention of Behavioral and Conduct Disorders: Trends & Research Issues," *Behavioral Disorders*, vol. 22, 1996.

Katz, Mark. *On Playing a Poor Hand Well.* New York: W. W. Norton & Co., 1997.

Kutscher, Martin L. *The ADHD e-Book "Just Stop."* (www.PediatricNeurology.com)

Lickona, Thomas. *Educating for Character.* New York: Bantam Books, 1991.

Mayer, G. Roy, and Los Angeles County Office of Education—Division of Student Support Services Safe Schools Division. *Classroom Management: A California Resource Guide.* Los Angeles, CA, 2000.

McCarney, Stephen, Kathy Wunderlich, and Angela Bauer. *The Pre-Referral Intervention Manual (PRIM).* Columbia, MO: Hawthorne Educational Services, Inc., 1993.

McEwan, Elaine, and Mary Damer. *Managing Unmanageable Students.* Thousand Oaks, CA: Corwin Press, 2000.

McKay, M., P. Fanning, K. Paleg, and D. Landis. *When Anger Hurts Your Kids: A Parent's Guide.* Oakland, CA: New Harbinger Publications, Inc., 1996.

McKenzie, Robert J. *Setting Limits.* Rocklin, CA: Prima Publishing, 1998.

Meyen, Edward, Glenn Vergason, and Richard Whelan. *Strategies for Teaching Exceptional Children in Inclusive Settings.* Denver, CO: Love Publishing Co., 1996.

National Association of School Psychologists (NASP). *Behavioral Interventions: Creating a Safe Environment in Our Schools.* National Mental Health & Educational Center, Winter 2000.

Nelsen, Jane, Lynn Lott, and Stephen H. Glenn. *Positive Discipline in the Classroom.* Rocklin, CA: Prima Publishing, 1997.

Parker, Harvey. *Problem Solver Guide for Students with ADHD.* Plantation, FL: Specialty Press, 2002.

Pelham, William E. *ADHD: Diagnosis, Nature, Etiology, and Treatment.* Center for Children and Families, University of Buffalo, 2002.

Pelham, William E., Jr., and Gregory A. Fabiano. "Behavior Modification," *Child and Adolescent Psychiatric Clinics of North America*, vol. 9, no. 3, July 2000.

Pfiffner, Linda J. *All About ADHD.* New York: Scholastic Professional Books, 1996.

Phelan, Thomas. *1-2-3 Magic: Effective Discipline for Children 2-12.* Glen Ellyn, IL: Child Management, Inc., 1995.

Raser, Jamie. *Raising Children You Can Live With: A Guide for Frustrated Parents.* Houston, TX: Bayou Publishing, 1995.

Raser, Jamie. "Control the Interaction, Not the Child," National Educational Services: *Reaching Today's Youth—The Community Circle of Caring Journal*, 1999. (http://www.nes.org/rty/jn5.html)

Rhode, Ginger, William Jenson, and H. Kenton Reavis. *The Tough Kid Book.* Longmont, CO: Sopris West, 1992.

Rief, Sandra. *How to Reach and Teach ADD/ADHD Children.* West Nyack, NY: The Center for Applied Research in Education, 1993.

Rief, Sandra. *The ADD/ADHD Checklist: An Easy Reference for Parents and Teachers.* Paramus, NJ: Prentice Hall, 1997.

Rief, Sandra, and Julie Heimburge. *How to Reach and Teach All Students in the Inclusive Classroom.* Paramus, NJ: The Center for Applied Research in Education, 1996.

Robinson, Kristin E. "Compliance, It's No Mystery," CHADD: *Attention*, vol. 7, no. 1, July/August 2000, 38–43.

Setley, Susan. *Taming the Dragons: Real Help for Real School Problems.* St. Louis, MO: Starfish Publishing Co., 1995.

Sewell, Karen. *Breakthroughs: How to Reach Students with Autism.* Verona, WI: Attainment Company, Inc., 1998.

2-18 (*continued*)

Shore, Kenneth. *Special Kids Problem Solver.* Paramus, NJ: Prentice Hall, 1998.

Sprick, Randall S. *Discipline in the Secondary Classroom: A Problem-by-Problem Survival Guide.* West Nyack, NY: The Center for Applied Research in Education, 1985.

Sprick, Randall, and Lisa Howard. *The Teacher's Encyclopedia of Behavior Management.* Longmont, CO: Sopris West, 1998.

Stewart, John. *Beyond Time Out—A Practical Guide to Understanding and Serving Students with Behavioral Impairments in the Public Schools.* Gorham, ME: Hastings Clinical Associations, 2000.

Taylor, John F. *Creative Answers to Misbehavior* (A Family Power Series Book). Warminster, PA: Mar-Co Products, Inc., 1992.

Taylor, John F. *From Defiance to Cooperation.* Roseville, CA: Prima Publishing, 2001.

Walker, Hill M. *The Acting-Out Child: Coping with Classroom Disruption.* Longmont, CO: Sopris West, 1997.

Walker, Hill, and Janet Eaton Walker. *Coping with Noncompliance in the Classroom.* Austin, TX: Pro-Ed, 1991.

Walker, Hill M., and Robert Sylvester. "Reducing Students' Refusal and Resistance," *Teaching Exceptional Children*, vol. 30, no. 6, July/Aug. 1998, 52–58.

Wallace, Ian. *You and Your ADD Child.* Sydney, Australia: HarperCollins Publishers, 1996.

White, Richard B., and Mark A. Koorland. "Curses! What Can We Do About Cursing?" *Teaching Exceptional Children*, Summer 1996, 48–52.

Wright, Diana Browning, and Harvey Gurman. *Positive Interventions for Serious Behavior Problems.* Sacramento, CA: Department of Education, 1998.

Zionts, Paul, Laura Zionts, and Richard Simpson. *Emotional and Behavioral Problems: A Handbook for Understanding and Handling Students.* Thousand Oaks, CA: Corwin Press, 2002.

Websites on Behavioral Supports and Interventions

Center for Effective Collaboration and Practice—The Center's mission is to support and promote a reoriented national preparedness to foster the development and the adjustment of children with or at-risk of developing serious emotional disturbance. http://cecp.air.org/

Center for the Prevention of School Violence—This serves as a primary resource for dealing with the problem of school violence. The Center focuses on ensuring that schools are safe and secure, free of fear, and conducive to learning. http://www.ncsu.edu/cpsv/

Center for the Study and Prevention of Violence—CSPV was founded in 1992 with a grant from the Carnegie Corporation of New York to provide informed assistance to groups committed to understanding and preventing violence, particularly adolescent violence.
http://www.colorado.edu/cspv/

Collaborative for Academic, Social, and Emotional Learning—site for emotional intelligence in the schools.
http://www.casel.org

GLARRC Early Prevention of Violence Database—The database consolidates information on resources related to the early prevention (years 0–6) of violence.
http://128.146.206.233/Resources/EPVD.cfm

Institute on Violence and Destructive Behavior—The mission of the Institute is to empower schools and social service agencies to address violence and destructive behavior at the point of school entry and beyond, in order to ensure safety and facilitate the academic achievement and healthy social development of children and youth.
http://darkwing.uoregon.edu/~ivdb/index.html

The Kentucky Behavior Home Page, The Kentucky Dept. of Education (KDE) and the Department of Special Education and Rehabilitation Counseling at UK (SERC)—A collaboration on student behavior. The purpose is to provide a format that allows school personnel, parents, and other professionals to gain access to information, to share effective practices, and to receive ongoing consultation and technical assistance concerning behavior problems and challenges in school and community settings.
http://serc.gws.uky.edu/
http://www.kde.state.ky.us/

The Online Academy, at the University of Kansas—Web-based modules and other technology innovations for moving validated educational interventions from research to practice. The resources are designed to empower teacher educators in the areas of reading, technology, and positive behavioral support. The Online Academy is funded by the Office of Special Education Programs in the U.S. Department of Education to support preservice teacher education programs nationwide.
http://onlineacademy.org

OSEP Technical Assistance Center on Positive Behavioral Interventions and Supports (PBIS)—Established by the Office of Special Education Programs, U.S. Department of Education, to give schools capacity-building information and technical assistance for identifying, adapting, and sustaining effective schoolwide disciplinary practices.
http://www.pbis.org/

The School Mental Health Project, UCLA Dept. of Psychology—SMHP was created in 1986 to pursue theory, research, practice, and training related to addressing mental health and psycho-social concerns through school-based interventions.
http://smhp.psych.ucla.edu

Note: See List 8-10 for more information and sources available on the Internet.

Section 3

INSTRUCTIONAL STRATEGIES, ACCOMMODATIONS, AND SUPPORTS

3-1

ADAPTATIONS, ACCOMMODATIONS, AND MODIFICATIONS: WHAT'S THE DIFFERENCE?

WHAT ARE ADAPTATIONS?

Adaptations are any adjustments in the curriculum, instructional components, environmental elements, and requirements/expectations of the student that may be needed. In inclusive classrooms, such adaptations are simply part of teaching to meet the needs of diverse learners.

A good teacher will always attempt to differentiate instruction and make adjustments to enable *all* students to succeed. The purpose of such adaptations is to help increase a student's performance, achievement, and social/emotional/behavioral functioning.

Adaptations in the general education curriculum for children with disabilities, as intended by federal laws (IDEA and Section 504), are changes that allow the student equal opportunity to obtain access, results, and benefits in the least restrictive setting.

This might involve making adaptations in the following:

- Materials
- Methods
- Teaching strategies
- Pacing
- Environment
- Assignments
- Task demands
- Grading
- Testing/evaluation
- Feedback
- Lesson presentation

- Reinforcement
- Input
- Output
- Student response opportunities
- Location
- Scheduling
- Level of support
- Degree of participation
- Time allotted
- Size/quantity of task or assignment

Adaptations include *accommodations* and *modifications,* and it is important to understand the difference between the two.

3-1 (*continued*)

WHAT ARE ACCOMMODATIONS?

Accommodations do *not* fundamentally change the performance standards, instructional level, or the content of what the student is expected to learn. The curricular content and expectations for performance/mastery are the same as for other students in the class or grade. Accommodations simply are provisions meant to enable the student to:

- Better access the general education curriculum.
- Learn and demonstrate mastery of the content.
- Meet the same performance goals that other students of the classroom/grade level are expected to achieve.

Accommodations typically include adaptations/adjustments such as:

- Providing extended time to complete tasks
- Providing visual supports (such as an outline or graphic organizer) to supplement auditory presentations (lectures)
- Using writing tools/supports (note-taking assistance, computer access, pencil grips)
- Preferential seating so students can better focus during class, and receive more direct and frequent prompting, monitoring, and feedback from the teacher

WHAT ARE MODIFICATIONS?

Modifications *do* alter or change in some way *what* the student is learning (the content or part of the curriculum). They also change to some degree the performance standards, the expectations for that student compared with what is required of his or her peers in the classroom/grade.

Note: If the student has not been taught the same content or at the same instructional level, then such modifications in content/curriculum will affect the ability of the student to be fairly assessed on district and state achievement tests.

Accommodations should generally be tried first (to enable the student to succeed in the general education curriculum) before more significant modifications in curriculum or work expectations are made.

SOURCES AND RESOURCES

Deschenes, Cathy, David Ebeling, and Jeffrey Sprague. *Adapting Curriculum & Instruction in Inclusive Classrooms.* Bloomington, IN: An ISDD-CSCI Publication, 1994.

Nolet, Victor, and Margaret J. McLaughlin. *Accessing the General Curriculum.* Thousand Oaks, CA: Corwin Press, 2000.

Wright, Diana Browning. Diagnostic Center, Southern California: Behavior/Discipline Trainings, 2000. (dwright@supreme.cde.ca.gov)

Wright, Diana Browning. "Preventing School Disruption: Using Positive Behavioral Interventions and Strategies." National Association of School Psychologists Convention. Las Vegas, Nevada; April 1999.

3-2
INSTRUCTIONAL INTERVENTIONS AND ACCOMMODATIONS

Many of the lists throughout this book contain instructional strategies and accommodations. Classroom management and behavioral lists also include instructional techniques and supports that are helpful in reducing or preventing behavioral problems in the classroom. See the related lists in addition to the following:

■ Assist student in getting started on assignments.

■ Use discreet verbal and nonverbal cues as prompts in order to help the student stay on-task and control disruptive behavior.

■ Provide frequent breaks.

■ Provide access to a less distracting location for independent work (such as a table in the corner of the room or an "office area").

■ Provide note-taking assistance (supplemental copy of peer notes, teacher notes or outline).

■ Increase monitoring of student understanding and work production.

■ Provide directions/instructions that are clear and listed step-by-step with a few words and pictures if appropriate.

■ Provide student with a task card of things-to-do for independent seatwork.

■ Adjust and extend time, as needed, for completion of tasks/assignments and testing/assessments.

■ Reduce the need to copy from the board or book onto paper. Provide a photocopy or copying assistance instead.

■ Utilize people supports (aides, cross-age tutors, peer tutors, parent volunteers, special education teacher) for more intensive direct assistance.

■ Assign a student buddy or peer partner (preferably a tolerant, patient classmate).

■ Modify timed assignments (give extra time if possible).

■ Reduce paper-and-pencil tasks. Provide accommodations to bypass written output difficulties, and allow students to show their mastery/understanding of subject matter through other means (demonstrations, verbal responses). (5-12)

■ Structure tasks by dividing them into shorter segments (given one at a time), and provide feedback on each segment before proceeding to the next.

■ Allow for movement and controlled talking opportunities during instruction (for example, to ask a peer partner for clarification).

■ Use attention-getting signals. (2-3, 2-5, 2-6, 3-3)

- Be certain that each student in the classroom is able to access the information. For example, when reading the grade-level core materials, if a child cannot read the text independently, use alternative methods (partner reading; listening to the chapter on tape at a listening post while following along in the book). (3-5, 5-3)

- Provide clear models/examples of expected "at standard" work.

- Differentiate instruction to address individual levels and needs of students.

- Provide texts to students, as needed, that are color highlighted for main ideas and vocabulary.

- Increase the amount of practice opportunities (for example, using computer software, learning games, drill, tutoring).

- Utilize graphic organizers to focus thinking and attention to key concepts and ideas, supporting details, sequence, and so forth.

- Increase response opportunities, using a variety of questioning techniques that are alternatives to raising hands and calling on one student at a time. (3-3, 5-5)

- Provide the opportunity (for example, with resource teacher) to preview new material before it is taught and discussed in class.

- Use technological tools, computer software, and other means of individualized or programmed instruction as appropriate. See List 5-12 regarding assistive technology.

- Provide audiotapes of lessons, lectures, literature read in class, and content book chapters as needed.

- Use direct, systematic instruction to build skills in areas of identified weakness.

- Consult with a special education teacher or other staff for strategies and suggestions on how to teach concepts/skills in a different way.

- Increase use of visuals, charts, models, and exemplars for easy reference.

- Use multisensory techniques to present information.

- Supplement instruction by using alternative approaches for teaching the concept/skill.

- Utilize books on tape. The student listens and follows along with the text.

- Explicitly teach active reading strategies and study/learning strategies (such as SQ3R, note-taking). (4-2, 5-5)

- Allow use of calculators, graph paper (to align numbers), charts, manipulatives, and other aids for math.

- Teach math facts using mnemonics and other memory techniques. (4-1, 5-14)

- Provide structures and scaffolds to explicitly teach different writing genres, prewriting strategies, handwriting, mechanics, editing, and so forth. (5-7, 5-8, 5-9, 5-11)

3-3
Strategies for Engaging Students' Attention and Active Participation

Getting and Focusing Students' Attention

- Try playfulness, silliness, use of props, and a bit of theatrics to get attention and pique interest.

- Use storytelling, as students of all ages love to hear stories—especially personal ones.

- Ask an interesting, speculative question; show a picture; tell a little story; or read a related poem to generate discussion and interest in the upcoming lesson.

- Use mystery by bringing in an object relevant to the upcoming lesson in a box, bag, or pillowcase. This is a wonderful way to generate predictions and can lead to excellent discussions or writing activities.

- Model excitement and enthusiasm about the upcoming lesson.

- Signal students in an auditory fashion:
  - Ring a bell or chimes.
  - Use a clap pattern.
  - Play a bar of music on the piano, keyboard, or guitar.

- Use a clear verbal signal ("Freeze . . . This is important . . ." "Everybody . . . Ready . . ." or "1, 2, 3, eyes on me").

- Use your voice to get attention, making use of effective pauses and tone variation (whispering also works).

- Use visual signals:
  - Flash the lights.
  - Raise your hand (which signals the students to raise their hands and close their mouths until everyone is silent and attentive).

- Use visual prompts and cues. See the Appendix for examples. These can be used to call attention to the steps of a routine, classroom behavioral expectations (hands and feet to self), and so forth.

- Use colored pens on dry-erase boards and transparencies for the overhead projector.

- Use visuals by writing key words or pictures on the board or overhead projector while presenting.

- Illustrate, illustrate, illustrate. You do not have to draw well to illustrate throughout your presentation. Give yourself and students permission and encouragement to *draw* even if everyone lacks the skill or talent. Drawings do not have to be sophisticated or accurate; in fact, often the sillier, the better.

- Use pictures, diagrams, gestures, manipulatives, demonstrations, and high-interest material.

- Point with a dowel, stick/pointer, or laser pointer to written material you want students to focus on.

- Cover or remove visual distractions. Erase unnecessary information from the board and remove visual clutter.

- Use overhead projectors. These are among the best tools for focusing students' attention in the classroom because they enable you to:

  - Frame important information.

  - Block unnecessary information (covering part of the transparency).

  - Face students and maintain eye contact (not turning back on students to write on the board).

  - Avoid instructional lag time while writing on the board and erasing.

  - Prepare transparencies in advance, saving instructional time.

- Move around in the classroom, maintaining your visibility.

- Present at a snappy pace with enthusiasm.

- Project your voice and make sure you can be heard clearly by all students.

- Be aware of competing sounds (noisy heaters or air conditioning units) in your room environment.

- Call students up front and close to you for direct instruction (such as seated on the carpet near the board or chart stand).

- Position all students so they can see the board and/or overhead screen. Always allow students to readjust their seating and signal you if their visibility is blocked.

- Use a flashlight or laser pointer. Turn off the lights and get students to focus by illuminating objects or words with the laser/flashlight.

Maintaining Students' Attention Through Active Participation

- Use study guides/sheets that are partial outlines. While you are presenting a lesson or giving a lecture, students fill in the missing words based on what you are saying and/or writing on the board or overhead.

- Have students write brief notes or illustrate key points during instruction.

- Spend less time lecturing and make efforts to significantly increase student responses (saying and doing something with the information being taught).

- Format lessons to include a variety of questioning techniques that involve whole class, partner, and individual responses.

- Before asking for a verbal response to a question, have all students jot down their best-guess answer. Then call for volunteers to verbally answer the question.

- Use direct instruction techniques and other methods of questioning that allow for high-response opportunities (choral/unison responses, partner/buddy responses).

3-3 (continued)

- Make frequent use of group or unison responses when there is one correct and short answer. While presenting, stop frequently and have all students repeat back a word or two.

- Use response cards to elicit unison responses:

  1. Cards are prepared for each student with answers already written on each section of their card, depending on the content of the lesson. For example: parts of speech (noun, verb, adjective, adverb); final punctuation marks (period, question mark, exclamation mark); and math symbols (add, subtract, multiply, divide).

  2. After posing a question, pause enough time for students to mark with a clothespin their choice on the prepared cards.

  3. Then give a signal indicating students are to hold up their response cards.

- Use response fans. A fan is made up of several cards with responses written on them, single-hole punched, and held together by a metal ring. Students hold up the response card they feel best answers the question.

- Utilize alternatives to simply calling on students one at a time. Instead, have students respond by telling their partner; writing down or drawing their response; and so on.

- Use partners (pair-shares), probably the most effective method for maximizing student engagement. Partner format ensures that everyone is actively involved, not just a few. This format is ideal for predicting, sharing ideas, clarifying directions, summarizing information, previewing information, drilling/practicing (vocabulary, spelling words, math facts), sharing reading of text, discussing reading material, and sharing writing assignments. For example:

  - "Pair up with your neighbor and share your ideas about . . ."

  - "Turn to your partner/neighbor and . . ."

  - After giving partners a chance to respond, ask for volunteers to share with the whole class: "Who would be willing to share what you or your partner thought about . . .?"

- Keep students engaged and participating during lessons with cooperative learning groups. Be sure to follow the proper structure of cooperative learning groups (assignment of roles, individual accountability) because it is *not* just group work. ADHD students do not typically function well in groups without clearly defined structure and expectations. See information in Sources and Resources about cooperative learning resources.

- Allow students to use individual chalkboards or whiteboards throughout the lesson, as these are motivating to students and help maintain attention. If used properly, they are also effective in checking for students' understanding and determining who needs extra help and practice.

- Use higher-level questioning techniques. Ask questions that are open-ended and stimulate critical thinking and discussion.

- Use motivating computer programs for specific skill building and practice. These programs should provide for frequent feedback and self-correction.

- Vary the way you call upon students. For example: "Everyone wearing earrings, stand up . . . this question is for you." Students from that group may answer or have the option to pass.

- Motivate all students to actively participate by differentiating instruction in the classroom. Provide many opportunities for student choices of activities/projects and ways to demonstrate their learning.

- Differentiate instruction through use of learning centers, flexible grouping, interest groups, independent projects/study, and a variety of other instructional strategies, structures, and accommodations.

RELATED LISTS

- See Lists 3-2, 3-4, 3-7, 3-9, 4-2, 5-3, 5-5, 5-10, and 5-14 for more strategies related to engaging students' attention and active participation.

SOURCES AND RESOURCES

Harmin, Merrill. *Strategies to Inspire Active Learning.* White Plains, NY: Inspiring Strategies Institute, 1998.

Heward, William, Ralph Gardner, Rodney A. Cavanaugh et al. "Everyone Participates in This Class," *Teaching Exceptional Children*, vol. 28, no. 2, Winter 1996, 4–10.

Kagan, Spencer, Miguel Kagan, and Laurie Kagan. *Reaching Standards Through Cooperative Learning* (series of books for each content area). Port Chester, NY: National Professional Resources, Inc., 2000.

Rief, Sandra. *How to Reach and Teach ADD/ADHD Children.* West Nyack, NY: The Center for Applied Research in Education, 1993.

Rief, Sandra, and Julie Heimburge. *How to Reach and Teach All Students in the Inclusive Classroom.* Paramus, NJ: The Center for Applied Research in Education, 1996.

Silberman, Mel. *Active Learning—101 Strategies to Teach Any Subject.* Boston: Allyn & Bacon, 1996.

Sousa, David A. *How the Brain Learns.* Thousand Oaks, CA: Corwin Press, 2001.

3-4
STRATEGIES FOR INATTENTIVE, DISTRACTIBLE STUDENTS

Environmental Factors and Accommodations to Keep in Mind

- Provide preferential seating—up front, within cueing distance of the teacher, and away from as many environmental distractions as possible (doors, windows, high-traffic areas of the room, enticing learning centers, and visual displays).

- Seat distractible students near well-focused peers who are good role models.

- Provide options for a less distracting work area through the use of study carrels, "office areas," partitions, privacy boards, and so on. These should not be used if they are viewed by the students in the class as punitive measures or as accommodations for students with special needs only.

- Be aware of and try to reduce unnecessary environmental noises in the classroom.

- Allow the use of earphones or earplugs for distractible students at certain times of the day (such as during seatwork time). Keep a few sets available for students to access, as well as *requiring* use of earphones when working on classroom computers or listening centers.

- See List 2-4 for more environmental strategies and accommodations.

Instructional Factors and Accommodations to Keep in Mind

- Increase visual, auditory, and physical cues/prompts to gain attention and help refocus inattentive, distractible students:
  - Put your hand on student's shoulder or back.
  - Use a private, prearranged visual signal (for example, point to and tap your chin to mean "watch my face and pay attention").
  - Point to or tap next to a visual symbol/prompt (posted on wall chart or on a desk card). See the Appendix for examples, such as pictures designating behaviors: "Sit up. Eyes forward (or on work). Busy working."
  - Use private, prearranged signal words.
  - Use nonverbal signals (flashing lights, ringing bell).

- Frequently make direct eye contact with inattentive students.

- Increase your proximity in order to facilitate attentiveness (standing near or seated close by).

- Present lesson at a snappy, lively pace using voice modulation to maintain students' attention.

- Keep brevity in mind (brief instruction and explanation).

- Color-highlight directions and important words in the assignment.

- Provide a study guide or some graphic tool for students to use accompanying verbal presentation. Jotting down a few words or filling in missing words in a guided format is helpful for maintaining attention.

- Have student(s) clear desk of distracters, allowing only essential items for the current task on the desk. *Note:* It is not uncommon for children with ADHD to have the need to touch or have some kind of object in their hands. For many children, this actually helps with self-regulation and staying alert. Consider providing certain students with something to hold and manipulate while seated and listening, such as a small squishy ball or a piece of Wikki Stix® (colored wax-covered yarn—see Sources and Resources). This should be permitted as long as it stays within their hand and is not bothering others. Another option is attaching something to a belt loop (such as a key chain with small object attached) to accommodate this need to touch and fidget.

- Utilize a high degree of multisensory teaching strategies (color, movement, graphics) and variety throughout instruction to hold interest.

- Significantly increase opportunities for active student involvement in the lesson and utilize questioning techniques that engage all students.

- See Lists 3-2, 3-3, and 3-7 for more instructional strategies that engage and accommodate the learning needs of inattentive, distractible students.

Increase Motivation to Better Focus and Attend to Task

- Use behavior-modification techniques with positive reinforcement/incentives (table points, individual charts for teacher initials, stickers, points, contracts) for motivating and reinforcing attentive, on-task behavior. (2-1, 2-9, Appendix)

- Utilize an individual contract for on-task behavior with positive incentives.

- Call positive attention to the student when focused ("I like the way Nick is following along and is on the right page." "See how nicely Sarah is sitting up and looking at the board").

- Reward for a certain number of completed items that are done with accuracy.

- Include a target behavior, such as "seatwork completed within the designated time," for monitoring and reinforcement of on-task behavior on a daily report card (or other form of monitoring/incentive plan).

Increase On-Task Behavior During Seatwork

- Provide guided practice before having students work independently on seatwork activities.

- Make sure directions are clearly understood before students begin their seatwork.

- Make sure necessary supplies are available.

- Send student(s) to their seat with a written task card or checklist.

3-4 (*continued*)

- Provide desk examples (such as math problems assigned) for reference.

- Give a manageable amount of work that the student is capable of doing *independently*.

- Give other "fail proof" work that the student can do in the meantime if he or she is stumped on an assignment and needs to wait for your attention or assistance.

- Block or mask some pages of assigned seatwork by covering up part of the page or folding the page under so lesser amounts are visible at one time.

- Actually cut (with scissors) assignments or work pages in half or smaller segments and pass out one part at a time. Blocking or cutting apart pages of work may help reduce the frustration a student feels upon seeing a paper that appears lengthy and overwhelming.

- Assign study buddies or partners for clarification purposes during seatwork, especially when you are instructing another group of students while part of the class is doing seatwork.

- Prepare some kind of signal to be used from the child's desk to indicate "I need help!" One method is to provide a red card that students place on their desk when they want to alert you (or any other adult) scanning the room that they need assistance.

- Scan the classroom frequently, as all students need positive reinforcement. Frequently give positive comments, praising students specifically whom you observe to be on-task. This serves as a reminder to students who tend to have difficulty.

- Consider using a timer for students who work well with a "beat the clock" system. Reward for the completion of a task during a designated time segment.

- See Lists 2-3, 3-2, 3-3, and 3-5 for more strategies.

Teach Self-Monitoring of Attention, Listening, and On-Task Behavior

- Use an auditory signal (such as an audiotape that has intermittent beeps). Whenever there is a beep, students mark a recording form at their desk with a plus (+) if they had been paying attention/on-task or a minus (−) if not. See Sources and Resources and the Appendix (for a sample self-monitoring form).

- Use picture prompts and cues at the student's desk. For example, prepare a prompt card showing picture icons or words indicating such behaviors as sitting properly in seat, book open, pencil in hand, eyes on paper. See the Appendix for picture examples.

- Teach students to self-monitor work production and to set individual short-term goals for improvement.

- See *125 Ways to Be a Better Listener* (see Sources and Resources) for teaching students to monitor and regulate their "Listening Attention Levels" (LAL). This is the term Graser uses in describing the amount of energy needed to pay attention in various situations. Some suggested strategies for raising one's LAL include:

  - Changing posture
  - Sitting up straight in the chair

- Putting both feet on the floor
- Raising head off shoulders
- Taking a quick, deep breath (to get a burst of oxygen)
- Tracking/observing closely the speaker's facial expressions and gestures
- Moving in closer to the speaker (if possible)

SOURCES AND RESOURCES

Graser, Nan Stutzman. *125 Ways to Be a Better Listener*™. East Moline, IL: LinguSystems, 1992.

Parker, Harvey. *Listen, Look and Think—A Self-Regulation Program for Children.* Plantation, FL: Impact Publications, Inc. Available at www.addwarehouse.com.

Rief, Sandra. *The ADD/ADHD Checklist: An Easy Reference for Parents and Teachers.* Paramus, NJ: Prentice Hall, 1998.

Wikki Stix® products are manufactured by Omnicor, Inc. in Phoenix, Arizona. Contact: 800-869-4554 or www.wikkistix.com.

3-5
ADAPTATIONS AND MODIFICATIONS
OF ASSIGNMENTS

There are many strategies and recommendations in a number of other lists throughout this book addressing the topic of adapting and modifying assignments. In addition, try the following, as needed:

- Reduce paper-and-pencil tasks.

- Shorten assignments.

- Provide a copy of another student's class notes.

- Allow student to use cursive handwriting or printing (whichever is easier for the student and more legible to read).

- Allow student to dictate responses while someone else records/transcribes.

- Allow different ways to answer other than in writing (orally, matching).

- Reduce the amount of required copying from the board.

- Reduce the amount of required copying from books.

- Allow the use of a computer for written tasks (and provide computer access).

- Allow demonstration of mastery through alternatives to writing (such as oral exams, demonstrations, visual displays).

- Back up oral directions with written instructions.

- Simplify complex directions.

- Block sections of the work. For example:
  - Fold under part of the page or cover it partially.
  - Cut the page into parts (for example, rows of math problems handed out one row at a time).

- Use highlighted texts.

- Monitor closely as student begins assignments to ensure understanding.

- Structure assignments so that they are broken down into a series of smaller segments and assign one part at a time.

- Check assignments midway through (or sooner for corrective feedback).

- Break long-term assignments into segments. Provide interim due dates and help with time management and monitoring of project timelines. (4-6, 4-8)

- Use an individual contract and positive reinforcement for work completion.

- Initiate a daily report card or other individualized monitoring form between home and school. Indicate work production as one of the behaviors to be monitored, evaluated, and reinforced at home and school. (2-1, 2-9, Appendix)
- Provide extended time for completion of assignments, as needed.
- Use taped texts.
- Adjust the reading level of the assignment.
- Offer choices in assignments (such as various topics and levels of difficulty; ability to work independently or with a partner or small group).
- Offer project/assignment options that draw upon a range of student strengths and interests.
- Limit number of choices in tasks, topics, and activities so as not to overwhelm.
- Assist student in determining the amount of time the assignment should take to complete.
- Provide in-school assistance getting started on homework assignments.
- Modify homework as needed, being responsive to parent feedback.
- Adapt textbooks by color highlighting key words and information. (3-6)
- Allow student to tape-record assignments/homework.
- Provide an assignment calendar or sheet and assistance, ensuring assignments are recorded daily and taken home. (4-6, 4-8)
- Provide samples and models of "at standard" and exemplary work.
- Provide a rubric detailing your expectations, including the specific criteria that will be used to evaluate students.
- Modify/adjust the length of tasks.
- Increase the novelty of the task by turning it into a game or providing different materials for student use (dry-erase boards/colored markers rather than paper/pencil).
- Provide handouts that have fewer items on a page and are easy to read.
- Reduce the number of problems on the page.
- Enlarge the print size and spacing on the page.
- Increase direct assistance and support. This includes peers and cross-age tutors.

3-6
ADAPTATIONS AND MODIFICATIONS
OF MATERIALS

Use Materials that Increase the Rate and Immediacy of Feedback

■ Make answer keys accessible for immediate self-correction.

■ Use flashcards with answers on the back for immediate checking and correction.

■ Utilize educational software for the computer, particularly interactive CDs and programs, which are excellent for teaching and reinforcing academic skills.

■ Use computer programs for drilling and practicing all basic skills (such as spelling, word recognition, math facts, grammar, and vocabulary).

■ Provide access to information/resources available through computers (Internet, CD encyclopedias).

Note: The element of self-correction, self-pacing, and competition against oneself or the computer (not another peer) is much less threatening for children with learning difficulties and low self-esteem. The immediate feedback and reward, color and sound, graphics, and novelty in the programming are highly motivational, perfect for holding the interest of children with ADHD.

Use the Tape Recorder as an Adaptive Device

■ Record directions and specific instructions to tasks so student(s) may listen as many times as necessary.

■ Record text chapters or literature so that students may listen to them (preferably while following along with the text).

■ Record test questions for student(s) to respond to verbally or in writing.

■ Record lectures, assignments, and class reviews prior to exams.

■ Give self-reminders.

■ Provide alternative methods of presentation (such as oral presentations with the use of sound effects).

Structure Materials to Enhance Students' Attention and Focus

■ Block the page or fold in such a way that only part of the print is shown at one time.

■ Frame the material.

■ Highlight, underline, circle, and draw arrows and boxes in vivid colors.

■ Provide clear, clean copies of handouts that are well organized and easy to read.

- Use illustrations and graphics.
- Enlarge the print/font size and spacing on the page.
- Provide markers (strips of cardboard or index cards) to students when reading.
- Provide an outline of the lesson.
- Rearrange the page format to simplify.

Compensate for Writing Difficulties

- Permit writing directly on the page or test booklet rather than having to copy answers onto another page or answer sheet.
- Have students try a variety of pencil grips.
- Have students use a mechanical pencil.
- Provide a clipboard.
- Make use of the computer/word processor.
- Experiment with different-sized graph paper and lined paper. Some children with writing difficulties can write neater and easier within smaller/narrower lines; others do better with wider lines.
- Provide photocopied pages rather than requiring copying from the board or book onto paper.
- Allow an upper-grade student to write in manuscript (print) rather than cursive, if it is easier and faster for him or her to do so.
- See List 5-12 for more related accommodations and for recommendations on assistive technology.

Use Math Material Supports and Adaptations

- Reduce the number of problems on the page.
- Use frames, boxes, or windows to separate and space problems.
- Use graph paper to structure placement of numerals and help with alignment and organization of problems.
- Use an assortment of colorful, concrete, manipulative materials (pattern blocks, tiles, cubes, counters, number lines, "more/less than" spinners, dice, beans/cups) to teach and reinforce number concepts of whole numbers, fractions, geometry, quantity, patterning, and so forth.
- Use calculators for problem solving and for checking work after paper-and-pencil calculations.
- Allow the use of and provide student(s) with multiplication tables/charts, a chart of formulas, and a list of measurements/conversions.
- Use compensatory techniques and materials for computation such as Touch Math™ and Semple Math. (5-14)

3-6 (*continued*)

Additional Suggestions

- Use creative learning center activities with hands-on, motivating materials for students to work on independently, with partners, or small groups. *Note:* The Sources and Resources contain numerous center activities appropriate for early childhood through middle school.

- Organize your materials by placing in tubs/bins, self-locking plastic bags, or colored boxes, and clearly labeling them for students (in words or pictures).

- Create as many hands-on activities, games, and puzzles as possible that teach and reinforce skills.

- Have an array of learning materials and books that span the developmental levels of students. For example, if the class is studying inventors, have an assortment of biographies and resources on inventors available at an easy reading level through more challenging levels. Regardless of the readability level, students can learn the same general concepts and information.

- Use word walls of vocabulary.

- Use tactile materials (writing/tracing on various surfaces and textures, salt/sand trays, pudding/frosting).

- Use games, games, games!

- Use high-interest supplemental materials.

RELATED LISTS

- See Lists 3-8, 5-10, 5-11, and 5-12 for more strategies and recommendations related to modifying materials.

SOURCES AND RESOURCES

Fetzer, Nancy, and Sandra Rief. *Alphabet Learning Center Activities Kit.* Paramus, NJ: The Center for Applied Research in Education, 2000.

Rief, Sandra, and Julie Heimburge. *How to Reach and Teach All Students in the Inclusive Classroom.* Paramus, NJ: The Center for Applied Research in Education, 1996.

3-7
STRATEGIES FOR PRESENTING LESSONS

- Introduce lessons with strategies to gain students' attention and interest, and "set the stage" for learning.

- Model enthusiasm and interest in the lesson or topic.

- Clearly state the lesson's purpose and relevance and exactly what students will be learning. Indicate content standards being addressed in the lesson.

- Set learning and behavioral expectations for lessons, as well as materials needed.

- Relate information to students' prior experiences and background information.

- Have students share what they already know about a topic before instructing on that topic. See KWL strategy and others in List 5-5.

- Limit the number of new concepts introduced at one time.

- Pause during oral presentations/lectures and allow students a few minutes to work with partners in order to briefly discuss the content and share their understanding.

- Summarize key points and let students know what is important for them to remember.

- Pause throughout instruction to question students' understanding of concepts.

- Frequently monitor and assess (formally and informally) students' understanding and mastery, reteaching and providing intervention when necessary.

- Increase "wait time" to *at least* five seconds when asking a student to respond to a question.

- Use questioning strategies that encourage student success without humiliation: probing techniques; providing clues; asking students if they would like more time to think about the question; and so forth.

- Expand on students' partial answers ("Tell me more.").

- Ask open-ended questions that allow for a variety of acceptable answers and encourage sharing of different perspectives.

- Speak slower and avoid giving directions when not directly facing the class.

- Be aware of your use of complex sentence structure and sophisticated vocabulary, which students may have difficulty comprehending.

- Paraphrase using similar language.

- Adjust lessons in response to student performance.

- Increase student-response opportunities significantly by using unison, partner, and small-group responses. (3-3)

- Teach with fewer words and greater use of visuals.

- Monitor and vary your rate, volume, and tone of voice.

3-7 (*continued*)

- Move throughout the room and provide individual assistance (clarification, cueing/prompting, redirection, and feedback) as needed.

- Use a variety of graphic organizers and techniques such as webbing, graphing, clustering, mapping, and outlining. (5-5, 5-7)

- Use a lot of role-playing, demonstrations, and experiential learning.

- Alternate activities to allow for variety and change of pace.

- Teach from concrete to abstract.

- Frequently review and make connections to information and concepts that have been previously taught.

- Teach thematically across the curriculum whenever possible because students better grasp the connection and learn most effectively when information is integrated and interrelated.

- Supplement verbal presentation with visuals, graphics, and demonstrations.

- Significantly increase the use of hands-on, active learning.

- Increase the amount of teacher modeling and guided practice.

- Increase use of gestures, hand signals, and other forms of nonverbal communication.

- Increase the amount of immediate feedback to students.

- Repeat important information.

- Move around, yet remain visible throughout the lesson presentation.

- Present lessons in short, brief segments and time blocks, giving students opportunities to respond in some format with high frequency throughout the lesson.

- Provide as many opportunities as possible for small-group instruction.

- Design lessons so that students experience a high rate of success.

- Vary the structure of presentation and student-response opportunities: direct teacher instruction (whole class or small group), cooperative (fours, triads, partners), independent, verbal/nonverbal responses, and so on.

- Use an overhead projector with transparencies of key points during lesson presentation, or write/illustrate the main information on the board.

- Project an outline of the lesson on the overhead or write the topic outline on the board for students to follow.

- Give students framed outlines to follow your lectures, and have them fill in the key points during the lecture. This framed outline can be projected on an overhead with you or individual students filling in directly on the transparency throughout the lesson.

- Teach students about "multiple intelligences" and "learning styles"—how we all learn differently, and have strengths and weaknesses in different areas. Provide numerous opportunities for student choices and options (projects, activities, tools/materials) to accommodate individual learning styles and interests. (3-5, 3-9)

- Provide student projects and assignments that have options, including music, drama, art, construction, designing, writing, speaking, use of technology, research, and any other means of creative expression.
- Use multisensory techniques throughout the lesson.
- Use a lot of color, movement, and graphics.
- Vary instructional techniques. Remember to incorporate variety and novelty into lesson presentations.
- Utilize a variety of audio–visual materials and resources.
- Present many models and examples.
- Teach strategically and model effective thinking, questioning, and planning/organizational processes.
- Know the skill level of your students and assign tasks at an appropriate level.
- Differentiate instruction and design activities that can span the developmental skill and ability range of students, providing choices and levels of complexity in assignments to meet the needs of *all* students in an inclusive classroom.
- Highlight in color important concepts, vocabulary, and key points.
- Use a game format for drill and practice activities.

RELATED LISTS

- Many of the lists throughout this book share related strategies. See Lists 3-2, 3-3, 3-4, 5-5, 5-10, and 5-14 for additional strategies that maximize attention, active engagement and participation, and learning outcomes for students.

3-8

ADAPTATIONS AND MODIFICATIONS OF TESTING

GENERAL TESTING RECOMMENDATIONS

The following is an extensive list of possible adaptations to be considered when trying to provide a fair assessment of students' learning. Included are some recommendations you should keep in mind when preparing exams for *all students*. Some of the other interventions should be considered as special accommodations for students with moderate to severe reading, writing, math, or attention difficulties, who are unable to demonstrate their comprehension or mastery of the content material under normal testing conditions and criteria.

- Prior to testing, *review, review, review*.
- Provide students with all handouts and test copies that are easy to read (typed, clear language, at least double-spaced, clean copies, ample margins).
- Avoid handwritten tests.
- Eliminate unnecessary words and confusing language in the test.
- State directions in clear terms and simple sentences.
- Underline or color-highlight directions or key words in the directions.
- Provide many opportunities for short-answer assessment (multiple choice, matching).
- On vocabulary tests, give the definition and have the student supply the word, rather than providing the word and the student needing to write out the definition.
- For fill-in-the-blank tests, provide a word bank from which students can select the correct word for the blanks.
- Provide students with examples of different types of test questions they will be responsible for on the exam.
- Administer frequent short quizzes throughout the teaching unit, reviewing the next day, and thus providing feedback to students on their understanding of the material. These short quizzes do not need to be graded for a score, but rather to help students in their learning and confidence prior to the exam.
- Read aloud the directions for the different parts of the test before students begin the exam.
- Teach students the strategies and skills for taking a variety of tests (true/false, multiple-choice, fill-in-the-blank, essay, fill-in-the-bubble).

- Give students the opportunity to write their own test questions in a variety of formats.

- Practice all types of testing formats, sharing and discussing "test-taking strategies."

- Use more short-answer testing formats (fill-in-the-blank, matching, multiple-choice). When giving essay questions, be willing to make accommodations for students with written output disabilities.

- Test only what has been taught.

- Provide additional workspace on the test (particularly for math tests).

- Avoid questions that are worded in a way to deliberately trick the student.

- Write multiple-choice questions with choices listed vertically rather than horizontally, as it is easier to read that way.

- Utilize portfolio assessment, whereby progress is evaluated on individual performance and improvement as opposed to comparing with other students.

- For a change of routine, assign take-home tests on occasion.

- Reduce weight of a single test grade. Have several shorter and more frequent quizzes rather than a lengthy unit test.

- Allow students to use graph paper or other paper to solve math problems and attach to test rather than requiring computation to be done on the limited workspace directly on the test.

- Divide a test in parts, administering each part on different days rather than rushing students to complete lengthy tests in one class period.

- Allow students to retake the test orally after given in written form to add points to their score if they are able to demonstrate greater knowledge/mastery than shown on the written test (especially for essay questions).

- Don't penalize for spelling and grammar on tests that are measuring mastery of content in other areas.

- Color the processing signs on math tests for students who do not focus well on details and make careless errors due to inattention. (For example, you might highlight: yellow = addition; green = subtraction; blue = multiplication).

- Utilize privacy boards at desks during test-taking time, and/or find other means of reducing distractions when students are tested.

INDIVIDUALIZED TESTING RECOMMENDATIONS

- Take the exam in the classroom, and then in a small group or with a special education teacher. Average the two grades.

- Substitute an oral for a written test as appropriate.

- Allow taped tests if needed, and permit student(s) to tape-record answers to essay questions rather than write them.

3-8 (continued)

- Read test items orally to student(s).

- Read the directions again to those students who need additional clarification.

- Before providing the final grade on a test, point out the test items you spot as incorrect and allow student(s) to try self-correcting careless errors before scoring.

- Give reduced spelling lists for students who struggle with spelling (for example, 15 words rather than 20 or 25). When dictating the words on the test, dictate those 15 words in any order first; then continue with the other words for the rest of the class. Those students on modified lists have the option of trying the additional words for bonus points. (5-10)

- Score tests for number correct out of the total number assigned per student (which can be shortened assignments or tests for individual students).

- Eliminate need for students with writing difficulties to copy test questions from the board or book before answering.

- Collaborate with special educators to rewrite the tests for students with special needs (shorter sentences, simplified vocabulary, easier-to-read format).

- Seat the student near you or in optimal location for your monitoring and focusing.

- Administer the test in a different location (such as the resource room).

- Administer the test at a different time of the day.

- Provide extended time for testing (one and a half times or twice the amount of time).

- Allow calculator and multiplication charts and tables on math tests that are assessing problem-solving skills, not computation.

- Encourage students to double- and triple-check their tests for careless errors (skipping items, getting mixed up on numbering, writing numerals and letters/words legibly, filling in next to the correct corresponding number, and so on).

- Administer the test, if necessary, in a separate location either individually or in a small group.

- Administer the test in shorter intervals in a few different sessions.

- Revise the test format, as needed, for certain students (reducing the number of items on a page, enlarging print, increasing the spacing between items).

- Allow students to directly write in the test booklet if needed.

- Permit brief breaks during testing if needed.

- Permit the use of earplugs or some other device to block out auditory distractions during testing.

3-9

ACCOMMODATIONS FOR LEARNING STYLES

Not everyone learns in the same way. Our "learning styles" encompass a number of factors, such as cognitive styles and sensory modality preferences (visual, auditory, tactile-kinesthetic). Modality preferences are the sensory channels through which it may be easier for a person to learn and process information. It does not mean that one has an impairment or weakness in the other modalities/channels, but that one favors a particular means of receiving information (input) or in showing his or her understanding (output).

The following describes what it means to be a "visual learner," "auditory learner," or "tactile-kinesthetic learner." Most people learn through a combination of all of the above. It is important for teachers to recognize the different types of learners, as well as the need to use a variety of teaching strategies that address students' diverse learning styles and draw upon their different strengths.

VISUAL LEARNERS

This type of student learns best by:

■ Seeing, watching, observing, viewing, and reading

■ Visual stimulation: pictures, images, graphics, and printed words

Support visual learners by providing and encouraging the use of:

■ Graphic organizers

■ Written directions (including pictures)

■ Maps, charts, diagrams

■ Handouts

■ Flashcards

■ Films, videos/CDs/DVDs, multimedia presentations

■ Advance organizers, framed outlines

■ Modeling, demonstrating, illustrating

■ Color-highlighted materials

■ Overhead projector

■ Dry-erase, flannel, and magnetic boards

■ Clustering, webbing, diagramming

■ Strategic use of color (organizing and highlighting important information to remember)

3-9 (*continued*)

- Letter cards (arrange into words), word cards (arrange into sentences), and sentence strips (arrange into paragraphs)

- Circling, underlining, drawing boxes, and using visual symbols next to important information

- Outlining the configuration of word shapes and color-coding structural elements (prefixes, syllables, suffixes, vowels) to aid with word recognition and spelling

- Prompting students visually ("Can you see what I mean?" "Look at this . . .")

- Visual cues to alert, get attention, and remind student. (See the Appendix for examples.)

  - Tape a target behavior card on the child's desk.

  - Point to a visual prompt of the routine or expectation.

AUDITORY LEARNERS

This type of student learns best by:

- Verbalizing, listening, explaining, and discussing
- Asking and answering questions
- Studying with a partner or small group
- Thinking out loud/self-talking

Support auditory learners by providing and encouraging the use of:

- Music (rhythm, beat, and melody) to reinforce learning of information
- Rhyming/verse/song
- Drama
- Stories
- Speeches
- Debates
- Books on tape/access to listening post
- Brainstorming
- Oral reports
- Word games
- Paraphrasing
- Verbal repetition
- Spelling bees
- Audiotapes

- Phonics
- Reader's Theater
- Cooperative learning (working with partners or small groups)
- Think-pair-share
- Discussions
- Study groups
- Reciprocal teaching
- Auditory cues to alert, get attention, and remind student.
  - A brief verbal message, such as "Listen . . . this is important" or stating child's name
  - Nonverbal auditory signals (chimes, bell)

TACTILE-KINESTHETIC LEARNERS

This type of student learns best by:

- Touching, doing, moving (physical activities)
- Hands-on learning

Support tactile-kinesthetic learners by providing and encouraging the use of:

- Frequent movement opportunities
- Learning games
- Experiential learning
- Field trips
- Project-oriented, active learning
- Objects to touch/manipulatives
- Lab experiences
- Performances, role-playing, simulations
- Construction crafts
- Various arts/crafts
- Computers and other technology
- Concrete examples for abstract concepts (such as arm-wrestling to demonstrate the conflict between protagonists and antagonists in a story)
- Tracing with fingers on sandpaper, carpet, and other textures/surfaces
- Studying information by reciting, rehearsing, and, if possible, by reading while in motion (walking, riding a bike, jumping rope, bouncing a ball, jotting down notes)
- Tactile-kinesthetic cues to alert, get attention, and remind student (such as a hand on shoulder)

3-9 (*continued*)

OTHER STYLES

Learning styles are also comprised of *cognitive* styles, as well as the above modality preferences. For example:

- **Analytic learners** tend to be sequential processors who learn best by:
  - Working from parts to whole
  - Making lists
  - Following step-by-step in a process
- **Global learners** tend to be simultaneous processors of information who learn best by:
  - Seeing the "big picture" (given examples of the end product)
  - Focusing on the whole or main concepts first, and then tackling the details
  - Clustering, webbing, mind mapping, and using other such techniques

ENVIRONMENTAL FACTORS

Environmental factors are another element of learning style. For example, some students are more productive with music in the background, while others need complete quiet in order to concentrate.

RELATED LISTS

- See Lists 2-4, 3-2, 3-4, 3-5, 3-6, and 3-7 for strategies related to accommodating different learning styles.

SOURCES AND RESOURCES

Moore, Lorraine. *Inclusion: A Practical Guide for Parents.* Minnetonka, MN: Peytral Publications, 1996.

Rief, Sandra, and Julie Heimburge. *How to Reach and Teach All Students in the Inclusive Classroom.* Paramus, NJ: The Center for Applied Research in Education, 1996.

Sousa, David A. *How the Special Needs Brain Learns*, Thousand Oaks, CA: Corwin Press, 2001.

- Consequently, the best way to remember new information and material is to use it immediately, preferably by teaching it to someone else.

RELATED LISTS

- See Lists 3-2, 3-5, 3-7, 3-8, 4-6, 4-7, 4-8, 4-9, 5-5, and 5-14 for a variety of accommodations that address academic areas affected by memory weaknesses (such as homework, time management, reading comprehension, math, spelling, and class work production).

SOURCES AND RESOURCES

Cipriano, Jeri. *Good Apple Homework Helper.* Torrance, CA: Good Apple, 1996.

Division for Learning Disabilities & Division for Research of the Council for Exceptional Children. *Current Practice Alerts: A Focus on Mnemonic Instruction.* Issue 5, Summer 2001. (www.dldcec.org/alerts)

King-Sears, M. E., C. D. Mercer, and P. T. Sindelar. "Toward Independence with Keyword Mnemonics: A Strategy for Science Vocabulary Instruction," *Remedial and Special Education*, 13, 22–23; 1992.

Levin, J. R. "Mnemonic Strategies and Classroom Learning: A Twenty-Year Report Card," *The Elementary School Journal*, 94 (2), 235–244; 1993.

Liautaud, Judy, and Dave Rodriguez. *Times Tables the Fun Way!* Sandy, UT: City Creek Press, 1999. (www.citycreek.com)

Mehring, Teresa A., and Alison K. Banikowski. "Strategies to Enhance Memory in Students with Disabilities," *CEC Today*, vol. 9, no. 1, June/July 2002. (www.cec.sped.org)

Memory Joggers™. Available from: 24 Nuevo, Irvine, CA 92612.

Rief, Sandra. *The ADD/ADHD Checklist.* Paramus, NJ: Prentice Hall, 1998.

Sousa, David A. *How the Brain Learns.* Thousand Oaks, CA: Corwin Press, 2001.

Student Academic Services, California Polytechnic State University, San Luis Obispo (http://sas.calpoly.edu/asc/ssl/memorization.html)

Wallace, Rosella R. *Smart-Rope Jingles (Jump Rope Rhymes, Raps, and Chants for Active Learning).* Tucson, AZ: Zephyr Press, 1993.

Wood, Donna K., and Alan R. Frank. "Using Memory-Enhancing Strategies to Learn Multiplication Facts," *Teaching Exceptional Children*, vol. 32, no. 5, 200; 2000.

4-2
METACOGNITIVE AND LEARNING STRATEGIES

LEARNING STRATEGIES AND STUDY SKILLS

Students with ADHD benefit greatly from being taught specific learning and study strategies for school success.

Metacognitive Strategies

Students develop self-awareness about how they are learning, how they approach a learning task, and self-evaluating the strategy effectiveness. Among these metacognitive strategies are:

1. Previewing and planning for how to go about learning or studying the material.
2. Organizing for the task, getting ready, and setting goals.
3. Monitoring one's own attention, production, and comprehension.
4. Self-assessment and evaluation of how well goals were met and learning took place.

The Strategies Instructional Approach developed by researchers at the University of Kansas for Research on Learning (Schumaker, Deschler et al., 1981) provides a number of research-validated strategies such as RAP.

RAP involves the following steps:

- *Read* the paragraph.
- *Ask* self to identify the main idea and two supporting details.
- *Paraphrase* or *put* the main ideas and details into one's own words.

Note: There are more metacognitive learning strategies from the University of Kansas described in other lists. See Related Lists.

Journal Responses

There are a variety of ways to use journals to engage students in thinking, questioning, making associations, and so forth *during* their reading, and responding and reflecting *after* their reading.

- *Double-Entry Journals:* The paper is divided into two columns. Notes are taken in the left column, citing anything of particular interest to the reader (quote, description, metaphor) along with the page number. In the right-hand column, the reader comments and records personal thoughts, interpretations, connections, and questions triggered by that section of the text.

- *Metacognitive Journal/Learning Log:* The page is divided into two columns. The left column is labeled "What I Learned." The right column is labeled "How I Learned This." This assists students in thinking about and analyzing their own learning process. The right-hand column can state other things, as well, such as "How This Affects Me" or "Why This Was Difficult (Easy) for Me." The key is reflection and analysis of one's own learning.

Reading Logs

Students can write their feelings, associations, connections, and questions in response to the reading. They may be given specific prompts to guide what is recorded in their logs; for example: "What did you learn?" "How did this make you feel?" "How did this relate to any of your own life experiences?" "What did you like/dislike about the author's style of writing?"

Think Aloud

This is another important approach for teaching students the metacognitive skills of thinking about their learning. Basically, it involves externalizing and making overt the thinking processes used when reading. Students have a model of what it might sound like to internally grapple with the text.

Note: For ADHD students with executive functioning weaknesses that may impair their use of inner language (1-2), this is an important teaching strategy to model.

- Orally read to the students as they generally follow along with the text.
- Model the process of interacting with the text (stopping to guess what will happen next/making predictions, asking questions of self or author, describing what is visualized, working through problems to figure out unknown vocabulary, making connections, and so forth).
- Clearly model how to self-monitor comprehension by stopping periodically and asking: "Is this making sense to me?"
- Have students practice some of these strategies with partners.

SQ3R

SQ3R increases comprehension and retention of textbook material (expository or informational), and involves the following steps:

1. *Survey*—Briefly look through the reading assignment at the titles, chapter headings, illustrations, charts, and graphs. Skim through the assignment and read the chapter summary and/or end-of-chapter questions.

2. *Question*—Turn the headings and subheadings of the text into questions. For example: **Producing Antibodies** can become: "How do our bodies produce antibodies?" **Organic motor fuels** can become: "What are the different organic motor fuels?"

4-2 (continued)

3. *Read*—Read to find the answers to the questions developed above. Identify the main ideas and jot down any questions, notes, or unknown vocabulary.

4. *Recite*—At the end of each chapter section, state the gist of what was read. *Note:* Restating or summarizing into a tape recorder is often very effective.

5. *Review*—Check recall of important information from the reading. To that end, a study guide of some kind may be created.

SQ4R

This is the same as SQ3R except that an additional step is followed—*Write*. The SQ4R procedure is: survey, question, read, recite, write, and review. After a brief verbal summary of what the reading passage was about, one must write the answers to the questions (in step 2) and then review.

RCRC

This is a study strategy involving the steps:

1. Read.
2. Cover.
3. Recite.
4. Check.

For example, the student first reads a portion of the material. Then the passage is covered (by hand or paper) and the student restates it in his or her own words. Finally, the student checks for accuracy by looking at the text again.

ADDITIONAL STRATEGIES

■ **Use resource and reference materials** (dictionary, atlas, encyclopedia, Internet) to locate information. There are prerequisite skills to using many resource materials: knowing alphabetical order and understanding use of guide words; being able to read and understand the legend of a map; and learning basic research skills.

■ **Note taking:** This requires listening and simultaneously writing down major ideas and key information in a useful format so the information can later be accessed. There are a variety of note-taking techniques. One example is the Cornell note-taking method, which involves the following:

1. Students divide a paper into two columns.
2. The first column (which is about one-fourth to one-third of the width of the paper) is where key terms, questions, additions, and corrections are written after the class period. It is used for recall of important information.

3. The right column is about three-fourths or two-thirds of the width of the paper. This is where the lecture notes are written (on the front side of the page only).

4. Students are to review their notes within 24 hours (preferably within three hours) after the lecture. During this time, they reread and then fill in key terms, make additions, corrections, and so on in the left column.

5. In addition, space is left at the bottom of the page for a summary. Good note-taking requires learning how to make abbreviations and use symbols.

RELATED LISTS

■ See Lists 2-6, 2-13, and 3-4 for listening strategies.

■ See List 5-5 to create concept webs and semantic maps.

■ See Lists 4-4 through 4-7 for organization and time-management strategies.

■ See List 4-1 for memorization strategies.

■ See the additional metacognitive strategies for reading in List 5-5, for math in List 5-14, and for writing in Lists 5-8 and 5-9.

■ See List 5-8 for information about the Self-Regulated Strategy Development Approach pioneered and researched by Harris and Graham with support from the U.S. Office of Special Education, and more strategies developed by researchers at the University of Kansas.

SOURCES AND RESOURCES

Archer, Anita, and Mary Gleason. *Skills for School Success*. North Billerica, MA: Curriculum Associates, 1990.

Barbee, Bruce (ed.) and presenters of Academic Support Workshops, UCLA, College of Letters & Science Counseling. *The Essential Handbook for Academic Success Skills*. Dubuque, IA: Kendall/Hunt Publishing Co., 1998.

Bell, Nanci. *Visualizing and Verbalizing for Language Comprehension and Thinking*. Paso Robles, CA: Academy of Reading Publications, 1991.

Bromley, K., L. Irwin-DeVitis, and M. Modlo. *Graphic Organizers: Visual Strategies for Active Learning*. New York: Scholastic, 1995.

Chamot, A., and J. O'Malley. *The CALLA Handbook: Implementing Cognitive Academic Language Learning*. Reading, MA: Addison-Wesley, 1994.

Consortium on Reading Excellence, Inc. (CORE). *Literacy Training Notebook*. Emeryville, CA: Core, Inc., 1998.

Davis, L., and S. Sirotowitz, with H. Parker. *Study Strategies Made Easy*. Plantation, FL: Specialty Press, 1996.

4-2 (continued)

Forte, Imogene, and Sandra Schurr. *Standards-Based Language Arts Graphic Organizers, Rubrics, and Writing Prompts for Middle Grade Students.* Nashville, TN: Incentive Publications, 2001.

Graser, Nan Stutzman. *125 Ways to Be a Better Listener.* East Moline, IL: LinguiSystems, 1992.

Greene, Victoria E., and Mary Lee Enfield. *Project Read—Language Circle.* Bloomington, MN: Language Circle Enterprise, 1994.

Howard, Deane. *Student Survival.* San Diego, CA: Educational Resources Publishing Co., 1991.

Polloway, Edward A., James R. Patton, and Loretta Serna. *Strategies for Teaching Learners with Special Needs.* Upper Saddle River, NJ: Merrill/Prentice-Hall, 2001.

Schumaker, J. B., D. D. Deschler, S. Nolan et al. "Error Monitoring: A Learning Strategy for Improving Academic Performance of LD Adolescents (Research Report No. 32)." Lawrence: University of Kansas, Institute for Research on Learning Disabilities, 1981.

Stockdale, Carol, and Carol Possin. *Solving Reading Problems.* East Moline, IL: LinguiSystems, 2000.

Strategic Teaching and Learning: Standards-Based Instruction to Promote Content Literacy in Grades Four through Twelve. Sacramento: California Department of Education, 2000.

Waring, Cynthia Conway. *Developing Independent Readers: Strategy-Oriented Reading Activities for Learners with Special Needs.* West Nyack, NY: The Center for Applied Research in Education, 1995.

4-3
ADHD: STRUGGLES WITH ORGANIZATION, TIME MANAGEMENT, AND STUDY SKILLS

The majority of people with attention deficit disorders experience difficulties to varying degrees with disorganization and time management. For ADHD students, weakness in these important skills often significantly affects school performance. In families of children or teens with ADHD, tears and battles over homework are often chronic problems.

Organization, time management, and study skills are directly affected as a result of core symptoms of the disorder (for example, resisting distractions, sustaining attention to task), and impairments in executive functions such as memory, motivation, and self-monitoring. (1-2, 1-5) It is common for students with ADHD to demonstrate many of the following behaviors/traits that negatively affect homework and classwork production:

- Disorganized (desk, work area, locker, room, backpack, notebook)
- Cannot find, forgets to bring, or loses important things (books, materials, and assignments needed)
- Poor planning, scheduling, and pacing
- Lack of awareness of time passing and how they spend their time during the day
- Inadequately estimating how long a task will take (such as completing an assignment)
- Not adequately prepared
- Misses deadlines/due dates
- Not on time (to class, activities, appointments)
- General difficulty keeping track of things and pacing themselves
- Poor management of long-term projects/assignments (book reports, research projects)
- Procrastinates
- Slow to get started/initiate the task
- Difficulty prioritizing activities and things that need to be done
- Forgets to record assignments (or difficulty doing so without help)
- Forgets to take home books and needed supplies for homework
- Forgets to turn in assignments (even when completed)
- Distracted by more desirable activities (watching TV, playing, talking on phone) when work is not yet completed
- Slow/tedious written organization and output
- Difficulty persevering on difficult or boring tasks
- Not clearly understanding the work assigned

4-3 (*continued*)

With regard to classwork and homework production, teachers need to factor in that it often takes students with ADHD *two or three times longer* to complete the work than it does their non-ADHD classmates. Homework is particularly a challenge because of the child's fatigue and frustration at the end of the day. Without the provision of home structures and supports (and often some medication), it is unlikely that much work is able to be accomplished by the end of the day/evening.

RELATED LISTS

■ See Lists 4-7, 4-8, and 4-9 for a number of strategies and supports recommended for parents and teachers to help with homework, and to build important organization, time management, and study skills.

4-4
WHAT TEACHERS CAN DO TO HELP WITH ORGANIZATION

Students with ADHD often have significant difficulty with organization, time awareness, and time management. Fortunately, there are many strategies that both teachers and parents can employ to build these skills, and, consequently, improve school success.

ORGANIZE STUDENTS' WORKSPACE AND MATERIALS

Supplies and Materials

- Require the use of a 3-ring binder or notebook starting in third grade (fourth grade the latest).

- Require the use of colored subject dividers and a pencil pouch for the notebook (include a few sharpened pencils with erasers and other small supplies/essentials).

- Have younger students (kindergarten through second grade) use a pocket folder for carrying papers to and from school.

- Require students to carry a backpack or book bag and to bring notebook/binder to and from school daily.

- Teach students how to keep their papers organized by placing them in the appropriate subject section of their notebooks.

- Require the use of a monthly assignment calendar/planner or daily/weekly assignment sheet to be kept at all times at the front of the notebook. Whichever is used (calendar, student planner, or assignment sheet), it should be 3-hole punched for storage in the notebook. Utilize it consistently for recording all classroom assignments. Model and monitor its use. See samples of assignment sheets in the Appendix.

- Have a consistent location in the notebook for storing homework assignments (or work "to do" or work to "turn in"). There are a variety of ways for doing so.

  - Use colored pocket folders (single pocket or double) that are 3-hole punched and inserted into the notebook. For example, a red pocket folder can be labeled "homework" and contain all homework; a different colored folder may be for graded and returned papers, or anything to "leave at home."

  - Use large laminated envelopes that are 3-hole punched and inserted into the notebook for homework, assorted project papers, and so forth.

- Encourage students to keep a supply of notebook paper handy in a consistent location of their binder.

4-4 (*continued*)

- Keep spare supplies available so that time isn't wasted with students searching or asking around to borrow from classmates. Consider "charging" students (they must pay you from their class money/tokens) or fining (points) in some way for not being prepared and needing to borrow supplies from you.

- Provide handouts to students that are always 3-hole punched in advance.

- Give students a clipboard for anchoring papers on the desk.

- Attach a pencil to the child's desk (either with string or Velcro™).

- Provide containers (bins, pencil cases, boxes, buckets, organizing trays, baskets, coffee cans covered in self-stick vinyl) as needed for materials/supplies on desks or tables.

- To help keep papers stored appropriately in the notebook, provide adhesive hole reinforcers for ripped-out papers, and plastic sleeves for papers that you do not want to 3-hole punch.

- Encourage students who need daily reference tools (times tables chart, frequently misspelled words list, dictionary) to keep them in a section of their notebook.

Desk and Work Area

- Provide students with a work area that has as much desktop space as possible.

- Limit the amount of materials/clutter on each student's desk or work area.

- Some very disorganized students do better with a basket on the floor next to the desk for keeping needed papers and books easily accessible and visible but not on the desktop until needed.

ORGANIZE THE CLASSROOM

- Use clearly labeled shelves, files, and bins so that you and the students know precisely where things belong and can easily locate them.

- Clearly identify certain places in the room (trays, color-coded folders or boxes) where students know consistently where to turn in assignments or store unfinished work.

- See Lists 2-3 and 2-4.

USE VISUAL REMINDERS AND MEMORY CUES

- Color-coordinate by subject area to make location of subject materials quicker and easier. For example, the science text is covered in yellow paper or has a yellow adhesive dot on the binding; the science notebook/lab book or folder is yellow; the schedule with science class period and room number is highlighted in yellow; and the tab/divider for science in the 3-ring notebook is yellow.

- Utilize brightly colored file folders for different subjects.

- Prepare important notices and handouts on colored paper, preferably color-coded for certain categories; for example: weekly/monthly newsletters in blue, spelling lists in pink, and so on.

- Use brightly colored paper for project assignments, providing details and due dates. Give two copies (one for the notebook and one to be posted at home).

- Use visual/pictorial cues for showing expected materials and daily routines and schedule. See examples in the Appendix of a morning routine and pictures that can be used for visual prompts. (2-3, 2-4, 2-5)

- Encourage students to use self-stick notes for reminders to themselves. Have them adhere the notes to book covers, in their lockers, planners, and so forth.

USE MONITORING, SUPPORTS, AND INCENTIVES

- Have periodic (weekly or every other week) desk and notebook checks.

- Positively reinforce (prizes, certificates, and privileges such as "no homework tonight" passes) for passing inspection of notebook/workspace checks as an incentive.

- Reward students who are organized and prepared. (2-1, 2-2, 2-7, 2-9)

- Provide bonus points or some other reward for improved organization, and reward your disorganized students who, upon request, are able to quickly locate a certain book or paper in their desk/notebook.

- Provide time and assistance, as needed, for cleaning out/sorting.

- At the end of the day, check that students have the necessary books/materials in their backpacks to take home.

- Provide assistance (another student or adult) to help disorganized students sort through desks, backpacks, and notebooks. It helps to dump everything into a shopping bag and bring to another area while working on this. Recycle unnecessary papers; apply adhesive paper reinforcers as needed; refile miscellaneous papers in the appropriate section of the notebook; throw away dried-up pens and markers; and so forth.

- Provide in-school help and adult assistance for putting together projects. Many students with ADHD and/or learning disabilities have a hard time laying out the pieces of projects, and impulsively glue papers to boards without first planning for the amount of space they have. Help with the little extras (nice lettering on the computer; cutting papers straight with a paper cutter rather than scissors), as this will make projects look so much better.

ASSIST WITH STUDENTS' PLANNING AND THINKING

- Provide advanced organizers and study guides to help organize thinking about key topics of the lesson.

4-4 (continued)

- Use visual/graphic organizers with high frequency (sequence charts, story maps, sentence maps, webs, clusters, flow charts, Venn diagrams).

- Provide framed outlines for filling in missing words and phrases during instruction. (5-5)

- Help students organize their ideas (prewriting, preplanning) with the use of self-stick notes, whiteboards/dry-erase pens, tape recorders, and questioning/prompting.

- Encourage the use of software that helps students plan and organize their written work. For example, the programs Inspiration™ and Kidspiration™ enable the child to easily web and organize ideas and outline them. (5-12)

- With all writing assignments, provide a scoring rubric to help the student in planning, organizing, and producing work at standard with grade-level expectations.

CHECK OUT THESE ADDITIONAL ORGANIZATIONAL TIPS

- Encourage students to organize materials upon arriving to class and before dismissal at the end of the school day.

- Teach and provide models of how to organize papers (headings, margins, spacing).

- Provide models of well-organized projects, science boards, and so forth.

- Consider loaning an extra set of books to keep at home if the student has trouble remembering to bring books to and from school.

- Provide direct assistance getting started on homework assignments and projects at school.

- If using a daily assignment sheet or planner, have students transfer to a monthly calendar any of the due dates for projects, tests, special events such as field trips, or other important dates for the month.

- Require labeling of materials/supplies with students' names.

- Allow for natural consequences of not having materials. *Do not* positively reinforce students who are unprepared by giving or loaning them new, desirable materials/supplies. Only let students borrow from a supply of less desirable materials. For example, many teachers keep a box of golf pencils and/or old pencils and erasers for this purpose.

SOURCES AND RESOURCES

Archer, Anita, and Mary Gleason. *Skills for School Success.* North Billerica, MA: Curriculum Associates, 1990.

Bos, Candace S., and Sharon Vaughn. *Strategies for Teaching Students with Learning and Behavior Problems.* Boston: Allyn & Bacon, 1988.

Dendy, Chris Zeigler. *Teaching Teens with ADD and ADHD.* Bethesda, MD: Woodbine House, 2000.

Rief, Sandra. *The ADD/ADHD Checklist.* Paramus, NJ: Prentice Hall, 1998.

Rief, Sandra, and Julie Heimburge. *How to Reach and Teach All Students in the Inclusive Classroom.* Paramus, NJ: The Center for Applied Research in Education, 1995.

Shore, Kenneth. *Special Kids Problem Solver.* Paramus, NJ: Prentice Hall Press, 1998.

Zentall, Sydney S., and Sam Goldstein. *Seven Steps to Homework Success.* Plantation, FL: Specialty Press, 1999.

4-5

WHAT PARENTS CAN DO TO HELP WITH ORGANIZATION

Disorganization and lack of time awareness are common characteristics of ADHD. Your child or teen is likely to be weak in these skills and will need your help, support, and "coaching" in order to be successful in school. Try not to be critical; instead, keep in mind that this is part of the disorder.

ORGANIZE YOUR CHILD'S WORKSPACE AND MATERIALS

Supplies and Materials

- Provide your child with a backpack and notebook/binder according to the teacher's specifications.

- It is recommended that beginning in third grade your child use a 3-ring binder with colored subject dividers and a plastic pouch for pencils and other small supplies. Students in kindergarten through second grade should use a soft pocket folder for storing their papers.

- Your child's planner, monthly calendar, or assignment sheet should be hole-punched and kept in the front of the notebook.

- If needed, provide a spelling dictionary or list of common and frequently misspelled words, a multiplication chart, and any other useful reference materials.

- Provide your child with plastic sleeves that can be inserted into the notebook for storing important papers that are not 3-hole punched.

- Colored folders that are 3-hole punched and can be inserted into the notebook are recommended for storing and easily locating papers. For example, a red pocket folder can be labeled "homework" and contain all homework, and a different colored folder may be for graded and returned papers, or anything to "leave at home."

- Another technique is to use large laminated envelopes that are hole-punched and inserted in the binder for homework, assorted project papers, and so on.

- Provide the necessary supplies to help your child be organized at school (you will likely have to replace and replenish supplies often). Have your child take inventory of what needs replacement, or ask the teacher.

- Provide all necessary supplies for homework and keep them readily accessible. (See the Homework Supply Kit recommendations on page 218.)

Room and Work Area

- Together with your child, choose a place in the home that has adequate lighting, is comfortable for working, and is as free from distractions as possible.

- Carefully examine your child's workspace. Make sure there is a large working surface (desktop) available that is free from clutter. If your child has a computer, do not place it on the desk, as it considerably cuts down on his or her working surface area. Instead, place the computer on a separate desk or table.

- Have your child clear out desk drawers and shelves of work, projects, and papers that were from different school years. Together, decide on what you would like to keep and store out of the way (in colored boxes, zipper portfolios) in order to make room for current papers and projects.

- Provide your child with a corkboard and pins to hang up important papers.

- Keep trays and bins for storing supplies/materials that will remove some of the clutter from the desktop.

- Provide the necessary storage space (shelves, closet space, bins, trays, drawers) for organizing your child's room efficiently.

- Label shelves and storage bins.

- Keep a 3-hole punch and electric pencil sharpener easily accessible.

- Besides a master family calendar (in kitchen), provide your child with a desk calendar that serves as an overview of important dates, activities, and events.

USE VISUAL REMINDERS AND MEMORY CUES

- Dry-erase boards are helpful to hang in a central location of the home for all phone messages and notes to family members. In addition, hang one in your child's room for important reminders and messages.

- Write notes and reminders on colored self-stick notes and place on mirrors, doors, and other places where your child is likely to see them.

- Encourage your child/teen to also write himself/herself notes and leave them on the pillow, by the backpack, by car keys, and so forth.

- Use electronic reminders and organizers.

- Use color strategically. Provide a file with color-coded folders in which your child can keep papers stored by category.

- Color-coordinate by subject area. For example, the history notebook and book cover for history text can be in green, the schedule with time/room number of history class highlighted in green, tab of subject divider in notebook for history is in green.

- Color-code entries on a calendar for school-related, sports, and social activities.

4-5 (*continued*)

CHECK OUT THESE ADDITIONAL ORGANIZATIONAL TIPS

- Make the time to help your child clean and organize his or her backpack, notebook, desk, and room. Help with sorting and dumping.
- Assist your child with cleaning and organizing by at least starting the job together.
- Offer a reward or incentive for straightening and organizing materials, putting away belongings, and so forth.
- If using a token economy system/behavior modification at home, give points, tokens, and so on for meeting an organizational/clean-up goal.
- Label your child's materials and possessions with his or her name.
- Avoid early morning rush and stress by developing the routine of your child getting as much as possible organized and ready for school the night before (clothes/outfit to wear, lunch prepared, everything loaded into the backpack). Shower or bathe in the evening.
- Place the backpack in the same spot every night.

MAKE A HOMEWORK SUPPLY KIT

You can help your child considerably in cutting down on wasted time spent searching the house for necessary homework supplies and materials. Not only is it a frustrating waste of precious minutes, but it also causes a major break in productivity, pulling children unnecessarily off-task.

This Homework Supply Kit can be stored in anything portable, preferably a lightweight container with a lid. Some children work at their desks; others at kitchen or dining room tables; and still others prefer to spread out on their beds or the floor. With this system, it does not matter the location of where your children choose to study. The necessary supplies can accompany them anywhere.

Recommended Supplies (depending on age of child)

Plenty of paper	Paper clips
Sharpened pencils with erasers	1-hole punch
Pencil sharpener	3-hole punch
Ruler	Dictionary
Crayons	Thesaurus
Paper hole reinforcers	Electronic spell-check
Glue stick	Self-stick notepads

Colored pencils

Colored pens and markers (thick and thin points)

Stapler with box of staples

Clipboard

Highlighter pens

Index cards

Calculator

RELATED LISTS

■ See Lists 4-7 and 4-9.

SOURCES AND RESOURCES

Academic Skills Center (http://www.sas.calpoly.edu/asc/ssl)

Barbee, Bruce (ed.) and presenters of the Academic Support Workshops, UCLA, College of Letters & Science Counseling. *The Essential Handbook for Academic Success Skills.* Dubuque, IA: Kendall/Hunt Publishing Co., 1998.

Bos, Candace S., and Sharon Vaughn. *Strategies for Teaching Students with Learning and Behavior Problems.* Boston: Allyn & Bacon, 1988.

Dendy, Chris Zeigler. *Teaching Teens with ADD and ADHD.* Bethesda, MD: Woodbine House, 2000.

Flick, Grad L. *Homework Skills Improvement Kit.* Biloxi, MS: Seacoast Publications, 2001.

Power, Thomas, James Karustis, and Dina Habbousha. *Homework Success for Children with ADHD.* New York: The Guilford Press, 2001.

Rief, Sandra. *The ADD/ADHD Checklist.* Paramus, NJ: Prentice Hall, 1998.

Shore, Kenneth. *Special Kids Problem Solver.* Paramus, NJ: Prentice Hall Press, 1998.

Zentall, Sydney S., and Sam Goldstein. *Seven Steps to Homework Success.* Plantation, FL: Specialty Press, 1999.

4-6
WHAT TEACHERS CAN DO TO HELP WITH TIME MANAGEMENT

Lack of time awareness is very common among individuals with ADHD, as they often underestimate how much time they have to complete a task or to arrive somewhere on time. In addition, ADHD students tend to be oblivious to deadlines and due dates. Remember that this is part of the disorder and not apathy or deliberate misbehavior.

Time Awareness

■ Any opportunity to practice time estimation is very helpful toward increasing such awareness. For example, challenge your students to estimate how long it takes to walk to the office and back (without running), or any other task. Make a game out of predicting, timing, and checking the students' time estimates for various activities.

■ Encourage self-monitoring during independent seatwork by recording the start time on the paper. When the work period is over, record the time (regardless of how much work the student actually produced). This is helpful documentation with regard to how well the student is able to stay on-task and work productively.

Assignment Sheets, Calendars, Student Planners/Agendas

■ Communicate and maintain the clear expectation that all assignments are to be recorded on students' assignment calendars, and monitor that this is occurring.

■ Model the writing of assignments on the calendar using a transparency of the calendar. Take a few moments at the end of the subject period or school day to lead students in the recording of assignments on their calendars.

■ When using an assignment calendar, teach students to write the assignments on the day they are *due*. Walk them through recording on the correct date.

■ Monitor the assignment calendars (particularly monthly calendars of ADHD students). They tend to write things on the wrong date.

■ Provide assistance to students who have difficulty recording assignments in their calendar, planner, or assignment sheet.

■ Routinely ask table partners or groups seated together to check each other that everything is accurately recorded on calendars.

■ Assign study buddies so students can help each other. These partners can be responsible for checking each other to make sure assignments are recorded on calendars; and when absent, to have the buddy collect all handouts, notices, and assignments. Buddies exchange phone numbers to call each other when the other is absent and communicate about what was missed that day in class.

- Be sure to select a well-organized, tolerant, and helpful partner/study buddy for the ADHD student.

- Keep a master monthly calendar posted in the classroom, containing all the activities and assignments given.

- If using a daily agenda or assignment sheet, provide students with a single- or double-page monthly calendar. Have students transfer due dates of any projects, tests, class trips, or important activities/events onto their monthly calendar.

- Have students keep the monthly calendar clearly visible and easy to locate in the notebook. In addition, a class calendar should be posted and referred to.

Schedules

- Establish a daily routine and schedule for the classroom.

- Post all schedules and refer to them throughout the day.

- Walk through the schedule each day and point out any changes in the daily/weekly schedule or routine that will be taking place.

- With younger students, use a pictorial schedule depicting the daily routine.

- For students receiving special education/related services, write down their weekly schedule and tape it to their desks. Keep accessible each student's special schedules so that you know at all times the days and times they are pulled out of class, or when service providers are coming to the classroom to work with the student.

- Encourage students and parents to carefully plan a weekly schedule, including an established homework/study schedule. Ask parents to first help their son or daughter become aware of how much time he or she spends in a typical day on all activities from school dismissal until bedtime.(4-7)

Long-Term Projects

- Structure any long-term assignments (book reports, research projects, science fair projects) by breaking them into smaller, manageable increments.

- Make sure students have access to needed materials.

- Assign incremental due dates to help structure the timeline toward project completion. For example, assign separate due dates for stages of the project (getting a topic approved, outline submitted, research notes/resources listed, turning in first draft, and so on).

- Call close attention to due dates. Post those due dates and frequently refer to them as reminders.

- Call some parents to make sure they are aware of the projects, and have at least one copy of the handout explaining project guidelines, with its timeline and scoring rubric, to keep posted at home.

- Suggest to parents that they closely monitor timelines and help with pacing (such as getting started promptly on going to the library and gathering resources).

4-6 (*continued*)

- Monitor progress by asking to see what the student has accomplished so far, and provide a lot of feedback along the way.

- Consider providing some of your ADHD students and their parents advanced notice about upcoming projects and reports, enabling them to have a "head start" (especially with planning and research).

Other Ways Teachers Can Help with Time Management

- Provide students with a course outline or syllabus.

- Assist with prioritization of activities and workload.

- Teach students how to tell time and read a nondigital clock.

- Teach students how to read calendars and schedules.

- Make sure *all* assignments, page numbers, and due dates are presented to students both verbally and visually.

- Post all assignments in a consistent place in the room (corner of the board, separate assignment board).

- Utilize "things to do" lists, modeling for the class and teaching how to write down and cross off accomplished tasks. See the sample in the Appendix.

- Attach a "things to do" list on students' desks and monitor the practice of crossing off accomplished items.

- Provide enough time during transitions to put material away and get organized for the next activity.

- Set timers for transitions. (First state: "You have five minutes to finish what you are working on and putting away your materials." Then set the timer.). (2-5)

- Teach students how to self-monitor on-task behavior so that they are using class time effectively for getting work done. See the Self-Monitoring Form in the Appendix and the description in List 3-4.

- Include "seated by beginning bell time" or some other behavior, indicating student's punctuality on any home–school monitoring system (such as a daily report card or daily/weekly monitoring form). See Daily Report Card Information and examples in List 2-9 and the Appendix.

- If tardiness is an issue with the student, try an individual contract to motivate the student to improve behavior. (See the samples in the Appendix.)

- Provide extended time as needed, and consider more flexibility with regard to accepting late work.

- Encourage your school to establish a schoolwide expectation and organization/study skills program for consistency.

- Use frequent praise and positive reinforcement. Reward for meeting deadlines, finishing in-school assignments, and so on.

- Encourage students who take medication at school to have a beeper watch set for the time they need to go to the nurse's office.

- Allow for bypass strategies when writing speed is a problem. (5-12)

- Suggest to parents the recommendations and tips for homework, organization, and time management in Lists 4-5, 4-7, and 4-9.

RELATED LISTS

- See Lists 4-4 and 4-9.

- See Sources and Resources at the end of Lists 4-4 and 4-5.

4-7
WHAT PARENTS CAN DO TO HELP WITH TIME MANAGEMENT

Difficulty with adequately budgeting and managing one's time is certainly not unique to children, teens, or adults with ADHD. It is the greatest challenge, in fact, of most college students (including those in top universities).

For those with ADHD, time awareness and time management are often exceedingly difficult and problematic due to reasons associated with the disorder. Therefore, your child will typically need far more support and assistance than the average child.

Time Awareness

- Teach your child how to tell time and read a nondigital (analog) clock.

- Teach your child how to read calendars and schedules.

- Teach your child to use "things to do" lists (writing down and then crossing out accomplished tasks).

- Help to plan a "things to do" list when your child comes home from school, scheduling for the evening and estimating together with your child how long each assignment/activity should take. See the sample in the Appendix.

- Assist your child with prioritization of activities and workload.

- Let your child choose, but assist in planning what to do first, second, third, and so forth.

- Post a large calendar/wall chart in a central location of the home for scheduling family activities and events. Encourage everyone to refer to it daily. Each family member may have his or her own color pen for recording on the calendar.

- Expect your child to record assignments (see the teacher for help) and monitor that this is being done. Ask to see your son's or daughter's assignment calendars/sheets/planners every day.

- Help transfer important extracurricular activities/scheduling onto your child's personal calendar/planner.

Long-Term Projects

- Your assistance with time management and structuring of long-term school projects (book reports, science projects, research projects) will be critical to the success of your child. See the suggestions to teachers in Lists 4-6 and 4-8 as to how you should structure and provide supports to students.

- Help your child break down longer assignments into smaller, manageable chunks with deadlines marked on the calendar for incremental steps of the project.

- Pay close attention to due dates and post the project requirements. Together with your child, record on a master calendar the due date of the final project, and plan when to do the steps along the way (such as going to the library, getting resources and materials).

- Ask the teacher for feedback. Do not assume your child is working on a project at school, even if he or she is given some time in class to do it.

- Large and long-term projects can be easily overwhelming and discouraging for your child (and you). Your child will likely need your assistance, as well as help at school, with pacing and monitoring timelines toward project completion.

Schedules

- Help your child create a weekly schedule.

- For older students, a recommended time-management strategy is to begin the scheduling process by first examining and tracking how they spend their time during the entire 24-hour day. This obviously includes morning routine before school; hours spent between school dismissal and bedtime; and time spent sleeping. See the Student Weekly Planning Schedule in the Appendix.

- After a few days of examining his or her daily schedule, your child should have better awareness of how much time is typically spent on routine activities: meals, sleeping, grooming, walking to class, watching TV, talking on the phone, on the computer, recreational and social activities, and study/homework time.

- Schedule a time for homework. Some children like to come home and immediately get part or all of their homework done and out of the way. Others need a break before tackling any homework. Together with your child plan a schedule or time for homework that can be adhered to as consistently as possible.

More Time-Management Tips

- Morning and evening routines/rituals for getting ready for school and preparing to go to bed at night are very helpful. Clear reminders of the routine (through the use of a checklist of sequential tasks to complete) reduce the nagging, rushing around, and negative interactions at these times of the day. Checklists are great tools for time management and staying on schedule.

- With your child, decide on the steps of the routine that he or she is most comfortable with and list in that order. For example:
  1. Lay out clothes for tomorrow.
  2. Shower.
  3. Check master calendar and planner.
  4. Pack lunch.
  5. Load backpack.

- Cross off each task on the list or chart as it is completed.

4-7 (*continued*)

- Combine the above with a positive reinforcement system. If your child has all items complete and checked off by a certain time, he or she earns extra points or tokens as a reward. (2-1, 2-9, 2-14)

- Get your child a watch to wear and a clock that is accurate in his or her room. Providing your child with a watch that has an alarm is very helpful, especially if your child takes medication and needs to be reminded of when to go to the nurse's office during school.

- Use electronic devices with timers to help remember appointments, curfews, and keep on schedule.

- Consider "no phone call" times in the evening, as calls often interfere with staying on schedule.

- If organization and time management are areas of weakness for you, as well as your child, consider hiring an organizational coach.

RELATED LISTS

- See Lists 4-5 and 4-9.
- See Sources and Resources at the end of Lists 4-8 and 4-9.

4-8
HOMEWORK TIPS FOR TEACHERS

This list addresses ways that teachers can greatly assist ADHD students and their parents in homework success.

What to Be Aware of

- Children/teens with attention deficit disorders generally struggle with homework. This is a source of chronic stress and frustration in the home.

- See List 1-2 about executive function weaknesses and List 4-3 regarding ADHD and the struggle with organization, time management, and study skills.

- Keep in mind how much extra time it typically takes a student with ADHD to do the work. What takes an average child (without ADHD) about 15–20 minutes to complete, can easily take at least two or three times as long for this child (even with strong parental support, supervision, and assistance).

- Be responsive to parents reporting great frustration regarding homework and willing to make adjustments so that students with ADHD and/or learning disabilities (LD) spend a reasonable (not excessive) amount of time doing their homework.

- Realize that students with ADHD who receive medication during the school day (to help them focus and stay on-task) are often not receiving medication benefits in the late afternoon or evening hours. It is an *unreasonable* expectation that parents be able to get their child to produce at home at night what you were not able to get the student to produce all day at school.

Things to Avoid

- Avoid sending home unfinished classwork. Instead, provide the necessary modifications and supports so that in-school work is in-school work, and homework is homework.

- Avoid assigning homework involving new information that the student is supposed to figure out on his or her own, or that parents are expected to teach their children. Homework should be a time for *reviewing and practicing* what students have been taught in class.

- Avoid assigning "busy work." Make the homework relevant and purposeful so that time is not spent on obscure assignments that are not helping to reinforce skills or concepts you have taught.

- Avoid assigning homework as a punishment or consequence for misbehavior at school.

- Avoid unnecessary copying, recopying, or expectations for high standards of neatness with your ADHD and/or LD students.

- Avoid assigning homework that is not collected, checked, or returned with feedback.

4-8 (*continued*)

Support and Structure

- Make sure you have explained the homework, provided clear guidelines, and clarified any questions.

- Provide many structural supports for long-term projects/assignments, including clear guidelines for the project and help with time management. See Lists 3-5 and 4-6 about chunking large projects into manageable increments, due dates, and timely assistance and feedback.

- One of the most important things you can do to help *all* students (and their parents) keep on top of homework, tests, and long-term projects is to *require* use of an assignment calendar/sheet/planner. Then *guide, walk-through*, and *monitor* the recording of assignments. If this is a daily expectation and routine, it will help everyone. See the assignment sheet example in the Appendix.

- Require and help walk through the recording of all homework assignments in the student planner, calendar, or assignment sheet.

- Check and initial the assignment calendar/sheet/planner.

- Supervise ADHD students before they walk out the door at the end of the day. Make sure they have materials, books, and assignments recorded and in their backpacks.

- Visually post homework assignments in addition to explaining them. Write the assignments in a consistent location of the classroom (corner of the board, chart stand).

- Keep a master copy of the assignment calendar/student planner up-to-date and accessible for students to copy. This is especially important for students who are pulled out of the classroom at times of the day, or may be absent or late to class for various reasons.

- Model recording of assignments on a transparency of their assignment sheet/calendar. Have students copy.

- Provide any needed modifications and accommodations. Ask yourself:
  - "What is the goal?"
  - "What do I want the student to learn from the assignment?"
  - "Can this child get the concepts without having to do all the writing?"
  - "Can this student practice the skills in an easier, more motivating format?"
  - "Can this child practice the skills doing fewer problems?"

- Think in terms of shortening, cutting the written workload, and reducing the amount of written output required. See List 5-12 for written output accommodations.

- Work with your school about the possibility of having supervised study halls, homework labs, tutorials, and other assistance available for students who need it.

Increase Communication

- Require that parents initial the assignment calendar daily. This system is a good way for you to communicate with parents, as well. You may write a few comments or notes to the parent on the assignment sheet and vice versa.

■ Communicate regularly with the parents of students who are falling behind in homework. Work out a system of letting the students and parents know that they are not getting the homework turned in. See examples of monitoring homework chart/form in the Appendix.

■ See List 4-6 for recommended strategies regarding long-term projects, assigning study buddies for homework clarification, and so on.

■ Communicate with other teachers on your team. Students who have several teachers are often assigned a number of tests, large projects, and reading assignments all at the same time from their different classes. Be sensitive to this. Stagger due dates and coordinate, whenever possible, with other teachers to avoid the heavy stress of everything being due at once.

■ Be sure to collect homework and give some feedback. It is very frustrating for students and parents to spend a lot of time on assignments that the teacher never bothers to even collect.

■ If your school has modernized home–school communication by providing homework hotlines, teacher web pages on school websites, and voice mail, use them regularly. Keep information to parents and students up-to-date.

Increase Motivation

■ Try to make the homework assignments more interesting. One way to add interest and increase motivation to work on homework is to build in the component of student choice; for example: "Select 3 of the 5 questions to answer." "Choose from topics A, B, or C."

■ Include some homework that incorporates an element of play or fun (such as a learning game to reinforce or practice a skill).

■ Write a goal of improvement in homework performance together with the student (and parent if possible).

  ▪ If, for example, the child turns in less than 50% of homework assignments during the typical week, the initial goal might be to turn in 70% of weekly assignments.

  ▪ Write the goal into a contract or daily report card, with rewards for achieving the goal.

  ▪ Gradually raise the goal/performance standard when appropriate.

  ▪ See Lists 2-1 and 2-9 for more information.

■ If using a daily report card or weekly report with a student, include ratings for the behavior ("Turned in homework," "Was prepared for class with homework and needed materials"). See the Appendix for examples and more information about daily report cards.

■ Reward students for completed and turned in homework. (Use extra points, tangible treats, "one free homework" pass, "one late homework without penalty" pass, special privileges, or whatever students find positively reinforcing. (2-2, Appendix)

More Helpful Tips

■ If you have extra copies of texts to loan parents, do so for those students who are always leaving the books they need at home or school.

4-8 (continued)

■ Offer the opportunity for in-school tutoring or extra help on subjects causing students difficulty.

■ Share strategies for parents to help with homework completion, organization, and time-management skills. Refer to Sources and Resources and Lists 4-5, 4-7, and 4-9.

■ Realize how *critical* it is for students with ADHD and/or learning disabilities to participate in extracurricular activities. They need every opportunity to develop areas of strength (athletics, arts/crafts, music), which will be their source of self-esteem and motivation. These after-school activities are as important to the child's development as academics.

■ Keep in mind when assigning homework that many students with learning/attention difficulties have tutors, work with other professionals in the community (counseling), and participate in additional academic training programs outside of school.

RELATED LISTS

■ See Lists 4-4 and 4-6 for additional recommended strategies and interventions that support homework success.

SOURCES AND RESOURCES

Dendy, Chris Zeigler. *Teaching Teens with ADD and ADHD*. Bethesda, MD: Woodbine House, 2000.

Flick, Grad L. *Homework Skills Improvement Kit*. Biloxi, MS: Seacoast Publications, 2001.

Rief, Sandra. *The ADD/ADHD Checklist*. Paramus, NJ: Prentice Hall, 1998.

Rief, Sandra, and Julie Heimburge. *How to Reach and Teach All Students in the Inclusive Classroom*. Paramus, NJ: The Center for Applied Research in Education, 1995.

Zentall, Sydney S., and Sam Goldstein. *Seven Steps to Homework Success*. Plantation, FL: Specialty Press, 1999.

4-9
HOMEWORK TIPS FOR PARENTS

In most homes of children/teens with ADHD, homework is problematic and a source of frustration for both the student and parents. This stems from the core symptoms and executive function difficulties associated with ADHD, which affect organization, time management, and study skills. (1-2, 1-5, 4-3)

The following are suggested strategies and tips to enable your child to be more successful in homework.

Note: If your child is on medication during the school day, but *cannot* get through the homework once the medication effects wear off, consult with your doctor. Many children with ADHD are more successful in their ability to do homework with a small dosage of medication in the late afternoon, or switching to a prescription that is a long-acting formula (and maintains its positive effects into the after-school hours).

Create a Better Work Environment

- Make sure your child has a quiet workspace with minimal distractions and where it is easy for you to supervise and monitor work production.
- Limit distractions in the home during homework hours (reduce unnecessary noise and activity; buffer from siblings).
- Help your child avoid distraction by turning off the television.
- If your teen has his or her own phone, restrict use during homework hours, and consider using an answering machine during these times.
- Some children prefer and are more effective working on homework in a location with you in the vicinity (such as the dining room table), rather than secluded in their room.
- Be sure your child has the necessary supplies handy. (See List 4-5 for the Homework Supply Kit recommendations.)
- Experiment with music softly playing in the background, which helps some children block auditory distractions and concentrate better. Try various types of instrumental music, environmental sounds, and music of your child's choice. (2-4, 3-9)
- Consider building a special homework study carrel designed to be bright, motivating to work in, and conducive to productivity. (See Zentall and Goldstein, 1999.)
- See List 4-5 for more strategies to organize your child's workspace, materials, and assist with time management.

Develop Homework Routine and Schedule

- Together with your child, establish a specific time and place for homework. In order to develop a homework habit, it is important to adhere to a homework schedule as closely and consistently as possible.

4-9 (continued)

- In scheduling, consider a variety of factors: extracurricular activities, medication effects at that time, meal and bedtimes, other chores and responsibilities, your availability to supervise/monitor, and your child's individual preferences and learning styles.

- Some children prefer and are more productive if they start homework shortly after they come home from school. Others need time to play, relax first, and then start homework later. However, it is recommended to *not* wait until the evening to get started.

- It is best to schedule homework, if possible, when you (or someone else) is available to supervise and monitor.

- See List 4-7 for more information.

Help with Preparation and Structure

- Expect your child to have all assignments recorded. Request the teacher's help in making sure all assignments are recorded daily. It is recommended to ask the teacher, if possible, to initial or sign the student calendar or assignment sheet.

- Be sure to follow through by reviewing the recorded assignments with your child.

- Emphasize the importance of not leaving school until your child has double-checked the assignment sheet/calendar and made sure the backpack is loaded with all books and materials needed to do the homework.

- Have your child take the phone numbers of a few responsible students who may be called if there is a question about school work. Ask the teacher to assign a responsible buddy for this purpose.

- Many schools are modernizing their communication systems with homework hotlines, recording daily assignments on teachers' voice mail, and establishing school websites with each teacher able to post assignments online.

- Examine assignment sheet/calendar with your child after school. Help with planning a "things to do" list of tasks for the evening. (See the Appendix.) Some prefer to do the easiest, quickest tasks/assignments first; others like to tackle the hardest ones first.

- Encourage your child to cross off tasks as they are accomplished.

- Help your child to first look over all homework assignments for the evening and organize materials needed before beginning.

- If your child frequently forgets to bring home textbooks, ask if you can borrow another set for home. If not, consider purchasing one.

- Assist your child in dividing assignments into smaller parts or segments that are more manageable and less overwhelming.

- The biggest struggle is keeping on top of those dreaded *long-range homework assignments* (reports, projects). This is something you will need to be vigilant about. Do the following:
  - Ask for a copy of the project requirements.
  - Post these at home and go over them together with your child.

- Write the due date on a master calendar.

- Plan how to break down the project into manageable chunks, scheduling steps along the way.

- Get started *at once* with going to the library, gathering resources, beginning the reading, and so forth.

Help During Homework

- Of course, the amount of direct assistance required during homework will depend upon the age and needs of your child.

- Be available to answer questions, provide support, and help your child stay on-task.

- Assist your child in *getting started* on assignments (reading the directions together; color highlighting the key words in the directions; doing the first few items together; observing as your child does the next problem/item on his or her own; and offering feedback/help if needed). Then get up and leave.

- Monitor and give feedback without doing all the work together. You want your child to attempt as much as possible independently.

- Even with younger children, try to get your child started, and then check and give feedback on small segments of his or her independent work (after every few problems, or one row completed). Being available to help and assist as needed is wonderful; however, try not to get in the habit of having your child rely on you overseeing every minute.

- As tempting as it may be, even when homework time is dragging on and on, do not do the work for your child.

- As homework supervisor and coach, praise your child for being on-task, getting to work, and taking responsibility. Give extra praise for accomplishment and progress.

- Positively reinforce with rewards, incentives, and other motivation techniques described below.

Increase Motivation and Work Production

- Use a kitchen timer to challenge your child to stay on-task, and reward work completed with relative accuracy during that time frame. Tell your child that you will come back to check his or her progress on homework when the timer rings.

- A "beat the clock" system is often effective in motivating children to complete a task before the timer goes off.

- Ask to see what your child has accomplished after a certain amount of time, or to show you when a particular assignment is done. Praise and reward work upon completion.

- One motivating tool for a "beat the clock" technique (and for self-monitoring and time-awareness) is the visual timer software *Time Timer* (see Sources and Resources).

- Help your child in setting up mini-goals of work completion (read *x* number of pages; finish writing one paragraph; complete a row of problems). When accomplishing the goal/task, your child is rewarded with a break and perhaps points/tokens or other reinforcer (if using a token economy system at home). (2-9, 2-12, 2-14)

4-9 (*continued*)

- Remind your child to do homework and offer incentives: "When you finish your homework, you can watch TV (or play a game)." (2-12)

- Allow your child a break between homework assignments. In fact, your child can reward him- or herself with a snack and play/exercise break after completing each assignment or two.

- A contract for a larger incentive/reinforcer may be worked out as part of a plan to motivate your child to persist and follow-through with homework: "If you have no missing or late homework assignments this next week, you will earn . . ." See the examples in the Appendix.

- Praise and compliment your child when he or she puts forth good effort.

- Avoid nagging and threatening. Instead use incentives to support and motivate your child through the difficult task of doing homework.

- Enforce consequences such as loss of points (on token economy/behavior-modification system) when your child fails to bring home needed assignments and materials to do the homework.

- Withhold privileges (no TV) until a reasonable amount of homework has been accomplished.

Other Ways Parents Can Help

- It is not your responsibility to correct all of your child's errors on homework or make him or her complete and turn in a perfect paper.

- If the homework is too confusing or difficult for your child to do (or for you to understand from the directions what is expected), let the teacher know.

- If homework is a frequent cause of battles, tears, and frustration in your home, seek help from the teacher. Make an appointment to discuss the homework problems, and request reasonable modifications and adjustments in homework assignments (such as reduced amount, or other written output accommodations). (3-5, 5-12)

- Have the child work a certain amount of time and then stop working on homework. Do not force your child to spend an excessive and inappropriate amount of time on homework. If you feel your child worked enough for one night, write a note to the teacher attached to the homework.

- Allow your child to dictate to you while you do the writing and recording of responses for him or her. These accommodations to help bypass writing difficulties are reasonable for children with ADHD. Speak to the teacher.

- Communicate with the teacher and try to come to a reasonable agreement about daily homework expectations. Remind the teacher that children with ADHD often take two or three times longer to output the same amount of work as their peers, and some of the homework demands might exceed your child's capacity without enormous stress.

- Let the teacher know your child's frustration and tolerance level in the evening. The teacher needs to be aware of the amount of time it takes your child to complete tasks, and what efforts you are making to help at home.

- Many students with ADHD need homework accommodations written into a 504 Plan or IEP. (7-1 through 7-4)

- If your child's teacher is not willing to make reasonable accommodations, go to the administrator.

- Encourage and help your child get in the habit of putting all books, notebooks, signed notes, and other necessary materials inside the backpack before bedtime.

- Place the backpack in a consistent location (such as by the front door) that your child cannot miss seeing or tripping over when leaving the house in the morning.

- It is common for students with ADHD to fail to turn in their finished work. Naturally, it is very frustrating to know your child struggled to do the work, and then never got credit for having done it. Supervise that completed work leaves the home and is in the notebook/backpack. You may want to arrange with the teacher a system for collecting the work immediately upon arrival at school.

- Help your child study for tests. Use memory strategies to increase recall and retention of material. Practice and study using a variety of multisensory formats. (4-1, 4-2)

- If your child struggles with reading, help by reading the material together or reading it to him or her. (5-3, 5-4, and 5-5)

- Help your child with reading and comprehending content area textbooks by photocopying the chapter of the book your child is studying. It is much easier to write notes directly on the pages; underline; or color-highlight key vocabulary, main ideas, and so forth.

- Ask for progress notes or use of a daily/weekly report card that keeps you apprised as to how your child is doing. See List 5-12 and the Appendix for information and examples.

- Communicate your expectations that homework is a priority. In today's busy society, many families are overextended with the number of extracurricular activities in which they are involved. If there is very little time in the late afternoon/evening to devote to schoolwork, perhaps you need to reexamine your commitments and activities. "Something has to give."

- Many parents find it very difficult to help their own child with schoolwork. If that is the case, find someone else who can. Consider hiring a tutor. Often a junior or senior high school student is ideal, depending on the need and age of your child. There are even services online that provide homework support and tutoring for a fee. If using such services, you will, of course, want to check references.

- Check out the wonderful resources for homework help available on the Internet. (See Sources and Resources.)

4-9 (*continued*)

■ Encourage your child and emphasize effort as the most important criteria when doing his or her homework.

RELATED LISTS

■ See Lists 4-4, 4-6, and 4-8 for homework, organization, and time-management strategies for teachers.

SOURCES AND RESOURCES

Academic Skills Center (http://www.sas.calpoly.edu/asc/ssl)

Barbee, Bruce (ed.) and presenters of the Academic Support Workshops, UCLA, College of Letters & Science Counseling. *The Essential Handbook for Academic Success Skills.* Dubuque, IA: Kendall/Hunt Publishing Co., 1998.

Bos, Candace S., and Sharon Vaughn. *Strategies for Teaching Students with Learning and Behavior Problems.* Boston: Allyn & Bacon, 1988.

Dendy, Chris Zeigler. *Teaching Teens with ADD and ADHD.* Bethesda, MD: Woodbine House, 2000.

Dyson, Marianne J. *Homework Help on the Internet.* New York: Scholastic, 2000.

Flick, Grad L. *Homework Skills Improvement Kit.* Biloxi, MS: Seacoast Publications, 2001.

Power, Thomas, James Karustis, and Dina Habbousha. *Homework Success for Children with ADHD.* New York: The Guilford Press, 2001.

Rief, Sandra. *The ADD/ADHD Checklist.* Paramus, NJ: Prentice Hall, 1998.

Shore, Kenneth. *Special Kids Problem Solver.* Paramus, NJ: Prentice Hall Press, 1998.

Time Timer—visual timer software (www.timetimer.com)

Zentall, Sydney S., and Sam Goldstein. *Seven Steps to Homework Success.* Plantation, FL: Specialty Press, 1999.

Section 5

Academic Difficulties in Reading, Writing, and Math

5-1

COMMON READING DIFFICULTIES IN CHILDREN AND TEENS WITH ATTENTION DEFICIT DISORDERS

Because of the inherent difficulties associated with poor executive functioning and sustaining focused attention to task, it is common for individuals with ADHD to have difficulty with recall and comprehension of reading material. Though they may have strong decoding and word-recognition skills (if they do not have the coexisting learning disability of dyslexia), and *appear* to be skilled readers, it is still most common to find that individuals with ADHD are generally not strategic readers and have "spotty" comprehension.

COMMON READING DIFFICULTIES

The following are common difficulties many children and teens with ADHD and/or learning disabilities experience with reading:

- *Limited range of strategies* to access as an independent reader.

- *Failure to utilize metacognitive strategies.* This refers to the practice of self-monitoring comprehension while reading the text by addressing errors in comprehension as soon as they arise. Many people with ADHD have difficulty with this due to executive function weaknesses. (1-2)

- *Failure to utilize internal language and self-talk* to actively engage the text, such as asking self:
  - "What is the main idea?"
  - "What is the author trying to say in this paragraph?"
  - "What does that remind me of?"
  - "What do I predict is going to happen next?"

- *Poor working memory*, resulting in limited recall of the reading material. Obviously, this also affects comprehension of the text (ability to summarize, retell, and respond to questions related to the reading).

- *Inattention* (being drawn off-task) while reading results in missing words and important details, which consequently, impede comprehension.

- *Difficulty with silent reading.* Individuals with ADHD often need to subvocalize or read quietly to themselves in order to hear their voice and maintain attention to what they are reading. If you observe students doing this, permit them to do so. Many stu-

5-1 (*continued*)

dents need the auditory input to stay focused, as they struggle to process the text through silent reading.

■ *Lack of a "schema" or structure* to guide students in figuring out the critical elements and main ideas of what they are reading.

Maintaining attention during whole-class instruction is an area of difficulty for many students with ADHD, resulting in the following:

■ They often struggle paying attention to stories and text being read out loud in class.

■ When one person is orally reading, it is common for students with ADHD to have a hard time following along with the rest of the class.

■ They are frequently on the wrong page of the book, and especially struggle to follow the reader if he or she lacks fluency and expression.

Points to Keep in Mind

■ It is often more beneficial for the teacher to first read the text with fluency and expression to the entire class, and then have students reread with partners or small groups.

■ It is also helpful to first have students read passages along with a partner or a small group, and then reread sections in a large-group setting.

■ If possible, seat ADHD students among well-focused students during this part of instruction.

■ A large percentage of individuals with ADHD report having difficulty maintaining their train of thought while reading. Though they may have excellent decoding skills and fluency, their high level of distractibility impedes them from processing the information. This problem is compounded if the student is presented with dry, uninteresting, or difficult material.

■ Students with ADHD report having to reread the material numerous times. Metacognitive strategies and techniques, such as reciprocal teaching, brief note-taking, summarizing, and self-questioning, are helpful strategies to teach students. Any techniques that require active involvement and thinking about/responding to what is being read help maintain focus and attention.

■ There are numerous strategies that can be employed to engage students in the reading process. Many students with ADHD benefit greatly from explicit instruction in various reading comprehension and learning strategies—being taught *how to* be strategic, active readers/thinkers. (4-2, 5-5)

■ Difficulty visually focusing on the print and losing their place when reading (tracking) is a common problem for students with ADHD. Encourage students to use strips of cardboard for markers or to use their finger to track, if needed. Some students may benefit from using a "window box" (or card with a cut-out opening large enough to view a limited number of words at a time).

ADHD AND LEARNING DISABILITIES

■ Roughly 30–60% of children with ADHD also have specific learning disabilities. Among the various learning disabilities, reading disorders are most common. Some children have specific processing deficiencies (auditory or visual perception, short-term memory, phonological awareness, receptive/expressive language) that affect their acquisition of reading skills. Dyslexia is the most common reading disorder and is language-based, usually characterized by a deficit in phonological processing.

■ Many struggling readers lack fluency because they are unable to recognize many words at the automatic level—even the most common, high-frequency words. Therefore, they attempt to sound out every word, resulting in slow, choppy reading and difficulty processing the information.

■ It is very common for those who struggle with reading to be weak in phonetic word attack and word-identification skills (decoding). This results in slow, labored reading and lack of fluency. Such students may benefit greatly from the following:

- Intensive intervention in phonological awareness

- Systematic and explicit instruction in phonics and decoding skills

- Learning how to see and recognize the structure and common patterns in words

- Learning how to apply strategies for independently decoding new, unfamiliar words

- A well-designed program of instruction that uses a variety of multisensory strategies and mnemonics. (See Sources and Resources in Lists 5-3 and 5-10.)

■ Poor readers who struggle to decode unfamiliar words are generally weak in one or more of the cueing systems, knowing how to use:

- Semantic clues ("Does that make sense?")

- Syntactic clues ("Does that sound right grammatically?")

- Grapho-phonic clues ("What does that word look like?" "How do I sound out that word?")

■ Fairly recently, the converging evidence based on 30 years of research into reading has become available. Numerous studies investigated:

- How children learn to read

- Why some children struggle in learning how to read

- What can be done to prevent reading difficulties

RESEARCH AND READING DIFFICULTIES

■ An abundance of research has revealed that phonological awareness is absolutely critical. It is now known that children who have reading difficulties in first grade and higher have often never acquired the necessary auditory skills of phonological awareness needed in order to decode or read print. Phonemic and phonological awareness are actually prerequisite skills to reading.

5-1 (*continued*)

■ One of the main sources of the current information is that obtained from the National Institute of Child Health and Human Development (NICHD), National Institutes of Health. The high rate of illiteracy and reading difficulties in the United States (about 17–20% of the population) is not only considered an educational problem, but a major public health problem as well.

■ To address this issue, the NICHD has supported scientific research continuously since 1965 to understand normal reading development and reading difficulties. NICHD developed a research network consisting of 41 research sites in North America (and other parts of the world), which conducted numerous studies on thousands of children, many over a period of years.

Note: The findings from this wealth of research were presented as testimony by G. Reid Lyon, Ph.D. (Chief of the Child Development and Behavior Branch of the NICHD, National Institutes of Health) to the Committee on Labor and Human Resources, U.S. Senate, in 1998. He states:

> In the initial stages of reading development, learning phoneme awareness and phonics skills and practicing these skills with texts is critical. Children must also acquire fluency and automaticity in decoding and word recognition. Consider that a reader has only so much attention and memory capacity. If beginning readers read the words in a laborious, inefficient manner, they cannot remember what they read, much less relate the ideas to their background knowledge. Thus, the ultimate goal of reading instruction for children to understand and enjoy what they read may not be achieved. (2000)

In addition, more research findings on this topic come from the Committee on the Prevention of Reading Difficulties in Young Children, National Research Council. This committee was entrusted by the National Academy of Sciences to conduct a study of the effectiveness of interventions for young children who might be predisposed to reading difficulties. This committee reviewed several factors:

■ Normal reading development and instruction

■ Risk factors useful in identifying groups and individuals at risk of reading failure

■ Prevention, intervention, and instructional approaches to ensuring optimal reading outcomes

The results of its research findings is found in *Preventing Reading Difficulties in Young Children*. (See Sources and Resources.)

INFORMATION BASED ON RESEARCH

The following includes some of what is now known based on the scientific evidence. If interested in more information, refer to the Sources and Resources.

- Failure to read proficiently is the most likely reason that students drop out, get retained, or are referred to special education.

- Approximately 50% of reading difficulties can be prevented if students are provided effective language development in preschool and kindergarten, and effective reading instruction in the primary grades.

- There is a very strong association between a child's ability to read, and his or her ability to segment words into phonemes (hear and separate a spoken word into its individual sounds—"pig" as /p/ /i/ /g/).

- Kindergarten children's phonemic awareness can predict their levels of reading and spelling achievement even years later. It is a more powerful predictor of reading progress than IQ.

- By providing explicit instruction in alphabetic code, sound-spellings, and phonemic awareness, we may prevent many children from needing to enter special education programs. (As many as 80% of referrals to special education involve reading difficulties.)

- Learning letter–sound correspondence (necessary for reading and spelling) requires an awareness that spoken language can be analyzed into strings of separable words. These words are comprised of sequences of syllables; and syllables are made up of smaller units of sounds (phonemes).

- Most children with severe reading difficulties have substantial weakness in auditory-related skills (such as phonemic awareness), and associating those sounds with the printed letter (sound–symbol relationships).

- The most frequent characteristic observed among children and adults with reading disabilities is a slow, labored approach to decoding or "sounding-out'" unknown or unfamiliar words and frequent misidentification of familiar words.

- Children who are most at risk for reading failure enter kindergarten limited in their awareness of sound structure and language pattern, phonemic sensitivity, letter knowledge, and the purposes of reading, and have had little exposure to books and print.

- Effective prevention and early intervention programs can increase the reading skills of 85–90% of poor readers to average levels.

RELATED LISTS

- Lists 4-2 and 5-5 address the most necessary strategies for students with ADHD—reading comprehension and learning strategies that actively engage processing and interaction with the text.

- List 5-2 details the characteristics and types of skills and strategies employed by "good readers."

5-1 (*continued*)

- List 5-3 addresses the strategies that are also important for students with coexisting language disorders and dyslexia—building vocabulary and word recognition skills.

- List 5-4 contains additional strategies, techniques, and reading interventions.

SOURCES AND RESOURCES

Adams, M. J. *Beginning to Read: Thinking and Learning About Print.* Cambridge, MA: MIT Press, 1990.

Blake, Kevin. "Two Common Reading Problems Experienced by Many AD/HD Adults," CHADD: *Attention*, vol. 6, no. 5, May/June 2000, 30–36.

The California Reading Initiative and Special Education in California—Critical Ideas Focusing on Meaningful Reform, developed by the Special Education Reading Task Force, the California Department of Education, and the California State Board of Education. Sacramento: California Department of Education, 1999. See the full document at: www.cde.ca.gov/spbranch/sed/resources.htm.

Dendy, Chris A. Zeigler. "5 Components of Executive Function and How they Impact School Performance," CHADD: *Attention*, vol. 8, no. 4, February 2002, 26–32.

Feldman, Kevin. *Ensuring All Students Learn to Read Well: Linking Research to Practice in Effective Reading Programs.* Sonoma County, CA: Sonoma County SELPA, 2000.

Foorman B. R., D. J. Francis, J. M. Fletcher, C. Schatschneider, and P. Mehta. "The Role of Instruction in Learning to Read: Preventing Reading Failure in At-Risk Children," *Journal of Educational Psychology*, 90, 115; 1998.

Good, R. H., D. C. Simmons, and S. B. Smith. "Effective Academic Intervention in the United States: Evaluating and Enhancing the Acquisition of Early Reading Skills," *School Psychology Review*, 27 (1), 45–56; 1998.

Honig, Bill. "Reading the Right Way," *CORE Reading Research Anthology.* Novato, CA: Arena Press, Consortium on Reading Excellence, Inc., 1999.

Lyon, G. R. "Overview of Reading and Literacy Initiatives," testimony provided to the Committee on Labor and Human Resources, United States Senate. Bethesda, MD: National Institute of Child Health and Human Development, 1998.

Lyon, G. Reid. "The NICHD Research Program in Reading Development, Reading Disorders and Reading Instruction: A Summary of Research Findings," publication from *Keys to Successful Learning: A National Summit on Research in Learning Disabilities.* New York: The National Center for Learning Disabilities, 1999.

Lyon, G. Reid. "Why Reading Is Not a Natural Process," *Educational Leadership*, 55 (6), 14–18; 1998. Also found in *LDA Newsbriefs*, Learning Disabilities Association of America, LD Online Reading, 2000; www.ldonline.org/ld_indepth/reading/reading.html or www.ldonline.org/ld-indepth/reading/why-reading-is-not.html

Rief, Sandra. *Ready . . . Start . . . School: Nurturing and Guiding Your Child Through Preschool and Kindergarten*. Paramus, NJ: Prentice Hall Press, 2000.

Simmons, D. C., and E. J. Kame'enui. *What Reading Research Tells Us About Children with Diverse Learning Needs: Bases and Basics*. Mahwah, NJ: Lawrence Erlbaum Associates, 1998.

Slavin, R., N. Karweit, and B. Wasik. "Preventing Early School Failure: What Works?" *Educational Leadership*, 50 (4), 10–17; 1993.

Snow, Catherine E., Susan M. Burns, and Peg Griffin (eds.). *Preventing Reading Difficulties in Young Children*, National Research Council. Washington, DC: National Academy Press, 1998.

Torgesen, J. K. "Catch Them Before They Fall," *American Educator*, 22 (1 and 2), 32–39; 1998.

5-2
THE READING PROCESS: WHAT GOOD READERS DO

Reading is a complex process with the goal to acquire meaning from the printed word. "Good readers":

- Decode and recognize words at a rate that enables them to read with fluency and automaticity.

- Use all cueing systems (semantic, syntactic, and grapho-phonic) to figure out unfamiliar words or language.

- Understand and figure out challenging vocabulary and word meanings.

- Know how to read for specific purposes.

- Use whatever background or prior knowledge they have about the subject to make inferences and get meaning out of what they are reading.

- Make connections as they read the text to other books previously read, to their own life and experiences, and to other information/concepts they know ("This reminds me of . . .").

- Reflect as they read.

- Utilize effective metacognitive strategies to think about what they are reading, and self-monitor their comprehension and understanding.

- Check for their own comprehension and use self-correcting ("fix-up") strategies when realizing they are not getting meaning or making sense of what is being read.

- Constantly predict and either confirm or change their predictions as they read.

- Understand organization and structure for different types of text (narrative and expository).

- Understand organization/story structure (characters, setting, problem, action, resolution to problem) to aid comprehension of literary text.

- Understand the structures or schemas for various kinds of expository text.

- Visualize when they are reading (scenes, characters), and make mental images.

- Distinguish main ideas and important information from details and less important information in the text.

- Summarize and paraphrase after determining the key ideas of material read.

- Focus on the main content.

- Recognize and understand cause/effect, fact/opinion, and compare/contrast relationships.

- Make inferences and draw conclusions.
- Read from a variety of genres (such as mystery, historical fiction, folktales, biographies, science fiction, and fantasy).
- Self-select books of personal interest and find pleasure in reading books of choice.
- Apply a host of strategies in the process of actively reading for meaning.

RELATED LISTS

- See Lists 4-2, 5-1, 5-2, 5-3, 5-4, and 5-5 for a host of strategies to teach and build skills in all of the above.

5-3
STRATEGIES FOR BUILDING WORD RECOGNITION, READING VOCABULARY, AND FLUENCY

Lack of fluency in reading interferes with comprehension. In order to become a fluent reader, the child must first become skilled at decoding the printed word. Students who struggle to figure out unknown words and have poor word recognition (decoding skills) need direct instruction with strategies and interventions as early as possible.

Because many students with ADHD also have the learning disability "dyslexia," they need to be identified and provided with specialized instruction designed to build their reading skills. However, certainly not all children who have poor decoding skills and lack fluency are dyslexic. These students may have had minimal phonics and word analysis instruction, and simply may not have sufficiently been taught these skills and strategies.

BENEFITS OF DECODING PRINT

Students who receive help in learning how to decode print (in order to become fluent readers) benefit from the following:

- Phonemic awareness (the auditory recognition of individual sounds and the ability to manipulate those sounds)

- Alphabet knowledge

- Letter–sound association for all consonants, vowels, consonant blends (*br, sl*); consonant digraphs (*ch, sh*); vowel digraphs (*ai, oa, ea*) and diphthongs (*oi, ou*); r-controlled vowels (*ir, er, ur, or, ar*)

- Word families, onsets, and rimes [-*ack* words (*black, stack, quack, pack, Jack*)]. *Note:* Onsets are the letters before the vowel (*bl, st, qu*). Rimes are the vowel and following letters in single-syllable words (*ack*).

- Structural analysis of words (awareness of word parts such as root words, compounds, prefixes/suffixes)

- Strategies for decoding multisyllabic words (first breaking the word into syllables and using phonic analysis to decode each syllable)

RECOGNIZING WORDS IN PRINT

Children who struggle to identify words need to be taught different strategies and cueing systems to recognize words in print:

■ *Semantic clues:* Determining if the word makes sense in the context of what is being read, and being able to self-correct (substitute a different word if it does not make sense).

■ *Syntactic clues:* Determining if the word sounds right grammatically, and being able to self-correct (substitute a different word that does grammatically fit in the context of what is being read).

■ *Grapho-phonic clues:* Using recognition of the printed letters (graphemes) and their corresponding sounds (phonemes) to figure out a particular word. Phonetic awareness of the sound associations for consonants, vowels, digraphs, and so on is critical in word recognition. So is the ability to take isolated sounds and blend them into words.

Children with reading disabilities are generally deficient in one or more of their cueing processes. They typically struggle with grapho-phonics and need a highly multisensory approach (using all of their senses) that incorporates mnemonic (memory) clues to help them learn and remember the sound–symbol associations.

Note: There are excellent programs and multisensory strategies that teach in this format and have a high success rate with children who have learning disabilities affecting their ability to read and spell. The following programs are also listed under Sources and Resources:

■ *Orton-Gillingham*

■ *Lindamood-Bell*

■ *Wilson Reading System*

■ *Project Read Language Circle—Phonology, Corrective Reading*

■ *Language!*

■ *Rewards*

■ *Stevenson Program*

Most research-validated reading programs for children with reading disabilities in decoding skills incorporate systematic instruction in phonics, direct instruction, and mnemonics (memory devices).

Many elementary schools use *Reading Recovery* (see Sources and Resources), a research-validated intervention in helping young readers learn and practice the cueing systems to figure out unknown words in the text.

LEARNING WORD RECOGNITION

Word-recognition instruction also involves teaching students the following:

■ *Observing word patterns:* Teach students how words can be grouped by rhyming sound families or visual patterns (rock/stock/flock, right/might/flight/bright) to build proficiency in reading and spelling. These are called "word families" or "onset and rimes."

5-3 (*continued*)

- *Structural clues:* Help students by directly teaching them structural analysis (recognition of prefixes, suffixes, base words, and their meanings). Focusing on the visual configuration of the word is a useful strategy for many readers. ("Does this word look like any other word I know?") Knowing how to break down a word into its component parts and syllables is crucial to word recognition.

- *Sight-word recognition:* A fluent reader must identify high-frequency words at an automatic level. Most can recall words commonly found in print, generally learning through a whole word approach. High-frequency words and words that cannot be sounded out phonetically are taught this way. Many struggling readers (especially with visual-sequential memory problems) do not have a large bank of words they know at the automatic level. The teacher must provide frequent practice in motivating game formats, through multisensory strategies, and *color* to help lock these words into the memory bank for instant recognition. (4-1, 5-10)

BUILDING A READING VOCABULARY

There are numerous strategies for building students' word banks and improving their recognition and understanding of reading vocabulary:

- "Word Sorts," a popular instructional technique for studying words and focusing on elements that are the same or different. Sort words into two or three categories according to features of the word (such as sounds within the word: long/short a, br/bl, ou/oi; different pronunciations of "ed" endings—walked, chilled, folded).

- Label words in the environment.

- Have children maintain their own card file of vocabulary words they are learning or have mastered.

- Use charts, posters, word walls, and as many visual displays as possible to enable children to recognize the printed word and its meaning.

INCREASING FLUENCY

The following are some recommended techniques for increasing fluency and practicing oral reading.

Choral Reading

- Have everyone in the class or group read together at the same time. This is an excellent strategy when using a short piece to focus on.

  1. Make a transparency of a poem or passage from the text (such as a humorous poem).

2. Model the oral reading with expression and fluency.

3. Have students read it together in unison in different variations (every other verse, line, boys/girls, left/right side of room, and so forth).

Cloze Technique

Read (or reread) a passage orally to the class, leaving out key words. The students fill in the missing words aloud.

Mirror (Echo) Reading

1. Read aloud while students follow along visually (in their book or on an overhead transparency).

2. After reading a sentence or part of a passage, have the students repeat it.

3. Stop model-reading after a few paragraphs or pages, and have students orally reread certain passages.

Repeated Readings

1. Provide a short, interesting passage.

2. Have students read and reread the passage until they achieve a certain level of fluency.

3. Have students record their progress on a graph, noting the fewer number of errors they make as they become more fluent in reading the passage.

4. Have students tape-record their improved reading fluency, which is very motivating.

5. Check out the reading program *Read Naturally* (see Sources and Resources) for building fluency.

Reread in a Variety of Situations

The process of rereading passages that have already been heard before increases fluency and comprehension, and is particularly helpful for students with reading difficulties. In response to teacher prompts and questioning, have students locate specific information and orally reread those passages. Try rereading in different formats:

- With partners
- Individually
- In small groups
- Into a tape recorder
- In unison (choral)
- With an adult (teacher, aide, parent volunteer)

5-3 (continued)

Buddy or Partner Reading

Have students read orally with partners, either in unison or alternating between paragraphs or pages. Try the following:

1. Have students share one book that is placed between them.

2. One reader points to the words while the other is following along.

3. Roles are then reversed.

4. Partners help each other with words and suggest strategies for figuring out unfamiliar words.

5. Partners question each other, discuss readings, and summarize.

6. Assign questions that each pair of students will need to be able to answer at the end of the reading assignment to encourage focused attention.

Improving Silent Reading

Another important strategy for building reading skills is to incorporate a period of uninterrupted time for everyone to be engaged in reading self-selected material at their independent reading level. In schools, this has a variety of names including Sustained Silent Reading (SSR) or DEAR (Drop Everything and Read). For those students who cannot read silently, they may be allowed to listen to a book on tape while following along at a listening post.

INDEPENDENT READING

This is an important component of a balanced literacy program. Rich classroom libraries containing various levels and genres of books are essential for enabling all students to access and select books of choice at each of their independent levels. Independent reading is critical for building fluency, but the book selected must be at an appropriate "independent level."

- One method of quickly determining if a book meets the criteria is the "Five-Finger Check":
  - The student reads one page from the book, holding up a finger when coming to a word he or she can't read.
  - If there are more than five fingers up, the book is too hard for independent reading.
- Another method is "One in Twenty":
  - Select a passage from a child's chosen book to read orally.
  - If the child makes less than one error in twenty words, the reading material is at the independent level.

During independent reading time, teachers generally have individual reading conferences with some of the students, which involve discussion and asking questions about their books.

VOCABULARY ENHANCEMENT

Some children with ADHD have language disorders as well, and may be weak in vocabulary skills and usage. Vocabulary can be taught through the following techniques and methods:

- Use a direct definition.
- Explain through words that are the same (synonyms) or opposite (antonyms).
- Use a description or metaphor.
- Teach the word through examples and non-examples.
- Use context clues.
- Instruct students to use a dictionary, glossary, or thesaurus to find the meaning.
- Read to students and provide other language experiences that will expose them to rich vocabulary.

Points to Keep in Mind

- A number of students have difficulty with the language/vocabulary of books at their grade level. However, all children should have the opportunity to hear and discuss literature and expository text that is interesting, motivating, and at a challenging level.
- Although the vocabulary may be difficult, a nonproficient reader can equally participate in reading of grade-level material through shared reading, read-alouds, teacher-guided reading, and the host of reading-comprehension strategies in which students collaboratively read the text. (5-4, 5-5)

SOURCES AND RESOURCES

Archer, Anita L., Mary M. Gleason, and Vicky Vachon. *Rewards (Reading Excellence: Word Attack & Rate Development Strategies)*. Longmont, CO: Sopris West, 2000.

Bear, D. R., M. Invernizzi, S. Templeton, and F. Johnston. *Words Their Way*. Columbus, OH: Merrill/Prentice Hall, 1996.

Bell, Nanci. *Visualizing and Verbalizing*. Paso Robles, CA: Academy of Reading Publications, 1991.

Blachowicz, Camille, and Peter Fisher. *Teaching Vocabulary in All Classrooms*. Paramus, NJ: Prentice Hall, 1996.

5-3 (*continued*)

Bornstein, Scott J. *Memory Techniques for Vocabulary Mastery.* Canoga Park, CA: Bornstein Memory Improvement Programs, 1988.

Brill, Sharon. *Literacy Made Easy: A Systematic Program for Children with Dyslexia and Other Reading and Writing Difficulties.* San Diego, CA: Educational Resource Specialists, 2002. (available at www.sandrarief.com)

Carnie, D. W., J. Silbert, and E. J. Kameenui. *Direct Instruction in Reading.* Columbus, OH: Merrill/Prentice Hall, 1997.

Clay, Marie. *Reading Recovery Program.* (www.readingrecovery.org)

Consortium on Reading Excellence, Inc. (CORE). *Literacy Training Manual.* Emeryville, CA: CORE, Inc., 1998. (www.coreread.com)

Cunningham, Patricia, and Dorothy Hall. *Working with Words—Month by Month Phonics.* Greensboro, NC: Carson-Dellosa Publishing Co., 1997.

Engleman, Zig et al., *Reading Mastery.* DeSoto, TX: SRA/McGraw-Hill (no date). (www.sra4kids.com)

Greene, Jane Fell. *Language!* 2nd edition. Longmont, CO: Sopris West, 2001.

Greene, Victoria E., and Mary Lee Enfield. *Project Read—Language Circle.* Bloomington, MN: Language Circle Enterprise, 1994.

Herrell, Adrienne. *Fifty Strategies for Teaching English Language Learners.* Upper Saddle River, NJ: Merrill, 2000.

Johnson, Gary, and Zig Engleman. *Corrective Reading.* DeSoto, TX: SRA/McGraw-Hill, 1978, 1980, 1988, 1989, 1999. (www.sra4kids.com)

Lindamood-Bell Learning Processes, San Luis Obispo, California (http://www.lblp.com)

Pinnell, Gay S., and Irene C. Fountas. *Word Matters.* Portsmouth, NH: Heinemann, 1998.

Read Naturally, St. Paul, Minnesota (www.readnaturally.com)

Recordings for the Blind and Dyslexic, Princeton, New Jersey (www.rfbd.org)

Rief, Sandra, and Julie Heimburge. *How to Reach and Teach All Students in the Inclusive Classroom.* Paramus, NJ: The Center for Applied Research in Education, 1996.

Stevenson, Nancy. *The Stevenson Program.* Attleboro Falls, MA: Stevenson Learning Skills, Inc., 1978, 1998.

Stockdale, C., and C. Possin. *Solving Reading Problems.* East Moline, IL: LinguiSystems, Inc., 2000.

Vurnakes, C. *Vocabulary Development: Using Roots and Riddles.* Torrance, CA: Frank Schaefer Publications, 1996.

Wilson, Barbara. *Wilson Reading System* (www.Wilsonlanguage.com)

5-4
READING TIPS AND STRATEGIES
FOR PARENTS

Try to read *to* and *with* your child every day. You can do "shared reading" in a number of ways.

■ Take turns reading the paragraphs or pages. For example, you read the pages to the left of the book, and your child reads the pages on the right.

■ Read together in unison with your child, with you as the lead reader running your finger under the words.

■ Try the following technique:

1. First, read a portion of the text ranging from a sentence or two to an entire paragraph.

2. Read at a normal rate while moving your finger smoothly under the words as your son or daughter watches.

3. Then read the same sentences or paragraph together while continuing to point to the words.

4. Finally, have your child read the same sentence or passage alone, as you listen and support with difficult words, as needed.

■ When listening to your son or daughter read, do not stop to correct or make your child sound out every single word. Coach your child in using different "cueing strategies." For example, when approaching a tricky word that your child cannot figure out, prompt to pass over that word and read to the end of the sentence. Then see if your child can go back and figure out the unfamiliar word. Ask questions such as:

• "Does that make sense?"

• "Did that sound right to you?"

• "What other word beginning with that sound would make sense here?"

■ If your child has the tendency to forget to bring books home from school, causing homework problems, consider purchasing or borrowing another set of books for home use.

■ Distractible children often lose their place easily while reading, so provide a bookmark to help keep their place. You might also block the page partially by placing a piece of cardboard, paper, or index card over part of the page.

■ Check out books on tape from your local library. If your child is receiving special education services due to reading disabilities, he or she is entitled to a service of being provided books on tape through Recordings for the Blind and Dyslexic. Contact the organization directly or ask your local chapter of the Learning Disabilities Association (LDA) for information on how you can apply for this service (see Sources and Resources).

5-4 (*continued*)

- Encourage your son or daughter to read to a younger child.

- Increase the motivation to read by allowing your child to choose material he or she is interested in.

- Remember that struggling readers are easily intimidated by lengthy books with few illustrations. Try these wonderful options:

  - Picture books that are interesting and appropriate for older children

  - Joke and riddle books

  - Comic books and magazines

  - Reference books with color pictures and short reading passages

  - Sheet music with lyrics of favorite songs and poetry

- Have your child participate in school book clubs, purchasing inexpensive books of choice on a regular basis. Purchase your child a subscription to a magazine (such as *Sports Illustrated for Kids, Ranger Rick, Cricket*).

- Consult with librarians and children's bookstore employees about popular titles and books that tap into your child's interests.

- Explore websites (see Sources and Resources) for more information about children's books and recommendations.

- Photocopy a chapter/unit from your child's textbook to make it easier to study the text. Encourage your child to color-highlight key information and take notes directly on those photocopied pages. For example, important vocabulary and definitions can be highlighted in one color (yellow); the main ideas can be highlighted another color (orange); and so forth.

RELATED LISTS

- Most children and teens with ADHD will particularly benefit from learning and applying reading comprehension and study strategies found in Lists 4-2 and 5-5.

- See all lists in the reading section as they provide information and specific strategies for both teachers and parents to help build reading proficiency.

SOURCES AND RESOURCES

Websites

American Library Association, 800-545-2433
www.ala.org/parents/index.html

Association for Library Service to Children, 800-545-2433
www.ala.org/alsc

Learning Disabilities Association, 412-341-1515
www.ldanatl.org

Parent's Picks
www.parentsoup.com/onlineguide/parentspicks/web.html

Recordings for the Blind and Dyslexic
www.rfbd.org

Video and Book

Rief, Sandra. *How to Help Your Child Succeed in School: Strategies and Guidance for Parents of Children with Learning Disabilities and/or ADHD.* San Diego, CA: Educational Resource Specialists; 800-682-3528; www.sandrarief.com. (This video demonstrates many of the above strategies, as well as others for helping your child in reading, math, writing, and homework.)

Rief, Sandra. *Ready . . . Start . . . School—Nurturing and Guiding Your Child Through Preschool and Kindergarten.* Paramus, NJ: Prentice Hall Press, 2001.

5-5
STRATEGIES FOR READING COMPREHENSION

It is vital that students with ADHD be actively engaged in the reading process, or they will struggle with reading comprehension. (5-1) They must be taught explicit strategies that develop their use of metacognition, and be involved in techniques to help them interact with the reading material.

To read for meaning and to gain comprehension, there are a number of strategies that are helpful and effective *prior to* reading (prereading), *during* reading, and *after* completing (postreading) the reading assignment.

READING COMPREHENSION STRATEGIES

Prereading Strategies

Prereading strategies are important for activating the reader's prior knowledge about the topic, building connections and comprehension of the text, and generating interest and the motivation to read the material.

■ Prior to reading, relate the story or reading material to the students' experience and background knowledge through class discussions, brainstorming, and charting prior knowledge ("What do we already know about . . . ?").

■ Set the stage and establish the purpose for what students are about to read; for example: "As you read, think about what you would do if . . ."

■ Lead the class through making/listing predictions prior to reading.

■ Generate interest and increase students' background knowledge and frame of reference before reading by using concrete objects and audio–visuals related to the topic of study (maps, music, photos, video).

■ Give time to students to preview the key information in the text (illustrations, captions, headings, chapter questions) before reading through the chapter/text. Previewing can also involve students listening to passages read aloud first before independently studying and rereading.

■ To activate prior knowledge, ask students to write down everything they know about the topic in their "learning log."

■ Discuss selected vocabulary that may be challenging for students.

■ Link prior knowledge to new concepts and information that will be studied. Use advanced organizers, anticipation guides, and other strategies such as KWL and semantic maps (as described later).

During-Reading Strategies

These should be taught and modeled in order to encourage the student to think about and interact with the reading material. This is crucial for comprehension and maintaining focus on text.

- Teach students how to paraphrase a paragraph, putting into their own words the main idea and significant details. Some students find that paraphrasing each paragraph and stating it into a tape recorder is a very helpful technique.

- Teach textbook structure (significance of bold print, italic print, headings, and subheadings).

- Teach how to find introductory paragraphs and summary paragraphs.

- Teach students how to rephrase main ideas and headings into their own words.

- Teach how to find the subject and main ideas, and sift out the key facts and important details from the irrelevant and redundant words/text.

- Provide students with a pad of self-stick notes. As they are reading, they can jot down notes, vocabulary words (to clarify), and questions by items they do not understand. The self-stick paper can be placed directly next to key points and main ideas for fast/easy reference.

- Teach story mapping: identifying the setting (time/place), characters, conflicts and problems, action/events, climax, and resolution of conflicts.

- Use any of the instructional strategies involving students with collaborative reading and analysis of the material (such as Reciprocal Teaching, Literature Circles).

- Encourage students to activate their imaginations and visualize while reading. Have students illustrate the scenes they visualize.

- Encourage questioning and self-questioning while reading. In this critical step, the reader must ask such questions as: "Where does the story take place?" "What is the problem?" "What will the character do next?" "Why did she (he) say that?" "What's the main idea?" "Does this make sense?" "What is the point the author is trying to make?" "I wonder what I would do in that situation."

- Use teacher-directed guided reading, which involves setting a purpose; sharing prior knowledge; making predictions; having students read silently for a while to answer a question the teacher posed; and then having a discussion, using the text to validate responses.

- Allow students to subvocalize (or read aloud softly to themselves). This auditory feedback often helps them focus on the reading material.

- Schedule breaks to increase motivation and sustained attention during independent reading. For example, encourage the child to set mini-goals in pacing his or her reading. Have the child read to a certain point in the text or to read for a predetermined amount of time. After reading to that point, the child rewards himself/herself by taking a brief break.

5-5 (*continued*)

- Use partner reading and cooperative learning formats in reading texts.
- Use instructional strategies such as "think-pair-share" and other buddy reading techniques.
- Try using a reading marker or strip of cardboard with students who lose their place in reading and have difficulty visually focusing on text.
- Teach clustering and webbing/semantic mapping to pull out the main idea and supporting details from the text.
- Enlarge a page of the book and make a transparency of it. Have students come up to the overhead and locate certain information by underlining it.
- Photocopy chapter pages and have students highlight important information.
- Provide study guides to aid in looking for key information in the text.
- Underline or circle important points in text.
- Color-code a master textbook for lower readers; for example: one color for vocabulary, another color for definitions, and a third color for important facts and topic sentences.
- Tape-record textbooks for individual use or group listening at a listening post. Use a good quality tape and a recorder with counter numbers. For ease in following text, have clear signals on the tape for when to turn the page, or include periodically on the recording the chapter and page number. Pages can be marked with the counter number at the beginning of each chapter.

Postreading Strategies

After-reading strategies should be utilized to involve the student in deeper thinking and exploration of the reading material:

- Use the information to complete filling out charts and graphic organizers.
- Have deep discussions about the concepts or events in the text, or in character analysis.
- Make connections through related writing activities.
- Do further extension activities related to the theme and content of the reading to apply the learning.

Many of the strategies used during reading are also continued or completed after the reading.

BUILDING READING COMPREHENSION

The following are a number of research-validated instructional formats and strategies that are highly effective in building reading comprehension.

Graphic Organizers (Graphic Outlines or Graphic Aids)

Numerous graphic displays can accompany reading of literature and textbook material to aid comprehension. These help students recognize and organize information in the book, and guide critical thinking by creating a graphic representation of the text.

- *Framed outlines*—Give students copies of a teacher-prepared outline that contains missing information. As they read, or later through subsequent discussion, students fill in the missing information. Ideally, this can be modeled on the overhead to teach the skill.

- *Storyboards*—Divide sections on a board or piece of paper and have students draw or write story events in sequence in each box/frame.

- *Story maps*—Include essential elements of a story (setting, characters, time, place, problem or conflict, actions or happenings, and resolution).

- *Story frames*—Develop sentence starters for students to fill in that provide a skeleton of the story or chapter. For example: "The setting of this chapter takes place ____. The character faced a problem when ____. First, he ____. Next, ____. Then ____. I predict in the next chapter ____."

- *Timelines*—Use these to help visualize chronological text and sequence of events.

- *Plot charts*—Develop the plot: Somebody . . . Wanted . . . But . . . And so . . .

- *Venn diagram*—Prepare two overlapping circles to display differences and similarities between characters, books, settings, topics, events.

- *Comparison chart*—Much like a Venn diagram, compare and contrast two or more items, events, concepts, characters, themes.

- *Flow chart*—Organize a series of items or thoughts in logical order.

- *Webs, cluster maps, semantic maps*—Place a central concept or main idea in the center of related subtopics, and extend further details from each of the subtopic areas. Use these to categorize or identify related information.

- *5 Ws chart*—After reading an article or excerpt from a text, have the student identify the 5 W elements (Who? What? When? Where? Why?) and record that information on the chart.

- *Other*—Use numerous other charts, such as main idea/supporting detail, cause/effect, sequence, classification matrix, and so on.

Anticipation Guide

This is a series of teacher-generated statements about a topic given to students in advance of the reading. Students individually respond to the statements (such as true/false) before reading about that topic. Typically, students are asked to discuss their choices briefly with

5-5 (*continued*)

partners or small groups prior to reading the passage. After reading the text material, they again discuss whether their beliefs have changed.

Directed Reading-Thinking Activity (DRTA)

This instructional framework guides active reading by taking students through the process of asking open-ended questions as they are reading and predicting what will happen next. Students are guided to make predictions about the passage. Then the passage is read (orally or silently) and, at predetermined points, students are asked to summarize the reading. At these points they are asked to confirm their predictions or revise them based upon their reading. In addition, students are asked to give reasons for their decisions with evidence located and cited from the text.

Imagery/Visualization

This technique aids comprehension by creating mental pictures of what is being read. Students are encouraged to create an image in their mind as they read. This skill can be taught through a series of guided questioning techniques that elicit from the child vivid detailed pictures as they move through the passage.

Note: See Nanci Bell's program under Sources and Resources. Examples of guided questions include: "What do you see?" "How does it feel?" "What does it look like?" "What colors?" "Where is he sitting?"

KWL

This strategy is used to guide reading throughout the process (prior, during, after). It involves a chart divided into three columns:

■ The first column (**K**) indicates what is already **known** about the subject/topic. This step activates students' prior knowledge. Ideas are recorded during a class brainstorm.

■ The middle column (**W**) is **what** the students want to learn about the subject. Discussion and guided questioning elicit topics to be recorded in this section. This column sets the purpose for reading, to find the answers to those questions.

■ The third column (**L**) is filled in on the chart as new information is **learned** from the reading or other teaching. This column can be entitled: "What We Learned/Still Need to Learn."

KWL Plus is the same except it also includes categorizing the information listed and mapping or organizing the information graphically. A summary is written based upon that graphic organization of ideas.

Literature Circles

In this instructional format, the class is divided into self-selected groups with students in each group reading a common book that is an unabridged version.

- After a period of independent reading, groups meet for discussion and analysis of their respective books.

- As students do their independent reading prior to meeting in their group, they are responsible for keeping notes and journals/logs.

- They are asked to record their responses to the literature, questions that they have, and other comments (for example, connections they make, feelings evoked).

- When the groups meet, they respond to the literature and the various literary elements.

There are often specific roles that individual members of the group may assume. For example, these may include:

- A group leader (discussion director), who is responsible for asking questions that require higher-order thinking skills

- A "book connector," who is responsible for making connections between what is read in the current book and other books read

- A person to locate interesting words and/or find the meaning of unknown words

- An artist/illustrator

- A summarizer

- A person to track where the characters have traveled to (and so forth)

OTHER ACTIVE READING/DISCUSSION FORMATS

Fishbowl

The class is divided into two circles (inner and outer). The inner circle actively engages in discussion about the book (or other topic). The outer circle observes and cannot contribute to the discussion. Their role is to note how well the inner group functioned in critical communication skills (listening to each other's point of view, asking relevant questions, asking for clarification, politely disagreeing, not interrupting). Roles are then reversed and the outer circle students are the ones participating in the discussion.

Jigsaw

Students are divided into "home" groups, each responsible for reading and understanding the same material. Each member is assigned a number (1–5) which corresponds to certain

5-5 (*continued*)

sections of the reading assignment. The students with the same number from each home group then meet in their "expert" groups in order to reread and study their section in depth. Expert groups work together in learning their portion of the material and planning how to teach that information and content to their home group members. Then everyone returns to their home group, and each member teaches his or her content to the home group peers.

Question-Answer Relationships (QAR)

Students are taught the different classification of questions: (1) right there, (2) think and search, and (3) on your own.

1. The answers to "right there" questions are stated directly in the text and simply require literal comprehension.

2. The answers to "think and search" questions are not so explicit and easy to locate, but are found somewhere within the text. Answering these questions requires interpretive or inferential comprehension and "reading between the lines." Finding the main idea of a passage is an example of inferential comprehension.

3. "On your own" questions are more abstract, and the answers cannot be found in the text. These questions require reading "beyond the lines" and involve higher-order thinking skills such as analyzing, evaluating, and creative thinking. Examples include comparing and contrasting, or answering questions such as: "What do you think caused ____ to happen?" "What other solution can you think of for that problem?"

Guided Reading

This is an instructional strategy in which students of approximately the same reading level are in reading groups (usually no more than six per group). The teacher selects books for each group to read together that are new to them and will involve working on strategies that students in that group specifically need to practice. Usually "leveled" books are used for guided reading groups, and are at the students' instructional level.

The teacher coaches students to apply strategies throughout the reading of the selected book with the purpose of teaching them how to read for meaning.

1. The procedure begins with an introduction to the book and "walking through" pages (looking at illustrations, making predictions, providing some background information, and focusing on some of the difficult vocabulary that will be encountered in the book).

2. Students then read *to themselves* as the teacher moves to each individual student and "listens in" as they read (asking them to read aloud softly).

3. The teacher provides prompts and asks questions to guide each student in using strategies for figuring out the text and problem-solving challenges they encounter in their reading. For example, "Reread that sentence. Does that make sense? What other

word would make sense there that starts with *ch*?" "Are there any little words you recognize in that big word?" "Sound it out."

4. Students are prompted to reread when they finish the initial reading, extending their comprehension and thinking about the book.

5. Teaching points and strategies are taught during and after the reading, depending upon what the teacher determines are the needs of the group.

Summarizing

This is one of the most important reading comprehension skills. It involves finding the main idea or topic sentence and supporting details. Sometimes the main idea is explicit and easy to find; other times it is implied or embedded in the passage. Techniques requiring students to stop at points in the reading to paraphrase in their own words or to summarize in one or two sentences provide excellent practice building this skill.

- Students can summarize verbally ("Tell your partner in one sentence what the paragraph was about.").

- Summaries can also be done by filling out graphic organizers (with provision of just a couple of lines to record key information only).

- Outlining is another summarizing technique.

- Students can also write a summary sentence or paragraph.

- Ask students to monitor their comprehension by responding to these kinds of prompts: "The main point of this was ____." "Overall, this was about ____."

GIST (Generating Interaction between Schemata and Text)

This strategy is used for comprehending informational text and determining the "gist" of the reading material.

1. Students read sections silently in cooperative groups.

2. When done reading a short section, the members of the group work together to write a one-sentence summary.

3. All group members then record that summary sentence.

4. Students continue in this fashion of reading a segment, stopping at logical points, jointly deciding upon a summary sentence, and then recording on their own papers.

5. Those papers can then serve as a study guide for the reading material.

Reciprocal Teaching

This is an instructional approach in which students take turns summarizing, questioning, and discussing small portions of the text. Students teach the material to each other section by section, and work together in cooperative groups to carry on a dialogue involving four processes:

5-5 (*continued*)

1. **Questioning** can involve any level of questions (literal, interpretive).

2. **Summarizing** requires identifying the main ideas and key points.

3. **Clarifying** involves discussing anything confusing in the passage.

4. **Predicting** elicits the group's best guesses or speculations of what will happen next.

The next passage or segment is then read, and the procedure continues with a student leading the discussion.

Narrative Text Structure

Students are taught story grammar or story mapping to understand the structure of literary text. This includes setting, characters, problem or conflict, sequence of major events (actions), and the resolution or problem solution. Younger students generally focus on the main characters, setting, and story structure (beginning, middle, and end).

Expository or Informational Text Structure

Students are taught how to identify the main ideas and supportive details in the text. They are explicitly shown that the main ideas are generally found in the chapter titles and headings, and that subheadings express the next biggest ideas and points. Learning how to use the glossary, table of contents, index, tables/graphs, as well as the techniques of scanning and skimming to find the answers, are important teaching points for helping students learn how to read and comprehend expository text.

SOURCES AND RESOURCES

Bell, Nanci. *Visualizing and Verbalizing for Language Comprehension and Thinking.* Paso Robles, CA: Academy of Reading Publications, 1991.

Bromley, K., L. Irwin-DeVitis, and M. Modlo. *Graphic Organizers: Visual Strategies for Active Learning.* New York: Scholastic, 1995.

Chamot, A., and J. O'Malley. *The CALLA Handbook: Implementing Cognitive Academic Language Learning.* Reading, MA: Addison-Wesley, 1994.

Consortium on Reading Excellence, Inc. (CORE). *Literacy Training Notebook.* Emeryville, CA: Core, Inc., 1998.

Forte, Imogene, and Sandra Schurr. *Standards-Based Language Arts Graphic Organizers, Rubrics, and Writing Prompts for Middle Grade Students.* Nashville, TN: Incentive Publications, 2001.

Fountas, Irene C., and Gay Su Pinnell. *Guided Reading.* Portsmouth, NH: Heinemann, 1996.

Greene, Victoria E., and Mary Lee Enfield. *Project Read—Language Circle.* Bloomington, MN: Language Circle Enterprise, 1994.

Polloway, Edward A., James R. Patton, and Loretta Serna. *Strategies for Teaching Learners with Special Needs.* Upper Saddle River, NJ: Merrill/Prentice-Hall, 2001.

Rief, Sandra, and Julie Heimburge. *How to Reach and Teach All Students in the Inclusive Classroom.* Paramus, NJ: The Center for Applied Research in Education, 1996.

Stockdale, Carol, and Carol Possin. *Solving Reading Problems.* East Moline, IL: LinguiSystems, 2000.

Strategic Teaching and Learning: Standards-Based Instruction to Promote Content Literacy in Grades Four through Twelve. Sacramento: California Department of Education, 2000.

Waring, Cynthia Conway. *Developing Independent Readers: Strategy-Oriented Reading Activities for Learners with Special Needs.* West Nyack, NY: The Center for Applied Research in Education, 1995.

5-6
WHY WRITING IS SUCH A STRUGGLE FOR STUDENTS WITH ADHD

It is rare for someone with ADHD not to have some degree of difficulty with writing. Children and teens with attention deficit disorders are often verbal and knowledgeable, but unable to communicate what they know on paper.

Weaknesses in written language are common in those with ADHD because the process is so complex. It involves the integration and often simultaneous use of several skills and brain functions (organization, spelling, fine motor, planning, self-monitoring, memory, language). Writing difficulties are manifested because the process requires the following skills.

Planning and Organization

Writing requires being able to generate, plan, and organize ideas. This stage of the writing process is often the most challenging and neglected, especially for those who experience difficulties with written expression. When given a written assignment, students with ADHD often get stuck here. They do not know what to write about, how to organize and begin, or how to narrow down and focus on a topic that will be motivating to write about.

Memory

Working memory is necessary in order to juggle the many different thoughts that one might want to transcribe onto paper. It involves:

- Keeping ideas in mind long enough to remember what you want to say.
- Maintaining focus on the "train of thought" so the flow of the writing won't veer off course.
- Keeping in mind the big picture of what you want to communicate, while manipulating the ideas, details, and wording.

The process of writing also requires:

- Retrieval of assorted information from long-term memory (for example, facts, experiences) to share about the writing topic.
- Recall of vocabulary words, spelling, mechanics, and grammatical usage.

Language

Writing requires the ability to:

- Express thoughts in a logical and coherent manner.

- Utilize descriptive sentences while maintaining proper sentence and paragraph structure.

- Fluidity of expressive language and facility with vocabulary usage.

Spelling

People with attention difficulties are often:

- Inattentive to visual detail, and do not notice or recall the letters, sequence, or visual patterns within words.

- Prone to making many careless mistakes.

Those who also have learning disabilities are typically weak in spelling due to:

- Auditory-sequential memory deficits (causing great difficulty learning letter–sound associations, as well as hearing/remembering and writing those sounds in the correct order).

- Visual-sequential memory (causing them difficulty recalling the way a word looks, and getting it down in the correct order/sequence). This results in misspelling common high-frequency words (*said, they, because*) that cannot be sounded out phonetically and must be recalled by sight.

Grapho-Motor Skills

Many children with ADHD and/or learning disabilities have impairments in grapho-motor skills. This affects the physical task of writing and organizing print on the page. They often have trouble:

- Writing neatly on or within the given lines

- Spacing/organizing their writing on the page

- Copying from the board or book onto paper

- With *fine-motor skills*, causing the act of handwriting to be very inefficient, fatiguing, and frustrating (affecting pencil grip, pressure exerted, legibility)

- Executing print or cursive with precision or speed

Note: Memory is also involved in fine-motor skills (remembering with automaticity the sequence of fine-motor movements required in the formation of each letter). Those with coexisting learning disabilities in visual processing also frequently reverse or invert letters (b/d, p/q, n/u) and form numerals/letters in strange, awkward ways.

Editing

Individuals with ADHD have significant difficulty during the revision and proofreading stage of the writing process. Many students with ADHD want to go directly from the ini-

5-6 (continued)

tial draft to the final draft without making revisions, as it is tedious to do (without the use of assistive technology and other assistance). They are typically inattentive to the boring task of finding and correcting errors. It is common to find lack of capitalization, punctuation, and complete sentences, along with numerous spelling errors in their written products.

Self-Monitoring

Fluent writing requires:

- Thinking and planning ahead
- Keeping the intended audience in mind and writing to that audience with a clear purpose
- Following and referring back to the specific structure of a writing genre (such as steps of a complete paragraph, narrative account, persuasive essay, friendly letter)
- Knowing how to read one's own work critically in order to make revisions and develop ideas more thoroughly

Speed of Written Output and Production

Some students with ADHD rush through writing assignments, often leading to illegible work with many careless errors. Others with ADHD write excruciatingly *slow*. Although they know the answers and can verbally express their thoughts and ideas articulately, they are unable to put more than a few words or sentences on paper. Needless to say, this is extremely frustrating. Part of the problem with speed of output may be due to:

- Impairments in impulsivity and inhibition
- Difficulty sustaining attention to task and maintaining the mental energy required in written expression
- Grapho-motor dysfunction

RELATED LISTS

- Lists 5-7 through 5-12 are packed with strategies that build writing skills and accommodate for writing difficulties.

SOURCES AND RESOURCES

Levine, Mel. *Developmental Variation and Learning Disorders.* Cambridge, MA: Educational Publishing Services, 1998. (www.allkindsofminds.org)

Misunderstood Minds. Writing Basics, Difficulties, Responses. WGBH Educational Foundation, 2002. (http://www.pbs.org/wgbh/misunderstoodminds)

Richards, Regina G. *When Writing's a Problem.* Riverside, CA: Richards Educational Therapy Center, Inc., 1995.

Rief, Sandra. "AD/HD: Common Academic Difficulties and Strategies that Help," CHADD: *Attention*, vol. 7, no. 2, 47–51; September/October, 2000.

5-7
STRATEGIES TO HELP WITH PREWRITING (PLANNING AND ORGANIZING)

Prewriting is a critical stage of the writing process—involving the generation, planning, and organization of ideas—and deciding "what" and "how" to express ideas before actually beginning to write. This is a challenge for many students with ADHD. The *prewriting* techniques below are designed to stimulate ideas, topic selection, and effective planning. They also provide much needed structure, organization, and motivation to write.

PREWRITING TECHNIQUES AT HOME

Parents can help their children think of possible writing topics.

- Look through family albums together and reminisce about people and events.
- Talk about happenings in the child's life (humorous incidents, scary moments, milestones) that he or she may not remember.
- Share family stories.
- Discuss current events.
- Ask leading questions that encourage the child to open up and share (feelings, fears, dreams, aspirations, likes/dislikes).
- Provide resources (books, reference materials, access to the library, Internet, and so on).

PREWRITING TECHNIQUES IN THE CLASSROOM

- *Brainstorming*—These sessions are very short and focused (no more than 3–5 minutes). Give a general theme or topic, and have students call out whatever comes to mind related to that topic while someone else records all responses.
- *Quickwrites*—Give students a few minutes (no more than 3–4) to write down everything they can think of related to a given topic. Model the same uninterrupted writing along with the students at this time.
- *Writing Topic Folders*—Have students maintain a folder, card file, or notebook of possible writing topics for reference purposes. Include hobbies, places visited, jobs they have done, personal interests, interesting/colorful family members, neighbors, friends, pets, and so forth.
- *Personal Collage Writing Folder*—Have students use words and pictures cut out from magazines, newspapers, and travel brochures. Laminate the folder when done. Students should include favorite places, foods, sports, hobbies, and so on.

- *Reference Books*—Pass out reference books to groups of students to look through for ideas of writing topics (mysteries of nature, airplanes, music, astronomy, mammals, dinosaurs, sports, fashion).

- *Writing Prompts*—Provide a stimulus, such as a poem, story, picture, song, or news item, to prompt writing. In addition, keep a file of pictures from magazines, old calendars, postcards, and so forth as stimuli for writing activities. It often helps to offer students a variety of sample topic sentences, story starters, and writing prompts when they are struggling for an idea.

- *Vocabulary Lists*—Have students generate a vocabulary list of words related to a theme or topic. For example, everyone might supply a word related to nature, climate, archaeology, words that make me shiver, words that make me hungry, soft words, angry words, and so forth.

- *Self-Questioning*—Teach students to talk themselves through the planning stage of their writing by asking: "Who am I writing for? Why am I writing this? What do I know? What does my reader need to know?"

- *Telling Personal Stories*—Have students in cooperative groups orally respond to prompts by telling personal stories. For example, "Tell about a time you or someone you knew got lost." After the oral telling and sharing of stories in small, cooperative groups, students write a rough draft or outline of the story they told.

- *Tape Recorder*—Encourage the use of a tape recorder with some students, so they can first verbalize what they want to say before transcribing ideas onto paper.

GRAPHIC ORGANIZERS

These are one of the most effective ways to help students generate their ideas, as well as formulate and organize their thoughts. For students with written language difficulties, use of a graphic organizer is a critical intervention in helping them plan before they begin to actually write. (5-5)

- *Clustering*—Write the main idea in a box or rectangle in the center of the page and surround the main idea box with bubbles containing all of the supporting ideas.

- *Writing frames*—Have students fill in blanks from a framed outline.

- *Mind mapping*—Draw a circle at the center of a page. The topic is written inside the center circle, and related ideas are written on lines stemming from the circle. This technique is also called webbing, and the graphic is called a web.

- *Diagrams*—For example, use Venn diagrams, which are graphics of overlapping circles that show a comparison between two or three items, topics, characters, or books.

- *Compare/contrast charts*—Use these to depict similarities and differences.

- *Story maps*—Use these in preplanning the critical elements (setting, characters, problem, action, and resolution) to be included when writing a story.

5-7 (continued)

ADDITIONAL PREWRITING TIPS

■ Model and provide guided instruction through the use of various types of graphic outlines; then practice its use with students, keeping the graphics readily available.

■ Present many models of good writing orally and visually.

■ Read examples of written works that demonstrate the skill you are emphasizing (for example, expanded, descriptive sentences; well-developed paragraphs; and use of metaphors/similes).

■ Teach and display steps of the writing process (prewriting, composing first draft, responding, revising, editing and proofreading, publishing).

■ Provide examples and display samples of several kinds of prewriting graphic organizers.

■ Use software such as *Inspiration*™ and *Kidspiration*™ for use in prewriting. See Sources and Resources at the end of List 5-12.

■ Stop students after a few minutes of writing and ask for student volunteers to share what they have written so far.

■ Provide models of papers containing an introduction, body, and conclusion.

■ Remember that planning and organization are some of the "executive functions" that are areas of weakness in many individuals with ADHD. Therefore, it is very important to provide instruction and support to guide them in the kind of thinking and questioning that is needed to effectively plan and organize before writing. (5-6)

A PREWRITING CHECKLIST

It is valuable to provide students a prewriting checklist that lists specific questions they need to ask themselves at this stage of the writing process. When creating a prewriting checklist, select a few of the following questions:

■ Have I brainstormed and written down a number of possible topics?

■ Have I selected my favorite topic among those choices, and can I write enough about it?

■ Have I identified my target audience?

■ Which writing genre am I going to use?

■ What style or voice will I write in?

■ Have I listed any words, ideas, or phrases related to my topic?

■ Have I narrowed down my topic?

■ Have I researched and collected enough interesting information from a variety of sources (books, newspapers, Internet, magazines)?

■ Am I taking sufficient notes from resources to support what I am writing about?

- Have I carefully documented the sources of any research information I might use so I will remember later where I found it and give proper credit?
- What are possible introductions that will excite and grab the attention of my audience?
- What details and examples might I use that will be interesting?
- If I'm writing a story:
  - Who will be the characters, and what will they be like?
  - What will my setting be (time, place)?
  - What is the main problem going to be?
  - What is the plot and action?
  - How will the problem be solved?
  - What will the ending be?
  - Will the main character have changed in some important way? How?

ORGANIZATION TIPS

- Take notes or write ideas on separate index cards. That makes it easier to spread out and group, organize, and sequence those thoughts and ideas.
- Break down notes into subtopics.
- If using *Inspiration*™ software, check out the built-in outlining feature. Categories listed in the graphic web format are automatically placed in outline form with the press of a button.

SOURCES AND RESOURCES

Kemper, Dave, Ruth Nathan, and Patrick Sebranek. *Writer's Express.* Wilmington, MA: Great Source Education Group, Inc., 1995.

Muschla, Gary Robert. *The Writing Teacher's Book of Lists.* Englewood Cliffs, NJ: Prentice Hall, 1991.

Rief, Sandra, and Julie Heimburge. *How to Reach and Teach All Students in the Inclusive Classroom.* Paramus, NJ: The Center for Applied Research in Education, 1996.

Rogers, Kathleen. *Writing to Inform.* Carthage, IL: Fearon Teacher Aids, 1987.

5-8
STRATEGIES FOR BUILDING SKILLS IN WRITTEN EXPRESSION

Written expression is the most common academic area of difficulty among students with ADHD. Several brain processes are involved and utilized simultaneously (language, attention, memory, sequencing, organization, planning, self-monitoring, critical thinking) when trying to compose a written piece of work. (5-6)

Students are expected to meet grade-level expectations and standards in a variety of writing formats and genres. Teachers are expected to differentiate instruction to teach writers of all levels and abilities. The teaching of writing requires knowing how to scaffold the instruction and provide the necessary structures and supports to students who need more help in the writing process. The following are strategies and tips for helping students become more successful writers.

VOCABULARY AND SENTENCE STRUCTURE

■ Teach sentence structure and build upon sentence writing skills, explaining that all complete sentences have a subject (noun) and a predicate (which includes a verb telling "what" about the subject).

■ Teach students to write more interesting, expanded sentences. Starting with a simple bare sentence, have them "dress it up" by adding colorful, descriptive adjectives and adverbs, more powerful verbs, and prepositional phrases.

■ Instruct students in the use of figurative language (metaphors, similes, personification, analogies) to enhance writing style. Display examples of different figures of speech for students to reference.

■ Teach words that are used to signal sequence (First of all, To begin, Furthermore, Meanwhile, Subsequently). Then display these words or provide a student desk copy for reference.

■ Teach transitional words and phrases (However, Consequently, In addition, Therefore, So, As a result). Display these words for reference or provide a copy for individual student use.

■ Point out to students such phrases as "I suggest . . ." or "I believe . . .," which signal an author's point of view; and words/phrases such as "nevertheless" or "on the other hand," which are used to compare and contrast two or more things. Provide a reference of such words to aid writing.

■ See List 5-3 for more strategies to build vocabulary (oral and written).

WRITING GENRES

The following are some of the genres that students are expected to write, depending upon the grade and developmental level.

- Paragraphs (summary, "how-to," compare/contrast, procedural, descriptive, and narrative)
- Friendly letter
- Business letter
- Informational or expository report (includes topic, main ideas, supporting details, and conclusion; often involves research, observations, and analysis)
- Narrative (requires presenting information in a story-like form with descriptive details, as well as a beginning, middle, and an end)
- Story (with literary story grammar: setting, characters, problem, sequence of events, climax, and resolution)
- Persuasive essay (writer tries to change the reader's point of view by presenting facts and opinions and arguing a point)
- Response to literature

SELF-MONITORING/METACOGNITION

Written expression requires a great deal of self-monitoring from students and putting themselves in the place of their potential readers. The writer needs to keep asking him- or herself:

- "Does this make sense?"
- "Is this clear?"
- "Do my ideas flow logically?"
- "Did I use the best choice of words?"

It is important to provide students with a checklist of structural components in every writing form and genre they are assigned. For example, when asking students to write an expository (nonfiction) piece, some questions they need to ask themselves in structuring the work and self-monitoring may include:

Opening

- How am I introducing the subject or topic?
- What will be the main idea(s) about my subject?
- What kind of "hook" can I use to capture the reader's attention?

Body

- How am I going to develop my main ideas?

5-8 (continued)

- What details and examples am I going to use?
- What will be my flow and sequence of ideas?

Conclusion

- What will be the final thought or wrap up?
- On what note am I leaving the reader?

The other writing strategy lists in this book include a number of self-monitoring questions:

- See List 5-7 for questions to ask in planning and organizing the written assignment.
- See List 5-9 for guiding questions to revise written work—expanding, changing, reorganizing, and clarifying; and for questions to self-monitor the proofreading process.

Explicitly teach students specific strategies to aid recall of steps and application of the process. One example is the POW strategy (by Karen Harris and Steve Graham):

> **P** = Plan what to say.
> **O** = Organize what to say.
> **W** = Write and say more.

Harris and Graham, with support from the U.S. Office of Special Education Programs (OSEP), pioneered the Self-Regulated Strategy Development (SRSD) approach, which includes POW and other strategies. With SRSD, students are explicitly taught how to use self-regulation procedures (goal-setting, self-monitoring, self-instruction, and self-reinforcement) in the process of writing. See Sources and Resources.

With OSEP support, Jeanne Schumaker and Don Deschler (University of Kansas) developed and evaluated four written-expression learning strategies: Sentence-Writing Strategy, Paragraph-Writing Strategy, Error-Monitoring Strategy, and Theme-Writing Strategy. See Sources and Resources.

See List 4-2 for more information regarding self-monitoring/metacognitive techniques.

GRAPHIC ORGANIZERS

Use graphic organizers and displays to structure the planning of each form of writing assignment. The following are a few examples:

Parts of a Business Letter

1. Heading
2. Inside address
3. Salutation

4. Body

5. Closing

6. Signature

Paragraph Structure

1. Topic sentence

2. At least three supporting detail sentences (answering the 5 W's)

3. Conclusion or summary statement

ADDITIONAL INSTRUCTIONAL RECOMMENDATIONS

■ Encourage students to frequently ask themselves the 5 W questions (who, what, when, where, why—and "how") as they write. Answering these questions will help ensure that they have provided enough vivid information for their readers.

■ Use the Writers Workshop approach, which provides class time for students to write on topics of their choice. In Writers Workshop:

  ▪ Students move through the following stages of the writing process: prewriting, drafting, revising, editing, and publishing.

  ▪ Model each stage with students and schedule writing groups to give feedback and suggestions.

  ▪ Students should interact and assist each other in revising, editing, sharing their writing, and so forth.

  ▪ Mini-lessons are taught as needed on specific skills and strategies.

■ Provide modeled writing and guided writing instruction as key components of a balanced literacy program.

  ▪ Even students with significant writing difficulties are often able to meet writing standards when they receive a high degree of explicit teacher modeling of writing skills and guided assistance.

  ▪ *Note:* The video *Successful Classrooms: Effective Teaching Strategies for Raising Achievement in Reading and Writing* (see Sources and Resources) demonstrates these highly effective writing strategies in elementary classrooms.

■ Provide students (when giving the assignment) any scoring guide/rubric that will be used to assess the written product when completed. This significantly helps students with writing difficulties, as it gives them a visual tool for planning, structuring, and self-monitoring their written work. It also helps the parents by explaining from the beginning exactly what the teacher expects in the writing assignment, and what is considered proficient performance for the grade level. (Rubrics are on a scale, such as 1–5, ranging from minimal performance to superior performance; or below standard to exceeded standard.)

5-8 (continued)

SOURCES AND RESOURCES

ERIC/OSEP. "Strengthening the Second 'R'—Helping Students with Disabilities Prepare Well-Written Compositions," *ERIC: Research Connections in Special Education*, no. 10, Winter 2002.

Fetzer, Nancy. *The Writing Program.* San Diego, CA: Fisher and Fetzer Educational Systems, 1999.

Fisher, Linda, Nancy Fetzer, and Sandra Rief. *Successful Classrooms: Effective Teaching Strategies for Raising Achievement in Reading and Writing* (video). San Diego, CA: Educational Resource Specialsts; 800-682-3528; www.sandrarief.com

Forte, Imogene, and Sandra Schurr. *Standards-Based Language Arts Graphic Organizers, Rubrics, and Writing Prompts.* Nashville, TN: Incentive Publications, Inc., 2001.

Harris, Karen, and Steve Graham. "Programmatic Intervention Research: Illustrations from the Evolution of Self-Regulated Strategy Development," *Learning Disability Quarterly*, vol. 22, 251–262; 1999.

Kemper, Dave, Ruth Nathan, and Patrick Sebranek. *Writer's Express.* Wilmington, MA: Great Source Education Group, Inc., 1995.

Miller, Wilma. *Reading and Writing Remediation Kit.* Paramus, NJ: The Center for Applied Research in Education, 1997.

Moore, Jo Ellen. *Paragraph Writing: Grade 2–4.* Monterey, CA: Evan-Moor Corp., 1997.

POW strategy (http://www.vanderbilt.edu/CASL). For more information about self-regulation strategy development, contact Karen Harris and Steve Graham at the University of Maryland.

Schirmer, Barbara, and Jill Bailey. "Writing Assessment Rubric: An Instructional Approach with Struggling Writers," *Teaching Exceptional Children*, vol. 33, no. 1, 52–59; September/October 2000.

SRSD approach. For more information on written expression learning strategies, contact Jeanne Schumaker and Don Deschler at the University of Kansas at Lawrence, Institute for Research on Learning Disabilities.

Terry, Bonnie. *Writer's Easy Reference Guide.* Auburn, CA: BT Learning Resources, 1999.

5-9
HELP WITH EDITING STRATEGIES AND OTHER TIPS

For students with ADHD, the editing stage of the writing process (revising, proofreading, and making corrections) is very difficult. Many are resistant to making changes once they have struggled to write the first draft. The following are strategies for both teachers and parents to help students in editing their written work.

■ Teach students the skills of proofreading and editing. One method is by making transparencies of anonymous students' unedited work, or using teacher samples of writing with errors in capitalization, punctuation, and so on. Edit the piece as a group.

■ Have students write rough drafts on every other line. This makes it much easier to edit and make corrections. *Note:* Revision requires self-monitoring and critically evaluating one's own work. Students with ADHD generally need a lot of direct instruction, modeling, and feedback to learn how to do so. Revising work is the step of the writing process that involves adding or deleting information, resequencing the order of sentences and paragraphs, and choosing words that better communicate what one wants to say.

■ Provide students with checklists to help self-monitor during the revision process. The following sample questions may be included in a self-editing checklist. Select some (not all) of the following questions in creating a list appropriate to the age and developmental level of the child:

1. Have I given enough information?
2. Have I identified my audience?
3. Have I written for my audience?
4. Does my introduction capture the attention of my readers?
5. Is my beginning interesting and exciting?
6. Did I develop my ideas logically?
7. Have I left out any important details?
8. Does everything make sense?
9. Did I stick to my topic?
10. Have I presented my ideas clearly?
11. Are the ideas in the right order?
12. Have I given details and examples for each main idea?
13. Have I included enough facts and details to support my subject?
14. Have I given enough information to my readers?

5-9 (*continued*)

15. Have I used descriptive words to make my writing interesting?

16. Do my paragraphs have a beginning, middle, and end?

17. Have I chosen the right words?

18. Does it read smoothly?

19. Do I need to insert, move around, or delete any ideas?

20. Did I write an interesting, powerful conclusion?

21. Did my conclusion restate the main ideas or refer back to the introduction?

22. Have I satisfied my purpose for writing?

23. Have I said everything I need to say?

More Useful Tips

■ Teach students to respond to their own writing. "My best sentence is _____. " "A simile or metaphor I used was _____."

■ Teach students to self-talk through the editing/revising stage of their writing: "Does everything make sense? Did I include all of my ideas? Do I need to insert, delete, or move ideas?"

■ Use peer editing. Have students work with a partner to read their work to each other:

   1. The partner listens and reads along as the author reads.

   2. The partner tells what he or she liked best.

   3. Then the partner questions the author about anything that does not make sense; suggests where more information is needed for clarification; and helps edit when he or she hears or sees run-on or incomplete sentences.

   4. Roles are then reversed.

■ Conduct teacher–student writing conferences:

   ▪ The teacher provides feedback, the student reflects on his or her own work, and both share what they like about the piece of writing.

   ▪ The student self-evaluates improvement and the skills to target for continued improvement. "My writing has improved in: _____ (sentence structure, paragraphing, fluency, creativity, organization, capitalization, punctuation, spelling). I plan to work on _____."

■ Provide students plenty of time to write in class. Give direct, supportive feedback.

■ Teach the skills needed to make choice of words more interesting (more descriptive adjectives, adverbs, verbs, and so on).

■ Provide lists and posted words for student reference (powerful verbs, alternatives to "said," transition and linking words/phrases).

■ Have students generate a class list of interesting words they find in the books they read; for example, "Locate 10 descriptive adjectives in the chapter."

- Display models and standards for acceptable written work.

- Provide a rubric with all writing assignments and show models of what written work looks like "at standard" and "exceeding standard."

- Display models of proper headings, spacing, and organization of written work.

- Teach sentence expansion and combination of sentences. Given a short phrase (two to three words), practice expanding the simple sentence frame by adding: "Where?" "How?" "When?" "Why?"

- Teach how to use the editing tools and options (thesaurus, spell-check, cut and paste) on a word-processing program.

- Allow and encourage writing on the computer, which makes editing and revising so much easier. Another benefit is being able to save various draft versions electronically, rather than storing paper, which helps maintain better organization and management of written work.

- Read or listen to the child read his or her writing. Then provide positive feedback consisting of something you like about the piece of writing, and any growth in skills that are apparent. Ask the child when something is confusing or unclear, and more information is needed.

Proofreading for Errors and Polishing the Final Product

- Provide direct instruction and guided practice in the skills of mechanics (punctuation and capitalization). Challenge students to find and correct the errors in capitalization and punctuation in a given sentence.

- Encourage parents to have their child self-edit by circling words he or she thinks were possibly misspelled, and then checking the spelling of those words together later.

- Encourage the use of an electronic spell-check device (such as those from Franklin) for use at home and school. (Franklin spellers are available from Franklin Electronic Publishers, http://www.franklin.com.)

- Tell students to add the "Midas touch" to their sentences and paragraphs, making them "golden."

- Teach editing symbols and provide a reference chart (insert, delete, capitalize, new paragraph).

- Provide a self-editing checklist for proofreading work for capitalization, sentence structure, and mechanical errors. The following are possible questions in developing a proofreading self-edit list for students:

  1. Did I use complete sentences?
  2. Did I begin all sentences with a capital?
  3. Did I end my sentences with a final punctuation mark (. ? !)?
  4. Have I capitalized all proper nouns?
  5. Have I checked my spelling for correctness?

5-9 (*continued*)

    6. Have I indented my paragraphs?

    7. Are verb tenses consistent?

    8. Did I check for run-on sentences?

    9. Is my paper neat and organized?

  10. Have I used adequate spacing?

  11. Have I erased carefully?

  12. Is my writing legible?

- Teach a mnemonic proofreading strategy to help students recall and apply an effective learning strategy. The COPS strategy developed by researchers Deschler and Schumaker (part of the Strategies Instructional Approach, University of Kansas) includes the steps of self-checking:

    C — Capitalization

    O — Overall appearance

    P — Punctuation

    S — Spelling

SOURCES AND RESOURCES

COPS strategy. For more information, contact Jeanne Schumaker and Don Deschler at the University of Kansas at Lawrence.

Fetzer, Nancy, and Naranca Elementary Staff. *Writing Level Guide.* San Diego, CA: Fisher & Fetzer Educational Systems, 1999.

Jacobson, Jennifer Richard. *How Is My Third Grader Doing in School?* New York: Fireside, 1999.

Kemper, Dave, Ruth Nathan, and Patrick Sebranek. *Writer's Express.* Wilmington, MA: Great Source Education Group, 1995.

Muschla, Gary Robert. *The Writing Teacher's Book of Lists.* Englewood Cliffs, NJ: Prentice Hall, 1991.

Rief, Sandra. *The ADD/ADHD Checklist: An Easy Reference for Parents and Teachers.* Paramus, NJ: Prentice Hall, 1998.

Rief, Sandra, and Julie Heimburge. *How to Reach and Teach All Students in the Inclusive Classroom.* Paramus, NJ: The Center for Applied Research in Education, 1996.

Schumaker, J. B., D. D. Deschler, S. Nolan, F. L. Clark, G. R. Alley, and M. M. Warner. *Error Monitoring: A Learning Strategy for Improving Academic Performance of LD Adolescents* (Research Report No. 32). Lawrence: University of Kansas, Institute for Research on Learning Disabilities, 1981.

5-10
MULTISENSORY SPELLING STRATEGIES AND ACTIVITIES

The following strategies motivate students to practice spelling words in a variety of multisensory formats.

Add Novelty with Fun Materials and Utilize Tactile (Feeling) Strategies

- Dip clean paintbrush in water and write words on tabletop or chalkboard.

- Write words in the air while sounding them out (sky writing).

- Write words in a flat tray or box of either sand or salt using one or two fingers.

- Write words in glue or liquid starch on pieces of cardboard. Then sprinkle any powdery material, glitter, yarn, beans, macaroni, or sequins to create textured, three-dimensional spelling words. Substances such as sand, salt, and glitter are good to use for students who benefit from tracing the words with their fingers. *Note:* The act of tracing with your fingers on a texture helps make a sensory imprint on the brain that increases memory and retention.

- Write words in a sandbox with a stick.

- Pair with another student and write words on each other's back with fingers.

- While sitting on the carpet, practice writing the words directly on the carpet with two fingers using large muscle movements.

- Practice writing words on individual chalkboards (or dry-erase boards) with colored chalk (or colored dry-erase pens).

- Finger-paint words using shaving cream on tabletops; or pudding, whipped cream, or frosting on paper plates.

- Type each word in a variety of different fonts and sizes. If you have a color printer, change the color of the words.

- Write the words using alphabet manipulatives and tactile letters (magnetic letters, sponge letters, alphabet stamps, alphabet cereal, letter tiles, linking letter cubes).

- Practice writing words with special pens (glitter pens, neon gel pens on black paper).

- Use a flashlight in a darkened room to "write" the words on a wall.

- Write words forming the letters with clay or Wikki Stix® (see Sources and Resources).

- Write words vertically in columns.

Use Song and Movement to Practice Spelling Words

- Pair movement while spelling words aloud (clap to each letter, bounce ball, yo-yo, jump rope, trampoline). Get creative!

5-10 (*continued*)

- Tap out the sounds or syllables in words (pencil to desk, fingertips to desk or arm, spelling word while tapping with one hand down the other arm [shoulder to hand].

- Use kinesthetic cues for letter/sounds and act out those motions or refer to those cues when segmenting words to spell. (See Fetzer and Rief, 2000. Their book features the "Holder & Fastie Alphabet" which provides kinesthetic cues and attention to how and where each sound of the alphabet is formed in the mouth.)

- Sing spelling words to common tunes/melodies.

- Spell words standing up for consonant letters and sitting down for vowels.

Use Color to Help Call Attention to Letters Within the Word and to Aid Memory

- Write words using the "rainbow technique" of tracing over each word at least three different times in different colored pencils, crayons, chalk, or markers. Then, without looking, write the word from memory.

- Color-code tricky letters (silent letters) in hard-to-spell words.

- Write the words by syllables in different colored markers.

- Write syllable by syllable, color-coding each one; for example, vowels in red.

- Write the first letter in the word in green, the last letter in red.

- Write silent letters (ghost letters) in white pen.

- After taking a pretest, color the known part of a word (correctly spelled letters) in one color. By the time the word is spelled correctly with further trials, the whole word should be written in color.

- Color consonants in one color and vowels in another.

- Color-code key elements/features of the word (such as prefixes/suffixes, final e).

Other Ways and "Choice Activities" for Students to Practice, Study, and Reinforce Spelling Words

- Make a word search on graph paper using all of the words. Include an answer sheet.

- Make a set of flashcards. Study each word with a partner (or parent). Leave out the words that were missed and restudy them.

- Say spelling words into a tape recorder. Spell them correctly into the recorder, and listen to the recording. Bring the tape to school.

- Make a rebus using some of the words. Use syllables and pictures to get ideas across clearly.

- Make a word picture with the spelling words. Lightly draw with pencil a basic shape. In thin black marker, write the words in small lettering around the basic outlined shape. Now erase the pencil marks and the words will form the shape!

- Give each letter of the alphabet a value (a = 1, b = 2, c = 3, d = 4, e = 5, and so forth). Then find the value of the words. Example: The value of the word *spelling* is 19 + 16 + 5 + 12 + 12 + 9 + 14 + 7 = _____.

- Find letters in magazines or newspapers. Glue each letter on a paper to form spelling words with a variety of printed letters.

- Make up word skeletons. Give them to a partner, who must figure out the words. Example: _ _ s _ r _ _ e _ t for the word *instrument*. You may need to give a clue if your partner is stumped. Check that your partner has spelled the words correctly.

- Place the words in alphabetical order.

- Write out each word. Circle the silent letters and underline the vowels.

- Study with a partner. Write your words on a dry-erase board. Have your partner write down how many words you get correct.

- Make up rhymes from the spelling words.

- Have someone dictate the words to you. Write your words using the Copy, Write, Cover, Check (CWCC) method.

- Trace words with a pencil while spelling the word. Then trace them with an eraser. Get up and do a brief physical activity (such as five jumping jacks). Now write the words and check for accuracy.

- Illustrate words and keep a notebook or card file of those words.

- Underline misspelled letters or trouble spots in words.

- Use the "Look, Say, Write" method of practice. Look at the word and trace it with your finger or pencil. Then say the word, spelling it out loud while copying it. Next, write the word without looking and check for accuracy. Fix any errors immediately because it helps with remembering the correct spelling of the word.

- Find as many little words within words as possible (words in sequence only). Examples: *incredulous* (in, red, us); *lieutenant* (lie, tenant, ten, ant).

Use These Instructional Suggestions in the Classroom

- Introduce words on the overhead projector. As a class, ask students to look at the configuration, little words within the word, and any mnemonic clues that would be helpful in remembering how to spell the word. Write the word in syllables in different colored pens. Discuss the word's meaning and use in context.

- When modeling and guiding students in sounding out a word in print:

  1. Cover up part of the word while demonstrating how to sound out one syllable at a time.

  2. Point to the individual sounds as you model decoding the word.

  3. Slide your hand or finger rapidly under the letters as you blend the sounds to quickly say the whole word.

- Have readily available several resources such as dictionaries, electronic spell-checkers, lists of commonly used words, and so on. (Franklin spell-checkers are available from Franklin Electronic Publishers, http://www.franklin.com.)

- Use commercial games that teach and reinforce spelling (Scrabble™, Boggle™, hangman). *Note:* When playing games in which correct spelling is not a requirement, extra

5-10 (*continued*)

bonus points can be awarded for words that *are* spelled correctly to add the incentive for spelling accuracy.

- Have students develop their own personal lists, word banks, word cards attached to a ring, notebooks, and card files for spelling words they wish to keep and practice. This is particularly useful when these personal spelling words are selected from misspelled words from the student's own written products.

- Teach students to look for patterns in words by using phonograms, word families, onsets, and rimes. Color-highlight patterns within the words.

- Provide systematic phonetic training to students who are deficient in this skill and are poor spellers. Many upper-grade students have not had sufficient, teacher-directed phonics instruction and are not firm on letter–sound associations and spellings. A large percentage of words in the English language are phonetically regular, and can be decoded and/or spelled correctly with phonetic knowledge and strategy application. (5-3)

- In addition to teaching words with different phonetic spelling patterns, teach words from high-frequency word lists. Make it a grade-level priority to teach and reinforce the spelling of a certain number of words from a list of high-frequency vocabulary words.

- Post in a highly visible location the high-frequency words that students are expected to spell correctly in their written work. In addition, provide student desk/notebook copies for reference.

- Maintain a Word Wall in the classroom that includes content area words, high-frequency words, and other words deemed important listed under each letter of the alphabet.

- Teach students to use every other line when writing rough drafts of papers. When writing, students can circle, put a question mark, or write "sp" above any words they think are probably spelled wrong. This helps them to self-monitor. They can also apply strategies for checking the spelling of those words. (5-9)

- Provide daily hands-on opportunities for active exploration of words (referred to as "word study"). Word-sorting activities are key word-study strategies. (See Bear et al., 1996.)

- Provide students with words on cards, sticky notes, or on a sheet to be cut out and sorted by a pattern, feature, or category. For example, sort words by letter combinations: ar/or; ea/ee; ng/nk; ch/sh/th; tion/sion; open syllable/closed syllable words. The word sorts depend upon the student's stage of spelling development and skills that need to be practiced and reinforced (such as sorting by beginning sounds, short vowels/long vowels, prefixes/suffixes).

- Word sorts are helpful in calling the student's attention to features of a word (spin/spine, win/wine, grim/grime) and noting the pattern.

- Use mnemonics whenever possible to help students remember and learn memory strategies to apply in the future. Example: He is a fri**end** to the **end**. (4-1)

- Use choral, unison techniques for practicing spelling of non-phonetic words. Chant words or clap out words and use voice inflections to help call attention to certain letters (emphasizing in a louder voice the tricky letters).

- When dictating words, stretch out the word and say it slowly. Model the technique and encourage students to use it when spelling, pulling apart the sounds to hear them more distinctly.

- Provide many peer tutoring and partner spelling opportunities (quizzing, practicing together in fun ways).

- Display models or examples of different phonograms for student reference (such as a picture of an eagle for **ea**; picture of a house for **ou**; picture of a train or snail for **ai**).

Use These Accommodations and Modifications

- Reduce the number of words required. Students with reduced lists may be tested only on the predetermined number of words (for example, 10 or 12 out of the 20). They may try all of the other words on the class test, however, which would be added bonus points if they answer any correctly.

- Instead of assigning some of the very difficult, low-frequency words on spelling lists, assign high-frequency words.

- Allow and encourage the use of a spell-check device such as those from Franklin Publishers.

- Increase the amount of practice.

- Grade content and spelling/mechanics separately.

RELATED LISTS

- See Lists 3-2, 3-4, 3-5, 3-6, 3-8, 3-9, and 4-1 for more strategies to increase memory and retention.

SOURCES AND RESOURCES

Bear, Donald R., Marcia Invernizzi, Shane Templeton, and Francine Johnston. *Words Their Way: Word Study for Phonics, Vocabulary and Spelling Instruction.* Upper Saddle River, NJ: Prentice Hall, 1996.

Fetzer, Nancy, and Sandra Rief. *Alphabet Learning Center Activities Kit.* Paramus, NJ: The Center for Applied Research in Education, 2000.

Harwell, Joan M. *Ready-to-Use Information and Materials for Assessing Specific Learning Disabilities.* West Nyack, NY: The Center for Applied Research in Education, 1995.

Rief, Sandra, and Julie Hemiburge. *How to Reach and Teach All Students in the Inclusive Classroom.* Paramus, NJ: The Center for Applied Research in Education, 1996.

5-10 (*continued*)

Setley, Susan. *Taming the Dragons.* St. Louis, MO: Starfish Publishing Co., 1995.

Stowe, Cynthia. *Spelling Smart: A Ready-to-Use Activities Program for Students with Spelling Difficulties.* Paramus, NJ: The Center for Applied Research in Education, 1996.

Wikki Stix® products are manufactured by Omnicor, Inc. in Phoenix, Arizona. Contact: 800-869-4554 or www.wikkistix.com.

5-11

Strategies for Improving Fine-Motor Skills, Handwriting, Written Organization, and Legibility

When a student struggles with handwriting and written organization, it interferes with production and being able to "show what you know." Paper-and-pencil tasks are a source of great frustration for many children with ADHD. When the physical act of writing is so tedious—and the result of one's efforts are messy and illegible—it is no wonder that children with ADHD often hate to write, and resist doing so.

FINE-MOTOR SKILLS

The small muscle movements required in writing are often weak in children with ADHD (and/or learning disabilities). Of course, with fine-motor difficulties, handwriting is directly affected.

Symptoms of Fine-Motor Problems

- Difficulty holding and positioning fingers on a pencil or writing tool.
- Numerous erasures often leading to ripped or crumpled paper.
- Slow speed in writing and copying.
- Wrist is held in a strange, awkward position.
- Lots of pressure is exerted when writing (pencil lead breaks frequently).
- Easily fatigues when doing paper-and-pencil tasks.
- Poor spacing on lines and page.
- Inconsistency in letter size, shape, and formation.
- Difficulty maintaining correct posture when writing.
- Grip release is not controlled (for example, too quick).
- Difficulty in fine-motor tasks such as stringing beads, buttoning, pulling up and down a zipper, tying shoelaces, putting paper clips on a paper, picking up small objects with fingers, and cutting with scissors.
- Does not form letters automatically; thinks about them or looks at model.
- Does not control writing tool well with just slight finger movements; moves arm muscles as well.

5-11 (_continued_)

Activities and Tips for Building Fine-Motor Skills

- Do finger warm-up exercises (open/shut, snapping, touch each one at a time to the thumb quickly) and finger-play activities (such as "Eensy Weensy Spider").

- Roll out and form clay or play dough into snakes and other shapes.

- Squeeze a stress or squishy ball to build strength in the hand muscles.

- Do activities requiring placement of paper clips, clothespins, or clamps on objects.

- Build things with small Lego® pieces.

- Build with various types of blocks and linking manipulatives.

- Use jigsaw puzzles.

- Do stringing, lacing, and threading activities (such as making necklaces from stringing beads).

- Use sewing cards.

- Learn how to knit or crochet.

- Practice buttoning and opening/closing snaps on clothing.

- Sort small objects (buttons, dried cereal, shells) into an egg container or ice cube tray by category.

- Pick up small objects with tweezers and tongs.

HANDWRITING, WRITTEN ORGANIZATION, AND LEGIBILITY

One of the reasons children struggle in writing is because they do not automatically recall the muscle movements and motor-planning skills involved in forming strokes (curves, loops, counterclockwise motion), and sequencing the steps involved to form each letter. They also may not have formed a clear mental picture of how each letter looks to reproduce from memory, and are constantly seeking a visual model.

Strategies and Tips for Teaching Handwriting and Improving Legibility of Written Work

- When teaching letters (print or cursive), group them by similarity of formation (l/t/i; a/c/d; v/w). Introduce those letters that are more frequently used (s, m, r) before those less commonly found in words (j, q, z).

- Point out and discuss similarities and differences in letters.

- Have children trace letters and then write a few independently. Afterward, have students circle their best one.

- Check out the highly recommended program for teaching print and cursive to children with writing difficulties called _Handwriting Without Tears_™, developed by Jan Olsen, an occupational therapist. (See Sources and Resources.) She uses numerous multisensory techniques and mnemonic cues for helping children learn proper letter formation.

The program also structures the sequence of letters introduced by clusters. For example, cursive *o*, *w*, *b*, and *v* are taught together as the "tow-truck letters" because of their special high endings.

■ Check out another recommended handwriting program called the *CASL Handwriting Program*, developed at Vanderbilt University by Lynn and Doug Fuchs, and research-validated as successful for children with disabilities. (See Sources and Resources.)

■ Use dots, numbered arrows, highlighter, and so forth to provide extra visual cues and supports.

■ Teach appropriate grasp of a pencil (pencil grip) in the early grades. If the child struggles to hold and manipulate a pencil, there are a variety of pencil grips that can be used to make it easier (triangular plastic; molded clay; and soft foam cushion that pencil slides through).

■ Try self-drying clay to mold a pencil grip to the size/shape of the child's fingers.

■ Experiment with the metal pencil frame found in the Zaner Bloser catalog (http://www.zaner-bloser.com). It enables the child to lightly grasp a pencil with a proper angle of the wrist to the paper, and to glide the pencil easily across the page.

■ Try mechanical pencils for older students who frequently break their pencil tips from applying too much pressure.

■ If a child is observed to struggle with the physical task of writing, consult a specialist (occupational therapist or special education teacher). An evaluation, consultation, or direct service from an occupational therapist and/or special education teacher may be needed.

■ Use real-life situations to stress the need for legible writing (job applications, filling out checks).

■ Stress how studies have proven that teachers tend to give students the benefit of the doubt and grade higher if their papers look good as opposed to being sloppy or hard to read. Neatness and legibility make a positive impression.

■ Provide students sufficient time to write in order to avoid time pressures.

■ Set realistic, mutually agreed-upon expectations for neatness.

■ Allow students to write using narrow-ruled paper (shorter line height) than paper that has wider-ruled lines, if needed.

■ Teach placing of index finger between words (finger spacing) to help students who run their words together without spacing.

■ Use special paper with vertical lines to help space letters and words appropriately.

■ Remind the child to anchor his or her paper with the non-writing hand or arm to keep it in one place while writing.

■ Try a clipboard if the student's paper is frequently sliding around.

■ Make sure there is always a sufficient supply of sharpened pencils and erasers available.

5-11 (*continued*)

■ Provide a strip or chart of alphabet letters (print or cursive) on the student's desk for reference of letter formation. Draw directional arrows on the letters the child finds confusing and difficult to write.

TACTILE-KINESTHETIC TECHNIQUES

The following are strategies that reinforce the "feel" of how to correctly form letters.

■ Make a "gel bag" by placing some hair gel in a self-locking plastic bag. With a permanent marker, write each letter for practice on the outside of the bag. While tracing the letter, the student feels the interesting texture of the gel inside of the bag (especially when gel or ooze bag is refrigerated).

■ Color-code the strokes of a letter on the outside of the gel bag. The first phase of the stroke can be one color (purple), the second phase can be another color (yellow). Arrows can be drawn indicating the directions of the letter formation, as well.

■ Practice correct letter formation by tracing letters written on a variety of textures (puff paint, sandpaper).

■ Many upper-grade students have not mastered cursive letters, and struggle with formation or speed. Provide guided practice for students in need by modeling on the overhead projector in color while talking through the steps.

■ Model letter formation (print or cursive) in color while writing on paper on an easel, dry-erase board, or overhead projector.

■ Write letters in the air with large muscle movements while giving a verbal prompt. Holding the child's wrist, write in large strokes in the air while talking through the strokes. For example, with the letter B, give the following instruction:

  ▪ Start at the top.

  ▪ Straight line down.

  ▪ Back to the top.

  ▪ Sideways smile. Sideways smile.

  ▪ Then repeat without guiding the child's hand, but observe that the formation is correct.

  See Fetzer and Rief (2000) and Rief (2001) for several more strategies for teaching letter formation.

■ Trace letters in sand or salt trays, on the carpet, or other textures using two fingers.

ADDITIONAL HANDWRITING TIPS FOR TEACHERS AND PARENTS

■ Provide a lot of practice at home and school when children are learning how to print or write in cursive. Observe carefully as children are practicing, and intervene immediately when you notice errors in letter formation. Gently correct if you observe children making the strokes incorrectly (bottom-to-top rather than top-to-bottom; circles formed clockwise rather than counterclockwise).

- Provide parents with a model of how the letters are being taught in class (for example, arrows indicating steps of letter formation and any verbal prompts) to be consistent.

- Provide prompts for correct letter formation/directionality by placing a green dot indicating where to begin and arrows indicating in which direction to write the strokes of the letter(s).

- Allow for frequent practice and corrective feedback using short trace-and-copy activities.

- Allow students to print if cursive is a struggle.

- Encourage appropriate sitting, posture, and anchoring of paper when writing.

- Add variety for motivational purposes, using different sizes, shapes, textures, and colors of paper; also experiment with fancy stationery and different writing instruments. Have students write on individual chalkboards with colored chalk or dry-erase boards with colored pens.

- Provide students with a slant board (for better wrist position). You can make one by covering an old 3-ring notebook completely with self-stick vinyl. The child then places his or her paper on the slant board when writing.

- Allow students to sometimes show their work by providing them with a blank transparency and requiring them to do their neatest writing in color to be shared with the class on the overhead.

- Teach and post standards of acceptable work in your classroom, whatever those standards may be (such as writing on one side of paper only; rough draft papers written on every other line; math papers with two or three line spaces between problems; heading on upper right section of paper).

- Encourage final drafts to be typed on a computer, providing assistance as needed.

- See List 5-12 for bypass strategies to use if handwriting is too tedious and difficult.

- Display and provide individual copies of handwriting checklists for students to self-monitor their own written work for legibility. The following are possible questions that may be included on a student handwriting checklist (depending on age/developmental level and grade-level standards):

  1. Are my letters resting on the line?
  2. Do tall letters reach the top line, and do short letters reach the middle line?
  3. Do I have space between words?
  4. Are my letters the right size (not too small, not too large)?
  5. Am I writing within the lines?
  6. Are my words in lowercase, unless there is supposed to be a capital?
  7. Am I consistent in my letters—all print or all cursive, not mixed?

5-11 (*continued*)

  8. Is my writing neat?

  9. Have I stayed within the margins of the paper?

SOURCES AND RESOURCES

Currie, Paula, and Elizabeth Wadlington. *The Source for Learning Disabilities.* East Moline, IL: LinguiSystems, 2000.

Fetzer, Nancy, and Sandra Rief. *Alphabet Learning Center Activities Kit.* Paramus, NJ: The Center for Applied Research in Education, 2000.

Fuchs, Lynn, and Doug Fuchs. *CASL (Center on Accelerating Student Learning),* Vanderbilt University. (http:// www.vanderbilt.edu/CASL/reports.html)

Graham, Steve, Karen Harris, and Barbara Fink. "Extra Handwriting Instruction: Prevent Writing Difficulties Right From the Start," *Teaching Exceptional Children*, vol. 33, no. 2, November/December, 2000.

Landy, Joanne M., and Keith R. Burridge. *Fine Motor Skills & Handwriting Activities for Young Children.* Paramus, NJ: The Center for Applied Research in Education, 1999.

Olsen, Jan Z. *Handwriting Without Tears™.* www.hwtears.com; 301-983-8409.

Richards, Regina G. *When Writing's a Problem—A Description of Dysgraphia.* Richards Educational Therapy Center, Inc., 190 E. Big Springs Road, Riverside, CA 92507.

Rief, Sandra. *Ready . . . Start . . . School—Nurturing and Guiding Your Child Through Preschool and Kindergarten.* Paramus, NJ: Prentice Hall Press, 2001.

Sousa, David A. *How the Special Brain Learns.* Thousand Oaks, CA: Corwin Press, 2001.

5-12
STRATEGIES FOR BYPASSING AND ACCOMMODATING WRITING DIFFICULTIES

There are numerous writing strategies and accommodations found in lists throughout this book. The following are also recommended for children and teens with writing disabilities.

■ Substitute nonwritten projects such as oral reports for written assignments.

■ Give students options and choices that do not require writing, choosing instead to draw upon individual strengths. This can be accomplished through hands-on, project-oriented assignments that involve investigating, building, drawing, constructing, creating, simulating, experimenting, researching, telling, singing, dancing, and so on. (3-5, 3-9)

■ Provide worksheets (math papers, tests) with extra space and enlarge the space for doing written work. (3-6)

■ Stress accuracy, not volume.

■ Follow written exams with oral exams and average the grades for those students. (3-8)

■ Allow oral responses for assignments/tests when appropriate.

■ Permit students to dictate their responses and have someone else transcribe for them.

■ Permit students to print if cursive is a struggle.

■ Do not assign a large quantity of written work.

■ Provide in-class time to get started on assignments.

■ Assign reasonable amounts of homework. If parents and students report that an inordinate amount of time is spent on homework most evenings, be willing to make adjustments. (4-8)

■ Allow students to use a tape recorder instead of writing for summarizing learning, responding to questions, planning, and recording ideas.

■ Provide access to a computer and motivating writing programs with a variety of fonts and graphics.

■ Provide note-taking assistance by assigning a buddy who will take notes, share, and compare with the struggling student.

■ Provide multiple-copy carbonless paper for the designated buddy note-taker to use. Students (including those with ADHD) should still take notes in the classroom, but be allowed to *supplement* their own notes with the more detailed and organized copies from their buddy.

■ Make photocopies of teacher notes or from designated students who take neat, organized notes. Share them with students who struggle copying information from the board or taking notes from class lecture.

5-12 (*continued*)

- Teach proper keyboarding/typing skills and provide many practice opportunities to increase skills. See software recommendations given later.

- Teach word-processing skills including the use of editing options (cut and paste) and various format options.

- Provide assistance for typing/printing final drafts of papers.

- Accept modified homework with reduced amounts of writing.

- Help students get started writing by sitting with them and talking or prompting them through the first few sentences.

- Have the student dictate while an adult writes the first few sentences to get the student started.

- Reduce the need to copy from the board or book.

- Permit and encourage subvocalizing or talking out loud while writing, as auditory feedback often helps the student to stay focused and self-monitor. (5-6)

- Provide word processors with speech-recognition programs, if needed, so students can dictate their written work.

- Increase time for completing written tasks.

- Provide extended time for testing, particularly written assessments (such as essay questions).

- Provide a variety of pencil grips for students in need. (5-11)

Use Assistive Technology

- Provide access to the computer for written work.

- Teach keyboarding/typing skills so children learn the proper finger positions. Some recommended programs for keyboarding/typing include:

  - *Type to Learn* (Sunburst Communication)

  - *UltraKey* (Bytes of Learning, Inc.) (http://www.bytesoflearning.com)

  - *Keyboarding for Individual Achievement* (Teachers' Institute for Special Education) (http://special-education-soft.com)

- Teach word-processing skills and encourage the use of spell-check and grammar-check.

- Allow the use of a handheld electronic spell-check (such as the Franklin Speller, available from Franklin Electronic Publishers, http://www.franklin.com).

- Use speech recognition/speech synthesis computer programs that translate words typed by the user into speech.

- Use word-prediction computer programs that "predict" what word the user intends to write based on the first few letters typed.

Note: For an excellent source of information on adaptive technology, check out: ldonline.org/ld_indepth/technology/techguide.html.

Recommended Computer Programs

- *AlphaSmart 3000* is a portable keyboard with a 4-line display that serves as an inexpensive substitute for laptop computers for individual student use. AlphaSmarts are user-friendly and allow the student to type and store material until it is later transferred to their personal computer for editing and revising. For more information, see http://www.alphasmart.com.

- *Inspiration™* and *Kidspiration™* (both available at www.inspiration.com) are user-friendly, motivational software programs that are research-validated as effective in helping students to develop written expression. Both programs allow students to do the following:
  - Create their own graphic organizers (concept maps, webs, flow charts).
  - Brainstorm ideas with pictures and words.
  - Organize and categorize information visually.
  - Plan and organize ideas prior to writing.

- The company Don Johnston (www.donjohnston.com) is one of the leaders in products for students with reading and writing difficulties. It carries the following recommended products to help struggling and reluctant writers:
  - *Write:Outloud®*—This is an easy-to-use talking word processor. This program reads each word out loud as students write, and also reads any electronic text. One feature is that it highlights as it reads, connecting the spoken word to the text. Another is that it contains electronic spell-checkers to help writers use expanded vocabulary and to find the phonetic errors.
  - *Co-Writer 4000*—This is a talking word-prediction program that coaches in spelling and grammar, enabling writers to build better sentences.
  - *Draft:Builder™*—This helps the student produce a first draft by: (1) outlining and mapping, (2) organizing notes that are entered, (3) building a logically sequenced draft.

- For young children, the program *PixWriter* by Slater Software, Inc. is wonderful. It allows the beginning writer to pick pictures or select words supported by pictures.

- Another useful tool is the *QuickLink Pen* by Wizcom Technologies. This allows students to electronically scan notes from print and transfer this information to computers for use in writing and editing papers. It can be very helpful when doing research.

Note: A description of many of the recommended technology products are found on the Don Johnston, Inc. website: http://www.donjohnston.com

5-12 (*continued*)

SOURCES AND RESOURCES

Berninger, V. "The Write Stuff for Preventing and Treating Writing Disabilities," *Perspectives*, 25 (2), 1999.

Dendy, Chris Zeigler. *Teaching Teens with ADD and ADHD.* Bethesda, MD: Woodbine House, 2000.

ERIC/OSEP. "Instructional Approaches that Improve Written Performance: Integrating Technology with Writing Instruction," ERIC/OSEP: *Research Connections in Special Education*, vol. 10, Winter, 2002.

Rief, Sandra. *The ADD/ADHD Checklist: An Easy Reference for Parents and Teachers.* Paramus, NJ: Prentice Hall, 1998.

5-13
MATH DIFFICULTIES ASSOCIATED WITH ADHD

Many students with ADHD and/or learning disabilities struggle academically with mathematics, as multiple processes and brain functions are involved in executing math problems. Some math challenges may be specifically related to weaknesses with ADHD (such as inattention, organization, working memory). Others may result more directly from a learning disability (such as sequential learning, perceptual-motor, language). Remember, some children have both ADHD and coexisting learning disabilities.

The following are impairments associated with ADHD and learning disabilities, and how they negatively affect performance in math.

MEMORY WEAKNESS

With math, active working memory is involved, so any memory weakness makes it a struggle to hold information in their heads long enough to utilize it throughout the steps of the problem. Long-term memory is also involved through the retrieval of processes and math vocabulary learned in the past. Memory weaknesses cause problems with:

- Learning and acquisition of basic math facts.

- Being able to recall math facts and retrieve those math facts quickly and accurately.

- Computing multistep problems (forgetful of sequence and recalling where they are in the process).

- Recalling rules, procedures, algorithms, teacher instruction, and directions.

ATTENTION WEAKNESS

Problems with attention result in numerous careless errors and inconsistent performance, even when the student is skilled at solving the math problems. Attention weaknesses cause problems with:

- Noticing processing/operational signs in math problems (for example, being aware that the + sign changes to −).

- Paying attention to other details (such as decimal points and other symbols).

- Self-correcting and finding own errors in computation.

- Being able to sustain the focus and mental effort necessary to complete the problems with accuracy.

5-13 (*continued*)

SEQUENCING WEAKNESSES

Sequencing weaknesses cause problems with:

- Being able to do algebra and other step-by-step equations.
- Executing any multistep procedure.
- Being able to do skip counting (3, 6, 9, 12, 15 . . .; multiples of other numbers).
- Recognizing and using patterns.

PERCEPTUAL, VISUAL-MOTOR, FINE-MOTOR, AND SPATIAL-ORGANIZATION WEAKNESSES

These weaknesses cause problems with:

- Copying problems from the board or book onto paper.
- Aligning numbers, decimal points, and so on accurately on paper.
- Writing and computing within the minimal amount of given space on the page; spacing between problems; leaving enough room.
- Remembering and using correct directionality for solving math problems (such as beginning with the column to the right and moving right to left; regrouping accurately).
- Recognizing and not confusing symbols (+, ×, 6/9, 38/83).
- Speed of writing down problems and answers (often either too fast and illegible, or too slow and cannot keep up or complete assignments/tests).
- Difficulties in the above result in numerous errors and need for frequent erasing and correction, causing the student much frustration.

LANGUAGE WEAKNESS

Difficulties with language cause problems with:

- Understanding and relating to the numerous abstract terms in math.
- Solving word problems (interpreting and understanding what is being asked; separating relevant from irrelevant information provided).
- Following directions.

In addition, as writing is infused in all curricular areas in today's classrooms, students are generally expected to write about their thinking processes, and how they solved problems. Consequently, a student who may be strong with numbers and mathematical problem solving, but struggles in written expression, may do poorly in math class as a result of language and writing difficulties.

SELF-MONITORING AND SELF-MANAGEMENT WEAKNESSES

These important executive functions, which involve self-awareness, metacogitive skills, and self-management, cause problems with:

- Taking time to plan strategies for solving a problem.
- Realizing if something is not working or making sense (for example, answer is not close to estimate) and readjusting or trying another strategy.
- Being aware of time and time management in pacing and working the problems given.
- Maintaining the level of attention and perseverance necessary to complete problems with accuracy.
- Being able to check for errors and self-correct.

RELATED LISTS

- See List 5-14 for math strategies and interventions.

SOURCES AND RESOURCES

Misunderstood Minds. WGBH, Educational Foundation, 2002; http://www.pbs.org/wgbh/misunderstoodminds/mathstrats.html.

Nicholls, C. J. "The Link between AD/HD and Learning Disabilities in Mathematics," CHADD 13th Annual Conference, October 17–21, 2001, in Anaheim, California.

Rief, Sandra. *How to Reach and Teach ADD/ADHD Children.* West Nyack, NY: The Center for Applied Research in Education, 1993.

5-14
MATH STRATEGIES AND INTERVENTIONS

Students with ADHD and/or learning disabilities have difficulties that affect success in math computation and problem solving. (5-13) Fortunately, there are a number of ways that teachers and parents can help. Here are strategies to strengthen and build math skills, as well as appropriate modifications and accommodations to support struggling students.

Make the Abstract More Concrete

■ Provide many kinds of manipulatives (cubes, chips, tiles, counters, beans, base-ten blocks, number line) to help students visualize and work out math problems.

■ Introduce mathematical concepts with demonstrations using real-life examples and motivating situations. For example, cut a sandwich into 5 equal parts to share in a small group (1/5 per student); or first count the total and then equally divide a bag of candy among a number of students (32 pieces divided by 5 kids = 6 each with 2 left over).

■ Teach multiplication, relating things that come in sets of a certain number (4's—quarters in a dollar or legs on a dog; 5's—fingers on a hand or days in a school week).

■ Model the use of drawing, diagramming, and labeling in the problem-solving process. Encourage students to use those strategies.

■ Use concrete references, such as the technique used in Semple Math (see Sources and Resources) of "Whole Number Street" in the teaching of place value, with different houses of numbers (unit house, thousands, millions house, and so on):

  ▪ Semple Math also provides mnemonic associations and spatial anchors. For example, "kids" are referred to as the numbers in the units place, "teens" are numbers in the tens place, and "adults" are numbers in the hundreds place.

  ▪ Users of Semple Math quickly can identify which "house" the number lives in, and how to consequently read and write that number.

  ▪ There is also a brick wall symbol on the right side of the paper as a cue, which helps the children remember how to place the numbers in relation to "standing near the wall."

■ Give as many opportunities as possible at home and school for using math in the context of real-life situations (using money, balancing a checkbook, determining mileage on a fantasy road-trip, comparison shopping, ordering a meal with tax and tip).

■ See Rief and Heimburge (1996) for more than 60 "Survival Math" activities that are motivating to students.

Compensate for Memory Difficulties and Increase Recall of Math Facts/Procedures

■ Use multiplication fact sheets, charts, and tables, and keep them readily available for reference.

■ Allow and encourage the use of calculators. Have students use them to check their work.

■ Teach children the "counting up method" on their fingers for a reliable back-up system to memorizing addition and subtraction facts to 18.

■ Use mnemonic devices (memory clues, images, and associations) to help students remember facts, sequential steps, procedures, and abstract concepts/vocabulary.

■ Use a variety of rhymes, chants, raps, and songs to help students memorize the multiplication tables. Students can make up their own or use those commercially available.

■ Use mnemonics such as **D**ead **M**onsters **S**mell **B**adly; **D**ear **M**iss **S**ally **B**rown; or **D**ad, **M**om, **S**ister, **B**rother for learning the steps of long division (**D**ivide, **M**ultiply, **S**ubtract, **B**ring down).

■ Teach the different "finger tricks" available for learning ×6, ×7, ×8, and ×9 tables. (See Sources and Resources.)

■ Use mnemonic programs that incorporate picture associations and clever stories to help master multiplication facts. (See Sources and Resources.)

■ Use Semple Math and its very creative associations and mnemonics.

■ Give students a blank multiplication chart and have them fill in the facts they know. Look for patterns and shortcuts. The rows of zeros, ones, fives, and tens are easily identified and eliminated from the list of multiplication facts that must be memorized.

■ Once students know multiples of ×0 through ×5, teach ×9s. When students are able to recognize and recall the commutative property of multiplication ($3 \times 7 = 7 \times 3$), it significantly reduces the stress and feeling that there are so many facts to learn. Actually, there will only be 12 more facts left to memorize ($4 \times 4, 4 \times 6, 4 \times 7, 4 \times 8, 6 \times 4, 6 \times 6, 6 \times 7, 6 \times 8, 7 \times 4, 7 \times 7, 7 \times 8, 8 \times 8$).

■ Have students practice one sequence of multiples at a time (×2s, ×3s) in a variety of multisensory formats until mastery.

■ Encourage keeping a card file of specific math skills, concepts, rules, and algorithms taught, along with specific examples of each on the card for reference.

■ Practice and review facts in frequent, brief sessions (5 minutes per session, a few times each day).

■ Daily timings of basic facts can be great practice and motivation *if* students compete against themselves, *not* their classmates. Have students chart their own progress and mastery. *Don't* display visually for the whole class to see, which is demoralizing and embarrassing for students who struggle to pass timings.

5-14 (*continued*)

- Touch Math® (see Sources and Resources) is an excellent supplementary or compensatory technique for children with ADHD and/or learning disabilities. Through the use of touch points strategically placed on numerals 1–9, students learn to rapidly visualize and accurately compute without having to pull up their fingers. This is a very useful bypass strategy and technique for students who struggle with learning basic facts.

  Note: Poor mastery of basic facts should not prevent students from being taught grade-level math curriculum and higher level concepts. Provide compensatory tools (math tables/charts) to help them past this hurdle, while continuing to teach, practice, and review math facts on a regular basis.

- See List 4-1 for more memory strategies.

Compensate for Spatial Organization and Perceptual-Motor Difficulties

- Encourage students to write and solve their computation problems on graph paper rather than notebook paper. Experiment with graph paper of varying square/grid sizes.

- Turn notebook paper sideways (with lines running vertically rather than horizontally). This makes it much easier for students to keep numbers aligned in columns, and reduces careless errors.

- Reduce the requirement of copying problems from the board or book by photocopying the page or writing out the problems on paper for certain students.

- Require struggling students to copy from the board/book just the first three or four problems for practice. Then give them a photocopy or assistance recording for the remaining problems of the assignment.

- Remove individual pages from consumable workbooks. Give one page at a time instead of the entire workbook.

- Provide a large workspace on tests. If necessary, rewrite test items on other paper with lots of room for computation.

- Provide scratch paper for student use in computation.

- Provide lots of space on the page between problems and at the bottom of the page.

- See Lists 3-6 and 5-11.

Use Instructional and Assessment Strategies and Modifications

- Allow extra time on math tests so students are not rushed, which can lead to careless errors.

- Avoid the anxiety of timed tests and drills (especially those posted for all students in the class to see). Or extend the amount of time permitted for certain students as "passing."

- Grade by number of correct problems over the number assigned (which could be different for students receiving modified homework/classwork).

- Provide frequent checks for accuracy. Set a certain number of problems to complete (such as one row only, or 4–5 problems) and then check before student is permitted to continue. This reduces the frustration of having to erase and fix a number of problems done incorrectly.

■ List steps/procedures to multistep problems and algorithms. Display clear numbered steps and/or give students a desk copy model of steps to solve problems.

■ Cut up a page of problems into strips/rows, and give to the students one strip at a time.

■ Have review problems prepared on cards (3–5 per card). Students choose a card to complete.

■ When testing long division or multiplication problems that involve using several digits and regrouping, give problems with numbers for which most all students know the math facts. Example: $6274 \times 52 =$ ____. Most students know the ×5 and ×2 tables. This way students are tested on their understanding of the process, and are not penalized because they have poor memory skills.

■ Provide models of assignments and criteria for success (rubrics).

■ Provide immediate feedback whenever possible. Go over homework assignments the next day, allowing students to comfortably ask questions and work any problems that they did not understand together as a class.

■ Encourage students to come for help when needed (before, during, or after class). Do not allow students to remain confused without providing any necessary reteaching and/or tutorial assistance.

■ Keep sample math problems on the board and have students keep them in a notebook for reference.

■ Work problems on an overhead projector or dry-erase board, using color to make the steps and processes more visually clear.

■ Reduce the number of problems assigned (half page, evens only, odds only).

■ Provide time in class for checking work.

■ Provide frequent review of skills.

■ Instruct with a teaching model of demonstrating, working together, working independently, and checking.

■ Use cooperative learning structures and formats in math instruction:

1. *Partners:* Working in pairs, one works a problem while the other coaches. Roles are reversed. Then, after a couple of problems are completed, partners pair up with another set of pairs and compare answers/check each other.

2. *Groups/Teams:* Teams of four work a problem together and check each other's understanding on one or more problems. Then the team breaks into two pairs who continue to work together to solve the next couple of problems. Students then continue independently working similar problems.

■ Use choral responses in instruction (chanting in unison: multiples, evens/odds, place value, names of geometric figures).

■ See Lists 3-2, 3-5, 3-7, 3-8, and 3-9.

5-14 (*continued*)

Increase Focus and Attention

- Color-highlight or underline keywords and vocabulary in word problems (*shared, doubled, product, average, larger, slower, difference, altogether, equal parts*).

- Color-dot the ones (units) column to remind students the direction of where to begin computation.

- Color-highlight processing signs for students who are inattentive to change in operational signs on a page. For example, color addition signs yellow, subtraction signs pink, and so forth.

- Color-highlight place value. For example, given the number 16,432,781, write the hundreds (781) in green, the thousands (432) in orange, and the millions (16) in blue.

- Reduce the number of problems on a page.

- Block part of the page while working on problems, or fold the paper under to reveal just one or two rows at a time.

- Softly say steps of the problem out loud to keep attention focused.

- Allow the child to stand up and stretch, or take a break of some kind after a certain number of problems are completed and checked for accuracy.

- See Lists 3-2, 3-3, 3-4, and 3-7.

Use Word Problem–Solving Strategies

- Teach steps needed for solving math problems. Clearly list steps and keep a visible chart of various problem-solving strategies.

- Teach and model a number of strategies for solving word problems:

  - Read the problem out loud.

  - Read at least twice before beginning.

  - Restate in own words.

  - Look for and color-highlight significant clue words (*altogether, how much more, faster than, part of*).

  - Draw pictures, diagrams, and sketches representing the problem.

  - Cross out irrelevant information.

  - Circle, underline, or color-highlight the numbers that are important.

  - Write the kind of answer needed (for example, miles per hour, degrees, dollars/cents).

  - Use objects/manipulatives.

  - Construct a chart or table.

  - Make an organized list.

  - Act it out.

- Look for a pattern.
- Make a model.
- Work backwards.
- Eliminate possibilities.
- Guess (estimate) and check.

■ Teach how to first estimate and then evaluate the answer to determine if it is reasonable or not.

■ Show how to reason whether or not an answer should be larger or smaller than the numbers given.

■ Teach important math vocabulary and keywords that indicate the process or strategy needed; for example: *total, sum, altogether* (addition/multiplication); *more/less, fewer, difference, what's left? missing? larger than/faster than/smaller than* (for subtraction); *what part of/per unit* (indicating division).

■ Make up word problems using student names, situations, and interests.

■ Encourage thinking of different ways to solve a problem.

■ Talk through the steps of problem solving.

■ Let students use their own methods for solving problems (mental, pictorial, fingers, manipulatives, paper/pencil).

■ Always build in time during the lesson for students to share how they solved the problem, and emphasize that there are a variety of ways, not just one method.

■ Provide many opportunities for students to make up their own word/thought problems to share with the class, and do as a group, whenever possible, within the context of the classroom activities. For example, when planning a class party or field trip, the students can work in teams deciding how many cars/drivers are needed, how many bottles of soda or juice need to be bought, how many dozens of cookies are to be baked, and so forth.

Use Self-Monitoring and Metacognitive Strategies

■ Provide direct instruction to help students think about their approach to problem solving.

■ Help students self-monitor their level of alertness when working, so they maintain attention to task, stay paced, and work problems with accuracy.

■ Model how to first read problems (particularly word problems) and plan a strategy for solving before beginning the work.

■ Teach how to work each problem carefully and check for accuracy.

■ Teach how to estimate and determine whether an answer given is reasonable or not.

■ Encourage students to stop after completing a few problems and check for accuracy (independently, with a partner, or teacher).

5-14 (*continued*)

- Use math portfolios/assessment. Have students keep a journal of their thinking, reasoning, questions, and understanding of math concepts. Also, have students write their understanding about mathematical concepts before and after the unit is taught.

- Guide students through the steps of the problem, modeling what to ask oneself when solving. For example: "Where do you always start?" (ones column). "Read the ones column" (5 minus 9). "Can you do that? Can you have 5 and take away 9?" (No). "So, what do we have to do next?" (Regroup, or borrow from the tens column).

- Model talking out loud while reasoning out or thinking about a mathematical problem. Encourage students to do the same, externalizing their thinking and verbalizing while solving problems. Listen to students as they think out loud, and correct gaps in their comprehension when possible at this point.

- Teach students to think about what they are being asked to figure out in the problem and to state it in their own words.

- See Lists 2-9 and 4-2, and the Self-Monitoring Form in the Appendix.

Increase the Amount of Practice and Review

- Review previously learned skills with high frequency.

- Make sets of practice/review problems (a few per page) with answers on the back for independent practice.

- Use computer software games for drill and practice of math skills. Computer practice is ideal in that most programs are adjusted for speed and level of difficulty. They provide immediate feedback and are fun, nonthreatening, and motivating to students.

- Pair students to practice and quiz each other on skills taught.

- Motivate the practicing of skills through the use of board games, card games, and other class games. Try using as many games as possible that do not have a heavy emphasis on speed of recall, or the type of competition that will discourage struggling students from even trying.

Increase the Motivation

- Give students a choice of computing with a calculator, paper and pencil, or mentally.

- Play team math games in class.

- Use board games (Uno™, Battleship™) and card games for building math skills (counting, logic, probability, strategic thinking).

- Let students choose what problems to do first, or to cross out or eliminate any two problems in the assignment they wish.

Points for Parents to Keep in Mind

- Since there is not enough time during a school day for the needed daily practice of math drill and rote memorization, parents should try to spend at least five minutes a day practicing at home in a variety of formats. They should practice with their child in a fun, relaxed manner, without pressure or tension.

■ Many children with ADHD and/or learning disabilities are not proficient with functional math skills (measurement, time concepts, counting money/change). Parents and their child should practice as much as possible at home. These are critical skills that teachers often do not have enough time to teach until mastery. Parents can include their child in such activities as cooking/baking, constructing, sewing, gardening, and home improvements, as these all involve measurement and other functional math skills.

RELATED LISTS

■ See all lists in Section 3 as well as List 4-8.

SOURCES AND RESOURCES

Baratta-Lorton, Robert. *Patterns & Connections in Mathematics.* Saratoga, CA: Center for Innovation in Education, 1993.

Burns, Marilyn. *Math By All Means.* New Rochelle, NY: The Math Solution Publications, 1991.

Curie, Paula, and Elizbeth Wadlington. *The Source for Learning Disabilities.* East Moline, IL: LinguiSystems, Inc., 2000.

Kagan, Spencer, Miguel Kagan, and Laurie Kagan. *Reaching Standards Through Cooperative Learning in Mathematics.* Port Chester, NY: National Professional Resources, Inc., 2000.

Polloway, Edward, James Patton, and Loretta Serna. *Strategies for Teaching Learners with Special Needs* (7th ed). Upper Saddle River, NJ: Merrill/Prentice Hall, 2001.

Rief, Sandra. *How to Reach and Teach ADD/ADHD Children.* West Nyack, NY: The Center for Applied Research in Education, 1993.

Rief, Sandra, and Julie Heimburge. *How to Reach and Teach All Students in the Inclusive Classroom.* Paramus, NJ: The Center for Applied Research in Education, 1996.

Rodriguez, Dave, and Judy Rodriguez. *Time Tables the Fun Way: A Picture Method of Learning the Multiplication Facts.* Sandy, UT: Key Publishers, Inc., 1999; 800-585-6059.

Semple, Janice L. *Semple Math—A Basic Skills Mathematics Program for Beginning, High-Risk and/or Remedial Students.* Attleboro, MA: Stevenson Learning Skills, Inc. (Levels I–III, 1986; Level IV, 2001).

Setley, Susan. *Taming the Dragons (Real Help for Real School Problems).* St. Louis, MO: Starfish Publishing Company, 1995.

5-14 (*continued*)

Touch Math®. Innovative Learning Concepts, 6760 Corporate Drive, Colorado Springs, CO 80919-1999; 800-888-9191.

Yates, Donnalyn. *Memory Joggers—Multiplication and Division Learning System*, 24 Nuevo, Irvine, CA 92612; 888-854-9400.

Section 6

Collaborative Care and Practices to Support Students with ADHD

6-1
THE NECESSITY OF A TEAM APPROACH

The success of children/teens with ADHD is dependent upon a *team effort* in a number of situations.

The Diagnostic Process Involves a Team

- Parent information is provided through interviews, rating forms, and questionnaires. (1-14, 1-19)

- School information/data is gathered from classroom teachers and other school personnel directly working with the student or observing the child's functioning in various school settings. (1-14, 1-15, 1-18, 1-19, 6-2)

- The multidisciplinary assessment (IEP) team (special education teacher/resource specialist, school psychologist, speech/language therapist, school nurse) may conduct a more formal evaluation of the student. (7-1 through 7-5)

- A physician or mental health professional evaluates the child for ADHD.

The Treatment Plan Involves a Team

- The most effective approach in treating ADHD is multimodal, involving a number of interventions from a variety of different professionals and service providers. (1-22, 1-23)

- Treatments outside of school may include counseling for the ADHD child/teen, his or her parents, or the family. Often it involves a combination, with counseling of various types as needed at different times in the child's life.

- School interventions are generally provided through a variety of school personnel and other resources that may include classroom teachers, school counselors, social workers, the school nurse, special education teachers, speech/language therapists, adapted P.E. teachers, occupational therapists, school psychologists, administrators, tutorial service providers, instructional aides, guidance aides, peer tutors, cross-age tutors, and parent or community volunteers.

- Medical intervention can be provided by different medical doctors (pediatricians, family practitioners, child psychiatrists, and neurologists).

- It is important for the child/teen to participate in activities that build upon his or her interests and strengths, and provide an emotional and/or physical outlet. This may require a variety of the following: coaches, trainers, instructors, youth group leaders, scout leaders, mentors, and others working with the child/teen in extracurricular activities.

- The child may be involved in other treatments to address specific needs (such as social skills training or private academic tutoring).

6-1 (*continued*)

- Parent training groups (for example, on behavioral therapy) may be provided by various community professionals/trained facilitators in behavior management and positive discipline strategies.

- The school's SST/504 Team should be monitoring and revising, as needed, any intervention plans that had been developed for the student. (7-1, 7-3)

- If the child is in special education, then the school's IEP team/service providers will be involved in the implementation of all aspects of a child's IEP. (7-1, 7-2, 7-4, 7-5)

- Support groups for parents of children/teens with ADHD will be comprised of a number of people who can serve as a resource and support, a very helpful intervention for parents.

- It is critical that in the diagnostic process, as well as *any* treatment and intervention provided, there be close communication among all parties: home, school, physician, and other service providers in the community.

- Most students with ADHD require close monitoring between the home and school to be successful:

  - Teachers need to keep parents well informed about work assignments; upcoming tests and projects; how the student is performing and keeping up with daily work; as well as behavior and other issues. See daily report cards and other monitoring and reporting forms in the Appendix and List 2-9.

  - Parents need to communicate with teachers regarding how the child/teen is functioning at home, the child's stress level, and other issues. In addition, they need to stay on top of monitoring that homework is being done and followed through with any home–school plans (to aid and reinforce behavior, work production, and organization skills).

- Any child/teen taking medication requires close monitoring and communication between the teacher(s), school nurse, parents, and physician. (1-25, 6-5)

- Most children with ADHD will be educated in general education classrooms. Some will be receiving special education services, and others will not. However, collaboration and consultation between special education and classroom teachers regarding effective strategies and accommodations is helpful in addressing the child's needs.

- Teachers who team-teach different subject areas, plan and team as a grade level, or team for special projects and/or disciplinary purposes, often report much greater job satisfaction. In addition, the students benefit from the opportunity to have more than one teacher, especially when teachers are able to enthusiastically share their areas of interest, strength, and expertise with students.

- Of course, the child/teen must be included in the team effort. Once students are old enough, they need to learn about ADHD and understand the reason for the various treatments/interventions. The older child/adolescent needs to take an active role in his or her treatment, and learn how to advocate for him- or herself in an effective manner. There are wonderful resources available for the child with ADHD. (8-10)

6-2
THE STUDENT SUPPORT TEAM (SST) PROCESS

Most schools have a team process for assisting teachers in devising instructional and behavioral strategies and supports for students experiencing difficulties in general education. This process and team is referred to by many names:

- **SST** can stand for "Student Support Team," "Student Study Team," or "Student Success Team."

- In some districts the team is called the "SAT" (Student Assistance Team), "SIT" (Student Intervention Team), "IST" (Instructional Support Team), or "TAT" (Teacher Assistance Team).

- In others it may be called the "Consultation Team," "Child Guidance Team," "Child Study Team," or "Multidisciplinary Intervention Team."

- Throughout this book, this team process will be referred to as SST.

The SST (or whatever name the district chooses to use) is *not* a special education process or procedure, but rather a function of regular/general education to strategize and brainstorm about ways to help students who are experiencing difficulty (academic, behavioral, social/emotional). The SST process and protocol differs from district to district and school to school.

The SST is a process and forum for teachers to meet with a team typically comprised of some support personnel, an administrator, and generally the parents in order to share input regarding children about whom they have concerns. The SST is noted by the following:

- The team brainstorms possible supports, interventions, and strategies that can be tried to assist the student.

- A few of those strategies/interventions are selected to be implemented for a period of time.

- Every SST meeting is intended to result in an action plan with a follow-up date to monitor its effectiveness in addressing the concerns.

Depending on the support personnel available at the school (and their schedules), the members of the team vary. Generally they include:

- The school psychologist, school counselor, special education teacher (resource specialist), school nurse, administrator, and classroom teacher(s).

6-2 (*continued*)

- The speech/language therapist and adapted P.E. teacher are other members of the team who may perhaps not be in attendance at all team meetings, but participate when the team will be discussing a student with issues involving speech/language or motor skill development.

- Some schools have social workers, reading specialists, and others with various areas of expertise who are able to join the team.

The SST meets on a regularly scheduled basis (such as once a week for approximately 60–90 minutes).

It is important to note that a school professional may refer a child to special education without an SST meeting, because the meeting is not required by law. However, schools generally discourage their school staff from doing so. SSTs are recommended for the following reasons:

- Schools that have effective and efficient SSTs in place can be very proactive in identifying children with needs and intervening early with various supports, adaptations, and safety nets.

- Most districts advise teachers and other school personnel to first discuss and plan for the child with any general education supports that may be provided before referring a child to special education (which begins the IEP process).

- Most districts require that schools document interventions and strategies that have already been tried as part of the referral process to special education. The SST is a perfect vehicle for doing so.

THE ROLE OF PARENTS

- If parents inquire about an evaluation for special education, they may be *asked* if they are willing to first discuss their concerns at an SST meeting (which should be scheduled very quickly and timely).

- It is important to understand that parents cannot be denied the immediate initiation of the IEP process if they choose to do so and make that request/referral. Parents *always* have the right to bypass the SST and directly request a formal assessment for special education and related services under IDEA or Section 504. (7-1 through 7-4)

- Sometimes schools will initiate the IEP evaluation process and still concurrently schedule the SST meeting to discuss and document what has already been tried, and the effectiveness of those strategies/interventions.

- Parents may or may not be in attendance at SST meetings, as this depends on the school/district protocol.

- Some schools prefer to meet initially without parents (generally for efficiency purposes) in order to discuss more students within the designated amount of time. It is harder to keep to a tight time schedule when parents are in attendance. Such schools will inform parents prior to a meeting as well as immediately after regarding any plan of action, and then will generally invite parents to attend a follow-up meeting.

■ Many schools request that parents attend the SST meeting. Parent input is extremely important and helpful in the problem-solving/strategy-planning process. Generally parents appreciate being invited to SST meetings, regardless of whether or not they are able to attend.

■ In all cases, it is necessary to inform parents when the SST meeting will be taking place, and also to reveal the outcome of the meeting (which usually involves a written plan of action).

■ Parents will be asked to share their perceptions of the child's functioning at home and school, areas of strength/interest, areas of difficulty, needs, and so forth. If behaviors are exhibited at school that are of concern, parents will be asked if any of these behaviors are observed outside of school.

■ Any information parents are willing to supply that can assist in determining an appropriate plan of action for the child is very helpful. Parents may be asked what they have found to be effective in motivating and reinforcing their child.

■ If parents are not attending the SST meeting, it is recommended that the school obtain their input by phone interview or by sending home a parent input form prior to the meeting.

THE ROLE OF THE SCHOOL

Note: SSTs are sometimes perceived as the "gatekeeper" to special education, as teachers may view the process as extra "hoops to jump through" before a child is referred. This is a misconception because SSTs are not intended to significantly delay appropriate referrals to special education.

The school's SST process has the potential of being a highly effective method for early intervention, providing much needed support to struggling students and their teachers. The benefits to the school include:

■ Provides teacher with access to a group of colleagues who share information and expertise in order to help the teacher better meet the individual needs of students.

■ Assists the teacher in problem-solving, strategizing, and developing a plan of appropriate classroom interventions.

■ Facilitates student access to additional schoolwide and perhaps community-wide supports and safety nets (as needed).

■ Provides teachers with an expanded "toolbox" or repertoire of instructional and behavioral strategies, and adaptations/accommodations useful for students in the general education classroom.

■ Provides the necessary pre-referral intervention documentation if a formal referral for special education is required.

6-2 (*continued*)

- Enhances the home–school partnership in efforts to collaboratively address student needs.

Because there are many schools with a large population or high percentage of students in need of support, a once-a-week SST meeting with a single team is not sufficient. To be effective, schools must be creative in finding ways to meet more frequently and consistently, as well as expand upon the resources and personnel in the building who can contribute and participate in the SST.

Some schools are using very creative models to increase the number of SST meetings to discuss and plan for student needs without overtaxing the members of the schoolwide SST. The following are some examples:

- Establishing multiple teams in the building with different members of support staff, administration, and teachers assigned to each team.
- Utilizing a layered or tiered SST process/structure. Students are first discussed and strategies/interventions designed in grade-level teacher teams, cluster teams, or house teams. If problems are not resolved at this level, then a schoolwide SST is scheduled with parents and other SST members.

Note: Sandra Rief has been very involved in working with schools (especially those with high levels of student needs) to establish effective processes/structures as noted above. For more information, see contact information in Sources and Resources.

THE ROLE OF TEACHERS

It is very helpful for teachers to follow through on preliminary steps prior to the SST meeting:

- Implement some strategies/interventions and document effectiveness.
- Communicate with previous teachers.
- Review the cumulative records and student data.
- Collect work samples.
- Share concerns and action taken with appropriate SST members at the informal level.
- Establish communication with parents—notify them of observations, concerns, attempts to assist, and so on.

With pre-referral steps taken, then the SST meeting is more productive. The team is in a position to recommend "next step" interventions. Teachers will be asked to complete a referral/SST request form prior to the meeting. The facilitator of the meeting generally makes a copy of the completed form to distribute to team members either before or at the time of the meeting. A typical SST Request (or Referral) form generally asks the teacher to:

- Describe the child's strengths/interests.

- Identify the areas of greatest concern.

- Identify strategies tried so far to help address those concerns/student needs.

- Document that the parents/guardians have been contacted and teacher has made an effort to share concerns and work together with parents.

DURING THE SST MEETING

- The team typically examines records: past report cards, assessment data, portfolio of work collected (if available), current work samples, attendance record, health records, vision and hearing screenings, and so on.

- Members of the team share their observations of the student in different settings. Any strategies and interventions that have been implemented are evaluated.

- Any strategies and interventions that have been implemented are evaluated.

- The teacher shares information about the student's performance, observed areas of strength and weakness, and may be asked to identify what he or she has learned to be effective in motivating and reinforcing the student.

- There is a designated recorder at the team meeting, even though typically everyone takes his or her own notes.

- One team member is responsible for facilitating the meeting. It is advised that a time-keeper be appointed as well.

- A plan of action, consisting of a targeted goal for improved student outcome and a few strategies or interventions for achieving that goal, is typically written during the meeting. The plan should include a follow-up date to examine the effectiveness of the strategies and interventions designated in the plan.

- Either a follow-up SST meeting (scheduled in a specified number of weeks) or a less formal follow-up between the teacher, parents, and one or two members of the team is appropriate.

The information generated and recorded at the meeting generally includes:

- Student strengths/interests
- Background information
- Areas of concern (needs)
- Goal/desired student outcome
- Interventions/strategies tried
- List of possible strategies/interventions (from brainstorming)
- Actions from the above-mentioned list selected for implementation
- Who is responsible for each strategy

6-2 (continued)

- When it will take place
- Follow-up date (usually three to six weeks later)

Points to Keep in Mind

- If it appears that the student may have ADHD, the SST meeting is often the perfect forum to share information and resources with parents, and discuss what is involved in an evaluation. A diagnostic evaluation can be initiated at this time if parents are so inclined. (1-17, 1-18)
- For an SST to be effective, it has to be a priority in the school. Administrators must make all efforts to resolve scheduling issues by taking such measures as providing coverage for classroom teachers if the meetings take place during school hours.
- A good SST action plan for a child with ADHD can be similar to a 504 plan. After assessing and determining eligibility, many 504 plans involve basically rewriting the SST interventions/strategies that are proven to be effective, and adding any other agreed-upon accommodations, supports, and information onto a district 504 form.
- For an action plan to be effective (whether it is one generated at an SST meeting, a 504 plan, or an IEP), there must be *follow-up* for accountability. The best of plans fail if we don't revisit the plan and assess how effective it is.

"SAFETY NETS" AND SUPPORTS FOR GENERAL EDUCATION STUDENTS

It is important for schools to provide interventions, special programs, and "safety nets" to students in need among the general education population so that special education is not the *only* means of getting additional assistance.

Schools will do their students a great service and reduce the number of children in need of special education if they get proactive and provide early intervention to their "at-risk" students (including remedial/tutorial help). Proactive schools find the means and resources to establish an array of interventions and safety nets (during the school day and extended hours) to address the various needs of their students. These include such programs and interventions as:

- Homework clubs
- Organization and study-skills assistance
- Computer lab for developing research skills, learning to type, and so on
- Practicing/reinforcing basic skills
- Assistance from cross-age tutors, parents, and community volunteers
- Small-group reading programs
- Extra guided reading and writing

- Math lab and tutoring
- Mentor or "special friend" programs
- Activity clubs, service clubs, sports and recreation, creative and performing arts, and so on

SSTs are most effective when they not only help the classroom teacher with designing and implementing effective classroom strategies, but can also offer students additional school supports to address their needs (as part of the general education program).

SOURCES AND RESOURCES

A Training Manual on Prevention & Support Services in General Education: Instructional Support Teams. New York State Education Department, 1999.

Rief, Sandra. *Instructional Support Team Manual* (developed for Community School District 10, Bronx, New York), 2000. For information, contact the author through www.sandrarief.com.

Rief Sandra, Linda Fisher, and Nancy Fetzer. *Successful Schools—How to Raise Achievement and Support "At-Risk" Students.* (video) San Diego, CA: Educational Resource Specialists; 800-682-3528; www.sandrarief.com.

6-3
WHAT SUPPORTS AND TRAINING DO TEACHERS NEED?

Parents and administrators need to realize that teachers frequently have several students in a classroom who need extra assistance, support, and attention, including:

- Children with ADHD, learning disabilities, and other neuro-biological, developmental, or behavioral disorders
- English-language learners (students who are not yet proficient in English)
- Children with social/emotional/behavioral problems due to trauma or situations in their personal lives
- Students with a wide range of skill and developmental levels

It is by no means an easy job to be an effective teacher and address the diverse needs of students in the classroom. There are high demands/expectations on teachers to be accountable for student achievement. However, there are often shrinking resources and support available to do so.

The following are some of the supports that teachers need in order to meet the needs of students with ADHD (and *all* students in the classroom).

Training

- Regarding the special needs of his or her student population, specifically about ADHD.
- Awareness training as well as specific skill-building training that is ongoing.
- In behavior-management strategies and interventions.
- In differentiating instruction to reach and teach diverse learners.
- Opportunities to attend workshops, seminars, and conferences on ADHD.

Teaming with Colleagues

- Buddying with a partner teacher to exchange ideas and re-energize each other.
- To team-teach different subject areas or do "guest" lessons and exchange classes to teach and share their areas of strength/interest.
- For disciplinary purposes (such as sending a student for a brief timeout in the buddy teacher's class).

Administrators who:

- Provide teachers and support staff with the *time* and *opportunity* (for example, through creative scheduling) in order to meet, plan, team, and collaborate with each other.
- Provide teachers with staff development opportunities that are practical and useful to teachers.
- Provide assistance for teachers who are overloaded with more than their fair share of "challenging" students (such as fewer number of students in the class, more prep time, scheduling preferences, more push-in help from support staff or school aides).
- Allow/encourage teachers to "experiment" with various strategies and techniques to find what works for an individual child.

Support personnel who:

- Are knowledgeable about children with ADHD.
- Are responsive and helpful when teachers express concerns and seek assistance.
- Strategize and help teachers plan appropriate actions/interventions for students.
- Follow-through and provide timely feedback.

Parents who:

- Share responsibility in the education of students.
- Understand the teacher's responsibility to all students in the class.
- Keep in mind what is reasonable when making requests.
- Communicate to their children the expectation that they respect and follow school and classroom rules.
- Cooperate in reinforcing appropriate behavior and work production goals.
- Communicate closely and openly with the teacher.
- Ensure that the child is coming to school "ready to learn" (adequate sleep, prepared with books, materials, homework).
- Treat the teacher with courtesy and respect.

Resources Available

- A lending library of materials teachers and parents can access, including books, videotapes, and other resources on ADHD.

Extra Assistance in the Classroom

- When there are children in need of 1:1 assistance in the classroom, it is very helpful to have another person (instructional assistant/paraprofessional, student teacher, parent volunteer, cross-age tutor) in the room to provide extra support.

6-3 (*continued*)

■ Parent volunteers who are willing to donate time to assist in the classroom (or work on projects at home that are requested by the teacher) are excellent sources of much needed teacher support.

OTHER SUPPORTS

■ Teachers need academic interventions that are not part of a special education program (tutorial assistance, extra direct-reading instruction) that they can access for students in need. Such supports can also serve as pre-referral interventions that teachers can try prior to referring a student for special education.

■ Teachers should be able to observe other teachers and have mentor/peer coaching assistance if needed or requested.

■ It is beneficial to have an idea/material swap and periodic opportunities for exchanging information, lessons, and so forth.

■ Teachers need to be cheered on to keep on learning and growing. The best support is being able to associate with positive, upbeat, and enthusiastic colleagues who love to teach and are committed to their students.

■ Teachers need to be treated as professionals whose opinion and input are solicited and listened to for site-based decision-making and district policy.

■ Being human, we all need to know that our efforts are recognized and appreciated. A positive comment from a colleague, parent, administrator, or student means a lot to teachers. Parents, if your child's teacher is trying hard to help and teach your son/daughter, take the time to thank that teacher.

6-4
WHAT SUPPORTS AND TRAINING DO PARENTS NEED?

Parenting a child with ADHD is generally far more challenging and stressful than it is to parent the average child. (1-20) Most people (including relatives, neighbors, and friends) do not understand what is involved in being able to effectively manage the behaviors of a child with ADHD. It is common for parents of children with ADHD to be unfairly judged by others who assume the child's behaviors are due to poor parenting or a lack of discipline.

ADHD is a chronic disorder that affects the child and the entire family. The following are some of the supports and training that parents of children with ADHD need to help cope with the challenges, and become better equipped to help their child:

■ Parents need to become experts about ADHD, and obtain as much knowledge and training as they can by attending conferences and seminars, as well as reading books, magazines, and information available on reputable websites. Knowledge about ADHD and the treatments that work will empower parents with the necessary confidence, hope, and skills.

■ Parent training in behavior modification and positive discipline are important components of effective treatment. Parents need such training available to them, provided by skilled professionals in their community. (1-22, 2-1, 2-2, 2-9 through 2-18, 8-5)

■ It is recommended that parents seek counseling to attend to personal problems or family issues, which compound the difficulty in the home.

■ Many families experience marital strife and family crises due to some of the issues surrounding the ADHD child's behavior. Parents need to support each other and do everything they can to function as a team, getting professional help when necessary. (1-22, 8-5)

■ Among the best supports for parents are organizations such as CHADD (Children and Adults with Attention Deficit Disorders). It is highly recommended that parents seek information about CHADD in their community, and attend a local meeting to learn more. (8-10)

■ Some communities have other kinds of support groups or regular meetings available for parents of children with ADHD and/or learning disabilities (through schools, agencies, hospitals, etc.).

■ Support groups/organizations such as CHADD are very helpful in that parents can network with other parents and learn from each other. Just hearing "you aren't alone" from other parents who are dealing with similar struggles can be reassuring and a great source of help.

6-4 (*continued*)

- Parents of children with ADHD are often the best sources for referrals to professionals in the community, and in advising how to best access support and services for their child at school. In addition, at CHADD meetings (or other groups) there is frequently a guest speaker from the community addressing various relevant topics and issues.

- Parents need to "share the load" with household responsibilities, as well as all parenting issues (homework, monitoring, discipline, and so forth).

- Single parents need to find support wherever possible (friends, relatives, neighbors, after-school tutoring programs).

- Providing parents with some respite by volunteering to baby-sit for a while or inviting the child to your home for a weekend is a wonderful gift from a relative or good friend.

- With a very challenging child in the home, it may be necessary to hire two baby-sitters.

- It may be necessary to hire help in the home for housekeeping, carpools, homework, and so forth.

- Parents need to feel comfortable asking for help, as it is hard to cope with stress and frustration alone. When feeling physically or emotionally overloaded, it is important to seek assistance.

- It is crucial for families to find ways of having fun together. Play games, participate in recreational activities, and appreciate the "good times."

- Parents must be educated in the school laws (IDEA and Section 504 of the Rehabilitation Act). Children with ADHD may be eligible for special education, related services, and/or accommodations in the classroom. With awareness of these laws, parents can help their child obtain school supports. (7-1 through 7-5)

- Parents need various support from teachers:
  - Willingness to communicate clearly
  - Monitoring their child's daily performance
  - Providing feedback
  - Sensitivity and responsiveness to struggles with homework issues
  - Flexibility regarding accommodations/modifications as needed for their child

- Parents need the support (communication and teamwork) of other school staff members who provide service or interventions to their ADHD child.

- It is highly recommended that any professionals with whom the parents choose to work (physicians, psychologists, educational therapists) exhibit the following qualities:
  - Experience and training working with children/families with ADHD.
  - An understanding of family issues with regard to a child/family member who has a disability.
  - Familiarity with the surrounding issues and common coexisting conditions/disorders with ADHD. (1-1)

- Awareness of the AAP Guidelines in diagnosis and treatment.
- A firm belief in a multimodal treatment approach.
- A strong interest in working together as a team (with parents and school personnel).

SOURCES AND RESOURCES

CHADD (Children and Adults with Attention Deficit Disorders)
8181 Professional Place, Suite 201
Landover, Maryland 20785
800-233-4050
http://www.chadd.org

With over 22,000 members in 225 affiliates nationwide, CHADD is the nation's leading nonprofit organization serving individuals with ADHD. Through collaborative leadership, advocacy, research, education, and support, CHADD provides science-based, evidence-based information about ADHD to parents, educators, professionals, the media, and the general public.

6-5

GROUNDBREAKING ADVANCES IN THE COLLABORATIVE CARE OF CHILDREN WITH ADHD

The author has been privileged to be on the faculty of a very exciting national program to improve the care of children with ADHD. The following is a description of this program, conducted under the leadership of the National Initiative for Children's Healthcare Quality (NICHQ), which we hope will serve as a research-validated model that will transform the quality of care for children with ADHD in the United States and worldwide. Information provided below is adapted with permission from sources copyrighted by the National Initiative for Children's Healthcare Quality.

- The National Initiative for Children's Healthcare Quality (NICHQ) is an independent, not-for-profit, education and research organization dedicated solely to improving the quality of health care provided to children. Founded in 1999, NICHQ's mission is to eliminate the gap between what is and what can be in health care for all children.

- NICHQ began as a program of the Institute for Healthcare Improvement (IHI), an organization that for over a decade has been the leader in improving health care in the United States and abroad. The IHI's mission is to help lead the improvement of health-care systems, to increase continuously their quality and value.

- Choosing the care of children with ADHD as one of its first areas of focus, NICHQ seeks to achieve a broad transformation in practices that care for children with ADHD by developing, testing, and deploying new methods of care.

- NICHQ's overall strategy for improving care is accomplished by:
  - Raising awareness
  - Conducting research to identify the best practices in pediatric care
  - Serving as a premier resource for the most effective methods and approaches in improving health care for children
  - Providing tools and methods to improve systems of care
  - Enabling physicians and their staffs to make changes based on the best available evidence for good practice

---

Permission granted by NICHQ (National Initiative for Children's Healthcare Quality) to publish the information in this list.

REASONS FOR THE NICHQ COLLABORATIVE ON ADHD

- Excellent evidence exists about what elements of care are effective to improve outcomes for children with this disorder. This evidence has been summarized in clinical practice guidelines by the American Academy of Pediatrics and others.

- These guidelines make key recommendations for clinicians, including:

  - Careful assessment of children with behavioral and learning concerns, including eliciting input from both parents and teachers and an assessment for coexisting conditions. (1-3, 1-11, 1-14)

  - Choice of an evidence-based approach to treatment, including appropriate use of medication, behavioral therapy, or a combination of both. (1-23)

  - Placing treatment within a comprehensive approach to chronic care management, which includes attention to family education and longitudinal follow-up. (1-22)

- Dismaying evidence exists that most children with this disorder do not receive the type of care that this best evidence would suggest.

- Most children with ADHD are diagnosed and managed by primary-care clinicians; some complex cases also involve the mental health system. The majority of children with ADHD also receive special education or counseling services in their schools.

- Efforts to enhance care and outcomes for these children must be focused on primary care but must also encompass the mental health and education systems. Currently the primary-care system is not well designed to manage children with ADHD.

MISSION OF THE INITIATIVE

The ADHD NICHQ Collaborative (currently in progress) began in the fall of 2001. The 1st International Summit on Improving Care for Children with ADHD took place in November 2002.

- At the outset of the collaborative, participating practices and the NICHQ staff and faculty committed to work together for a minimum of 12 months to implement a model of care for children with ADHD. This model was based on:

  - Currently available scientific evidence

  - *American Academy of Pediatrics Guidelines for the Diagnosis and Management of ADHD* (1-14, 1-16)

  - A model for the optimal delivery of care for persons with chronic conditions developed by Dr. Ed Wagner and colleagues

- In addition, teams committed to apply methods for implementing and spreading organizational change across the practice.

- In order to fulfill these commitments, each primary-care organization established an improvement team. These improvement teams consist of:

6-5 (*continued*)

- A physician "champion"
- A nurse or other member of the practice with day-to-day leadership for the successful performance of the initiative
- Someone from the practice with administrative expertise (such as information systems, medical records, or billing)
- In this particular initiative, teams also included, when possible:
  - A representative from the school system (school nurse, assistant principal, school district health administrator)
  - Mental health provider
  - ADHD parent representative
- NICHQ assembled an expert multidisciplinary faculty to lead the teams (see below). NICHQ also provided an extensive set of tools and materials to facilitate appropriate diagnosis and treatment, as well as communication with parents and schools.

MEASURING SUCCESS

- Teams reported on a monthly basis a limited number of measures, focusing on the key changes that they were asked to make, and the most important outcomes for children. Some of the measures for the collaborative assessed:
  - Key processes of care (for example, use of a written management plan for families and teachers)
  - Important outcomes (for example, improvement in symptoms and in overall function)
- Teams selected goals to achieve at the start of the collaborative, and used the monthly reports to track their progress towards these goals.
- Participating teams were required to address the following components from the *Care Model for Child Health* in their efforts to improve care for children with ADHD.

Community Resources and Policies

- Form partnerships with schools and mental health providers.
- Identify key contacts at school for each child with ADHD seen in their practice/clinic.
- Seek input from school staff for assessment, diagnosis, monitoring, and treatment plans.
- Educate parents about their rights and requirements for obtaining appropriate educational services/supports.

Family and Self-Management Support

- Emphasize the patient's and parent's active and central role in managing their child's ADHD.

- Enable parents and child to begin an educational process about ADHD management.
- Enable parents to establish connections for support (such as CHADD groups).
- Develop a written ADHD Management Plan for every child with ADHD and practice shared goal setting with child and family.

Decision Support

- Establish links with other specialists.
- Embed evidence-based AAP Guidelines into daily clinical practice.
- Partner with mental health provider.
- Provide effective behavior-management strategies to parents and teachers to target specific behaviors at home or school.
- Provide referral to behavior-therapy programs if warranted.

Delivery System Design

- Define roles and delegate tasks.
- Provide care in planned visits based on AAP Guidelines.
- Share written management plan (see the Appendix) with the school and mental health professional.
- Ensure regular follow-up care.

Clinical Information Systems

- Identify patients with ADHD and use ADHD registry to track useful and timely information.
- Facilitate communication with patients to assure timely planned follow-up.
- Facilitate individual patient care planning.

Health-Care Organization

- Include measurable goals for improving health care for children with ADHD as part of the organization's annual business plan.
- Allocate leadership and resources to pilot team and for spread of improvements after pilot.
- Create incentives for providers to improve ADHD care and implement Care Model for Child Health.

Note: The above model is adapted from Institute for Healthcare Improvement's Breakthrough Series Collaborative: Improving Care for People with Chronic Conditions, chaired by Dr. Ed Wagner, Group Health Cooperative of Puget Sound.

In the course of the collaborative, teams made changes in their immediate delivery systems (their private practices, hospital clinics, or community health centers), as well as changes in their communities. Teams were encouraged to try changes on a small scale first and learn from the experience, rather than plan large changes.

6-5 (continued)

ENVIRONMENTAL POLICY CHANGES

One particularly promising component of the program was the active involvement of the North Carolina Department of Medical Assistance (Medicaid), which cosponsored the program. In observing the process of improvement, NC Medicaid clarified and modified several of its practices and procedures to enable the delivery of more appropriate services for children with this disorder. The agency was also seeking to influence its sister agency at the State, the Department of Education, to provide increased training and support for teachers to better meet the needs of children with this disorder and their families.

At the conclusion of the year-long initiative, NICHQ conducted an International Conference to showcase the accomplishments of the collaborative teams, and share other important perspectives gained by the faculty and other leading innovations in care in this field. In addition, NICHQ is seeking to provide additional collaborative support on a regional basis, and to work with national organizations to imbed the tools and approach in broader educational programs.

FACULTY FOR THIS INITIATIVE

Collaborative Chairs

Peter Jensen, MD

Mark Wolraich, MD

Core Faculty

Harlan Gephart, MD

Maureen Gill, MSW

Daniel Hyman, MD

Beth Kaplanek, RN, BSN

Carole Lannon, MD, MPH

Laurel K. Leslie, MD

William E. Pelham, Jr., Ph.D.

Karen Pierce, MD

Sandra Rief, MA

Guest Faculty

Janice Anderson, MSN, RN

Marian F. Earls, MD

Jane N. Hannah, Ed.D.

Maxwell Manning, Ph.D.

Michael Schoenbaum, Ph.D.

NICHQ Staff

Charles Homer, MD, MPH, NICHQ Executive

Pat Heinrich, RN, BSN, Director

Lloyd Provost, MS, Senior Improvement Advisor

Leslie Loeding, MS, Improvement Advisor

Sarah McGovern, Manager

Shawn Hatcher, Coordinator

For more information about this ADHD NICHQ Collaborative, contact:

National Initiative for Children's Healthcare Quality (NICHQ)
375 Longwood Ave., Third Floor
Boston, MA 02215
617-754-4875
www.nichq.org

Many of the resources developed by NICHQ for the American Academy of Pediatrics (AAP) ADHD Toolkit can be downloaded from the NICHQ web site.

Special Education, Related Services, or Other School Supports and Accommodations for Students with ADHD

7-1
EDUCATIONAL RIGHTS OF
CHILDREN WITH ADHD

It is important to be aware of the federal laws that protect children with disabling conditions (including ADHD) from discrimination. There are two main laws protecting students with disabilities:

1. Individuals with Disabilities Education Act of 1997 (known as IDEA)

2. Section 504 of the Rehabilitation Act of 1973 (known as Section 504)

IDEA is the special education legislation in the United States. Section 504 is a Civil Rights Statute enforced by the U.S. Office of Civil Rights.

Note: Another law that protects individuals with disabilities is The Americans with Disabilities Act of 1990 (ADA). This overlaps with Section 504 and is not so relevant to school-aged children. The federal regulations refer to ADD and ADHD.

Both IDEA and Section 504 require school districts to provide:

- A free and appropriate public education (FAPE) in the least restrictive environment (LRE) with their nondisabled peers to the maximum extent appropriate to their needs

- Supports (adaptations, accommodations, modifications) to enable the student to participate and learn in the general education program

- The opportunity to participate in extracurricular and nonacademic activities

- A free nondiscriminatory evaluation

- Procedural due process

Because there are different criteria for eligibility, services/supports available, and procedures and safeguards for implementing the laws, it is important for parents, educators, clinicians, and advocates to be well aware of the variations between IDEA and Section 504, and fully informed about their respective advantages and disadvantages.

See Lists 7-2 through 7-5 for a more thorough description of the two laws and how students with ADHD are protected under each.

BASIC INFORMATION ABOUT IDEA

- In 1975, Congress enacted a federal law entitled "Education for All Handicapped Children Act" (P.L. 94–142). This important special education legislation was amended in June 1997, and is now called Individuals with Disabilities Education Act (IDEA or

7-1 (*continued*)

IDEA '97). IDEA will be reauthorized a few months after this book goes to press; this may result in some changes to the information about IDEA provided here.

- IDEA provides special education and related services for those children who meet the eligibility criteria under one of 13 separate disability categories. (7-4)

- A child must have at least one disability listed in the statute, and this disability *must adversely affect the child's ability to benefit from the educational program, making special education necessary.*

Under IDEA, children who qualify for special education receive an IEP (individual education plan) that is:

- Tailored to meet the needs of the student

- Developed, reviewed, and revised in accordance with Section B of IDEA

- The guide for every educational decision made for the student with disabilities

Points to Keep in Mind

- The IEP process begins when a student is referred for evaluation due to a suspected disability, and a process of formal evaluation is initiated to determine eligibility for special education services.

- Children found eligible under IDEA are entitled to the special programs, related services, modifications, and accommodations the IEP team determines are needed for educational benefit.

- The IEP is very specific in terms of goals, short-term objectives, and benchmarks. There are progress reviews during the school year, and then an annual review (or sooner if requested) of the IEP.

- At all stages, parents are an integral part of the process and team. The IEP does not go into effect until parents sign the IEP and agree to the plan.

ADDITIONAL KEY FEATURES OF IDEA

- Provision of necessary supports and services to enable students to succeed (to the maximum extent possible) in the *general education curriculum*

- Consideration of students' strengths, participation in district and state assessments, and special factors (such as behavioral factors and needs, proficiency in English, and language needs)

- Review and determination of whether behavior was caused by the child's disability (manifestation determination) when disciplinary actions involving removal for more than ten days are being considered by the school. (7-5)

ELIGIBILITY CRITERIA FOR STUDENTS WITH ADHD

- On September 16, 1991, the U.S. Department of Education and Office for Civil Rights issued a joint policy clarification memorandum confirming that:
  - Children whose "ADD is a chronic or acute health problem that results in limited alertness which adversely affects educational performance" could qualify for special education and related services under IDEA.
  - Even if a child did not qualify for special education and related services under IDEA, he or she may be considered a "qualified handicapped person" under Section 504 (if ability to learn or to otherwise benefit from his or her education is substantially limited due to the ADD/ADHD).

- Sometimes students with ADHD qualify for special education and related services under the disability categories of "Specific Learning Disability" (SLD) or "Emotional Disturbance" (ED). For example, a child who has ADHD who also has coexisting learning disabilities may be eligible under the SLD category. (7-2)

- Many students with ADHD are eligible for special education and related services under the IDEA category of "Other Health Impaired" (OHI). Eligibility criteria under this category requires that:
  - The child has a chronic or acute health problem (ADD/ADHD).
  - This health problem causes limited alertness in the educational environment (due to heightened alertness to environmental stimuli).
  - This results in an adverse effect on the child's educational performance to the extent that special education is needed. *Note:* The adverse effect on educational performance is not limited to academics, but can include impairments in other aspects of school functioning (for example, behavior) as well.

- On March 11, 1999, ADD and ADHD were formally and explicitly listed in the IDEA Regulations under the category OHI. This clears up any ambiguity school districts may have had regarding whether or not students with ADHD can qualify for special education under this disability category.

- See List 7-2 for more detailed information about OHI and how students with ADHD qualify for special education under OHI criteria.

SECTION 504

Section 504 protects the rights of people with disabilities from discrimination by any agencies receiving federal funding, which includes all public schools.

7-1 (*continued*)

Eligibility Criteria for Students with ADHD

- Children with ADD/ADHD who may not be eligible for services under IDEA (and do not qualify for special education) are often able to receive accommodations and supports in school under a Section 504 Plan.

- As noted earlier, Section 504 differs from IDEA in criteria for eligibility, procedures, safeguards, and services available to children. The educational provisions and protections for students with attention deficit disorders covered under Section 504 (as well as specific eligibility criteria, assessment, and so forth) are detailed in List 7-3.

- In short, Section 504 protects children if they fit the following criteria:
  - The student is regarded or has a record of having a physical or mental impairment.
  - The physical or mental impairment substantially limits one or more major life functions (for example, learning).

Section 504 entitles eligible students to:

- Reasonable accommodations in the educational program
- Equal access to education and commensurate opportunities to learn as nondisabled peers

Points to Keep in Mind About Section 504

- The implementation of the plan is primarily the responsibility of the general education school staff.

- The 504 Plan could also involve modification of nonacademic times (such as lunchroom, recess, P.E.).

- Supports under Section 504 might also include the provision of services (for example, counseling, health, assistive technology).

In contrast to the IEP, the 504 process:

- Is simpler and less regulated
- Is generally easier with regard to student evaluation and determining eligibility
- Requires much less with regard to procedures, paperwork, and so forth

Note: Children who qualify under IDEA eligibility criteria are automatically covered by Section 504 protections; however, the reverse is not true. Even though students found to be ineligible for special education services under IDEA *may* be found eligible under Section 504, they are *not automatically* covered.

WHICH IS MORE ADVANTAGEOUS FOR STUDENTS WITH ADD/ADHD—IDEA OR SECTION 504?

This is a decision that the team (parents and school personnel) must make considering eligibility criteria and the specific needs of the individual student. For students with ADD/ADHD who have more significant school difficulties, IDEA is usually preferable for the following reasons:

- IEPs provide more protections (procedural safeguards, monitoring, and regulations) with regard to evaluation, frequency of review, parent participation, disciplinary action, and other factors. (7-2, 7-4, 7-5)

- Specific goals and short-term objectives addressing the student's areas of need are written in the IEP and regularly monitored for progress.

- There is a much wider range of program options, services, and supports available.

- Funding is provided for implementation of IEP for programs and services. Section 504 is nonfunded.

Generally speaking, an IEP carries more weight and is taken more seriously by school staff.

For students who have milder impairments and do not *need* special education, a 504 Plan is a faster, easier procedure for obtaining accommodations and supports. The 504 Plan can be highly effective for those students whose educational needs can be addressed through adjustments, modifications, and accommodations in the general curriculum/classroom.

7-2
IDEA AS IT APPLIES TO STUDENTS WITH ADHD

- List 7-1 explains the federal law IDEA (Individuals with Disabilities Education Act), under which many students with attention deficit disorders qualify for special education and related services.

- List 7-4 details the IEP process, which is mandated and regulated by IDEA.

- Students with ADHD are often subject to disciplinary actions at school as a consequence of their behaviors. List 7-5 addresses the provisions under IDEA '97 with regard to children with disabilities and discipline.

- When IDEA is reauthorized (a few months after this book goes to press), there may be changes in the law and the information that follows.

The key features of IDEA as they apply to children with ADD/ADHD are summarized in this list.

QUALIFYING FOR SPECIAL EDUCATION AND RELATED SERVICES

The school multidisciplinary team must determine the following:

1. The child has one of the 13 disabilities under IDEA. (7-4)

2. The disability significantly interferes with school performance such that the student requires special education and related services.

Of the 13 disability categories listed under IDEA, there are three disabilities that may apply to students with ADHD:

1. Specific Learning Disability (SLD)

2. Emotionally Disturbed (ED)

3. Other Health Impaired (OHI)

WHAT IS SLD?

Specific Learning Disabilities (SLD) is a disorder in one or more of the basic psychological processes involved in understanding or in using language, spoken or written, that may manifest itself in an imperfect ability to listen, think, speak, read, write, spell, or do mathematical calculations. SLD may include such conditions as dyslexia, perceptual disabilities, brain injury, minimal brain dysfunction, dyslexia, and developmental aphasia.

ELIGIBILITY CRITERIA FOR SLD

Due to the fact that many children with ADHD also have coexisting learning disabilities, they often qualify for special education under the category of SLD.

A team may determine that a child has an SLD if the child does not achieve commensurate with his or her age and ability levels in one or more of the following areas:

1. Oral expression
2. Listening comprehension
3. Written expression
4. Basic reading skills
5. Reading comprehension
6. Mathematics calculation
7. Mathematics reasoning

In addition, to qualify as an SLD, the severe discrepancy between ability and achievement may *not* be primarily due to:

1. A visual, hearing, or motor impairment
2. Mental retardation
3. Emotional disturbance
4. Environmental, cultural, or economic disadvantage

Note: Most states and districts currently use a "discrepancy formula" in determining eligibility for special education under the SLD category. This means they require a significant discrepancy between the child's measured ability level (IQ score) and academic achievement on individual achievement tests administered.

WHAT IS ED?

Emotional Disturbance (ED) is a condition exhibiting one or more of the following characteristics over a long period of time and to a marked degree that adversely affects a child's educational performance:

- Inability to learn that cannot be explained by intellectual, sensory, or health factors
- Inability to build or maintain satisfactory interpersonal relationships with peers and teachers

7-2 (continued)

- Inappropriate types of behavior or feelings under normal circumstances
- A general pervasive mood of unhappiness or depression
- A tendency to develop physical symptoms or fears associated with personal or school problems

WHAT IS OHI?

Other Health Impairment (OHI) means that the child has limited strength, vitality, or alertness due to chronic or acute health problems that adversely affect school performance.

- When applied to students with ADHD, this includes the child's heightened alertness to environmental stimuli that results in limited alertness with respect to the educational environment.
- Students with ADD/ADHD have been able to qualify for special education and related services under the OHI category (if they meet the criteria) for many years. However, not until the final regulations of IDEA '97 were published in 1999 were ADD and ADHD specifically named on the list of chronic health problems.
- In the past, many school districts have refused to consider ADD/ADHD in the category of OHI. Fortunately, the 1999 regulations eliminated any ambiguity and excuse for school districts to deny students with attention deficit disorders who need special education their right to receive services under OHI. (7-1)

Determining OHI

- Most states and school districts require a medial diagnosis of ADHD and a physician's statement of such to qualify a student under OHI; however, this varies from state to state and district to district, depending on how OHI is interpreted.
- Some states and districts do not require a medical diagnosis to determine that a child has an attention deficit disorder *for educational purposes.*
- Check with your local school district regarding specific requirements for OHI.
- See List 1-18 for information on a school-based evaluation of the disorder and Lists 1-15 and 1-19 for other supports required from the school in diagnosing ADHD.

DISCIPLINING STUDENTS WITH ADHD UNDER THE LAW AND ADDRESSING BEHAVIORAL DIFFICULTIES

With the 1999 regulations of IDEA, important new disciplinary protections and behavioral supports for students with disabilities were included in the special education law. This is highly relevant to students with ADHD. See List 7-5, which addresses disciplinary protections and procedures. This includes information regarding Manifestation Determination Review, Functional Behavioral Assessment, and Behavioral Intervention Plans.

Points to Keep in Mind

- Children with ADD/ADHD do not automatically qualify for special education services under IDEA.

- It must be determined that the disability or condition significantly impairs a child's educational performance resulting in a need for special education and related services.

- However, proving a negative impact on educational performance does not require failing grades or test scores; it can also involve other aspects of the student's functioning at school (such as impairments in social/emotional/behavioral functioning, and deficient study skills and work production affecting learning).

SOURCES AND RESOURCES

"Behavior and Discipline Q and A," *Teaching Exceptional Children*, vol. 30, no. 4, March/April 1998, 32–35.

Cohen, Matthew. "Section 504 & IDEA—What's the Difference: Limited vs. Substantial Protections for Children with ADD and Other Disabilities," CHADD: *Attention*, Summer 1997.

Cohen, Matthew. "Educational Rights for Children with AD/HD," *The CHADD Information and Resource Guide to AD/HD*. Landover, MD: CHADD, 2000.

Cohen, Matthew. "Individuals with Disabilities Education Act: What You Need to Know About AD/HD Under the Individuals with Disabilities Education Act," *The CHADD Information and Resource Guide to AD/HD*. Landover, MD: CHADD, 2000.

Cohen, Matthew, and Elliott Portnoy. "Beginning School Advocacy for Parents of the ADHD Child," CHADD's Ninth Annual Conference, October 1997, in San Antonio, Texas.

Cohen, Matthew D. "Looming Reauthorization Battle Threatens Rights of Kids with Disabilities Under IDEA '97," CHADD: attention@chadd.org; vol. 9, no. 1, August 2002, 17–20.

Gartland, Debi. "Effective IEP Development for Students with AD/HD," CHADD: *Attention*, vol. 7, no. 2, September/October 2000, 56–61.

"Individualized Education Programs & IDEA '97." http://www.ldonline.org/ld_indepth/iep/idea97.html

"IDEA '97 Final Regulations to Provisions," *Teaching Exceptional Children*, vol. 32, no. 1, September/October, 1999, 88–89.

7-2 (*continued*)

"IDEA Re-Authorization Issues: LDA Guiding Principles," *LDA Newsbriefs,* vol. 37, no. 4, July/August 2002, 3. (no author cited)

Lachs, Sheila. "Changes to the Individuals with Disabilities Education Act and What They Mean for Children with ADD," CHADD: *Attention,* vol. 4, no. 4, Spring 1998, 18–24.

"Legal Rights and Services for Children with ADD," *CHADD Fact Sheet.* http://www. chadd.org/facts/add

Martin, Reed. "Advocacy Strategies for Students with ADD." http://www.reedmartin.com

"Special Education Rights of Parents and Children Under the IDEA, Part B." California Department of Education, Special Education Division: *The GRAM,* Spring 1999.

U.S. Department of Education in cooperation with the Council for Exceptional Children. www.ideapractices.org
www.ed.gov/offices/OSERS/OSEP/index.html

Wrightslaw. www.wrightslaw.com

Wright, Pam, and Pete Wright. *From Emotions to Advocacy—The Special Education Survival Guide.* Hartfield, VA: Harbor House Law Press, 2002.

Wright, Peter, and Pamela D. Wright. *Wrightslaw: Special Education Law.* Hartfield, VA: Harbor House Law Press, 2000.

7-3
HOW SECTION 504 APPLIES TO STUDENTS WITH ADHD

Note: Some of the information in this list is also included in List 7-1, Educational Rights of Children with ADHD. Read both lists for a thorough understanding of Section 504 and the protections and accommodations many students with attention deficit disorders are entitled to under this law.

WHAT IS SECTION 504?

- Section 504 of the Rehabilitation Act is a federal civil rights law that prohibits discrimination against people with disabilities. It states that no individual can be discriminated against based on his or her disability; and applies to all organizations, programs, or agencies that receive federal financial aid.

- The Office of Civil Rights (OCR) enforces Section 504. Even though there is no funding for providing services required under Section 504, the OCR can withhold federal funds to any programs or agencies (for example, school districts) that do not comply.

- Section 504 provides individuals with disabilities protection against discrimination in school (preschool through postsecondary), as well as in the workplace and other major life activities.

Many of the same protections under Section 504 are mandated under the Individuals with Disabilities Education Act (IDEA):

- Section 504 also requires public school districts to provide a "free and appropriate public education" (FAPE) to every "qualified handicapped person" residing within their jurisdiction.

- FAPE must be designed to meet the individual needs of the child as adequately as the needs of students without disabilities, and at no cost to parents.

- Qualified students under Section 504 are entitled to "reasonable accommodations" which generally means provision of accommodations in the classroom, but may also include specialized instruction and related services.

- As with IDEA, Section 504 also requires placement in the "least restrictive setting" (LRE). This means the child's education "must be provided in the regular education classroom unless it is demonstrated that education in the regular environment with the use of supplementary aids and services cannot be achieved satisfactorily."

7-3 (*continued*)

- The child has a right to: a nondiscriminatory evaluation by the school district, procedural due process, the opportunity to participate in extracurricular and nonacademic activities, and a plan to support the student in general education.

HOW ARE STUDENTS WITH ADHD FOUND ELIGIBLE UNDER SECTION 504?

- Eligibility for Section 504 is based on the existence of an identified physical or mental condition or impairment that substantially limits a major life activity.

- Section 504 defines an individual with a disability as any person who: (1) has a physical or mental impairment, (2) has a record of, or (3) is regarded as having such an impairment.

- Section 504 eligibility is dependent upon the determination that the condition or impairment substantially limits a major life activity (such as walking, breathing, speaking and/or hearing, seeing, *learning*, performing manual tasks, and caring for oneself).

- As learning is considered a major life activity, children diagnosed with ADHD are entitled to the protections of Section 504 if the disability substantially limits their ability to learn.

- Students with ADHD who may not be eligible for services under IDEA (because they do not meet eligibility criteria for special education) are often able to receive support and intervention under Section 504.

- Students who do qualify for special education services under IDEA are also automatically protected under the broader eligibility criteria of Section 504, but not vice versa.

- Eligibility for Section 504 may occur when the child needs special education *or* related services. IDEA criteria requires that the student needs special education *and* related services. So, children receiving 504 Plans (not IEPs) are typically those who have less severe disabilities.

- Section 504 and IDEA have different criteria for eligibility, procedures, safeguards, and services available to children.

- Many children/teens with attention deficit disorders may fit the definition of "handicapped," depending upon the severity of their disorder. If the ADD/ADHD *does not* significantly affect or limit their learning or school functioning, they would not be considered eligible under Section 504.

- If their ADD/ADHD *does* significantly limit their learning or functioning, the child/adolescent would be eligible for reasonable accommodations and support.

- This typically means developing a plan of appropriate interventions within the general education program, designed to accommodate some of the student's special needs. The implementation of the plan is primarily the responsibility of the general education school staff.

To determine the existence of the disability and the impact on learning, the school is required to do an assessment under Section 504. It is typically much less extensive than that conducted for the IEP process, and requires/involves the following:

■ Evaluation procedures that are nondiscriminatory

■ Generally a review of records (school, medical) and various assessment data, standardized testing, evaluation of work samples, behavioral rating scales)

■ Assessment tools that are validated for their stated purpose and accurately reflect the child's ability

■ Information from more than one test and a variety of sources, in order to determine that the child does have a disability that adversely affects learning/educational performance

■ Often, the school's SST is the same team responsible for 504 evaluation, determination of eligibility, and writing the 504 Plan. (6-2)

Note: Section 504 contains fewer regulations than IDEA with regard to testing. It does not address the procedures, frequency, role of outside evaluations, or require parental consent for testing.

Parents seeking service for their children may ask the school to consider whether or not their son or daughter may be eligible for any accommodations or supports under Section 504 if not under IDEA.

If parents or the school suspects a child has ADHD that is adversely affecting the child's educational performance (which can include behavioral performance as well as academic), an evaluation needs to be done for the purposes of determining eligibility for services and supports under either IDEA or Section 504. Many schools have established procedures and protocols specifically for ADHD evaluations. (1-17, 1-18)

WHAT IS A 504 PLAN?

■ A student found eligible under Section 504 must have a 504 Plan designed to meet the child's educational needs. This is different from an IEP, as it is much simpler and falls under the responsibility of general education, not special education.

■ A 504 Plan is intended to provide what is necessary for a child with disabilities to have equal access to education and opportunities to learn commensurate with that of his or her nondisabled peers.

A 504 Plan generally lists and summarizes the reasonable and appropriate accommodations and interventions to be provided to the student. These are the classroom interventions that the teacher is responsible for providing, and can also include:

■ Accommodations provided in other school settings (playground, cafeteria, school bus)

■ Program modifications

7-3 (*continued*)

■ Supplementary aids and services (such as equipment/assistive technology, health, counseling, consultation)

Even though it is often interpreted that a 504 Plan means exclusively classroom accommodations, that is not the case according to the law. The school team must consider how to address *all* of the student's educational needs.

WHAT ARE REASONABLE ACCOMMODATIONS AND MODIFICATIONS?

Reasonable accommodations, supports, adaptations, and modifications are provided throughout this book. Here is a brief summary of some commonly needed accommodations:

■ *Environmental* (providing a structured learning environment, preferential seating, reducing/minimizing distractions) (2-4, 3-9, 8-1)

■ *Behavioral* (increased structure, supervision/monitoring, extra cueing and private signals, use of daily report card or weekly report between home and school, assistance/support during transitions) (2-1, 2-3, 2-5 through 2-11, 2-16, 3-4, and Appendix)

■ *Testing/assessment* (extended time, alternative times for test completion, modified format, administered in shorter sessions) (3-8, 5-12, 5-14)

■ *Instructional* (break assignment into series of smaller assignments, use of highlighted texts, advance organizers, note-taking assistance, peer tutor, tailoring assignments) (3-2, 3-5, 3-6, 3-7, 4-2)

■ *Organizational* (assistance with structuring of materials/workspace and assignments, help recording assignments, establishment of home–school monitoring system of class and homework assignments) (4-4 through 4-9, and Appendix)

■ *Writing accommodations/supports* (use of graphic organizers, teacher/peer editing assistance, permission to dictate while someone else records, alternatives to written assignments such as oral or hands-on/demonstrations) (5-7 through 5-12)

Points to Keep in Mind

■ A case manager is assigned to monitor the child's progress under the 504 Plan.

■ Though annual reviews are expected (and typical), in contrast to IEP regulations, 504s are not regulated as to the frequency of monitoring and review of the plan.

■ Every school district is required to have a 504 Coordinator who serves as the key contact person.

■ Information regarding Section 504 (eligibility, rights, procedural safeguards, and so on) should be available upon request from the school district. There is also generally a designated person in the school responsible for 504s (often the school counselor).

- Parents can file a complaint with the Office of Civil Rights as well as request an impartial due-process hearing if they feel their rights are being violated under Section 504.

- See List 7-5 about the rights of students with disabilities when being faced with disciplinary actions. Section 504 provides less protection than IDEA in these cases. For example, there is no "stay put" provision under Section 504.

- Parents can file a request for a due-process hearing if they disagree with the school's proposed change of a child's placement (suspension in excess of ten days, expulsion, interim placement). But unlike IDEA protections, the student is not granted the right to stay in the current placement while the hearing is pending.

- Classroom teachers need training in order to develop the skills necessary for teaching students with disabilities in inclusive settings. They need to understand the rationale and be willing and conscientious to make the necessary adaptations, modifications, and accommodations for their students with special needs.

- School personnel need to be informed about the law and made aware that when students are on plans governed by legal mandates (IEPs, 504s), their compliance with what is written into the plan is *not optional*. They are *required* under the law to make those provisions and carry out the plan. If they refuse to do so, they are opening up themselves to the potential of personal liability.

SOURCES AND RESOURCES

Cohen, Matthew. "Section 504 & IDEA—What's the Difference: Limited vs. Substantial Protections for Children with ADD and Other Disabilities," CHADD: *Attention,* Summer 1997.

Cohen, Matthew. "Educational Rights for Children with AD/HD," *The CHADD Information and Resource Guide to AD/HD.* Landover, MD: CHADD, 2000.

Cohen, Matthew, and Elliott Portnoy. "Beginning School Advocacy for Parents of the ADHD Child," CHADD's Ninth Annual Conference, October 1997, in San Antionio, Texas.

Disability Rights Education and Defense Fund. http://www.dredf.org

EDLAW Center. http://www.edlaw.net

Legal Rights and Services for Children with ADD," *CHADD Fact Sheet.* http://www.chadd.org/facts/add

Martin, Reed. "Advocacy Strategies for Students with ADD." http://www.reedmartin.com

National Association of Protection and Advocacy Systems. http://www.protectionandadvocacy.com

National Information Clearinghouse on Children and Youth with Disabilities. http://www.nichcy.org

7-3 (continued)

Parent Advocacy Coalition for Educational Rights (PACER Center). http://www.pacer.org

Wright, Pam, and Pete Wright. *From Emotions to Advocacy—The Special Education Survival Guide.* Hartfield, VA: Harbor House Law Press, 2002.

Wright, Peter, and Pamela D. Wright. *Wrightslaw: Special Education Law.* Hartfield, VA: Harbor House Law Press, 2000.

7-4

THE IEP AND THE
SPECIAL EDUCATION PROCESS

This list contains detailed information about the special education process and IEPs. For more information about the federal law (IDEA) that governs the IEP process, see List 7-1. The application of IDEA with regard to students with ADD/ADHD is detailed in Lists 7-2 and 7-5.

As noted in List 7-1, IDEA will be reauthorized sometime during 2003, which may result in changes to the information in this list.

WHAT IS AN IEP?

- Stands for "Individual Education Program or "Individualized Education Plan"
- Refers to the special education process
- Serves as the written plan for every child with a disability that must be reviewed and revised in accordance with IDEA
- Applies to all public school students receiving special education and related services
- Enables the child to participate and progress in the general curriculum
- Requires collaborative team effort for designing an educational program
- Improves educational results and outcomes for children with disabilities

IDEA sets clear eligibility standards that school districts must follow in determining whether a child qualifies for special education or related services. As such, the child must fit one of the classification criteria as having a disability, and that disability must be significantly affecting the child's ability to learn or educational performance. This is an IEP team decision based upon the data collected; assessment; and the input of parents, educators, and other team members.

The 13 disability categories under IDEA include:

1. Autism
2. Deaf-blindness
3. Deafness
4. Emotional disturbance
5. Hearing impairment
6. Mental retardation
7. Multiple disabilities
8. Orthopedic impairment
9. Other health impairment
10. Specific learning disability
11. Speech or language impairment
12. Traumatic brain injury
13. Visual impairment, including blindness

7-4 (continued)

PARENTS AND DUE PROCESS

- At all stages, parents are key members of the IEP team and integral part of the IEP process. Parental input and permission must be obtained throughout (for example, with regard to assessment plan, programs, services, goals and objectives, and placement). In fact, IEP does not go into effect until parents agree to it and sign it.

- Whenever there is a dispute or disagreement between parents and the school regarding a child's special education plan or program, there are various avenues for resolving the differences. Disagreement may arise over evaluation, goals, services, placement, and other issues.

- In most cases, these issues can be worked out in a regular meeting format by sharing concerns and utilizing a cooperative team approach. However, if necessary, parents have other options:
  - Mediation
  - Formal complaint
  - Due-process hearing

- The mediation process is highly recommended for resolving disputes for the following reasons:
  - Approaches problem collaboratively (nonadversarial in nature)
  - Resolves conflicts without need for litigation
  - Focuses on child's needs
  - Tends to be cost effective

- Parents may file a formal complaint if they believe the school district is violating their rights regarding the laws and regulations pertaining to students with disabilities (evaluation, provision of services, implementation of plan, and so on). To that end, parents should request a copy of their legal rights from the school or district special education department.

THE BASIC SPECIAL EDUCATION PROCESS UNDER IDEA

When IDEA is reauthorized a few months after this book goes to press, there may be some changes to the current law, effective in 2003. Most of the following information is summarized from "A Guide to the Individualized Education Program," published by the Office of Special Education and Rehabilitative Services, U.S. Department of Education, July, 2000. (http://www.ed.gov/pubs/edpubs.html)

The special education process that the school system is responsible for under IDEA is as follows:

1. **Identify child as possibly needing special education and related services.** Generally, a referral is made by a parent, teacher, or other school professional requesting an evaluation to see if a child has a disability. Then an assessment plan is developed by the school's multidisciplinary evaluation team, addressing all areas of suspected disability. The assessment plan must be developed within a reasonable amount of time (such as 15 calendar days), and parents must give their written consent to the assessment plan before proceeding further.

2. **Evaluate child.** The evaluation is generally referred to as a *psycho-educational evaluation* and may involve a battery of tests to measure cognitive ability; academic achievement; and perceptual-motor, memory, language, and other processing skills. A multidisciplinary team of school professionals (school psychologist, special education teacher/educational evaluator, school nurse, speech-language specialist) is involved in the evaluation. Results will be used to decide the child's eligibility for special education and related services and to make decisions about an appropriate educational program for the child.

3. **Decide eligibility.** Based upon the results of the above evaluation, as well as other information provided by the parent (such as reports from evaluations conducted outside of school), the team decides whether the child is "disabled" as defined by IDEA. *Note:* If parents disagree with the school's evaluation, they have the right to take their child for an Independent Educational Evaluation (IEE), and can ask the school system to pay for it. Parents may also request a hearing to challenge the eligibility decision.

4. **Find child eligible for services.** If found to be a "child with a disability" as defined by IDEA under any of the 13 disability categories, the child is eligible for special education and related services. Within 30 calendar days after determining that a child is eligible, the IEP team must meet to write an IEP for the child. *Note:* This timeline is translated in different ways by school districts across the United States. For example, the timeline may be: (a) Within 15 calendar days after receiving a request/referral, the school proposes a written assessment plan and informs parents of their due-process rights; (b) The parents must agree with the school district's assessment plan or request a different one. Once the parent signs the assessment plan, the school has 50 days, not counting school vacations, to perform and complete the assessment and hold the IEP meeting.

5. **Schedule IEP meeting.** The school schedules the IEP meeting with parents, teacher(s), other IEP service providers, and student (if appropriate). Parents must be given sufficient notice about the meeting and be informed of its purpose, as well as who will be attending from the school district. Parents have the right to invite people to the meeting who have special expertise and are knowledgeable about their child.

6. **Hold IEP meeting and write the IEP.** The team meets to discuss the child's strengths, areas of need, and present levels of performance. By the end of the meeting, an IEP is written with input from all participants. Parents must give their consent to *all* aspects of the IEP (the special education program, related services, placement,

7-4 (continued)

goals/objectives, and so forth). If parents disagree and cannot work out their differences with the school district, a mediation process must be available. If that fails, parents may choose to file a complaint with the state education agency and request a due-process hearing.

AFTER THE IEP IS WRITTEN

1. **Provide services.** The school must make sure that the IEP is being carried out as it was written. Each teacher and service provider must have access to the IEP and know his or her specific responsibilities for implementing all aspects of the IEP. This includes all supplemental aids, services, program modifications, and accommodations.

2. **Measure progress and report to parents.** As mandated in the IEP, the child's progress toward annual goals is measured. Parents are informed regularly of progress and whether the child is on pace to achieve the written goals by the end of the year. Per IDEA '97, progress toward IEP goals must be reported at least as often as parents of nondisabled students are informed of their children's progress.

3. **Review IEP.** This is done at least annually to determine whether the child has fulfilled the goals/objectives set forth. The IEP may be reviewed at any time if requested by either parents or school personnel. In all cases, parents must agree and sign their permission for any changes in the plan (services rendered, placement, and so forth). If parents don't agree with any of the aspects of the IEP, they should discuss their concerns with members of the IEP team. There are several options including: additional testing, independent evaluation, mediation, or due-process hearing. Parents may also file a complaint with the state education agency.

4. **Reevaluate child.** The student must be reevaluated at least every three years (triennial evaluation) to determine whether he or she continues to be a child with a disability and to assess his or her current educational needs. In addition, the student may be reevaluated more often if deemed necessary based upon his or her condition, or if the child's parent or teacher requests a reevaluation.

WHAT ARE THE CONTENTS OF THE IEP?

By law, the IEP must include certain information about the child and the educational program designed to meet his or her unique needs.

- *Present levels of educational performance* derived from testing and observing how the child is currently doing in school. This includes information about how the child's disability affects his or her involvement and progress in the general curriculum.

- *Annual goals* that are measurable and reasonable for the child to accomplish in a year. The goals are further broken down into measurable short-term objectives or benchmarks.

- *A listing of the special education and related services* to be provided to the child or on behalf of the child. This includes supplementary aids and services that the child needs. It also includes modifications to the program or supports for school personnel, such as training or professional development that will be provided to assist the child.

- *Participation with nondisabled children.* The IEP must explain the extent (if any) to which the child will *not* participate with nondisabled children in the regular class and other school activities.

- *Participation in state- and districtwide tests.* The IEP must state what modifications in the administration of these tests the child will need to participate. If the IEP team determines an assessment is not appropriate for the child, it must state why and how the child will be tested instead.

- *Dates and places.* The IEP must state when, where, and how often services will be provided, as well as how long they will last.

- *Transition service needs.* Transition planning begins by the age of 14 (sometimes younger). This involves helping the student plan his or her courses of study so that the classes lead to the student's post-school goals:
  - The team must write a statement of the transition service needs based upon the student's courses of study (advanced placement courses, vocational education) into the IEP.
  - Beginning when the child is age 16 (or younger), the IEP must initiate transition services that provide the student with a coordinated set of services to help move him or her from school to adult life.
  - Services focus upon the student's needs or interests. A statement of interagency responsibilities or any needed linkages must be included in the IEP.

- *Age of majority.* Beginning at least one year before the student reaches the age of majority, the IEP must include a statement that the student has been told of any rights that will transfer to him or her at the age of majority.

- *Measuring progress.* The IEP must state how the child's progress will be measured and how parents will be informed of that progress.

WHAT ARE RELATED SERVICES?

The following are some related services/benefits a student may receive from special education. Related services, as listed under IDEA, include (but are not limited to):

- Speech/language pathology services
- Transportation
- Occupational therapy
- Orientation and mobility services
- Parent counseling and training
- Physical therapy
- Audiology services
- Counseling services

7-4 (*continued*)

- Early identification and assessment of disabilities in children
- Medical services
- Psychological services

- Recreation
- Rehabilitation counseling services
- School health services
- Social work services in schools

WHO ARE THE MEMBERS OF THE IEP TEAM?

IDEA requires that certain individuals are part of the IEP team and involved in the development and writing of the child's IEP. An IEP team member may fill more than one of the team positions if properly qualified and designated. These team members include:

- *Parents/guardians* (key members of the team!).
- *General/regular education teacher(s).* At least one of the child's general education teachers must be on the IEP team.
- *Special education teacher(s)/or providers.*
- A *person who can interpret evaluation results* (in terms of designing appropriate instruction). This member must be able to talk about the instructional implications of the child's evaluation results. This is usually the school psychologist and/or educational evaluator/learning specialist.
- A *school-system representative* who knows a great deal about special education services and necessary school resources. This is often the principal or administrator from the district's special education department.
- *Student* (as appropriate).
- *Transition services agency representatives* (if appropriate).
- *Others with knowledge or special expertise about the child.*

WHAT ARE THE SPECIAL FACTORS TO CONSIDER?

According to IDEA, the following "special factors" (when appropriate) must be considered when developing the IEP for each individual student.

- If the child has *limited proficiency in English*, the IEP team will consider the child's language needs as they relate to his or her IEP.
- If a child's *behavior* interferes with his or her learning or the learning of others, the IEP team will consider strategies and supports to address the child's behavior.
- If the child is *blind or visually impaired*, the IEP team must provide for instruction in Braille or the use of Braille, unless determined after an appropriate evaluation that the child does not need this instruction.

- If the child has *communication needs*, the IEP team must consider them.

- If the child is *deaf or hard of hearing*, the IEP team must consider his or her language and communication needs. This includes the child's opportunities to communicate directly with classmates and school staff in his or her usual method of communication (such as sign language).

- The IEP team must always consider the child's need for *assisted technology* devices or services.

Points to Keep in Mind About Special Education, IDEA, and IEPs:

- IDEA is enforced by the U.S. Office of Special Education Programs (OSEP). Compliance is monitored by the State Department of Education and the Office of Special Education Programs.

- IDEA has a provision called "child find" which requires that every state must identify, locate, and evaluate all children with disabilities who need special education and related services. The responsibility is placed upon the school districts to identify children suspected of having disabilities who reside in the school district. Parents can also call the "child find" system and ask for an evaluation.

- There are important new provisions under IDEA '97 regarding discipline policies and behavioral interventions involving students with disabilities. See List 7-5 for more information about these protections for students with ADHD who have behavioral challenges resulting in possible suspensions or expulsion.

- IDEA requires schools to consider the findings of an outside evaluator and, in some cases, pay or reimburse parents for the independent evaluation.

- As discussed in List 7-1, children under IDEA are guaranteed the right to an education in the "least restrictive environment":

  - This means that whenever possible, children should be able to participate in activities and be educated with their nondisabled peers.

  - Children with disabilities are to be removed from general education only if supplemental aids, modifications, and additional services are not sufficient to educate the child in a satisfactory manner in the regular education program.

  - IDEA also requires that the child be educated as close to home as possible.

- Special education services are defined as "specially designed instruction," which may be available within a range of settings:

  - Special education is not a *place*, but a *service* that can be provided anywhere—including the general education classroom.

  - In fact, most children with ADHD and other mild to moderate disabilities can be effectively served within an inclusive model with the proper modifications, supplemental aids and services, and direct and indirect assistance from special educators.

  - However, inclusive education does not mean that the special education child must *only* be served throughout the day within the classroom. For example, pullout services for small-group instruction are appropriate and effective for many students.

7-4 (*continued*)

■ School districts must provide a wide range of options such as full inclusion, pullout services, and special day classes for students whose needs are best served in a special education class for the majority of the school day. A very small population of students with disabilities will require even more restrictive educational settings (such as residential placements) to meet their severe needs.

SOURCES AND RESOURCES

"A Guide to the Individualized Education Program," published by the Office of Special Education and Rehabilitative Services, U.S. Department of Education (July, 2000) is available free of charge from:

ED Pubs
Editorial Publication Center
U.S. Department of Education
P.O. Box 1398
Jessu, MD 20794-1398
877-4-ED-PUBS
http://www.ed.gov/pubs/edpubs.html

Document is also available online: http://www.ed.gov/offices/OSERS

Cohen, Matthew. "Individuals with Disabilities Education Act: What You Need to Know about AD/HD Under the Individuals with Disabilities Education Act." The CHADD Information and Resource Guide to AD/HD, Landover, MD, 2000; 98–100.

Council for Exceptional Children. http://www.cec.sped.org

Disability Rights Education and Defense Fund. http://www.dredf.org

The EDLAW Center. http://www.edlaw.net

ERIC Clearinghouse on Disabilities and Gifted Education (ERIC EC). 800-328-0272; http://ericec.org

Federal Resource Center for Special Education. http://www.dssc.org/frc

Harbor House Law Press, Inc. http://www.harborhouselaw.com

ILIAD/ASPIRE. Adapted by Laura Reilly, Information Manager, ILIAD/ASPIRE Projects.

"IDEA '97 Final Regulations to Provisions," *Teaching Exceptional Children*, vol. 32, no. 1, September/October, 1999, 88–89.

IDEA Local Implementations by Local Administrators (ILIAD), The Council for Exceptional Children. 877-CEC-IDEA; www.ideapractices.org

"Individualized Education Programs & IDEA 97." http://www.ldonline.org/ldindepth/iep/idea97.html

Latham, Peter, and Patricia Latham. *Documentation and the Law.* Washington, DC: JKL Communications, 1996.

Luger, Susan, and George Zelma. "Understanding Special Education and the Law." http://www.aboutourkids.org/world/may00/02

National Association of Protection and Advocacy Systems (NAPSA). http://www.protectionandadvocacy.com

National Association of School Psychologists (NASP). http://www.naspweb.org/index.html

National Information Clearinghouse on Children and Youth with Disabilities. http://www.nichcy.org

The Policy Maker Partnership (PMP) for Implementing IDEA '97, National Association of State Directors of Special Education. 703-519-3800; www.nasdse.org

"Special Education Rights of Parents and Children Under the IDEA, Part B," California Department of Education, Special Education Division: *The GRAM*, Spring 1999.

Technical Assistance for Parent Centers—the Alliance, PACER Center. 888-248-0822; www.taalliance.org

U.S. Department of Education (in cooperation with the Council for Exceptional Children).
www.ideapractices.org
www.ed.gov/offices/OSERS/OSEP/index.html

Wright, Pam, and Pete Wright. *From Emotions to Advocacy—The Special Education Survival Guide.* Hartfield, VA: Harbor House Law Press, 2002.

Wright, Peter, and Pamela D. Wright. *Wrightslaw: Special Education Law.* Hartfield, VA: Harbor House Law Press, 2000.

Note: The following are regional resource centers:

Northeast Regional Resource Center (NERRC)—Serving: Connecticut, Maine, Massachusetts, New Hampshire, New Jersey, New York, Rhode Island, and Vermont.
http://www.trinityvt.edu/nerrc

Mid-South Regional Resource Center (MSRRC)—Serving: Delaware, Kentucky, Maryland, North Carolina, South Carolina, Tennessee, Virginia, District of Columbia, and West Virginia.
http://www.ihdi.uky.edu/msrrc

7-4 (*continued*)

Southeast Regional Resource Center (SERRC)—Serving: Alabama, Arkansas, Florida, Georgia, Louisiana, Mississippi, Oklahoma Puerto Rico, Texas, and the U.S. Virgin Islands.
http://edla/aum.edu/serrc/serrc.html

Great Lakes Area Regional Resource Center (GLARRC)—Serving: Illinois, Indiana, Iowa, Michigan, Minnesota, Missouri, Ohio, Pennsylvania, and Wisconsin.
http://www.glarrc.org

Mountain Plains Regional Resource Center (MPRRC)—Serving: Arizona, Bureau of Indian Affairs, Colorado, Kansas, Montana, Nebraska, New Mexico, North Dakota, South Dakota, Utah, and Wyoming.
http://www.usu.edu/mprrc

Western Regional Resource Center (WRRC)—Serving: Alaska, American Samoa, California, Federated states of Micronesia, Guam, Hawaii, Idaho, Nevada, Oregon, Republic of the Marshall Islands, and Washington.
http://interact.uoregon.edu/wrrc/wrrc.html

7-5
DISCIPLINING STUDENTS WITH DISABILITIES UNDER IDEA

IDEA provides protections for students with disabilities so they are not unfairly disciplined when misbehavior stems from the disability itself. This safeguard is particularly important to students with ADHD whose behavior frequently results in disciplinary action.

Before a student with a disability is suspended for more than ten days (see circumstances below which constitute a "change in placement"), expelled, or placed in another setting due to behavioral issues and violations of school rules, a "Manifestation Determination Review" must be conducted.

WHAT IS A "MANIFESTATION DETERMINATION REVIEW"?

■ This is a formal review by the IEP team that needs to take place no later than ten school days from the time the school makes the decision to change a student's placement.

■ The purpose of this mandatory meeting is to determine whether or not the problem behavior resulting in disciplinary action is a manifestation of the student's disability.

■ IDEA prohibits schools from expelling or suspending students whose behaviors result from their disabilities for more than ten days during a school year—except in circumstances involving weapons or drugs, or when the student is a threat to himself/herself or others.

■ If the behavior *is* related to the disability, the IEP team needs to determine and ensure appropriate services, interventions, and placement. Any disciplinary actions the school imposes must be appropriate for the student's disability.

WHAT ARE THE REQUIREMENTS OF THE REVIEW?

■ The school must observe the student and consider the special education evaluation, the IEP, and placement.

■ The school must decide if:

　• The IEP and placement were appropriate and effectively implemented.

　• Supplementary aids/services were provided.

　• Behavioral-intervention strategies were provided.

7-5 (*continued*)

- ▪ The student understood the consequences of his or her behavior.
- ▪ The student was able to control his or her behavior.
- ■ Of course, with ADHD, the issue of whether or not the child is able to inhibit and control his or her impulsive/hyperactive behavior is an important consideration in making this manifestation determination.

If a student who is suspected as having a disability (but was never identified) faces disciplinary action constituting a change of placement, he or she is protected under the provisional safeguards of IDEA under these circumstances:

- ■ If the school had prior knowledge or should have had knowledge that the child was a student with a disability
- ■ If the child's behavior or performance demonstrated the need for special education
- ■ If the parents stated in writing that the child needed special education or requested an evaluation
- ■ If the child's teacher expressed concern about the child's behavior or performance to other school personnel

CHANGE OF PLACEMENT

- ■ A "change of placement" with regard to suspensions is defined as more than ten consecutive days of suspension *or* multiple short-term removals/suspensions exceeding ten days during the school year that constitute "a pattern."
- ■ The length (and total amount) of time the student is removed, as well as the type of behaviors and incidents, are considered in determining the existence of a pattern.
- ■ Under IDEA, services must be provided to the student with an IEP after the tenth consecutive day of suspension (or nonconsecutive removals constituting a pattern that exceeds ten days) in order to help the child continue to progress in his or her IEP goals and general curriculum.
- ■ Schools can remove a student with disabilities up to 45 days for carrying or possessing a weapon, and for knowingly using, selling, or soliciting illegal drugs or controlled substances at school or school functions. These are the only circumstances that a school may exceed the 10-day suspension and the student be placed in an alternative setting for 45 days without an order from a hearing officer.
- ■ Parents have the right to ten days' notice before a school proposes changing the child's placement. They also may request an impartial due-process hearing if they disagree with the school's decision.

If the school believes the student presents a danger to self or others, an emergency order can be filed for the student's removal. An impartial hearing officer can order the child to be removed to an Interim Alternative Educational Setting (IAES) for up to 45 days if he or she determines:

- There is substantial evidence that the current placement is likely to result in injury to the child or to others.
- The school made reasonable efforts to minimize the risk of harm, including the use of supplementary aids and services.
- The IAES will provide the child the opportunity to continue to participate in the general curriculum with the services and modifications of his or her IEP.

Children with disabilities in alternative settings must continue to receive a free and appropriate public education.

IDEA regulations include a "Stay-Put" or "Frozen Placement" provision, meaning that:

- If either party requests an impartial due-process hearing, the child remains in the last agreed-upon (then current) placement until all administrative and legal proceedings are resolved.
- The "stay-put" provision applies to suspensions or expulsions that constitute a change of placement.
- It does not apply to cases involving drugs and weapons, or when the child is deemed a threat to self or others—which enables the school to place the child in the 45-day IAES.

If a student engages in behaviors that "impede his or her learning or that of others" around him or her, then the IEP team must consider appropriate strategies, supports, and interventions to address that behavior.

IDEA now requires that either before (but not later than ten days after) taking a disciplinary action resulting in a change of placement, the school is to conduct a Functional Behavioral Assessment (FBA) and implement a Behavioral Intervention Plan (BIP) for the student. If this has already been done prior to the behavior that resulted in the suspension, then the IEP meeting convenes to review and modify the plan to address the child's behavior.

WHAT ARE THE FBA AND BIP?

- A Functional Behavioral Assessment (FBA) requires examining the *antecedents* (conditions that exist or events that may be identified as triggers to the problem behaviors). (2-17)
- Antecedents involve any number of factors (such as environmental, physical, performance and skill demands, teacher–student interactions) that precede the problem behavior and may be adjusted to prevent or reduce reoccurrences of the misbehavior in the future. The FBA also looks at the *consequences* (positive and negative) that occur as a result of the misbehavior.

7-5 (continued)

- By examining these factors in the classroom and/or other school settings, a Behavioral Intervention Plan (BIP) is then developed specific to that student. The BIP is designed to use proactive strategies and interventions to avoid and reduce the likelihood of problematic behavior, and to teach the student appropriate strategies and skills.(See lists in Section 2 and the Appendix.)

- The team can also identify positive reinforcers to use with the student in the implementation of a behavioral plan that are meaningful to the individual student. (2-2, 2-14)

- Corrective consequences appropriate to the student's disability are included in the BIP and need to be implemented by those adults responsible for disciplining the student. (2-8)

THE VALUE OF THE FBA AND BIP

A great deal of student misbehavior can be reduced or eliminated by paying attention to triggering events or conditions and developing a well-thought-out plan of response to misbehavior and encouragement of positive behavior for the individual child. A proactive plan is generally far more beneficial than the typical school consequence of seeking such punishments as removing the child. Even though removal of students with behavioral problems is what many teachers and other school personnel prefer (and may alleviate the situation temporarily), it is not the answer.

Hopefully, more focus on the FBA and the BIP for students with behavioral challenges will become the norm, rather than the exception, as they currently are in most school districts. For this to happen, more resources need to be allocated: school psychologists, counselors, and other support staff who will be provided the time to observe (in classrooms), assess, and develop effective behavioral-intervention plans with teachers and parents.

SOURCES AND RESOURCES

"Behavior and Discipline," *Teaching Exceptional Children.* March/April 1998.

Cohen, Matthew. "Section 504 & IDEA—What's the Difference: Limited vs. Substantial Protections for Children with ADD and Other Disabilities," CHADD: *Attention.* Summer, 1997.

Cohen, Matthew. "Individuals with Disabilities Education Act 1999: What You Need to Know about AD/HD Under the Individuals with Disabilities Education Act." *Inside CHADD,* June/July 1999

Cohen, Matthew. "Educational Rights for Children with AD/HD," *The CHADD Information and Resource Guide to AD/HD.* Landover, MD: CHADD, 2000.

Gartland, Debi. "Effective IEP Development for Students with AD/HD," CHADD: *Attention,* September/October 2000.

"IDEA '97 Final Regulations to Provisions," *Teaching Exceptional Children,* vol. 32, no. 1, September/October 1999, 88–89.

Lachs, Sheila. "Changes to the Individuals with Disabilities Education Act and What They Mean for Children with ADD," CHADD: *Attention,* Spring 1998.

"Legal Rights and Services for Children with ADD," *CHADD Fact Sheet.* http://www.chadd.org/facts/add

Martin, Reed. "Advocacy Strategies for Students with ADD." http://www.reedmartin.com

National Association of Protection and Advocacy Systems (NAPSA). www.protectionandadvocacy.com

National Association of School Psychologists. http://www.naspweb.org/index.html

National Information Clearinghouse on Children and Youth with Disabilities. http://www.nichcy.org

"Special Education Rights of Parents and Children Under the IDEA, Part B," California Department of Education, Special Education Division: *The GRAM,* Spring 1999.

U.S. Department of Education in cooperation with the Council for Exceptional Children. www.ed.gov/offices/OSERS/OSEP/index.html

Wrightslaw. www.wrightslaw.com

Wright, Pam, and Pete Wright. *From Emotions to Advocacy—The Special Education Survival Guide.* Hartfield, VA: Harbor House Law Press, 2002.

Wright, Peter, and Pamela D. Wright. *Wrightslaw: Special Education Law.* Hartfield, VA: Harbor House Law Press, 2000.

Understanding, Supporting, and Improving Outcomes for Individuals with ADHD

8-1
WHAT STUDENTS WITH ADHD NEED FOR SCHOOL SUCCESS

- A structured, positive classroom that is welcoming, inclusive, and well managed
- To feel "safe" and comfortable in the classroom environment, knowing that they will be treated with dignity and respect, and not deliberately criticized, embarrassed, or humiliated in front of their peers
- Instruction and materials that motivate, engage their interest, and keep them involved, therefore minimizing both boredom and frustration (the sources of many behavior problems in the classroom)
- Clarity of expectations and predictability of schedules and routines
- Clearly defined and enforced rules and consequences
- Engaging and effective instruction with a high degree of active learning and high response opportunities
- Structuring of their work environment, tasks, and materials
- Assistance through transitions
- Assistance in helping to focus and maintain attention
- Discreet cueing, prompting, and reminders
- Help/training with organization, time management, and study skills
- Learning-style and environmental accommodations
- Escape-valve outlets
- Extra time to process information and output/perform tasks
- Creative, interesting, and challenging curriculum
- A great deal of modeling and teacher-guided instruction
- Meaningful learning experiences that help them to make connections and see the relevance
- Choices, options, and flexibility
- Teaching strategies that build upon their strengths and help bypass their weaknesses
- More frequent and powerful rewards
- Concrete, multisensory, experiential learning
- Direct, focused instruction
- Variety, variety, variety
- Confidence that their teacher cares about their needs and can be trusted

8-1 (continued)

- Opportunities to voice their feelings, concerns, and ideas
- Feeling they have choice and are involved in some decision-making
- Positive attention from teachers and peers
- Ongoing support, encouragement, and "coaching" for skills in which they are weak
- An emphasis on their own personal best efforts and self-improvement, rather than on competition against one another
- Help coping with feelings of frustration
- Direct support and teaching of learning/study strategies and self-management and self-monitoring techniques
- The opportunity to participate in school activities that showcase their areas of strength (art, music, P.E., creative electives) to their peers
- Close home and school monitoring with incentives/positive reinforcement for reduction of problematic behaviors and an increase in productivity
- Either a formal (IEP/504) or informal (SST Action Plan) school plan that is monitored and reviewed for effectiveness by school team and parents
- Teamwork and collaboration on the part of school personnel, parents, and medical/mental health providers
- Teachers who embody the following qualities:
  - Balance of firmness and flexibility (willing to make accommodations)
  - Kindness
  - Tolerance and a positive attitude
  - Fairness
  - Authority
  - Good communication and problem-solving skills
- Teachers who do the following:
  - Maintain high expectations, yet provide support, enabling students to achieve those expectations/standards.
  - Understand ADHD (from training) and recognize how it affects student behavior and performance.
  - Model self-control and the ability to stay calm (not react out of anger).
  - Make adjustments/modifications in homework and other performance demands if needed (particularly within the written workload).
  - Show they have a sense of humor and truly enjoy teaching.
  - Try to make learning fun.
  - Encourage and motivate students by seeing past the behaviors to the "whole child."

- Believe the child belongs in his or her classroom, and will do what it takes to help the student succeed.

RELATED LISTS

- Lists throughout this book address all of the above.

8-2
WHAT CHILDREN AND TEENS WITH ADHD NEED FROM PARENTS

It is common for children/teens with ADHD to receive a high degree of negative feedback and disapproval on a day-to-day basis at school and in the community. This can take its toll on their self-esteem. The family plays the most important role in providing the child with nurturing and loving support to develop the resilience they need to overcome obstacles and achieve success.

Children and teens need:

- The unconditional love and acceptance of their families
- To know they are "okay" and not deficient in the eyes of their parents
- Forgiveness
- Patience and tolerance
- Empathy and understanding
- Clear limits and structure
- Positive discipline
- Support and encouragement
- Consistency and logical consequences
- Predictability of schedules and routines
- Numerous opportunities to develop their areas of strength (sports, music, dance, arts)
- To be able to pursue their interests and participate in extracurricular activities
- Special time with parents (not contingent upon anything) for talking, having fun together, and building/strengthening the relationship
- To feel safe and comfortable, and be able to "let down their guard"
- To be able to express their feelings, worries, concerns, and ideas
- To feel they have choices and are involved in some decision-making
- Frequent positive feedback
- Help understanding and labeling their feelings (for example, "I'm frustrated," "I'm disappointed")
- To have their feelings validated by parents' active listening
- For parents to focus on important issues and downplay less critical ones
- An emphasis on their own personal best efforts and self-improvement
- Reminders and prompts without nagging, criticism, or sarcasm

- Parents' involvement and close communication with the school
- Help with coping skills and feelings of frustration
- Parent guidance, and coaching in appropriate behavior and skills
- Modeling and practicing of calm, rational, problem-solving approaches
- Fun and humor
- To hear and feel how much they are loved and appreciated
- Praise and recognition for what they are doing "right"
- To know that it is okay to make mistakes, as it is only natural, and for parents to acknowledge when they do so
- To be able to ask for help, and know parents will do what they can to provide it
- Buffering from unnecessary stress and frustration
- Fair, clear, and reasonable rules and expectations
- Supervision and follow-through
- Help with organization and study skills
- Structuring of their work environment, tasks, and materials
- Help getting chores, assignments, and projects started
- Preparation for changes and time to adapt and adjust
- Help with planning ahead, following schedules, and keeping on-target with deadlines and responsibilities
- Escape-valve outlets

RELATED LISTS

- See Lists 2-12, 2-13, 2-15, 2-18, 4-5, 4-7, 4-9, 6-1, and 8-9.

8-3
DO'S AND DON'TS FOR TEACHERS

- **Don't** assume the student is lazy or apathetic.

- **Do** realize that students with ADHD have neuro-biological reasons for their poor performance and lack of productivity in the classroom. (1-1, 1-2, 1-4, 1-7)

- **Don't** assume the student is deliberately not performing because you have observed that at times he or she is able to perform a particular task/assignment.

- **Do** remember that *inconsistency* is a hallmark characteristic of this disorder. Sometimes they can do the work; sometimes they cannot.

- **Don't** give up on using behavior-modification techniques.

- **Do** realize that you will need to revamp, revise, and modify aspects of the behavioral plan (for example, incentives, reinforcement schedule) to maintain the interest and motivation of ADHD students. It is well worth the time and effort! (2-2, 2-7, 2-9, 2-14, 2-18)

- **Don't** give up on any student.

- **Do** know how much it matters that you believe in them, maintain high expectations, and give your best effort to help them succeed (no matter how difficult and frustrating it may be). (8-1)

- **Don't** tell children what you want them *not to do*. ("Don't blurt out in class.")

- **Do** tell children what you want them *to do*. ("Raise your hand and wait to be called on.") (2-6)

- **Don't** focus the majority of your attention on a child's misbehaviors.

- **Do** attend to the student most of the time when he or she is behaving appropriately.

- **Don't** be afraid to ask questions and seek advice/support when you have concerns about a student.

- **Do** involve your support staff by communicating with school support personnel and bringing students to the SST for assistance. (6-1, 6-2, 6-3) Your team should support you in:
  - Making observations
  - Helping with behavioral management and classroom strategies
  - Attending meetings with parents
  - Providing information
  - Suggesting any school-based interventions that may be available and appropriate
  - Making necessary referrals

- **Don't** neglect to do everything you can to forge a collaborative relationship with the parents. (6-1, 6-4, 8-4)
- **Do** the following:
  - Invite parents to visit the school and observe their child in the classroom.
  - Communicate with parents regularly and make a plan for working together (such as using a Daily Report Card) on specific goals. (2-1, 2-9, 4-8, and the Appendix).
  - Let parents know that your primary goal is helping their child improve his or her school functioning and success.
- **Don't** surround yourself with negative peers who are critical of students, not open to new techniques and strategies, and not updating their skills.
- **Do** keep a positive attitude and associate with colleagues who also have a positive mindset. Keep learning and growing. Take advantage of professional-development opportunities.
- **Don't** listen to previous teachers who only want to pass on the negative traits and characteristics of their students to you.
- **Do** assume the best of the child. Allow each student to start the year with a fresh, clean slate.
- **Don't** forget the quiet student in the background who can easily go through the school year unnoticed and anonymous.
- **Do** realize that these are the students often in greatest need of support and intervention.
- **Don't** work alone.
- **Do** find buddies, share with colleagues, and collaborate!
- **Don't** put yourself in the position of suggesting to parents that their child has ADHD and needs to be evaluated (or medicated).
- **Do** the following:
  - State your objective observations regarding the child's behavior and performance in the classroom.
  - Request an SST meeting and involve your school's multidisciplinary team. (6-2)
  - Inquire about protocol at your school regarding ADHD concerns and how to proceed. (1-17)
- **Don't** be afraid to make various accommodations or adjustments (instructional, behavioral, and environmental) as needed for certain students.
- **Do** choose to make the adaptations and special arrangements it takes for students to succeed in the classroom. It is *okay* and *fair* to make accommodations/modifications for individual students with disabilities.

8-4
COMMUNICATING WITH PARENTS: TIPS FOR TEACHERS

It is much easier to discuss concerns with parents once you have opened the lines of communication in a positive manner.

- One of the best ways you can establish rapport with parents is to speak about their child's areas of strength and competence. Make every effort to learn about the child, identifying his or her individual strengths, interests, and positive characteristics.

- Clearly communicate to parents early in the year (first days of school) and on an ongoing basis via weekly/monthly newsletters regarding your classroom goals, policies, expectations, activities, and special events. Always invite and welcome parent participation.

- Be proactive:
  - Call or write notes home communicating positive messages to parents about their child (what you appreciate about the student).
  - Make yourself easily accessible and let parents know when and how they can best contact you.
  - Reach out to parents by letting them know they are welcome at school.
  - Communicate that you are eager to work with parents as a "team" to ensure that their child is successful in your class.

- When you have concerns about a student:
  - Make the personal contact and explain to parents what you are concerned about.
  - Again, try to always indicate something positive.
  - Describe how the child is functioning (academically/behaviorally).
  - State your observations objectively without "labeling" the behavior or child ("lazy" or "bad").
  - Be sure parents realize you are not blaming the child or anyone else.
  - Communicate your interest in doing everything possible to help the student do well in school.

- Ask parents if they have noticed (at home) any of the difficulties you have described or if previous teachers ever communicated these concerns in the past.

- Let the parents know what specific strategies and interventions you are currently utilizing and/or will begin to implement to address the areas of concern. Ask if they have any additional suggestions or information that can help you meet the student's needs.

- Tell parents that you will be in touch and let them know if things are improving. At this time (or through a follow-up contact), inform parents about the school's Student Support Team (SST) process. (6-2)

- Explain that at your school there is a process through which teachers consult with a team of their colleagues (other teachers, administrators, and support staff) to help develop a plan of strategies and interventions to assist students.

- Inform parents that you may be consulting with the team for more ideas and recommendations to ensure their child's success.

- To establish and build a positive relationship with parents:

  - Communicate in a manner that is respectful and nonjudgmental.

  - Welcome their "partnership."

  - Acknowledge that they are the "experts" on their son or daughter.

  - Value their input and any information/insights, as you truly care about their child.

8-5
PARENT ADVOCACY: TIPS AND STRATEGIES

Parents of children with ADHD will find that they need to learn advocacy strategies to ensure that their child receives the help he or she needs. ADHD is a long-term, chronic disorder requiring parents to take on the role of case manager for their child's care and treatment over the years. In order to do so effectively, parents need to educate themselves about ADHD. As a parent, it is your responsibility to step in and intervene on behalf of your child whenever the situation arises that your son or daughter needs more support, intervention, and understanding of his or her disorder.

- Learn about your child's rights under the law to a free, appropriate public education, and to accommodations and/or direct special services if the ADHD is affecting your child's ability to learn or perform successfully at school. (7-1 through 7-5)

- To be an effective advocate, you must establish a partnership with the school. You will have to communicate with school staff regarding your child to a far greater degree than is necessary for most other children. Your level of involvement with the school significantly increases when you have a child with any disability or special needs.

- Many parents feel uncomfortable at school meetings, particularly team meetings that involve several members of the school staff. Try to enter meetings with an open mind and cooperative attitude. Be willing to share your opinions, feelings, observations, suggestions, and any information about your child or family that may help with planning and intervention.

- Do not be afraid to ask questions and request that certain language (educational jargon) be explained. Ask for clarification on anything you do not understand.

- At certain meetings, such as Student Support Team (SST) and IEP meetings, you should receive a copy of any reports or paperwork to which staff members make reference. If not, request a copy. (6-2, 7-4)

- Take notes during meetings. In addition, it is helpful if you enter meetings prepared with a few notes to yourself regarding items you wish to share, discuss, or ask about.

- You are welcome to bring someone with you to meetings. It is most helpful if both parents can attend school meetings together, even if parents are divorced but share custody. Schools are used to working with sensitive family situations, and will do what they can to effectively communicate and work with parents and guardians.

- Avoid becoming defensive, aggressive, accusatory, or hostile with school personnel. Try to remain polite and diplomatic.

- One of the most effective ways to help your child is to provide resources and information about ADHD to teachers, coaches, and other adults directly working with your child on a regular basis. Much of the teacher training and public awareness regarding ADHD is a direct result of parents' strong efforts (through organizations such as CHADD) to educate others about the needs of their children. (6-4, 8-10)

- Often the best way to establish a positive relationship with the school is to be a helpful, involved parent who volunteers time and service to the school. There are countless ways that schools can use the direct or indirect services of parents. All schools are seeking parent involvement in the classroom or various school committees, programs, and projects. Become more involved in the school community and get to know staff members.

- Let teachers or other staff members who are making a strong effort on behalf of your child know that you are appreciative. It is generally the little things that make a difference.

- Communicate frequently with the classroom teachers. Find out as much as you can about how your child is functioning at school and ways you can support at home.

- You have a right to have your child's educational needs assessed by the school district. Speak with the classroom teacher, special education teacher, other members of the multidisciplinary team, the principal, or the director of special education about pursuing an evaluation.

- Submit to the school a written, dated letter requesting an evaluation, including the reason you want assessment (for example, concern about your child's educational performance). This will begin the IEP process and timeline. The evaluation will determine whether your child qualifies for special education/related services based upon an identified area of disability.

- It is generally recommended to first proceed through the SST process before requesting formal testing if this process is used at your school site; however, it is not a requirement to do so. (1-16, 6-2)

- Read the paperwork the school provides regarding procedures, the assessment plan, and your due-process rights under the law. If you have any questions, ask.

- After testing there will be an IEP meeting at which time the results of the evaluation will be shared with you and other members of the team. If your child qualifies for special education/related services, an Individual Education Plan (IEP) will be written with specific goals and objectives to address his or her areas of need. Again, question any of the test data, interpretations, or recommendations you do not understand. (7-2, 7-4)

- If your child qualifies for services or special education programs, ask for information about those services/programs.

- If you disagree with any part of the IEP, you do not have to sign it. You may also write your areas of disagreement on the IEP. Further, if you wish to include other information on the IEP or request additional goals, objectives, or accommodations to address the needs of your child, ask that they be included in the IEP.

- If the team's recommendation is to place your child outside the general education classroom, ask to visit and make observations of those special education classes/placements. As your child's advocate, you will want to make sure the program or placement is appropriate. You do not have to accept any services, programs, or placements. Know that you also have the right to discontinue any services/programs at any time.

8-5 (*continued*)

- Learn about Section 504 Plans and possible supports/accommodations your child may receive if eligible under Section 504. (7-1, 7-3)

- Keep a file on your child that includes all copies of testing, reports, IEPs, report cards, health records, immunization, and other important data.

- Include in a file a log of communication with the school and other professionals working with your child, including:

  - Dates of doctor appointments and medication logs.

  - Summaries of conversations and meetings; notification of disciplinary actions and referrals your child received at school; interventions promised to be put into effect; and so forth.

- Having the above-mentioned information easily accessible will likely come in handy at some time.

- To be an effective advocate for your child, prepare for meetings by trying to learn:

  - How your child is functioning at school (in classroom and other settings)

  - In what areas your child is struggling (academic, social-emotional, behavioral)

  - The kinds of supports and accommodations that may be helpful and available

- If through your health-care plan you are limited as to which doctors your child may see for an evaluation, be sure that the physician is aware of and follows AAP guidelines in the diagnostic and treatment process. (1-14, 1-16, 1-22, 1-23)

- Seek professionals in the community with whom you feel comfortable and confident. Get referrals from others who may be in the best position to recommend specialists dealing with ADHD-related issues.

- Be assertive in checking the level of expertise of the professionals you seek out. If you are uncomfortable with their treatment approach, express your concerns. If they do not appear committed to a team approach, you will be better off finding someone else. Your child's doctors and therapists should be in close communication with you and the school.

- To be an effective advocate for your child, you will need to monitor the plans as well as your child's progress. Request update meetings or parent–teacher conferences. If something is not working, it can always be changed. Attempt to solve problems using a cooperative team approach.

- Any plan—whether formal (504, IEP) or informal (SST Action Plan)—can be reviewed at any point during the school year. You do not have to wait until an annual review meeting or a quarterly/semester parent–teacher conference. Request a review of the plan or any services, programs, or special placements whenever you wish.

- Continuously remain in close communication with the school to monitor growth and progress and implement changes/modifications as needed.

SOURCES AND RESOURCES

Rief, Sandra. *The ADD/ADHD Checklist.* Paramus, NJ: Prentice Hall, 1998.

Snyder, Marlene. "Parent's Perceptions of School Services for Children with ADD: Communication is the Key!" CHADD: *Attention*, vol. 4, no. 1, Summer 1997, 10–12.

Welch, Ann. "Finding the Balance Between Advocacy and Excuses." CHADD International Conference, October 1999, in Washington, DC.

8-6
ADHD IN YOUNG CHILDREN

Most children with ADHD are not diagnosed until the elementary school grades. With very young children it is harder to distinguish the line between what is "normal" rambunctious, active, inattentive, and uninhibited early childhood behavior, and what may be abnormal (maladaptive and inconsistent with the child's developmental level). Those youngsters exhibiting very significant difficulties with ADHD symptoms may be identified in kindergarten, preschool, and even earlier.

- Teeter (1998) summarized the hallmarks of ADHD during the preschool stage, including the following:
  - Parental stress is at its zenith.
  - Hyperactivity and noncompliance are common.
  - Impulsive responding, hyperactivity during structured activities, and inattention and distractibility to tasks are high.
  - Peer rejection is common.
  - The number of environmental demands to sit down, be quiet, and follow directions in school increases.
  - The number of referrals to psychologists for difficult and challenging behaviors increases.

- Of course, parents should discuss concerns about their young child with their pediatrician and teacher. It is recommended to pursue an evaluation when symptoms are problematic and impairing, as early intervention (such as parent training/therapy, behavior management at home and school, and medication in some cases) can greatly improve the child's ability to function successfully.

- Children with ADHD often display other developmental difficulties (such as speech/language, gross-/fine-motor skills, learning). Parents and the school team should have the child's vision and hearing screened, and pursue an evaluation, as needed, for these other areas of concern.

- It is difficult for many parents to decide whether or not their child (particularly those with late birthdays) is ready to start kindergarten or wait another year. Parents should visit the kindergarten classes at the school, speak with teachers, seek advice from their pediatrician, and try to make the most informed decision based upon knowledge of their own child and his or her needs.

- When a child has ADHD, behaviors that affect social and academic performance generally do not improve by just providing more time to mature. Other interventions will be necessary to specifically target areas of weakness and build skills. Early intervention is always the most beneficial for children with disabilities and special needs.

- The same principles of parenting, effective behavior management, and problem prevention described in Lists 2-10 through 2-16 and 2-18 apply to parents of young children with ADHD.

- It is highly recommended for parents to start early in seeking help from specialists in learning how to cope with and manage their young child's challenging behaviors and more difficult temperaments. There are many resources available to help parents learn how to do so (for example, parenting classes, behavior-management training, counseling, parent support groups such as CHADD, books/videos, and other materials).

- Parents will need to provide the necessary structure and manage the environmental factors to help their child be successful, anticipating potential problems and planning accordingly. For example, parents of highly active young children will need to take great care to childproof the home for safety.

- Effective early childhood teachers, as all good teachers:

  - Provide a classroom environment that is loving, nurturing, comfortable, and safe.

  - Are generous with hugs, smiles, and praise/positive attention.

  - Maintain close contact and involvement with parents.

  - Are specific, firm, and clear in their expectations.

  - Provide structure, consistency, and follow-through.

  - Establish a predictable routine and schedule.

  - Are flexible, kind, and tolerant.

  - Offer children choices.

  - Teach with a great deal of multisensory techniques (movement, hands-on activities, music).

  - Use individualized discipline and behavior-management techniques.

  - Allow children time and opportunity to explore and make discoveries.

  - Are well planned and prepared.

  - Teach, model, and practice all behavioral expectations.

  - Use positive reinforcement with very high frequency.

  - Teach through fun, exciting curriculum and activities.

  - Create a room environment that takes into account different learning styles.

  - Adapt activities and provide for the needs of all students (whatever their developmental level may be).

  - Have a clear awareness that children's self-esteem and feeling good about themselves is of utmost importance.

  - Respect each child's individuality.

- In kindergarten, every behavioral expectation and social skill must be taught. Teachers need to explain and model each desired behavior and practice until all students know precisely what is expected from them. For example, children must learn how to:

8-6 (*continued*)

- Line up, stand in line, and walk in line.

- Move to groups and stations/learning centers.

- Sit on the rug or at the table.

- Get the teacher's attention (such as raise hand).

- Modulate their voice ("indoor/outdoor" voices).

■ Teachers need to model, role-play, and have children practice expectations. Examples: "Show me what to do when you have something you want to say." "Who wants to show us how we get our lunch boxes and line up for lunch?"

■ It helps to use literature that has manners and appropriate behavior as a theme, and to teach behavioral expectations and social skills through the use of puppets, music, games, visual display, role-playing, and so on.

■ Behavior-management techniques for kindergarten children with ADHD are similar to those in higher grades (using a high degree of feedback; visual prompting/cueing; proximity control; group positive-reinforcement systems; corrective consequences that are applied consistently; and individualized behavioral plans/supports). (2-1 through 2-11, 2-16, 2-18)

■ Sometimes children with ADHD are on sensory overload or are fatigued. It is important to allow time and space to settle, regroup, and get away from some of the overstimulation. It helps to have a "quiet space" area that is designed for this purpose (such as calming music they can listen to with earphones, pillows, stuffed animal, and so on). (2-10, 8-9)

■ Teachers may ask: "Do you need to move to _____?" "Is there a better place to do your work?" Redirect to a quieter, calmer area by whispering to the child, "Go to the pillow area and read a book." (2-11)

■ The perceptive teacher will watch for signs of children beginning to get restless, agitated, and so on, and try diverting their attention to redirect their behavior ("Sara, come help me turn the pages of this book.").

■ Most young children love to be the teacher's helper. They can be given a task to do, such as wiping down tables, putting up chairs, or passing out papers. It is important to find out what the child likes to do, identifying what is meaningful and motivating to that youngster. Some children do not care at all about stickers or other tangible/material reinforcers, but would be highly motivated to be able to earn the chance to blow bubbles, ride a tricycle in the playground, or care for the class pet. See List 2-2 regarding positive incentives/reinforcers.

■ As with older children, the best way to manage is through watching for positive behaviors, and recognizing children for what they are doing right. Besides specific praise from teachers, positive recognition and appreciation from peers is important as well. Examples: "Let's give a big round of applause to . . ." (Children clap finger-to-finger in a large circular movement). "Let's give ourselves a pat on the back." (Children reach over and pat themselves on the back.) "Let's give the silent cheer for . . ."

- Check for specific behaviors: "Are your eyes watching? Are mouths zipped? Are we sitting 'criss-cross applesauce'?"

- Use visual prompts for all behavioral expectations. For example, make class charts with pictures depicting the behaviors you want students to demonstrate. Point to and refer to those visuals frequently. See the Appendix for possible picture prompts to use for this purpose.

- Use individualized behavior-modification charts or daily report cards. Some children will need an individualized system for monitoring and reinforcing one or two specific behaviors. With young children, the reinforcement schedule must be frequent—short time segments for rewarding (with chance to earn a star, smiley face, stamp). See Lists 2-1, 2-7, and 2-9 for more information and the Appendix for sample charts.

- In addition, early childhood classrooms need to be:
  - Rich in oral language, with children exposed to a lot of rhyme and verse, patterned literature, and fun, interesting stories
  - Colorful, warm, and comfortable
  - Well equipped with enriching materials, centers, literature, and hands-on activities
  - Full of curriculum and activities/materials to enhance the development of language skills, fine-motor development, early literacy, and math (3-6, 5-3, 5-11, 5-14)
  - Clearly labeled, so children can access materials and clean up independently (4-4, 5-11)
  - Embedded with music and movement in all aspects of the curriculum throughout the day (use of songs, chants, motions to signal and use during transitions, to enhance body awareness and coordination, following directions, teach phonological awareness, help calm and redirect behavior)

SOURCES AND RESOURCES

Jones, Clare B. *Sourcebook for Children with Attention Deficit Disorder—A Management Guide for Early Childhood Professionals and Parents.* Tucson, AZ: Communications Skill Builders, 1991.

Reimers, Cathy, and Bruce Brunger. *ADHD in the Young Child—Driven to Redirection.* Plantation, FL: Specialty Press, Inc., 1999.

Rief, Sandra. *How to Reach and Teach ADD/ADHD Children.* West Nyack, NY: The Center for Applied Research in Education, 1993.

Rief, Sandra. *Ready . . . Start . . . School: Nurturing and Guiding Your Child Through Preschool and Kindergarten.* Paramus, NJ: Prentice Hall Press, 2001.

Teeter, Phyllis Anne. "Back to School Advice to Parents of Young Children with AD/HD." http://members.chaddonline.org/attention

Teeter, Phyllis A. *Interventions for AD/HD: Treatment in Developmental Context.* New York: The Guilford Press, 1998.

8-7
ADHD IN ADOLESCENTS

For most children with ADHD, the symptoms (to varying degrees) continue into adolescence. Many pre-teens/teens find these years to be the most difficult and stressful for them and their families.

■ Core symptoms of ADHD may diminish or manifest differently as the child matures. For example, a hyperactive teen will not be jumping out of his or her seat, but will probably appear restless and antsy.

■ Impulsivity, lack of self-control, and poor planning in adolescence are associated with many risk factors, including significantly more traffic violations, accidents, teen pregnancies, as well as conduct that results in conflict with school authorities, parents, and law enforcement. (1-6)

■ Some children with ADHD who were able to cope adequately with the work demands in elementary school are unable to do so any longer in middle and high school. Weaknesses in executive functions become more apparent in upper grades, negatively affecting academic performance. (1-2, 1-5)

■ It is very important for parents and teachers of ADHD students to be aware of conditions that commonly co-occur with ADHD, and may emerge in the middle and high school years. (1-11) Depression, anxiety, sleep disturbances, ODD, conduct disorder, and LD are common coexisting conditions.

■ It is important to reevaluate when other conditions are suspected, and implement whatever treatments and interventions (such as medical, psycho-social, educational) may be necessary at this time.

■ Adolescents with ADHD may appear mature physically and "grown up," but looks are deceiving. They are typically far less mature socially and emotionally than peers their own age, with a two- to four-year developmental delay in skills affecting their self-management.

■ Though they may be of an age when the expectation is to demonstrate more independence, responsibility, and self-control, the reality is that adolescents with ADHD take longer to exhibit those behaviors. They need more adult monitoring and direct supports than their peers.

■ Issues that tend to be problematic for middle school and high school students with ADHD include:
  • Poor organization and time management in keeping track of all assignments from five to six classes
  • Poor study skills (note-taking, test-taking, listening skills)

- Instruction (lecture; little opportunity for hands-on, active learning) that is not conducive to their learning styles

- Multiple teachers' behavioral expectations, classroom procedures, and work requirements

- Teachers in these grades more frequently have little or no training in ADHD, resulting in less empathy and willingness to accommodate students' individual needs

- Being more difficult to discipline than the average student

■ In addition, middle school and high school students with ADHD have the same struggles to cope with as all adolescents:

- Transitioning and adjusting to a new school

- Learning their way around campus

- Getting to know and deal with several teachers and many new classmates

- Intense social and peer pressure (need to be accepted and "fit in")

- Physical changes and raging hormones

- Stress related to home life and out-of-school factors

■ Students in these grades often complain about school being boring, and not seeing the connection between what is taught in school and their own lives. Instruction for *all* students at this level should be:

- Meaningful and relevant

- Challenging and motivating

- Eliciting active participation and student involvement

- Providing variety and choices

■ Parents of adolescents with ADHD often find themselves in great need of support and guidance. The adolescent years are challenging for most parents, and often far more so with a child who has ADHD. Dealing with the adolescent child often requires treatment and support for parents:

- Professional counseling in behavior-management strategies; setting and enforcing reasonable expectations; and coping with various issues.

- Treating problems parents may have of their own which make it more difficult to address the teen's needs. Remember, there is a much higher incidence among parents of children with ADHD of having mental health, marital, and substance-abuse issues.

- Organizations such as CHADD are highly beneficial for parents. They are a great source of support, information, and parent-to-parent guidance from others in similar circumstances.

■ Critical to the success of adolescents with ADHD is a teacher who:

- Is trained in, aware of, and understands ADHD

8-7 (continued)

- Uses effective classroom-management strategies (2-3, 2-4, 2-5, 2-7, 2-8)
- Monitors behavior and academic progress
- Is willing to work with the student and parents to provide extra support and follow-through (daily or weekly report cards, contracts, checking assignment calendar, organizing materials, and so forth) (2-9, 4-4, 4-6, 4-8, 6-1, 8-1, and examples in the Appendix)

■ Critical to the success of adolescents with ADHD is a parent who:

- Uses structure—with negotiable and nonnegotiable rules, reasonable expectations, and follow-through
- Uses a positive discipline approach and behavior-management strategies
- Monitors and supervises (although the adolescent may complain bitterly)
- Uses open channels of communication and makes real efforts to listen and involve the teen in decision-making
- Gives time and attention
- Is aware of the child's friends and activities
- Encourages and supports

Note: See Lists 2-12, 2-15, 4-5, 4-7, 4-9, and 8-2.

■ Adolescents with ADHD often need additional treatments and interventions, such as:

- Social skills training (2-16)
- Counseling
- Problem-solving, conflict-resolution, and anger-management training
- Medication (1-24, 1-25)
- Tutoring
- Coaching in setting goals, breaking down tasks, time management, self-monitoring, and self-reinforcement
- School evaluation for possible IEP or 504 Plan (7-1 through 7-4)

■ Teens with ADHD generally need an adult at school who serves officially or unofficially as a case manager—monitoring progress, advising, and intervening in school situations.

■ For students with IEPs, the special education teacher (resource teacher) is often the case manager. Sometimes it is a school counselor, homeroom teacher, or other staff member who serves this function.

■ It also helps if middle and high schools have in place supportive interventions or "safety nets" (mentors, homework assistance, study skills/learning strategies classes, tutoring) available to students in need. Teens with ADHD would benefit from such school supports, as well as the opportunity to participate in clubs, sports, and electives to build upon their interests and showcase their areas of strength.

Note: Most of the strategies and interventions for ADHD (instructional, environmental, organizational, and behavioral) recommended throughout this book are still effective and appropriate for adolescents as well.

SOURCES AND RESOURCES

Dendy, Chris A. Zeigler. *Teenagers with ADD—A Parent's Guide.* Bethesda, MD: Woodbine House, 1995.

Dendy, Chris A. Zeigler. *Teen to Teen: The ADD Experience* (video), 1999. www.chrisdendy.com

Dendy, Chris Zeigler. *Teaching Teens with ADD and ADHD.* Bethesda, MD: Woodbine House, 2000.

Dendy, Chris Zeigler. "Surviving the Ride—Parenting Teenagers with AD/HD," CHADD: *Attention*, vol. 8, no. 5, April 2002, 12–18.

Dendy, Chris Zeigler. "Finding the Joy—Parenting Teenagers with AD/HD," CHADD: *Attention*, vol. 8, no. 6, June 2002, 15–20.

Ellison, Phyllis Anne Teeter. "Strategies for Adolescents with AD/HD: Goal Setting and Increasing Independence," *The CHADD Information and Resource Guide to AD/HD.* Landover, MD: CHADD, 2000.

Flick, Grad L. *How to Reach and Teach Teenagers with ADHD.* Paramus, NJ: The Center for Applied Research in Education, 2000.

Fowler, Mary. *Maybe You Know My Teen.* New York: Broadway Books, 2001.

Greenbaum, Judith, and Geraldine Markel. *Helping Adolescents with ADHD & Learning Disabilities.* Paramus, NJ: The Center for Applied Research in Education, 2001.

Ingersoll, Barbara, Bruce Pfeiffer, Sharon Weiss, and Kathleen Nadeau. *ADD Adolescents in the Classroom: An Educator's Survival Guide* (videos/guide). CHADD of Northern Virginia, 1998.

Markel, Geraldine, and Judith Greenbaum. *Performance Breakthroughs for Adolescents with Learning Disabilities or ADD.* Champaign, IL: Research Press, 1996.

Nadeau, Kathleen. *Help 4 ADD @ High School.* Silver Spring, MD: Advantage Books, 1998.

Parker, Harvey. *Put Yourself in Their Shoes—Understanding Teenagers with ADHD.* Plantation, FL: Specialty Press, Inc., 1999.

Phelan, Thomas W. *Surviving Your Adolescents.* Glen Ellyn, IL: Child Management, Inc., 1998.

8-7 (*continued*)

Phelan, Thomas. "Lessons from the Trenches: 'Managing' the Teen with AD/HD," *The CHADD Information and Resource Guide to AD/HD.* Landover, MD: CHADD, 2000.

Quinn, Patricia. *ADD and Adolescents.* New York: Magination Press, 1995.

Robin, Arthur L. *ADHD in Adolescence: Diagnosis and Treatment.* New York: The Guilford Press, 1998.

Snyder, Marlene, and Rae Hamphill. "Parents of Teen Drivers with AD/HD: Proceed with Caution," *The CHADD Information and Resource Guide to AD/HD.* Landover, MD: CHADD, 2000.

Teeter, Phyllis A., and Paula Stewart. "Transitioning of the ADHD Child to Secondary School: A Multimodal Approach." CHADD's 9th Annual Conference, October 23–25, 1997, in San Antonio, Texas.

8-8
ADHD IN ADULTS

ADHD has a lifelong course with varying degrees of symptoms persisting into adulthood for most. (1-12) A large percentage of adults now diagnosed with ADHD struggled over the years with a disorder they did not know they had. Over the years they may have been misdiagnosed with other disorders, and unfairly labeled because of behaviors that were misunderstood.

■ Many adults suspect their own ADHD and seek an evaluation after one of their children is diagnosed with the disorder. Many other adults continue to try coping with ADHD-related symptoms that impair their daily functioning without the benefit of identification, diagnosis, or proper treatment.

■ As described in other lists, ADHD increases the risk for a number of other difficulties that result from poor self-control and ability to regulate one's behavior. Among the common issues many adults with ADHD must cope with are:

  ▪ Criticism and negative feedback

  ▪ Negative feelings (guilt, shame, embarrassment, anger, frustration)

  ▪ Difficulties with organization and time management

  ▪ Social and relationship difficulties

  ▪ Financial difficulties

  ▪ Frequent job changes

  ▪ Fewer job promotions

  ▪ Difficulties functioning in the workplace

  ▪ Job dissatisfaction (often settling for the wrong job)

  ▪ Underemployment and underachievement due to their abilities

  ▪ Higher incidence of depression, anxiety, other mood or personality disorders, and learning problems

  ▪ Higher rates of substance use and substance abuse

  ▪ Marital problems

  ▪ Challenge of raising one or more children who also have ADHD and possible coexisting conditions

■ As with ADHD in children and adolescents, adults also need a comprehensive evaluation before proper treatments can be implemented. Such an evaluation in adults should involve:

  ▪ Clinicians with expertise in ADHD and coexisting conditions

  ▪ A clinical interview of current symptoms and functioning

8-8 (*continued*)

- A clinical comprehensive interview of history (developmental, medical, work, educational, and psychiatric)

- Information obtained about functioning in multiple settings—from the adult being evaluated and, when possible, from others who know the person well (spouse, parent)

- Other objective information (such as records, past evaluations/reports)

- A determination of symptoms being chronic and pervasive

- A determination of other psychiatric diagnoses that may better explain symptoms than ADHD

- A determination of other possible coexisting conditions

- The following multimodal treatments are considered at this time to be among the most promising in treating adults with ADHD and helping them to best manage the symptoms of their disorder. An individualized treatment plan targeting the needs of the ADHD adult may include some of the following interventions:

  - Consultation with medical/mental health professional

  - Counseling/therapy (individual, couples, family)

  - Education about ADHD (for adult and significant others) to better understand the disorder, its effect on his or her behavior and life, and how best to manage the symptoms

  - Specific training in anger management and coping strategies, as well as social skills

  - Help setting achievable, realistic goals

  - Coaching (see below)

  - Help seeking treatment for possible coexisting conditions

  - Medication therapy (as with children/teens, stimulant medication for ADHD and possible other medications for coexisting disorders)

  - Vocational guidance/counseling to find a better match of strengths, learning styles, and preferences to the demands and environment of the job

  - Support groups (CHADD, ADDA)

  - Skill building and support in organization, time management, goal setting, and learning strategies

  - Workplace accommodations

- Strategies, supports, and accommodations (memory, organization, time management, reading comprehension, writing, and testing) effective for children and teens with ADHD described in lists throughout this book are also applicable and useful for adults.

- Coaching is a form of therapy that is popular among adults with ADHD. It involves an ongoing relationship between client and coach in which the adult with ADHD receives support and assistance from his or her coach in:

  - Helping to define his or her goals

- Discovering ways to maximize his or her strengths and talents
- Designing an action plan to achieve the goals
- Creating structures and strategies to optimize functioning and take action toward accomplishing goals
- Providing the external structure to help stay focused on their goals and overcome obstacles
- Breaking down long-term projects into short-term incremental steps
- Time management, organization skills, and other areas of weakness affecting work performance and production

■ See Sources and Resources for information and websites about coaching services that are related to adult interventions/resources.

■ Many adults with ADHD may be entitled to protection under the Americans with Disabilities Act of 1990 (ADA). As with Section 504 of the Vocational Rehabilitation Act of 1973, ADA also prohibits discrimination against any individual who has a physical or mental impairment that substantially limits one or more major life activities (including learning and working), or who has a record of such impairments.

■ Section 504 is the law under which students with disabilities may receive reasonable accommodations in school. ADA allows for qualifying individuals with disabilities to receive reasonable accommodations in the workplace.

■ Adults with ADHD will need to make the determination if it is in their best interest to pursue accommodations, which would require disclosing their ADHD to their employer.

■ Reasonable accommodations in the workplace might include such things as:
- Job restructuring (for example, altering when and/or how a job is performed)
- Providing a nondistracting workspace
- Allowing employee to do some work at home
- Giving instructions slowly and clearly
- Providing written as well as verbal instructions to employee
- Providing extra clerical support

There is much to learn about ADHD in adults. Only in the past few years has attention been paid to ADHD in this population. Fortunately, there is research currently taking place that hopefully will shed more light in the near future. There are also wonderful resources with information on this topic. See Sources and Resources.

SOURCES AND RESOURCES

Adamec, Christine. *Moms with ADD*. Dallas, TX: Taylor Publishing Co., 2000.

American Coaching Association. http://www.americoach.com

8-8 (continued)

Attention Deficit Disorder Association (ADDA). http://www.add.org/content/coach1.htm

"Attention-Deficit/Hyperactivity Disorder in Adults," *The CHADD Information and Resource Guide to AD/HD.* Landover, MD: CHADD, 2000.

Barkley, Russell. *Attention Deficit Hyperactivity Disorder: A Handbook for Diagnosis and Treatment.* New York: The Guilford Press, 1998.

Ellison, Phyllis A. Teeter, and Sam Goldstein. "Poor Self-Control and How it Impacts Relationships," CHADD: *Attention,* vol. 8, no. 5, April 2002, 19–24.

Goldstein, Sam. *Managing Attention and Learning Disorders in Late Adolescence and Adulthood. A Guide for Practitioners.* New York: John Wiley & Sons, Inc., 1996.

Hallowell, E. M., and J. J. Ratey. *Driven to Distraction.* New York: Random House, 1994.

Hope, Langner. "ADD: An Invisible Disability," *ADDvance,* vol. 3, no. 6, July/August 2000, 4–8.

Johnson, Mary Jane. "From the Coach's Toolbox," *ADDvance,* vol. 5, no. 2, November/December 2001, 4–8.

Kelly, K., and P. Ramundo. *You Mean I'm Not Lazy, Stupid or Crazy.* New York: Scribner, 1993.

Latham, Peter, and Patricia Latham. *Succeeding in the Workplace.* Washington, DC: JKL Communications, 1994.

Mooney, Jonathan, and David Cole. *Learning Outside the Lines.* New York: Simon & Schuster, 2000.

Murphy, Kevin. "Psychological Counseling in Adults with AD/HD." In Russell Barkley, (ed.), *Attention-Deficit Hyperactivity Disorder: A Handbook for Diagnosis and Treatment.* New York: The Guilford Press, 1998.

Murphy, Kevin, and S. LeVert. *Out of the Fog: Treatment Options and Coping Strategies for Adult Attention Deficit Disorder.* New York: Hyperion, 1995.

Nadeau, Kathleen. *Adventures in Fast Forward.* New York: Brunner/Mazel, Inc., 1996.

Nadeau, Kathleen. *ADD in the Workplace.* Bristol, PA: Brunner/Mazel, Inc., 1997.

Ratey, Nancy, and Theresa Laurie Maitland. *Coaching College Students with AD/HD.* Silver Spring, MD: Advantage Books, 2000.

Snowman, S. R. *Rising to the Challenge: A Styles Approach to Understanding Adults with ADD and other Learning Difficulties.* Plymouth, MA: Jones River Press, 1996.

Solden, Sari. *Women with Attention Deficit Disorder.* Grass Valley, CA: Underwood Books, 1995.

Weiss, Lynn. *A.D.D. on the Job.* Dallas, TX: Taylor Publishing Co., 1996.

Weiss, Lynn. *View from the Cliff—A Course in Achieving Daily Focus.* Lanham, MD: Taylor Publishing, 2001.

8-9
STRESS REDUCTION, RELAXATION STRATEGIES, AND EXERCISE

When you are hyperactive, emotionally overreactive, and/or anxious, it helps to learn relaxation and stress-reduction strategies. It can be particularly therapeutic and beneficial to teach children/teens with ADHD some of the following lessons and techniques, which are known to have health and psychological benefits.

FUN AND LAUGHTER

Laughter is one of the best ways to release stress and feel good. The chemicals released in the body through laughter reduce pain and tension. So, there is probably no substitute for finding ways to have fun and to laugh with our children.

BREATHING TECHNIQUES

Many of us know the positive effects of controlled breathing through our training in Lamaze or other natural childbirth classes. Controlled, conscious breathing has the benefit of relaxing muscles and reducing stress. Many believe it is useful in the management and, perhaps, cure of some physical ailments and disease.

- Teach children how to take conscious, deep breaths to relax, listening to the sound of the air coming in and out. Show them how to inhale deeply (preferably through the nose, but through the mouth is fine) and *slowly* exhale through the mouth. When inhaling, the abdomen rises and expands.

- Teach progressive muscle relaxation by isolating different body parts and relaxing them with each slow breath exhaled. For example, while lying on the floor, instruct them to tighten or squeeze their toes on the left foot, and then relax with a deep breath. Proceed in this fashion to the right side of the lower body, to the abdomen and upper body, each arm, hand/fingers, chest, neck, jaws, and face.

- Teach children that when their bodies are relaxed, they are better able to think and plan.

- It is particularly helpful for children to recognize that when they are nervous, stressed, and angry, they should feel the tightening of certain body parts. If they can recognize when fists clench, jaws tighten, and stomachs harden, they have the power over their bodies to relax and gain control.

- Children can begin to breathe deeply and "send" their breaths consciously to relax body parts. By sending the breaths to their hand, for example, the child can silently prompt him- or herself to relax the hand (until the fist is released and fingers are loose).

- Help guide students to visualize that with each breath they take in, their body becomes filled slowly with a soothing color, aroma, sound, light, warmth, or other pleasant, comfortable feeling.

- Ask students to think of a color that makes them feel very comfortable, peaceful, and relaxed. Then have them practice, with closed eyes, breathing in that color and "sending" it (blowing it) throughout the body. If a child, for example, chooses "turquoise," guide him or her to visualize the turquoise going down his or her throat, into the neck and chest, down to the stomach, and so on, until the child is filled with the beautiful, peaceful, wonderful turquoise . . . and is relaxed and in control.

YOGA AND SLOW-MOVEMENT EXERCISES

Various yoga postures and slow-movement games and exercises are fun and helpful for teaching children to relax, use controlled movements, and increase their imagination and imagery skills. Some simulated movements and postures may include: scaling through space; climbing a pyramid; carrying a fragile gift to someone; and being a scarecrow, rag doll, popped balloon, and so forth.

VISUALIZATION AND GUIDED IMAGERY

The ability to visualize colorful, vivid images with rich imagination and detailed action are natural skills of childhood. These same skills have been found to be useful in empowering people to help overcome obstacles in their lives, improve memory, enhance learning, and facilitate healing—physical, mental, and emotional. Imagery is also helpful in developing focus and concentration, calming oneself, coping with stress, and increasing positive study skills, social skills, and creative expression.

- Specialists are available who train individuals in these techniques and who use visualization and guided imagery as part of their therapy in treating different health, social, behavioral, and emotional problems.

- Books and resources are available that use these techniques for self-help and management. One of these resources is *Imagery for Kids—Discovering Your Special Place*, an audiotape combining gentle music and a guided journey (see Sources and Resources).

- Teach students to visualize themselves in situations where they are achieving and being successful. Once students have had practice with guided visualization, encourage them to use the techniques of deep breathing and visualizing themselves doing what they want to do. For example, prior to taking a test, have students visualize themselves:

8-9 (*continued*)

- Working diligently and confidently while taking the test
- Persistently reading each item carefully
- Being relaxed and not getting nervous or excited
- Being confident with their answers
- Finishing the test and going back to check for careless errors

MUSIC

- Music can be very helpful for relaxation, as a pre-visualization activity, to soothe away worries and distractions, and bring a sense of inner peace.
- Music also stimulates the brain in ways besides relaxation. Many people find that they are better able to focus, and are more productive and motivated when listening to the radio or some of their favorite music.
- Many teachers find that playing cassettes/CDs of classical music, Baroque, soothing environmental sounds, and instrumental arrangements are very effective in the classroom. Different forms of music have been found to be effective in increasing the ability to focus, soothe, and relax, and to enhance learning, creativity, and critical-thinking skills.
- There is evidence that certain kinds of instrumental musical arrangements and rhythmic patterns have therapeutic calming and focusing effects. Musical therapy is being used in different settings (such as pain clinics, hospitals). See Gary Lamb, REI Institute, and OptimaLearning® in Sources and Resources.
- Some artists whose music is calming include: Kitaro, George Winston, Steven Halpern, Hillary Stagg, Zamfir, Jim Chappell, among others.
- Environmental sounds (rainforest, oceans, waterfalls) are calming.
- Baroque music examples that are low energy and calming include *Clair de Lune* (Debussy) and *Four Seasons* (Vivaldi).

LEISURE ACTIVITIES, RECREATION, AND HOBBIES

Nurture a child's interest and encourage participation in calming leisure activities such as working with clay, knitting, fishing, and drawing. In addition, find recreation and leisure activities to enjoy as a family, such as bicycling, hiking, skating, and so on. There is nothing like having fun together as a family to reduce stress and strengthen loving, positive relationships.

EXERCISE

Exercise stimulates the central nervous system, increasing blood flow and oxygen to the brain. Some of the benefits include boost in mood, increase in focus and alertness, learning, and memory. For children who have an abundance of energy, exercise is a healthy positive way to expend that energy. It is particularly important, therefore, for children/teens with ADHD to exercise regularly. In fact, exercise in the morning (a before-school jogging program or some kind of aerobic workout) may increase a child's academic and behavioral performance.

SOURCES AND RESOURCES

Calming Rhythms. REI Institute, Inc., 800-659-6644.

Cheatum, Billye Ann, and Allison A. Hammond. *Physical Activities for Improving Children's Learning and Behavior.* Champaign, IL: Human Kinetics, 2000.

Huth, Holly Y. *Centerplay.* New York: Simon & Schuster, 1984.

Jensen, Eric. *Trainer's Bonanza.* San Diego, CA: The Brain Store, Inc., 1998.

Lamb, Gary. (Musical Compositions at 60 beats per minute) Santa Cruz, CA: Golden Gate Records. 800-772-7701.

Lanham, Geoff. "Leisure as a Positive Experience for Children with AD/HD," CHADD: *Attention*, vol. 7, no. 6, June 2001.

OptimaLearning®. *Baroque Music.* www.thebrainstore.com

Putnam, Stephen C. "Keeping Up the Motivation to Exercise," CHADD: *Attention*, vol. 8, no. 6, June 2002, 21–25.

Reznick, Charlotte. *Imagery for Kids—Discovering Your Special Place* (audiotape). 310-393-2416.

Rief, Sandra. *The ADD/ADHD Checklist.* Paramus, NJ: Prentice Hall, 1998.

Songs for Self-Regulation. The Alert Program/Belle Curve Records. 888-357-5867; www.bellecurve.com

8-10
RESOURCES ON THE INTERNET

Note: The following websites are not specific to the headings they are listed under, as categories overlap.

ADHD and/or Learning Disabilities

ADD Focus
http://www.healthyplace.com/Communities/ADD

ADHD Living Guide
http://adhdlivingguide.com

Attention.com
http://www.attention.com

Children and Adults with Attention Deficit/Hyperactivity Disorder
http://www.chadd.org

ADD Helpline
http://www.addhelpline.org

ADHD Online Community
http://www.adhd.com

All Kinds of Minds
http://www.allkindsofminds.org

Council for Exceptional Children (CEC)
http://www.cec.sped.org

Council for Learning Disabilities
http://www.cldinternational.org

Hello Friend: The Ennis William Cosby Foundation
http://www.hellofriend.org

The International Dyslexia Association
http://www.interdys.org

Kitty Petty ADD/LD Institute
http://www.kpinst.org

Learning Disabilities Association (LDA)
http://www.ldanatl.org

Learning Disabilities Information & Education Center
http://www.ldiec.net

(The author has an online course "Reaching & Teaching Students with AD/HD" available for university credit. Contact this site for more information.)

LD OnLine: An Interactive Guide to Learning Disabilities for Parents, Teachers, and Children
http://www.ldonline.org

LD Resources
http://www.ldresources.com

National Attention Deficit Disorder Association (ADDA)
http://www.add.org

National Initiative for Children's Healthcare Quality (NICHQ)—Collaborative on ADHD
http://www.nichq.org

One ADD Place
http://www.oneaddplace.com

San Diego ADHD Web Page
http://www.sandiegoadhd.com

Schwab Foundation for Learning
http://www.schwablearning.org

Medical and Mental Health

American Academy of Child and Adolescent Psychiatry
http://www.aacap.org/

American Academy of Pediatrics
http://www.aap.org

American Psychiatric Association
http://www.psych.org

American Psychological Association
http://www.apa.org

Athealth.com
http://www.athealth.com/consumer/disorders/ADHD.html

Bright Futures
http://www.brightfutures.org/mentalhealth

Center for Mental Health Services
http://www.mentalhealth.org

The Child Advocate
http://www.childadvocate.net

The Children's Health Council
http://www.chconline.org

Council for Children with Behavioral Disorders
http://www.ccbd.net/

8-10 (*continued*)

Federation of Families for Children's Mental Health
http://www.ffcmh.org

Mental Health: A Report of the Surgeon General (AD/HD)
http://www.surgeongeneral.gov/library/mentalhealth/chapter3/sec4

National Alliance for the Mentally Ill
http://www.nami.org

National Assembly on School-Based Health Care
http://www.nasbhc.org

National Association of School Nurses
http://www.nasn.org

National Association of School Psychologists
http://www.nasponline.org

National Center for Complementary and Alternative Medicine
http://nccam.nih.gov

National Institute of Child Health and Child Development
http://www.nichd.nih.gov

National Institute for Mental Health
http://www.nimh.nih.gov/publicat/adhdmenu.cfm

National Library of Medicine
http://www.nlm.nih.gov

National Mental Health and Education Center for Children and Families
www.naspcenter.org

Research & Training Center on Family Support & Children's Mental Health
http://www.rtc.pdx.edu

UC Davis M.I.N.D. Institute—Medical Investigation of Neurodevelopmental Disorders
http://mindinstitute.ucdmc.ucdavis.edu

UCLA School Mental Health Project
http://smhp.psych.ucla.edu/pdfdocs/Attention/attention.pdf

Vanderbilt Child Development Center
http://peds.mc.vanderbilt.edu/cdc/rating~1.html

Virtual Resource Center in Behavioral Disorders
http://www.coe.missouri.edu/~vcrcbd/

Individuals with Disabilities, the Law, and Special Education

Disability Rights Advocates
http://www.dralegal.org

EDLAW, Inc.
http://www.edlaw.net

Education Resources Information Center (ERIC)
http://ericir.syr.edu/

ERIC Clearinghouse on Disabilities and Education
http://www.cec.sped.org

Federal Resource Center for Special Education
http://www.dssc.org/frc

IDEA Local Implementations by Local Administrators (ILIAD)
http://www.ideapractices.org

IDEA Practices
http://www.ideapractices.org

IDEA Regulations
http://www.ed.gov/offices/OSERS/IDEA/getregs.html

Internet Resources for Special Children
http://www.irsc.org

National Center on Education, Disability, and Juvenile Justice
http://www.edjj.org/index.html

National Information Center for Children and Youth with Disabilities
http://www.nichcy.org

National Parent Network on Disabilities
http://www.npnd.org

Office for Civic Rights
http://www.ed.gov/offices/OCR

Office of Special Education & Rehabilitation Services
http://www.ed.gov/offices/OSERS

Parent Advocacy Coalition for Educational Rights (PACER Center)
http://www.pacer.org

Protection & Advocacy
http://www.protectionandadvocacy.com

More Associations and Resources on Disabilities/Special Needs

American Occupational Therapy Association (AOTA)
http://www.aota.org

American Speech-Language-Hearing Association (ASHA)
http://www.asha.org

Assistive Technology, Inc.
http://www.assistivetech.com

8-10 (*continued*)

Autism Society of America
http://autism-society.org

Internet Resources for Special Educators
http://specialed.miningco.com

Private Special Education Schools
http://www.spedschools.com

Recordings for the Blind and Dyslexic
http://www.rfbd.org

Special Education Resources on the Internet
http://www.hood.edu/seri/serihome.htm

Tourette Syndrome Association, Inc.
http://www.tsa.mgh.harvard.edu

More Educator Associations and Resources

American Association of School Administrators
http://www.aasa.org

American Federation of Teachers (AFT)
http://www.aft.org

Association on Higher Education & Disabilities
http://www.ahead.org

Center for Effective Collaboration and Practice
http://cecp.air.org

Classroom Connect
http://www.classroom.net

Council of Administrators of Special Education (CASE)
http://members.aol.com/casecec

Education World
http://www.education-world.com

National Association of Elementary School Principals
http://www.naesp.org

National Education Association (NEA)
http://www.nea.org

University of Kansas—Center for Research on Learning
http://www.ku-crl.org

University of Kansas—Special Education On Line
http://www.sped.ukans.edu

Behavioral Supports/Interventions and Violence Prevention

Center for the Study and Prevention of Violence
http://www.colorado.edu/cspv/infohouse/factsheets.html

Effective Behavioral Support
http://brt.uoregon.edu/ebs

OSEP Center on Positive Behavioral Interventions and Supports
http://www.pbis.org

More for Parents and Families

Association for Library Service to Children
http://ala.org/alsc

Family Education Network
http://www.familyeducation.com

50+ Great Sites for Kids & Parents
http://www.ala.org/parentspage/greatsites/50.html

Parent Patch
http://www.parentpatch.com

Parent Soup
http://www.parentsoup.com

Parent's Picks Websites
http://parentsoup.com/onlineguide/parentspicks/web.html

Note: See List 2-18 for numerous resources on this topic.

Books and Videos (many additional sources are available)

ADD Clinic
http://www.the-add-clinic.com

ADD Warehouse
http://www.addwarehouse.com

Educational Resource Specialists
http://www.sandrarief.com

(This site carries all of the author's books, videos, and additional resources and information.)

Newsletters and Magazines

ADDitude Magazine for People with ADD
http://www.additudemag.com

ADDvance Resource for Women and Girls with ADD
http://addvance.com

8-10 (*continued*)

The ADHD Report
http://www.guilford.com

ATTENTION
http://www.chadd.org

BRAKES: The Interactive Newsletter for Kids with ADHD, Magination Press
http://www.maginationpress.com

The National Center for Gender Issues and ADHD newsletter
http://www.ncgiadd.org

8-11
ABBREVIATIONS ASSOCIATED WITH ADHD

504	Section 504 of the Rehabilitation Act of 1973
AAP	American Academy of Pediatrics
ADA	Americans with Disabilities Act of 1990
ADDA	Attention Deficit Disorder Association
BIP	Behavioral Intervention Plan
CDC	Centers for Disease Control and Prevention
CHADD	Children and Adults with Attention Deficit Disorders
CNS	Central Nervous System
DAT 1	Dopamine Transporter Gene
DRC	Daily Report Card
DSM-IV	*Diagnostic and Statistical Manual, 4th edition*
ED	Emotional Disturbance
EF	Executive Functions
FAPE	Free and Appropriate Public Education
FBA	Functional Behavioral Assessment
IAES	Interim Alternative Educational Setting
IDEA	Individuals with Disabilities Education Act of 1997
IEE	Independent Educational Evaluation
IEP	Individual Education Program; also Individualized Education Plan
ISS	In-School Suspension
LAL	Listening Attention Levels
LD	Learning Disabilities
LDA	Learning Disabilities Association
LRE	Least Restrictive Environment
MTA	Multimodal Treatment Study of Children with ADHD

8-11 (continued)

NICHD	National Institute of Child Health and Human Development
NICHQ	National Initiative for Children's Healthcare Quality
NICHY	National Information Clearinghouse on Children and Youth with Disabilities
NIH	National Institutes of Health
NIMH	National Institute of Mental Health
ODD	Oppositional Defiant Disorder
OHI	Other Health Impairment
OSEP	U.S. Office of Special Education Programs
SAT	Student Assistance Team; also called SST (Student Support Team), SIT (Student Intervention Team), IST (Instructional Support Team), or TAT (Teacher Assistance Team)
SLD	Specific Learning Disability
SST	Student Support Team; also called Student Success Team. Refers to SAT and includes any school multidisciplinary team names.

Literacy Terms

COPS	Capitalization/Overall appearance/Punctuation/Spelling (5-9)
CWCC	Cover/Write/Cover/Check (5-10)
DRTA	Directed Reading/Thinking Activity (5-5)
GIST	Generating Interaction Between Schemata and Text (5-5)
KWL	Know/Want to know/Learned (3-5, 3-7)
POW	Plan/Organize/Write (5-8)
QAR	Question-Answer Relationships (5-5)
RAP	Read/Ask/Paraphrase (4-2)
RCRC	Reading/Covering/Reciting/Checking (4-1)
SQ3R	Survey/Question/Read/Recite/Review (4-2)
SRSD	Self-Regulated Strategy Development (5-8)

Appendix

CHARTS, FORMS, AND VISUAL PROMPTS

HOMEWORK ASSIGNMENT LOG

Week of: _____

Teacher's signature: _____   **Parent's signature:** _____

Date	Subject	Assignment	
		Assignment	
		Materials	**Due date:**
			Date turned in:
		Assignment	
		Materials	**Due date:**
			Date turned in:
		Assignment	
		Materials	**Due date:**
			Date turned in:
		Assignment	
		Materials	**Due date:**
			Date turned in:
		Assignment	
		Materials	**Due date:**
			Date turned in:

HOMEWORK ASSIGNMENTS

WEEK OF _____

Teacher's signature _____ Parent's signature _____

ASSIGNMENT	CLASS/ TEACHER	ASSIGNED DATE	DUE DATE

STUDENT WEEKLY PLANNING SCHEDULE

Student's name _____

Parent's signature _____

Time	Monday	Tuesday	Wednesday	Thursday	Friday	Saturday	Sunday
3:00-4:00							
4:00-5:00							
5:00-6:00							
6:00-7:00							
7:00-8:00							
8:00-9:00							
9:00-10:00							

THINGS TO DO
TODAY

DATE_____   **COMPLETED**

1. _____   ☐

2. _____   ☐

3. _____   ☐

4. _____   ☐

5. _____   ☐

6. _____   ☐

7. _____   ☐

8. _____   ☐

9. _____   ☐

10. _____   ☐

11. _____   ☐

12. _____   ☐

Classroom Procedures
What Do You Expect Students to Do When...?

- they need to sharpen a pencil_____
- they don't have paper or other needed supplies _____
- they finish work early _____
- they have a question during instruction _____
- they need to go to the restroom_____
- they want to throw something in the trash _____
- they have a question during independent work _____
- they need a drink of water_____
- announcements made on intercom, phone rings, other interruptions __
- they enter the classroom at beginning of day (period)_____
- they enter classroom after recess/PE/lunch_____
- they prepare to leave classroom at end of day (period)_____
- moving into or changing groups _____
- the bell rings _____
- they are late/tardy_____
- they return after being absent _____
- listening to and responding to questions_____
- you signal for attention _____
- working cooperatively (partner or small group)_____
- working independently _____
- turning in papers, passing papers, exchanging papers_____
- moving about the room_____
- lining up _____
- at learning centers _____

Procedures & Routines to teach immediately: signaling/getting their attention/quieting class; entering class & dismissal; how to/where to keep materials & belongings; preparing for class & homework assignments (e.g., paper headings/recording assignments on assignment calendar)

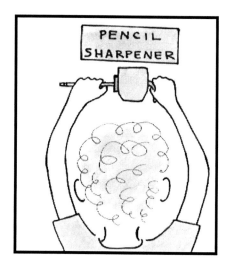

HOME NOTE

Today we _____
_____

I learned _____
_____

I had fun _____
_____

I need to work on _____
_____
_____

Date _____

Student _____

How to Establish a School-Home Daily Report Card

1. **Select the Areas for Improvement.**
   - Discuss the child's behavior with all school staff who work with the child.
   - Determine the child's greatest areas of impairment.
   - Define goals toward which the child should be working regarding the areas of impairment.
   - Key domains:

     –Improving peer relations

     –Improving academic work

     –Improving classroom rule-following and relationships with adults

2. **Determine How the Goals Will Be Defined.**
   - Identify specific behaviors ("target behaviors") that can be changed to make progress toward the goals easier.
   - Target behaviors must be meaningful and clearly defined/observed/counted by teacher and child.
   - Examples of target behaviors in the Key domains:

     –<u>Improving peer relations:</u> does not interrupt other children during their work time, does not tease other children, plays without fighting at recess

     –<u>Improving academic work:</u> has materials and assignments necessary to do tasks, complete assigned academic tasks, is accurate on assigned tasks, completes and returns homework

     –<u>Improving classroom rule-following and relationships with adults:</u> obeys the teacher when commands are given, does not talk back to the teacher, follows classroom rules
   - Additional target behaviors are listed on the attached sheet, Sample Report Card Targets.

3. **Decide on Behaviors and Criteria for the Daily Report Card.**
   - Estimate how often the child is doing the target behaviors by reviewing school records and/or observation.
   - Determine which behaviors need to be included on the report.
   - Evaluate target behaviors several times throughout the day.
   - Set a reasonable criterion for each target behavior (a criterion is a target level the child will have to meet in order to receive a positive mark for that behavior). Set criteria to be met for each part of the day, not the overall day (eg, "interrupts fewer than 2 times in each class period" rather than "interrupts fewer than 12 times per day").

4. **Explain the Daily Report Card to the Child.**
   - Meet with teacher, parents, and child.
   - Explain all aspects of the Daily Report Card (DRC) to the child in a positive manner.

NICHQ
©2002 National Initiative for Children's Healthcare Quality   Reference: Adapted from ©CTADD, Inc. Center for Children and Families, University of Buffalo, State University of New York

5. Establish a Home-Based Reward System.

- Rewards must be selected by the child.

- Arrange awards so that:

  −Fewer or less preferred rewards can be earned for fewer yeses.

  −More desired rewards can be earner for better performance.

- Give the child a menu of rewards (See "Child Reward Form"):

  −Select rewards for each level.

  −Label the different levels with child-appropriate names (eg, One-Star Day, Two-Star Day).

  −Use the "Weekly Daily Report Card Chart" to track weekly performance.

  −Some children need more immediate rewards than the end-of-day home rewards—in such cases, in-school rewards can be used.

6. Monitor and Modify the Programs.

- Record daily the number of Yeses the child received on each target.

- Once the child has regularly begun to meet the criterion, make the criteria harder (if the child is regularly failing to meet the criterion, make the criteria easier).

- Once the criterion for a target is at an acceptable level and the child is consistently reaching it, drop that target behavior from the DRC. (Let the child know why it was dropped and replace with another target if necessary.)

- Move to a weekly report/reward system if the child is doing so well that daily reports are no longer necessary.

- The report card can be stopped when the child is functioning within an appropriate range within the classroom, and reinstated if problems begin to occur again.

7. Trouble-shooting a Daily Report Card.

- If the system is not working to change the child's behavior, examine the program and change where appropriate (see "Trouble-shooting a DRC").

8. Consider Other Treatments.

- If, after trouble-shooting and modification, the DRC is not resulting in maximal improvement, consider additional behavioral components (eg, more frequent praise, time-out) and/or more powerful or intensive behavioral procedures (eg, a point system).

NICHQ
©2002 National Initiative for Children's Healthcare Quality   Reference: Adapted from ©CTADD, Inc. Center for Children and Families, University of Buffalo, State University of New York

Child's Name _____ Medication _____ Today's Date_____

Daily School Report Card
Circle Y(Yes) or N(No)

Subjects / Times

Y N	Y N	Y N	Y N	Y N	Y N	Y N
Y N	Y N	Y N	Y N	Y N	Y N	Y N
Y N	Y N	Y N	Y N	Y N	Y N	Y N
Y N	Y N	Y N	Y N	Y N	Y N	Y N
Y N	Y N	Y N	Y N	Y N	Y N	Y N
Y N	Y N	Y N	Y N	Y N	Y N	Y N
Y N	Y N	Y N	Y N	Y N	Y N	Y N

1. _____

2. _____

3. _____

4. _____

5. _____

6. _____

7. _____

Teacher's initials						
Total # of Yeses						
Total # of Nos						

Comments:

_____

_____

_____

_____

Reward Form (SAMPLE)

Child's Name:_____   Date:_____

	Daily Rewards:
Level 3 (50%-74% positive marks):	Choose 1 thing from daily menu
Level 2 (75%-89% positive marks):	Choose 2 things from daily menu
Level 1 (90%-100% positive marks):	Choose 3 things from daily menu
	Weekly Rewards
Level 3 (50%-74% positive marks):	Choose 1 thing from weekly menu
Level 2 (75%-89% positive marks):	Choose 2 things from weekly menu
Level 1 (90%-100% positive marks):	Choose 3 things from weekly menu

CLASSROOM BEHAVIORAL CHART

Name _____ _____ Date _____	on time	stays seated	on task	raises hand	follows directions
8:00 – 8:30	+ −	+ −	+ −	+ −	+ −
8:30 – 9:00	+ −	+ −	+ −	+ −	+ −
9:00 – 9:30	+ −	+ −	+ −	+ −	+ −
9:30 – 10:00	+ −	+ −	+ −	+ −	+ −
10:00 – 10:30	+ −	+ −	+ −	+ −	+ −
10:30 – 11:00	+ −	+ −	+ −	+ −	+ −
11:30 – 12:00	+ −	+ −	+ −	+ −	+ −
12:00 – 12:30	+ −	+ −	+ −	+ −	+ −
12:30 – 1:00	+ −	+ −	+ −	+ −	+ −
1:00 – 1:30	+ −	+ −	+ −	+ −	+ −
1:30 – 2:00	+ −	+ −	+ −	+ −	+ −
2:00 – 2:30	+ −	+ −	+ −	+ −	+ −

+ − + − + − + − + −

TOTAL										

TOTAL +	
TOTAL −	
NET	
TARGET	

1. CROSS OUT BOXES THAT ARE NOT APPLICABLE.
2. CIRCLE THE + OR − IN THE APPLICABLE BOXES.
3. ADD ALL + AND ALL −.
4. SUBTRACT TOTAL − FROM TOTAL +, AND ENTER AS NET.
5. STUDENT EARNS PREDETERMINED REWARD IF HE OR SHE REACHES THE TARGET OF
   _____% (e.g., 70%). OR USE THE LEVELED REWARD SYSTEM.

°Art is taken from Microsoft® clip art.

STUDENT DAILY BEHAVIORAL REPORT

Name _____ Date _____ Goal _____ Reward _____

| Total points earned for the day _____ |
| Total points possible for the day _____ |

10:00 AM

9:00 AM

8:00 AM

3:00 PM

2:00 PM

11:00 AM

12:00 PM

1:00 PM

On Task

Follows directions

Cooperates

On Time

Copyright © 2003 by Sandra F. Rief

1. Circle the applicable picture if student demonstrated that behavior.
2. Cross out pictures that are not applicable to the session.
3. Don't mark picture if behavior was not demonstrated.
4. Indicate a goal for the day (e.g., 70% to 80% of the total applicable pictures or possible points).
5. Student earns predetermined reward if he/she reaches the goal. Or use the Leveled Reward System.

Teacher _____ Parent _____

°Art is taken from Microsoft® clip art.

STUDENT WEEKLY PROGRESS REPORT

Name: _____ Class: _____ Teacher: _____ Week of: _____

| Daily Goal ____ | Weekly Goal ____ | Weekly Points Earned ____ | Reward ____ |

Period	MONDAY Conduct	MONDAY Classwork	TUESDAY Conduct	TUESDAY Classwork	WEDNESDAY Conduct	WEDNESDAY Classwork	THURSDAY Conduct	THURSDAY Classwork	FRIDAY Conduct	FRIDAY Classwork
1										
2										
3										
4										
5										
6										
7										
Earned points →										

	MONDAY	TUESDAY	WEDNESDAY	THURSDAY	FRIDAY
Student's Signature					
Parent/Guardian Signature					

CONDUCT: 1. Hands, feet, objects to yourself + or - 2. Respectful to adults & classmates + or - 3. Follow teacher directions + or - 4. Stays in your place unless you have permission + or -

CLASSWORK: 1. Participates in lessons & activities + or - 2. Comes to class prepared + or - 3. Gets started on assignments right away + or - 4. Stays on task and complete or almost complete assignments + or -

I. The student will earn points based on the following: Unsatisfactory = 1 point, Fair = 2 points, Good = 3 points, Excellent = 4 points.
II. The number of points earned are based on the number of pluses, 4 pluses = 4 points, 3 pluses = 3 points, 2 pluses = 2 points, 1 plus = 1 point.
III. Indicate a goal for the day and for the week (e.g., 70% to 80% of daily goal and 70% to 80% of the weekly goal).
IV. The possible points per period are 8 (must meet 4 behavior & conduct criteria) Total points per day = 8 multiply by the number of class periods. Total points per week = Total per day multiply by number of days student is in attendance.

CONNECT-THE-DOTS CHART

INDIVIDUAL/CLASS _____

DATE STARTED _____

DATE FINISHED _____

REWARD _____

HOW TO USE THE CHART

1. Select a class or individual goal (e.g., all homework turned in).

2. If you meet goal, color in and connect to next dot.

3. When chart is filled (all dots are colored), the reward is earned.

WEEKLY BEHAVIOR REPORT

BEHAVIOR	Monday		Tuesday			Wednesday			Thursday			Friday		
	Before Recess	After Lunch	Before Recess	After Recess	After Lunch	Before Recess	After Recess	After Lunch	Before Recess	After Recess	After Lunch	Before Recess	After Recess	After Lunch
I followed rules														
I did my work														

OR

3 points = Very good job

2 points = Nice job

1 point = So So

0 points = I had trouble

My goal is to earn _____

points/smileys by _____

so I can earn _____

Teacher signature _____

Parent signature _____

BEHAVIOR RATING SHEET

NAME: _____   DATE: _____

Time of Day: _____

Rate the student in the behavior(s) circled from the following list:

	Excellent	Good	Average	Below Average	Poor
Participates in the lesson/activity	5	4	3	2	1
Comes to class prepared	5	4	3	2	1
Follows teacher directions	5	4	3	2	1
Follows class rules	5	4	3	2	1
Follows rules out-of-classroom	5	4	3	2	1
Interacts appropriately with peers	5	4	3	2	1
Uses class time effectively	5	4	3	2	1
Completes tasks/assignments	5	4	3	2	1

Teacher signature: _____

Comments:

Student's overall behavior/performance today:

☐ Excellent - Wonderful day!
☐ Good - Nice job!
☐ Average - Satisfactory
☐ Below average - Some difficulty
☐ Poor - Significant difficulty

Daily Performance Record

NAME: _____   DATE _____

SUBJECT	BEHAVIOR	TURNED IN HOMEWORK	PREPARED FOR CLASS	USED CLASS TIME EFFECTIVELY
Teacher_____	Good Average Poor	YES NO	YES NO	Yes Somewhat No
Teacher_____	Good Average Poor	YES NO	YES NO	Yes Somewhat No
Teacher_____	Good Average Poor	YES NO	YES NO	Yes Somewhat No
Teacher_____	Good Average Poor	YES NO	YES NO	Yes Somewhat No
Teacher_____	Good Average Poor	YES NO	YES NO	Yes Somewhat No
Teacher_____	Good Average Poor	YES NO	YES NO	Yes Somewhat No

Please sign and return _____   _____

Parent/Guardian signature   Date

Student-Generated Progress Report

The following is a short progress report. Your child has evaluated him-/herself. My initials appear next to the evaluation if I am in agreement.

Behavior in Class

_____ Exceptional, splendid, excellent!
_____ Good
_____ Needs to improve

Homework

_____ Wow! Everything's done.
_____ Good. Almost everything is done.
_____ Help! I've gotten behind.

Classwork

_____ Quality stuff!
_____ Pretty good
_____ Could be better!

Notebook

_____ Neat!
_____ Okay
_____ Messy!

Student's signature _____

Parent's signature _____

Date _____

shared by Julie Heimburge, co-author with S. Rief of How to Reach & Teach All Students in the Inclusive Classroom

STUDENT GOAL SHEET

My goal for the day/week is:

_____

_____

_____

This is my plan for reaching my goal:

_____

_____

_____

- -

I would like to improve

_____

_____

_____

Student name _____ Date _____

SELF-MONITORING FORM

Name: _____   **Period:** _____ **Date:** _____

Select a behavior to self-monitor during Independent work time.

Example: I was working / on-task.

When you hear the signal on the tape, check √ yourself (**YES** or **NO**) and continue with your work.

YES	NO

Teacher Signature _____

RESPONSE COST CHART

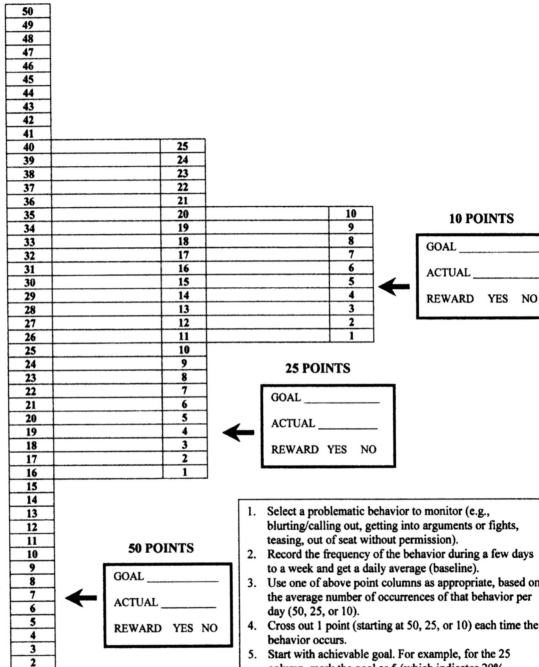

10 POINTS

GOAL _____

ACTUAL _____

REWARD   YES   NO

25 POINTS

GOAL _____

ACTUAL _____

REWARD   YES   NO

50 POINTS

GOAL _____

ACTUAL _____

REWARD   YES   NO

1. Select a problematic behavior to monitor (e.g., blurting/calling out, getting into arguments or fights, teasing, out of seat without permission).
2. Record the frequency of the behavior during a few days to a week and get a daily average (baseline).
3. Use one of above point columns as appropriate, based on the average number of occurrences of that behavior per day (50, 25, or 10).
4. Cross out 1 point (starting at 50, 25, or 10) each time the behavior occurs.
5. Start with achievable goal. For example, for the 25 column, mark the goal as 5 (which indicates 20% improvement).
6. If the student has 5 or more remaining points, reward is earned. Circle the yes.
7. Raise the goal for success until behavior has improved to a manageable level.

Note If the baseline frequency of the behavior does not fit in one of the 3 point columns above, use the 50-point column and adjust from there. For example, if you need 30, start from the 30 box and deduct points from there.

Pizza

Student Contract

Name _____   Week of _____

I will earn a sticker when I _____

with no more than _____ warning(s).   ☺ ☆ ✺

Monday	Tuesday	Wednesday	Thursday	Friday
AM	AM	AM	AM	AM
PM	PM	PM	PM	PM

When I have _____ stickers in a week,
I will celebrate!

Celebrate

My prize will be _____.

Signatures

Student _____

Teacher _____

Parent _____

STUDENT CONTRACT

I, _____, agree to do the following:
(Include criteria/standard for successful performance.)

_____

_____

_____

If I fulfill my part of this contract, I will receive the following reward(s):

_____

_____

_____

This contract is in effect from (date) _____ to (date) _____ .

It will be reviewed (daily__ weekly__ other_____).

Signed:

_____   _____   _____
    student   **teacher**   **parent**

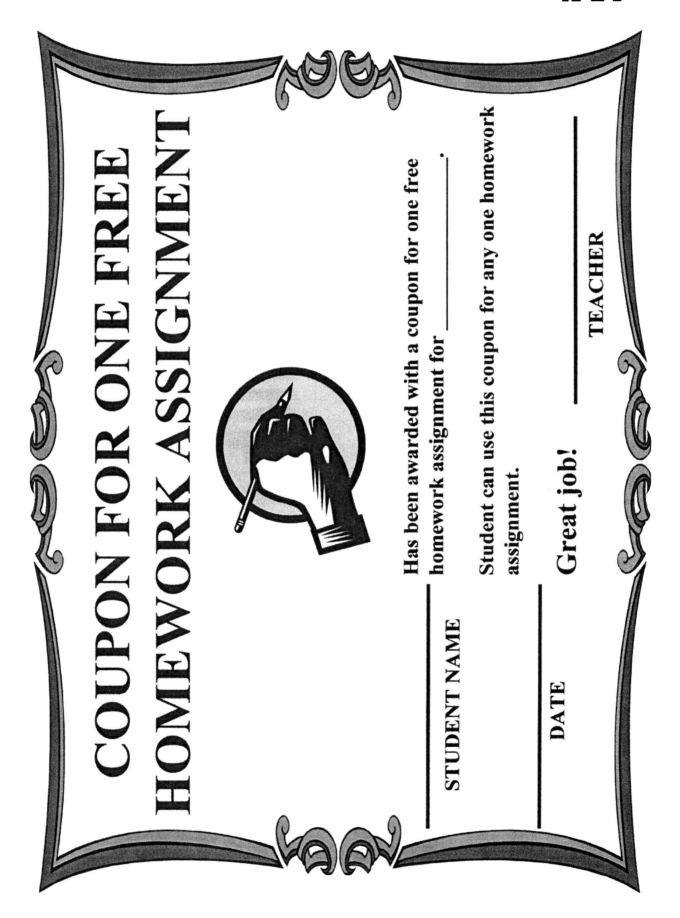

COUPON FOR ONE FREE HOMEWORK ASSIGNMENT

STUDENT NAME

Has been awarded with a coupon for one free homework assignment for _____.

Student can use this coupon for any one homework assignment.

DATE

Great job!

TEACHER

ADHD MANAGEMENT PLAN

DATE: _____

To the family of_____ , please refer to this plan between visits if you have questions about care. If you are still unsure, call us at _____ for assistance.

Patient _____ 's doctor is _____ Pager #_____

Parent/Guardian_____ Relationship_____

Contact Number(s)_____ , _____

School Name _____ School Phone No _____ Fax No. _____

Key Teacher Contact Name _____ Grade_____ Teacher's E-mail _____

GOALS What improvements would you most like to see? Specific behavior you would like to see improve:

At Home: _____

_____

At School: _____

_____

PLANS to reach this goal:

1._____

2._____

3._____

MEDICATION

1. _____ | Time _____ am/pm | Time _____ am/pm | Time _____ am/pm
Dose 1_____ mg | Dose 2 _____ mg | Dose 3_____ mg

2. _____ | Time _____ am/pm | Time _____ am/pm | Time _____ am/pm
Dose 1_____ mg | Dose 2 _____ mg | Dose 3_____ mg

❑ Medication to be given on non-school days   ❑ Medication given for _____ number of days

❑ School authorization signed by parent and MD   ❑ Rx written for duplicate bottle for administration at school

❑ Side effects explained/info given

Common Side Effects: Decreased Appetite, Irritability/Crankiness, Sleep Problems, Stomachache, Acting Out

Call your doctor immediately if any unusual side effects occur: Tics, Mood Swings, Changes in Personality

❑ School testing scheduled   date _____

❑ Parent and Teacher Vanderbilts   completed_____

❑ F/U Parent Vanderbilt given   completed_____

❑ F/U Teacher Vanderbilt given to parent   ❑ F/U Teacher Vanderbilt to be faxed to school   completed _____

❑ Behavioral Counseling Referral to _____

❑ Parenting Tips Sheet given   ❑ CHADD phone number given: (800) 233-4050

❑ Community Resources/Referrals: _____

NEXT FOLLOW-UP VISIT: _____

NICHQ Vanderbilt ASSESSMENT Scale –TEACHER Informant

Teacher's Name:_____ Class Time: _____ Class Name/Period: _____

Today's Date: _____ Child's Name: _____ Grade Level: _____

Directions: Each rating should be considered in the context of what is appropriate for the age of the child you are rating and should reflect that child's behavior since the beginning of the school year. Please indicate the number of weeks or months you have been able to evaluate the behaviors: _____.

Is this evaluation based on a time when the child ☐ was on medication ☐ was not on medication ☐ not sure?

SYMPTOMS	Never	Occasionally	Often	Very Often
1. Fails to give attention to details or makes careless mistakes in schoolwork.	0	1	2	3
2. Has difficulty sustaining attention to tasks or activities.	0	1	2	3
3. Does not seem to listen when spoken to directly.	0	1	2	3
4. Does not follow through on instructions and fails to finish school-work (not due to oppositional behavior or failure to understand).	0	1	2	3
5. Has difficulty organizing tasks and activities.	0	1	2	3
6. Avoids, dislikes, or is reluctant to engage in tasks that require sustained mental effort.	0	1	2	3
7. Loses things necessary for tasks or activities (school assignments, pencils, or books).	0	1	2	3
8. Is easily distracted by extraneous stimuli.	0	1	2	3
9. Is forgetful in daily activities.	0	1	2	3
Total number of questions scored "2" or "3" in question #'s 1-9:_____				
10. Fidgets with hands or feet or squirms in seat.	0	1	2	3
11. Leaves seat in classroom or in other situations in which remaining seated is expected.	0	1	2	3
12. Runs about or climbs excessively in situations in which remaining seated is expected.	0	1	2	3
13. Has difficulty playing or engaging in leisure activities quietly.	0	1	2	3
14. Is "on the go" or often acts as if "driven by a motor."	0	1	2	3
15. Talks excessively.	0	1	2	3
16. Blurts out answers before questions have been completed.	0	1	2	3
17. Has difficulty waiting in line.	0	1	2	3
18. Interrupts or intrudes on others (e.g., butts into conversations/ games).	0	1	2	3
Total number of questions scored "2" or "3" in question #'s 10-18:_____				
Total Symptom Score for question #'s 1-18:_____				
19. Loses temper.	0	1	2	3
20. Actively defies or refuses to comply with adult's requests or rules.	0	1	2	3
21. Is angry or resentful.	0	1	2	3
22. Is spiteful and vindictive.	0	1	2	3
23. Bullies, threatens, or intimidates others.	0	1	2	3
24. Initiates physical fights.	0	1	2	3
25. Lies to obtain goods for favors or to avoid obligations (e.g., "cons" others)	0	1	2	3
26. Is physically cruel to people.	0	1	2	3
27. Has stolen items of nontrivial value.	0	1	2	3
28. Deliberately destroys others' property.	0	1	2	3
Total number of questions scored "2" or "3" in question #'s 19-28:				

NICHQ Vanderbilt ASSESSMENT Scale –TEACHER Informant

Teacher's Name: _____ Class Time: _____ Class Name/Period: _____

Today's Date: _____ Child's Name: _____ Grade Level: _____

	Never	Occasionally	Often	Very Often
29. Is fearful, anxious, or worried.	0	1	2	3
30. Is self-conscious or easily embarrassed.	0	1	2	3
31. Is afraid to try new things for fear of making mistakes.	0	1	2	3
32. Feels worthless or inferior.	0	1	2	3
33. Blames self for problems; feels guilty.	0	1	2	3
34. Feels lonely, unwanted, or unloved; complains that "no one loves him/her."	0	1	2	3
35. Is sad, unhappy, or depressed.	0	1	2	3
Total number of questions scored "2" or "3" in question #'s 29-35: _____				

PERFORMANCE *Academic Performance*	Excellent	Above Average	Average	Somewhat of A Problem	Problematic
36. Reading	1	2	3	4	5
37. Mathematics	1	2	3	4	5
38. Written Expression	1	2	3	4	5
Classroom Behavioral Performance	Excellent	Above Average	Average	Somewhat of A Problem	Problematic
39. Relationship with peers	1	2	3	4	5
40. Following directions	1	2	3	4	5
41. Disrupting class	1	2	3	4	5
42. Assignment completion	1	2	3	4	5
43. Organizational skills	1	2	3	4	5
Total number of questions scored "4" or "5" in question #'s 36-43: _____					
Average Performance Score: _____					

COMMENTS:

PLEASE RETURN THIS FORM TO:_____

MAILING ADDRESS:_____

_____

FAX NUMBER:_____

Scoring Instructions for the NICHQ Vanderbilt Assessment Scales

These scales should NOT be used alone to make any diagnosis. You must take into consideration information from multiple sources. Scores of 2 or 3 on a single Symptom question reflect *often-occurring* behaviors. Scores of 4 or 5 on Performance questions reflect problems in performance.

The initial assessment scales, parent and teacher, have 2 components: symptom assessment and impairment in performance. On both the parent and teacher initial scales, the symptom assessment screens for symptoms that meet criteria for both inattentive (items 1–9) and hyperactive ADHD (items 10–18).

To meet *DSM-IV* criteria for the diagnosis, one must have at least 6 positive responses to either the inattentive 9 or hyperactive 9 core symptoms, or both. A positive response is a 2 or 3 (often, very often) (you could draw a line straight down the page and count the positive answers in each subsegment). There is a place to

record the number of positives in each subsegment, and a place for total score for the first 18 symptoms (just add them up).

The initial scales also have symptom screens for 3 other co-morbidities—oppositional-defiant, conduct, and anxiety/depression. These are screened by the number of positive responses in each of the segments separated by the "squares." The specific item sets and numbers of positives required for each co-morbid symptom screen set are detailed below.

The second section of the scale has a set of performance measures, scored 1 to 5, with 4 and 5 being somewhat of a problem/problematic. To meet criteria for ADHD there must be at least one item of the Performance set in which the child scores a 4 or 5; ie, there must be impairment, not just symptoms to meet diagnostic criteria. The sheet has a place to record the number of positives (4s, 5s) and an Average Performance Score—add them up and divide by number of Performance criteria answered.

Parent Assessment Scale	Teacher Assessment Scale
Predominantly Inattentive subtype ■ Must score a 2 or 3 on 6 out of 9 items on questions 1–9 <u>AND</u> ■ Score a 4 or 5 on any of the Performance questions 48–55	**Predominantly Inattentive subtype** ■ Must score a 2 or 3 on 6 out of 9 items on questions 1–9 <u>AND</u> ■ Score a 4 or 5 on any of the Performance questions 36–43
Predominantly Hyperactive/Impulsive subtype ■ Must score a 2 or 3 on 6 out of 9 items on questions 10–18 <u>AND</u> ■ Score a 4 or 5 on any of the Performance questions 48–55	**Predominantly Hyperactive/Impulsive subtype** ■ Must score a 2 or 3 on 6 out of 9 items on questions 10–18 <u>AND</u> ■ Score a 4 or 5 on any of the Performance questions 36–43
ADHD Combined Inattention/Hyperactivity ■ Requires the above criteria on both inattention and hyperactivity/impulsivity	**ADHD Combined Inattention/Hyperactivity** ■ Requires the above criteria on both inattention and hyperactivity/impulsivity
Oppositional-Defiant Disorder Screen ■ Must score a 2 or 3 on 4 out of 8 behaviors on questions 19–26 <u>AND</u> ■ Score a 4 or 5 on any of the Performance questions 48–55	**Oppositional-Defiant/Conduct Disorder Screen** ■ Must score a 2 or 3 on 3 out of 10 items on questions 19–28 <u>AND</u> ■ Score a 4 or 5 on any of the Performance questions 36–43
Conduct Disorder Screen ■ Must score a 2 or 3 on 3 out of 14 behaviors on questions 27–40 <u>AND</u> ■ Score a 4 or 5 on any of the Performance questions 48–55	**Anxiety/Depression Screen** ■ Must score a 2 or 3 on 3 out of 7 items on questions 29–35 <u>AND</u> ■ Score a 4 or 5 on any of the Performance questions 36–43
Anxiety/Depression Screen ■ Must score a 2 or 3 on 3 out of 7 behaviors on questions 41–47 <u>AND</u> ■ Score a 4 or 5 on any of the Performance questions 48–55	

The parent and teacher follow-up scales have the first 18 core ADHD symptoms, not the co-morbid symptoms. The section segment has the same Performance items and impairment assessment as the initial scales, and then has a side-effect reporting scale that can be used to both assess and monitor the presence of adverse reactions to medications prescribed, if any.

Scoring the follow-up scales involves only calculating a total symptom score for items 1–18 that can be tracked over time, and

the average of the Performance items answered as measures of improvement over time with treatment.

Parent Assessment Follow-up
- Calculate <u>Total</u> Symptom Score for questions 1–18.
- Calculate <u>Average</u> Performance Score for questions 19–26.

Teacher Assessment Follow-up
- Calculate <u>Total</u> Symptom Score for questions 1–18.
- Calculate <u>Average</u> Performance Score for questions 19–26.

American Academy of Pediatrics

DEDICATED TO THE HEALTH OF ALL CHILDREN™

NICHQ

National Initiative for Children's Healthcare Quality

McNeil

Consumer & Specialty Pharmaceuticals

Visual Prompts and Icons

Following are a variety of illustrations that may be used as visual prompts to help students remember appropriate behaviors and expectations. You may wish to use these illustrations when developing individual student behavioral charts or as reminders of expected behaviors taped to a student's desk. The illustrations may also be enlarged for a classroom poster.

Visual Prompts

A-27.1:   be friendly or respectful and polite; pay attention; work cooperatively; follow directions; be on-task; participate in the lesson

A-27.2:   keep hands and feet to self; cross legs while sitting on the rug

A-27.3:   (supplies/materials) backpack; paper/pencil; planner/calendar; sharpened pencils; notebook; book

A-27.4:   be on time; follow rules; be ready with materials; complete assignments; refrain from blurting out or other disruptive behavior

A-27.5:   listen; look ("eyes on me"); sit appropriately, be in seat; raise hand, participate

A-27.6:   line up appropriately; use quiet mouth

Icons

You may wish to use these reduced illustrations on forms, charts, behavioral contracts—the possibilities are endless.

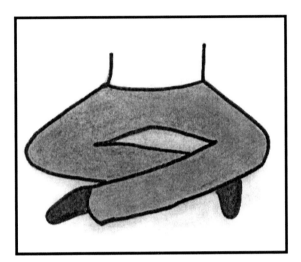

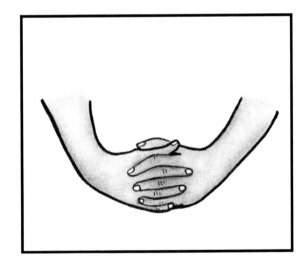

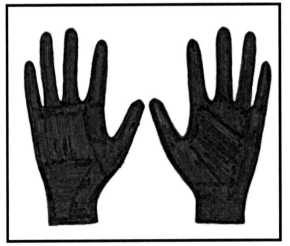

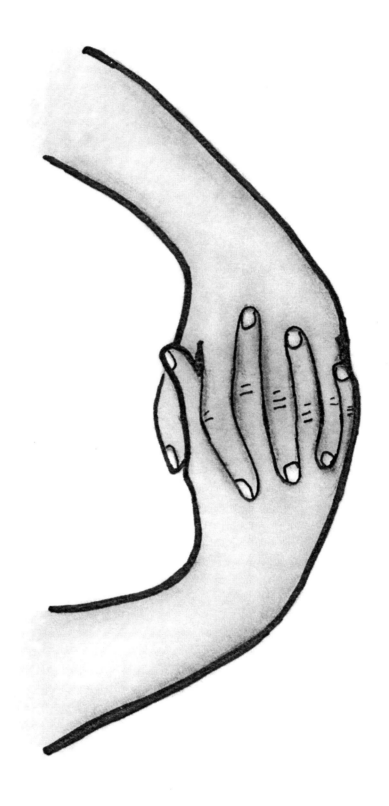

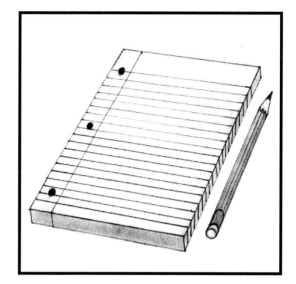

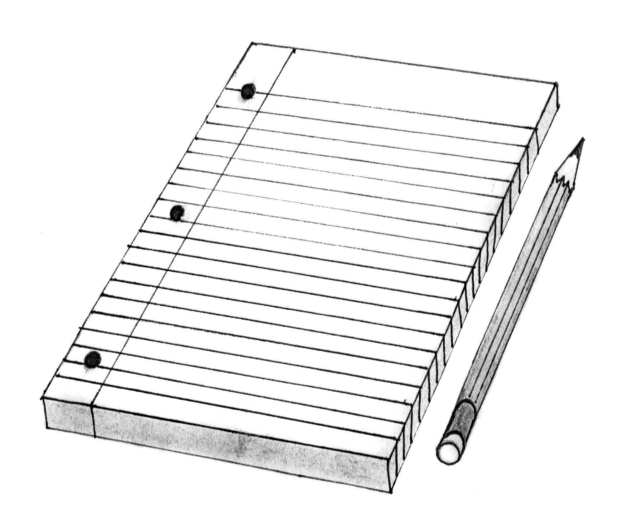

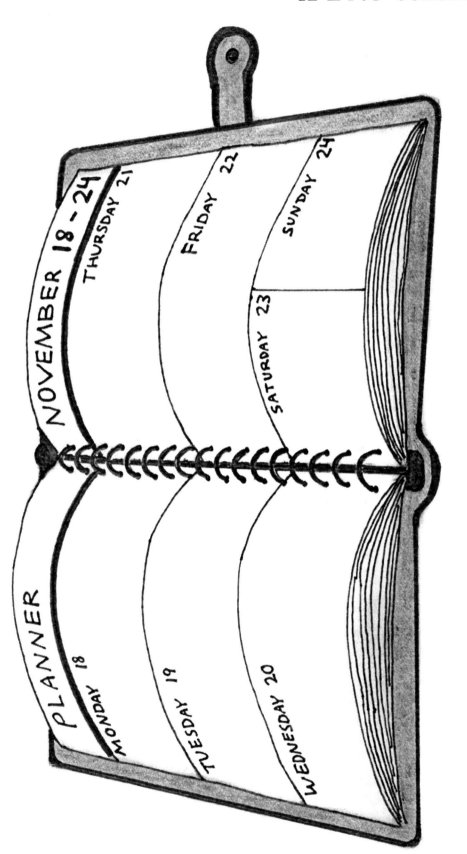

PLANNER

NOVEMBER 18 - 24

MONDAY 18

TUESDAY 19

WEDNESDAY 20

THURSDAY 21

FRIDAY 22

SATURDAY 23

SUNDAY 24

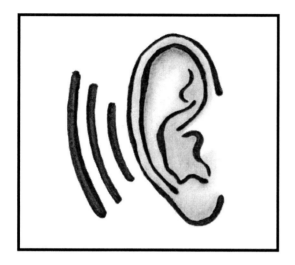
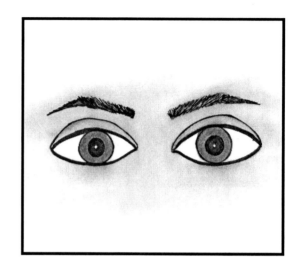

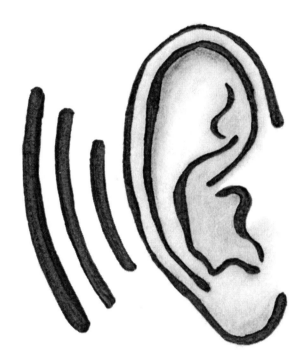

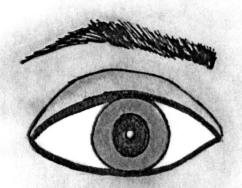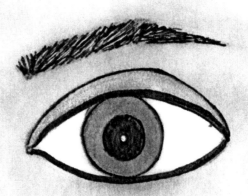

ZIP

Icons

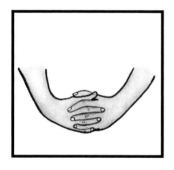  

CPSIA information can be obtained at www.ICGtesting.com
Printed in the USA
BVOW02n0422230913

331745BV00012B/21/P

9 780787 965914